ESSAYS
ON
THE MODERN LAW
OF WAR

By
L. C. Green

TRANSNATIONAL PUBLISHERS, INC.
Dobbs Ferry, New York

Leslie C. Green, LL.B., LL.D., F.R.S.C. is professor of political science and honorary professor of law at the University of Alberta.

Library of Congress Cataloging in Publication Data

Green, L. C. (Leslie C.), 1920-
  Essays on the modern law of war.

  Includes index
  1. War (International law)—Addresses, essays,
lectures. I. Title.
JX4511.G665   1984   341.6   84-23924
ISBN 0-941320-26-X

Manufactured in the United States of America

Let there be no perfidy, no falsehood in your treaties with the enemy, be faithful to all things, proving yourselves upright and noble and maintaining your word and promises truly.

Caliph Abu Bakr (c. 634 A.D.) to his troops

Attached to force are certain self-imposed, imperceptible limitations hardly worth mentioning, known as international law and custom, but they scarcely weaken it.

Clausewitz, *On War*, 1832.

La guerre n'est pas ce qu'elle était. Le droit n'est toujours pas ce qu'il devrait. L'une progresse dans la force de destruction, quand l'autre persiste dans la faiblesse des protections.

Furet, Martines and Dorandeau, *La Guerre et le Droit*, 1979.

For Anne
may she never know the horrors of war

CONTENTS

PREFACE

I first became interested in the law of armed conflict as a military lawyer in India during World War II. Later I was appointed Legal Adviser to the Canadian Delegation to the Diplomatic Conference on the Reaffirmation and Development of International Humanitarian Law applicable in Armed Conflicts, which was responsible for the adoption of the two Protocols additional to the Geneva Conventions of 12 August 1949. As a result of my experience at that Conference, I realised how important it was that students, as well as military personnel, should become aware of some of the special problems within the law of armed conflict. I soon discovered that my students in this field were lacking the raw materials for their study. Apart from comparatively few collections of documents and a number of out-of-date books, many of the more modern works dealing with armed conflict were either analyses of the Conference or excessively detailed studies of particular issues. What was lacking were relatively short studies of specific practical issues of the kind which would appeal to the ordinary student of the law of armed conflict, and which might prove useful to the man in the field, or those charged with instructing him in this branch of the law.

As a result of my own interest, I began writing on issues that appealed to me and which I felt were of general interest. These papers appeared in a variety of legal journals, and I realised how convenient it would be for my own students if some of these papers were available to them in a single volume. As a result of their difficulties, and after discussing the matter with a number of friends, including army officers, I decided that it might be helpful to bring some of these papers together.

The papers in this collection were written over a number of years as the particular subject matter struck me as relevant, or in response to a particular need. Inevitably, there may be a measure of overlap. But this is a field in which this cannot be avoided. Thus, the ban on "unnecessary suffering" arises in virtually every matter with which the law of armed conflict is concerned.

Chapter I, III, VI, X and XII originally appeared in the *Canadian Yearbook of International Law*; IV, V, VIII and IX in the *Israel Yearbook on Human Rights*; II in the *Revue de Droit de l'Université de Sherbrooke*; VII in the *Annals of Air Law*; and XI in *Chitty's Law Journal*. I am grateful to the editors and publishers of these journals for having allowed me to reproduce these papers, amended and brought up to date where necessary. Chapter VIII was written for this collection.

Finally, I must thank my secretary, Ms Leah Modin, who willingly gave up time to deal with such manuscripts as were necessary and who accepted any amendments and alterations, both trivial and important, without complaint. I must also thank Ms. Heike Fenton and Transnational Publishers for their cooperation in every respect with regard to the publication of this volume.

L.C.G., August, 1984

TABLE OF CASES

Hryhoriw v. R. (1954) 52

Indian National Army Trials (1945/6) 49
Interpretation of Peace Treaties (1950) 21
Ireland v. U.K. (1978) 93
Isayama, Re (1946) 139

Janson v. Driefontein Consolidated Mines (1902) 1
Jung and Schumacher, Re (1946) 269

Karadzole v. Artukovic (1958) 219
Kawasaki Kisen Kabushiki Kaisha of Kobe v. Bantham S.S. Co. (1939) xx, 1, 43, 229, 262
Keighley v. Bell (1866) 51, 218
Kidd Case (1701) 50
Killinger, Re (1945), 254
Klein, Re (1945) 120-121
Kolczynski, ex p. (1955) 219
Kuechenmeister, ex p. (1947) 2

La Reine des Agnès, The (1803) 264
Leeb, Re von (1948) 61-62, 248
Le Louis, The (1817) 239
Levy v. Parker (1973) xx, 133-134, 151
List, Re (1948) 62-63, 75-76
Llandovery Castle, The (1921) 27, 30-31, 56, 57, 59, 117-118, 121, 138, 244-245, 254, 262

MacKay v. The Queen (1980) 259
Marks v. Esperdy (1963/4) 185
Marquis de Somerueles, The (1813) 263
Masuda, Re (1945) 59
McCall v. McDowell (1867) 52
Mercoid Corp. v. Mid-Continent Investment (1944) 210
Meunier, Re (1894) 219
Meyer, Re (1945) 226-227, 250, 254, 269-271, 273
Milch, Re (1947) 60-61 120, 122
Military Prosecutor v. Omar Mahmud Kassem (1969) 9
Minorities in Upper Silesia (1928) 63
Mitchell v. Harmony (1851) 51
Mitchell v. Laird (1973) 229
Mohd. Ali v. Public Prosecutor (1968) 9
Möwe, The (1915) 29
Müller, Re (1921) 244, 245

Nancy, The (1805) 263
Natzweiler Trial (1946) 60, 121
Navios Corp. v. The Ulysses II (1958) 2
Neitz, Re (1946) 270
Neu v. McCarthy (1941) 53
Nga Myat Tha (1882) 46

ABBREVIATIONS

A.C.	Appeal Cases (U.K.)
A.L.R. Annot.	American Law Reports Annotated (U.S.)
Abb.	Abbot's Admiralty Reports (U.S.)
All E.R.	All England Reports (U.K.)
Am. Dec.	American Decisions (U.S.)
Ann. Dig.	Annual Digest and Reports of Public International Law Cases
Atl.	Atlantic Reporter (U.S.)
B.F.S.P.	British and Foreign State Papers
Black	Black's U.S. Supreme Court Reports
C.C.C.	Canadian Criminal Cases
C.F.P.	Canadian Forces Publication
C.L.P.	Current Legal Problems
C.M.A.R.	Court Martial Appeal Reports (Canada)
C.M.R.	Court Martial Reports (U.S.)
C. & P.	Carrington & Payne's English Nisi Prius Reports
Cmd.	Command Papers (U.K.)
Co.	Coke's Reports (U.K.)
C.Rob.	Christopher Robinson's Admiralty Reports (U.K.)
D.L.R.	Dominion Law Reports (Canada)
E.R.	English Reports
F.	Federal Reporter (U.S.)
F.Supp.	Federal Supplement (U.S.)
F. & F.	Foster & Finlason's Nisi Prius Reports (U.K.)
Fed.	Federal Reporter (U.S.)
Fed. Cas.	Federal Cases
Fed. Rep.	Federal Reporter
G.A.	General Assembly (United Nations)
G.L.R.	Ghana Law Reports
H.M.S.O.	His/Her Majesty's Stationery Office
Hague Recueil	Recueil des Cours, Académie de Droit International de La Haye

How.	Howard's U.S. Supreme Court Reports
I.C.J.	International Court of Justice
I.C.L.Q.	International and Comparative Law Quarterly
I.C.R.C.	International Committee of the Red Cross
I.L.A.	International Law Association
I.L.M.	International Legal Materials
I.L.R.	International Law Reports
K.B.	King's Bench Reports (U.K.)
Kelyng	Kelyng's English Crown Cases
L.N.T.S.	League of Nations Treaty Series
M. & S.	Maule & Selwyn's English King's Bench Reports
M.L.R.	Military Law Reporter (U.S.)
Mil.L.R.	Military Law Review
Mod.L.R.	Modern Law Review
Moore, Int'l Arb.	J.B. Moore, *International Arbitrations*
N.E.	North Eastern Reporter (U.S.)
N.Y.S.	New York Supplement (U.S.)
N.Z.L.R.	New Zeland Law Reports
O.R.	Ontario Reports (Canada)
P.	Probate Reports (U.K.)
P.R.	Punjab Reports (India)
P.C.I.J.	Permanent Court of International Justice
Prelim. Obj.	Preliminary Objection
Q.B.	Queen's Bench Reports (U.K.)
Q.R. & O.	Queen's Regulations and Orders (Canada)
R.S.C.	Revised Statutes of Canada
Res.	Resolution
S.A.L.R.	South African Law Reports
S.C.	Statutes of Canada
S.C. (Cape)	Supreme Court, Cape of Good Hope
S.C.R.	Supreme Court Reports (Canada)
S.E.	South Eastern Reporter (U.S.)
S.J.L.B.	Selected Judgments Lower Burma
S.W.	South Western Reporter (U.S.)
Schindler/Toman	D. Schindler and J. Toman, *The Laws of Armed Conflicts*, 1981
Stats.	U.S. Statutes at Large
St.Tr.	State Trials (U.K.)
Stewart	Stewart's Vice-Admiralty Reports, Nova Scotia (Canada)
Stockton	Stockton's Vice-Admiralty Reports, New Brunswick (Canada)
Term Rep.	Term Reports (U.K.)
U.N.T.S.	United Nations Treaty Series
U.N.W.C.C.	United Nations War Crimes Commission
U.S.	United States Supreme Court Reports
W.L.R.	Weekly Law Reports (U.K.)
W.W.R.	Western Weekly Reports (Canada)
War Crimes Reports	Law Reports of the Trials of War Criminals (U.N.W.C.C.)
Woods	Woods Circuit Court Reports (U.S.)
Y.B.I.L.C.	Yearbook of the International Law Commission

INTRODUCTION

The law relating to armed conflict is customarily divided into the *jus ad bellum*—the right to resort to war—and the *jus in bello*—the law during war. Consideration of the *jus ad bellum* would involve analysis of such instruments as the Kellogg Pact[1] or the United Nations Charter, the General Assembly's Definition of Aggression[2] and perhaps even its Declaration on the Principles of International Law Concerning Friendly Relations and Cooperation among States.[3] Further, to ascertain the *jus ad bellum* it becomes necessary to consider the legal definition of war as distinct from the factual existence of hostilities, and this takes us into examination of the interrelationship between war, armed conflict and self-defence.[4] It also necessitates examination of the status of those engaged in a conflict in order to determine whether they are belligerents entitled to enjoy the rights which flow from the *jus in bello* or are mere rebels or insurgents unprotected and largely unrecognized by international law.[5] To some extent this problem of classification has been evaded by the adoption in 1977 of Protocol I relating to Humanitarian Law in International Armed Conflict,[6] which extends the definition of an international armed conflict, and thus the *jus in bello*, to "armed conflicts in which people are fighting against colonial domination and alien occupation and against racist régimes in exercise of their right of self-determination, as enshrined in the Charter of the United Nations and the Declaration of Principles of International Law and Friendly Cooperation among States in accordance with the Charter of the United Nations." Moreover, Protocol II[7] adopted at the same time seeks to extend some of the basic humanitarian principles of the *jus in bello* to non-international armed conflicts, previously regarded as outside the ambit of that law.

1. The Pact of Paris—Treaty for the Renunciation of War, 1928, 94 LNTS 57, 4 Hudson, *International Legislation* 2526.
2. Res. 3314 (XXIX) 1974, 13 *I.L.M.* 710.
3. Res. 2625 (XXV) 1970, 9 *ibid*. 1292.
4. See, e.g., Green, "Armed Conflict, War and Self-Defence," 6 *Archiv des Völkerrechts* 1959, 387.
5. See, e.g., Green, "The Status of Rebel Armies," 3 Univ. of Malaya Law Rev. 1961, 223; "Le statut des forces rebelles en droit international," Revue Générale de Droit International Public 1962, 5.
6. See Schindler/Toman, *The Laws of Armed Conflicts* 1981, 551, Art. 1(4).
7. *Ibid*., 619.

Not only have the two Protocols extended the *jus in bello*, or parts thereof, to conflicts which would not previously have been considered as amounting to "war" in the sense in which that term was understood in international law, but Protocol I abjures the use of the word war entirely and refers simply to armed conflicts, thus obviating the need to determine whether a war exists or not. This trend towards extending at least the humanitarian part of the *jus in bello* to any armed conflict was already instituted in the Geneva Conventions, 1949,[8] to which the two Protocols have been annexed.

From the point of view of national law, the situation has not radically changed. In so far as problems arise relating to such matters as the frustration of contract,[9] the validity of an exemption clause in an insurance policy,[10] determination of the date when the law of peace has returned[11] or whether foreign enlistment legislation is applicable,[12] it may still be necessary to decide whether a war exists within the conception of the jurisprudence of the forum concerned. The trend in national law has been increasingly to look at the factual situation, and to accept the argument that if a conflict exists and there is an *animus belligerendi*, then, from the point of view of national law, the court should accept that a war exists and apply such national law as becomes relevant in such a situation. Although courts are looking more and more to the factual situation, they are still in many instances bound by the decision of their government as expressed in the opinions submitted from the relevant law officers.[13] In such circumstances, the conclusion that a war exists is based more on political than legal grounds.

In so far as the man in the field engaged in any particular conflict is concerned, he is not really affected by whether a "war" in the traditional legal sense exists or not. On the other hand, from a moral point of view he may contend that a war is unlawful and that, since his state is in breach of international law, he is exempt from participating.[14] The legal effect of such a contention is, however, decided solely in accordance with national law and we have yet to see a judicial officer decide that his country is involved in an illegal war justifying a decision by a citizen not to participate. Once the decision has been made by a state or some other authority entitled to make the decision that the forces under its command are to engage in conflict, it is irrelevant for the members of those forces whether a 'war' or an 'armed conflict' or a 'police action'[15] is in progress. From his point of view he is engaged in hostilities against an enemy—now generally known as an 'adverse party'[16]—and from then on his conduct towards that opponent should be in accordance with the laws of armed conflict—the *jus in bello*.

With the adoption of Protocol I in 1977 much of the traditional law of armed conflict changed. Even though the Protocol was directed at extending the scope of humanitarian law, it did in fact also amend the *jus in bello* in the strict sense of that term, since it included new regulations concerning the methods and means of warfare.[17] It is easy to

8. I—Wounded and Sick, II—Wounded, Sick and Shipwrecked, III—Prisoners of War, IV—Civilians, *ibid.*, 305, 333, 355, 427 resp.
9. See, e.g., *Kawasaki Kisen Kabushiki Kaisha of Kobe* v. *Bantham S.S. Co.* [1939] 2K.B.544.
10. See, e.g., *Shneiderman* v. *Metropolitan Casualty Co. of New York* (1961) 220 N.Y.S. 2d 947.
11. See, e.g., *R.* v. *Bottrill, ex p. Kuechenmeister* [1947] K.B. 41; *Bordier* v. *Lorilleux* (1960) 40 I.L.R. 434 (French Cour de Cassation).
12. See, e.g., *R.* v. *Jameson* [1896] 2 Q.B. 425.
13. See, e.g., Lyons, "Conclusiveness of the Foreign Office Certificate," 23 Brit. Y.B. Int'l Law 1946, 240; "The Conclusiveness of the 'Suggestion' and Certificate of the American State Department," 24 *ibid.* 1947, 116; "Conclusiveness of the Statements of the Executive: Continental and Latin-American Practice," 25 *ibid.* 1948, 180.
14. See, e.g., *Parker* v. *Levy* (1973) 1.M.L.R. 2130.
15. This is the term sometimes used to describe the U.N. action in Korea, see Ross, *The United Nations* 1966, 396. It is also the term used by Turkey to describe its invasion of Cyprus in 1974.
16. This is the term used in the 1949 Conventions and Protocol I.
17. Protocol I, Part III, Arts. 35-42.

spell out the law, but this does not mean that it is going to reach the soldier in the field whose conduct it regulates and whose rights it protects. One of the difficulties that has always confronted the fighting soldier, whether officer or man, has been that of ascertaining the law. While most armed forces, at least in the English-speaking countries, have published manuals of military law, of which part, normally, relates to the law of war,[18] these publications have not been readily available to the fighting men, having been issued for the main part to base offices or the members of the judge advocate's staff, who are rarely in the front-line. It is true that the Geneva Conventions and Protocol I contain provisions calling for the dissemination of their contents, but the extent to which this takes place varies from country to country and, perhaps, from unit to unit.[19] From the point of view of the soldier, the law of war is as binding upon him as his own system of national law, so that *ignorantia juris non excusat*[20] and from a practical point of view the fact that Protocol I provides for the employment of legal advisers does not really help him,[21] since these advisers have only to be "available, when necessary, to advise military commanders at the appropriate level."[22] The importance of making the fighting man aware of the substance of the law of armed conflict was appreciated by the Institute of International Law as long ago as 1880, when it drew up its *Oxford Manual* on the Laws of War on Land.[23] In the Preface to the *Manual*, the Institute stated

> . . . it has contented itself with stating clearly and codifying the accepted ideas of our age so far as this has appeared allowable and practicable.
>
> By so doing, it believes it is rendering a service to military men themselves. In fact, so long as the demands of opinion remain indeterminate, belligerents are exposed to painful uncertainty and endless accusations. A positive set of rules, on the contrary, if they are judicious, serves the interests of belligerents and is far from hindering them, since by preventing the unchaining of passion and savage instincts—which battle always awakens, as much as it awakens courage and manly virtues—it strengthens the discipline which is the strength of armies; it also ennobles their patriotic mission in the eyes of the soldiers and keeps them within the limits of respect due to the rights of humanity.
>
> But in order to attain this end it is not sufficient for sovereigns to promulgate new laws. It is essential, too, that they make these laws known among all people,

18. See British Manual of Military Law, Part III, The Law of War on Land, 1958; U.S. Dept. of the Army, The Law of Land Warfare, FM27-10, 1956; U.S. Dept. of the Air Force, International Law—The Conduct of Armed Conflict and Air Operations, AFP 110-13, 1976; see, also, German General Staff, "The Usages of War on Land," 1902, tr. Morgan as *The German War Book*, 1915.
19. For an example of such a teaching programme, see U.S. Dept. of the Army, 'The Geneva Conventions of 1949 and Hague Convention IV of 1907', ASubjScd 27-1, 8 Oct. 1970, summarised and commented upon in Green, "Aftermath of Vietnam: War Law and the Soldier," 4 Falk, *The Vietnam War and International Law* 1976, 147, 167-72; *The Law of Land Warfare—A Self-Instructional Text*, 27-200, 1972. See, also, Canadian Manual on the Geneva Conventions of August 12, 1949, CFP 122, 17 Jun. 1968; General Military Training, Vol. 4, "Unit Guide to the Geneva Conventions," CFP 318(4). The Canadian Defence Forces have now introduced lectures on the law of armed conflict and issue a series of pictorial representations of specific issues under the heading "You and the Law of War;" however, some of these leave much to be desired—Picture 3 portrays a soldier searching a surrendering German and states rightly "Do not attack enemy soldiers who surrender. Disarm them and treat them as prisoners of war," but the heading of the picture is "Enemy soldiers may possess valuable information;" picture 7 carries the title "Respect civilian property" and the picture carries the slogan 'Looting is forbidden', but this is stamped across a Reichsbank building guarded by two armed sentries; more to the point is picture 10 which shows a variety of weapons and ammunition, and carries the injunction "Do not alter your weapons and ammunition," while the explanation given is "Unnecessary suffering is not your objective."
20. See, "The Man in the Field and the Maxim *Ignorantia Juris Non Excusat*," ch. II *infra*.
21. See, "The Role of Legal Advisers in the Armed Forces," ch. IV *infra*.
22. Article 82.
23. Schindler/Toman, *op. cit.*, 35.

so that when a war is declared, the men called upon to take up arms to defend the causes of the belligerent States, may be thoroughly impregnated with the special rights and duties attached to the execution of such a command.

The Institute, with a view of assisting the authorities in accomplishing this part of their task, has given its work a popular form, attaching thereto statements of the reasons therefor, from which the text of a law may be easily secured when desired.

Aware of the asseveration by Cardinal Newman[24] that "there is such a thing as legitimate warfare: war has its laws; there are things which may fairly be done, and things which may not be done," this collection of essays does not purport to lay down any code of armed conflict law. It seeks, rather, to state in a relatively popular form the *jus in bello* as it exists on a number of specific issues which, for the main part, are of relevance to the man in the field.

24. *Apologia pro Vita Sua*, 1864.

I

The New Law of Armed Conflict*

In his *De Jure Belli ac Pacis*, Grotius, quoting Cicero, stated that "there is no Middle between War and Peace,"[1] and this sentiment seems to have received general agreement well into the twentieth century. Thus, in *Janson* v. *Driefontein Consolidated Mines*, Lord Macnaghten stated: "I think the learned counsel for the respondent was right in saying that the law recognises a state of peace and a state of war, but that it knows nothing of an intermediate state which is neither one thing nor the other—neither peace nor war."[2] One might have thought that the English courts would have abandoned this view in the light of their own experience during the Manchukuo incident, for by 1939 in *Kawasaki Kisen Kabushiki Kaisha of Kobe* v. *Bantham S.S. Co.*[3] the Court of Appeal was prepared to concede that "war" might exist for some commercial purposes but not in so far as other legal relationships were concerned. Acting on the advice of the Foreign Office that "the current situation in China is indeterminate and anomalous and His Majesty's Government are not prepared to say that in their view a state of war exists," the Court held that

> in the particular context in which the word "war" is found in the charterparty [under consideration], that word must be construed, having regard to the general tenor and purpose of the document, in what may be called a common-sense way. . . . To suggest that, within the meaning of this charterparty war had not broken out involving Japan . . . is to attribute to the parties to it a desire to import into their contract some obscure and uncertain technicalities of international law rather than the common sense of business men.

---

*The author was a member of the Canadian delegation to the 1975, 1976, and 1977 sessions of the Geneva Conference on Humanitarian Law in Armed Conflict. The views here expressed are his alone, and do not reflect those of the delegation or of the government of Canada.
[1](1625) *Inter bellum et pacem nihil est medium*—Lib. III, cap. XXI, s. 1 (Eng. tr. 1738, 715; Carnegie tr., 1925, 832).
[2][1902] A.C. 484, 497.
[3][1939] 2 K.B. 544, 558.

Nevertheless, when faced with a major political issue concerning the right to intern or deport to Germany a German as an enemy alien after the end of World War II and the unconditional surrender of Germany, the Court of Appeal took the line that since there had been no Peace Order in Council there must still have been a war.[4]

While the judges may have looked at the situation in a black/white relation, the jurists were having doubts. As early as 1925, having examined the comments of the writers and a number of real issues, McNair suggested that "perhaps it will be found possible to substitute for so technical a term as 'war' some more objective and physical test in the nature of acts of force."[5] During World War II, Professor Schwarzenberger went much further.[6] In his view,

> whether the state of peace continues with the State against which limited force is applied or not, depends on the latter's decision. Similarly, it is left to third States to decide for themselves whether, in their relations with the contending States, they prefer the laws of peace or neutrality. Even if all States directly and indirectly concerned acquiesced in the limited use of force, it appears to be a misnomer to call such a *pax bellicosa* by the name of peace. It is equally unwarranted to call war a state in which both contending States insist on the continuation of their peaceful relations, merely because third States wish to apply the law of neutrality to such a *bellum pacificum*. These constellations are incompatible with the states of peace and war; they constitute a state of their own, a *status mixtus*.

Perhaps the clearest example of this is to be found in the statement of the British Prime Minister on November 1, 1956, concerning the hostilities between the United Kingdom and Egypt. He said that, in the absence of any declaration of war, the two countries were "in a state of armed conflict."[7] A somewhat similar approach to the Suez operations was adopted by the court of a neutral country, the United States, in *Navios Corp.* v. *The Ulysses II.*[8] Similarly, during the Vietnam hostilities, the crews of Norwegian merchant ships calling at Vietnam ports received war risk allowances of 100 per cent of their pay and allowances.[9] On the other hand, after the cease-fire terminating the Suez operations of 1956 had been signed and become effective, the Appellate Division of the New York Supreme Court held that the death of an American photographer-journalist as a result of an Egyptian breach of the cease-fire was not an act "caused by any war or any act of war," such as would have fallen within the exception clause of an insurance contract.[10]

It is clear, therefore, that in practice states and courts will recognize that the old classification into war and peace as two distinct concepts is far too rigid.[11] Because of this, and particularly in the light of the conflicts that have taken place since 1945, which have rarely been accepted as wars in the traditional sense of international law, there has been a tendency to replace the concept of war by that of armed conflict.[12] Moreover, it has become clear that the traditional law as applied to war situations has become somewhat out of date if not irrelevant.

---

[4]*R.* v. *Bottrill, ex p. Kuechenmeister* [1947] 1 K.B. 41. See also, *In re Hourigan* [1946] *N.Z.L.R.* 1.

[5]"The Legal Meaning of War and the Relation of War to Reprisals," *Grotius Transactions for 1925*, 1, 17.

[6]"Jus Pacis ac Belli?" 37 *Am. J. Int'l Law* 460, 470 (1943).

[7]558 *Parliamentary Debates* (Commons), col. 1645.

[8](1958) 161 F. Supp. 932, 939-41.

[9]*The Times* (London), June 18, 1965.

[10]*Shneiderman* v. *Metropolitan Casualty Co. of New York* (1961) 220 N.Y.S. 2d 947.

[11]For a general discussion on this, see Green, "Armed Conflict, War and Self-Defence," 6 *Archiv des Völkerrechts* 387 (1957).

[12]See, e.g., Schwarzenberger, "From the Laws of War to the Law of Armed Conflict," 21 *Current Legal Problems* 239 (1968).

Apart from technological developments in the methods of warfare and with regard, for example, to the use of aircraft for evacuation of the wounded necessitating new regulations for the identification and protection of such machines, the period since 1945 has witnessed a series of armed confrontations between non-state entities, but of a character which could hardly be regarded as civil disturbances of the old domestic kind. At the same time, with the growth of the number of independent states which have felt an affinity for those still under colonial rule, an entirely new approach towards rebellions aiming at independence has become evident. Internal armed conflicts, whether of the traditional kind aimed at changing the party in power or the social structure of the state, or whether, like the American colonists in the eighteenth century, seeking independence from foreign rule, tend to be conducted with a vehemence that is not normally shown in classical dual wars, for, unless there is a basic conflict in ideological approach as on the eastern front between Nazi Germany and the Soviet Union, a modicum of humanity and even chivalry is still present. While the American Civil War with its *Andersonville Trial*[13] showed that, as between themselves and for very limited purposes in the field of criminal law, the parties might in fact apply some form of quasi-international law, for the most part there has been barely any room for international law. It is true that, in that conflict, problems arose between the United States and third powers concerning their neutrality,[14] or the legality of a blockade,[15] or issues of recognition,[16] or intervention and non-intervention, as in the Spanish Civil War,[17] too. However, international law considered that whatever happened within the borders of a state was subject to the sovereignty of that state, unless clearly removed therefrom. The manner in which an established government treated its rebels was therefore totally within the domestic jurisdiction of the state in question, while the attitude of the rebels has always seemed to reflect the views of John Harrington:[18]

> Treason doth never prosper; what's the reason?
> Why, if it prosper, none dare call it treason,

or of Montesquieu, who wrote of a king who, "having defeated and imprisoned a prince who disputed the crown with him, began to reproach him for infidelity and treachery. 'It was decided only a moment ago,' said the unfortunate prince, 'which of us was the traitor'."[19] In view of this, it is perhaps hardly surprising that a humanitarian movement like the International Committee of the Red Cross, which has been responsible for initiating and sponsoring so much of the humanitarian law of armed conflict, exercised itself to secure some measure of international agreement on the need to provide some legal regulation of internal conflicts.

Aware of the difficulties inherent in calling international conferences, particularly on issues that do not appear to be world-shattering or highly newsworthy, and conscious of the desire of many of the newly independent states to secure international recognition for the struggles for national liberation being waged by those still under colonial domination, the International Committee of the Red Cross in 1971 deemed that the time was ripe to commence careful study of the humanitarian law of war with a view to codifying

[13]*U.S. v. Wirz* (1865) H. R. Exec. Doc. No. 23, 40th Cong. 2d Sess., 1867-68, vol. 8.
[14]See, e.g., *Alabama Arbitration* (1872), 1 Moore, *Int'l Arb.* 653.
[15]*The Prize Cases* (1862) 2 Black 635.
[16]See 1 Moore, *Digest of Int'l Law*, s. 66; 1 Smith, *Great Britain and the Law of Nations* 302 (1932).
[17]See e.g., Padelford, *Int'l Law and Diplomacy in the Spanish Civil Strife* (1939).
[18]*Epigrams of Treason* (1618).
[19]*Persian Letters* (1721, tr. Healy, 1964), 174.

and developing it to the extent necessitated by current realities. After a series of meetings of governmental experts, the International Committee was able to draw up two draft Protocols additional to the Geneva Conventions of 1949[20] directed to the development of humanitarian law in armed conflict. Protocol I was concerned with international conflicts and sought to bring the Geneva law—the international law of war has frequently been divided into the Geneva law and the Hague law, the latter referring to the Conventions of 1899 and 1907, particularly Convention IV relating to the Laws and Customs of Warfare on Land—up to date in the light of the deficiencies that had become apparent during and after World War II. Protocol II was the more historic, in that for the first time an effort was made to produce an international convention to operate during non-international armed conflicts. In so far as this was concerned, two alternate lines of action were feasible. On the one hand, an attempt could be made to reproduce as far as possible the provisions of Protocol I, adapting where necessary the law of international armed conflict to non-international conflicts. There was even the suggestion that since the law was concerned with humanitarianism in armed conflicts, there was really no need to differentiate between international and non-international disputes and one convention could govern both. In contrast to this, there were some, and this was particularly true of the Canadian representatives, who emphasized that those engaged in non-international conflicts, at least in the anti-government faction, were likely to be unsophisticated from the military point of view, lacking the discipline of state armed forces, and knowing even less of the law of war than has normally been the case with such forces.[21] In their view, therefore, Protocol II should be drafted in simple and non-technical terms and should be as brief as possible, directed to securing observance of what might be termed the basic minimal principles of humanitarian law. Moreover, partisans of this approach were concerned that the type of non-international conflict to which this new Protocol should apply should possess as low a threshold as possible, that is to say, while not applying to ordinary riots and civil disturbances, it should come into operation long before the conflict reached the severity and level of the traditional civil law.

When the first session of the diplomatic Conference convened in Geneva in 1974 it became clear that the two Protocols were going to be similar in character, with the second almost mirroring the first. Four sessions were necessary before the Protocols were finally adopted in June 1977, and during this period a number of attempts were made to simplify Protocol II. In fact, the Canadian delegation actually presented a complete draft of a new Protocol II that reflected this aim. However, this draft as such was never discussed, although at the final session a number of non-aligned powers under the leadership of the head of the Pakistan delegation revived the idea of simplicity and based their new proposals on those of the Canadian draft, with the ultimate result that Protocol II no longer reflects the image of Protocol I.[22]

Although the Conference was devoted to the development of humanitarian law, it soon became clear that political pressures and interests, particularly concerning third world countries, were going to be of major significance. Among the earliest indications of this was the demand that national liberation movements be permitted to participate. After all, while it might be conceded that the Vatican was an automatic candidate for inclusion in humanitarian discussions, if the law of armed conflict was to be updated in any realistic fashion it would obviously have to take account of the interests and expe-

---

[20]1949, Schindler/Toman, 305, 333, 355, 427; 1977, 555, 609.

[21]See Green, "Humanitarian Law and the Man in the Field," 14 *Can. Y.B. Int'l. Law*, 1976, 96.

[22]Protocol I, Schindler/Toman, 551; Protocol II, 619. On the Canadian proposals, see "Canada's Role in the Development of the Law of Armed Conflict," ch. XIII *infra*.

riences of those who appeared to be most directly affected. There can be no gainsaying the fact that since 1945 most armed conflicts have in some way or another been concerned with problems of national liberation and self-determination. Since, however, the Conference was an inter-state affair it would not be possible for any of these movements to be included as full participants. Moreover, while various organs of the United Nations or other international organizations might be prepared to pass resolutions in praise and support of such movements and might even be willing to allow them something in the nature of a quasi-membership, it was hardly proper for a conference of this character to take such a highly controversial and political decision. As a result, a resolution was adopted agreeing to invite "recognized" national liberation movements as observers, but possessing in practice more rights than the observers sent by non-governmental organizations. While there has never been any authoritative definition of a national liberation movement, practice has tended to agree that a national liberation movement is that which is recognized as such by the regional organization concerned with the area in which the *soi-disant* national liberation movement (n.l.m.) is carrying on its activities—thus automatically excluding any movement not popular with the majority of the members of such an organization, and probably also any movement operating in an area where no such organization exists. In fact, it was only the Palestine Liberation Organization which played an active role during the Geneva Conference—to the extent of co-sponsoring amendments to the original draft and even making explanatory statements as to how it would have voted on particular issues had it been given the right to vote, the only discrimination to which it seemed to be subject.

Having decided to allow national liberation movements to participate on this basis, it was perhaps inevitable that the conference would ultimately be confronted with a claim that such movements should be allowed to sign the Final Act. A Final Act is nothing but a record of what has transpired at the Conference and an authentication of the documents that have been adopted.[23] It has been defined as "a formal statement or summary of an international conference, enumerating the treaties or related treaty instruments drawn up as the result of its deliberations, together with resolutions, or 'voeux,' adopted by the conference."[24] It "must not contain international commitments. A Final Act must be limited to such matters as a statement or summary of the proceedings of the conference, the names of the states that participated, the organization of the conference and the committees established, resolutions adopted, the drafts of international agreements formulated for consideration by governments concerned, and the like."[25] While it might appear, in view of this, that there is no reason for any participant in an international conference not to sign the Final Act, provided the basis on which it has participated in the Conference has been made clear,[26] it must be recognized that there is a certain political *cachet* attached to being permitted to sign an international instrument, however formal and non-legal, on the same basis as recognized members of the international community. The friends of the Palestine Liberation Organization were extremely anxious to ensure this privilege for the Organization. This ran into difficulties not merely from Israel and its sympathizers, but also from a number of states which considered it improper for this Conference to be the first to permit such action, which was considered highly political.

---

[23]See, e.g., Final Act of the U.N. Conference on the Law of Treaties, Vienna 1969, 8 *I.L.M.* 728-35 (1969).

[24]Satow, *Guide to Diplomatic Practice* 260 (Gore-Booth, ed., 1979).

[25]U.S. Dept. of State, Circular 175 Procedure (Foreign Affairs Manual, vol. 11, ch. 700, 1974), *Digest of U.S. Practice in Int'l Law 1974*, (Rovine ed.) 211.

[26]See, e.g., re revolutionary governments and governments in exile, Blix, *Treaty-Making Power*, ch. X, XI (1960).

Others questioned why some observers, namely the n.l.m.s, should be given this right when others, for example the High Commissioner for Refugees, and even the International Committee of the Red Cross, perhaps more intimately connected with the Protocols than any other entity including the participating states, were not to be so honoured. Ultimately, it was decided to include in the Final Act the text of the resolution extending the invitation to participate, with a further statement that this particular signature was in no way to be considered as a precedent. This proviso is, of course, completely without meaning. Once an act has been tolerated, or a decision taken, it must of necessity be a precedent, even though those affected by it declare that in their view it is a once-and-for-all act with no significance for the future. As to the actual signature, a number of states made it clear that, while willing to accept this compromise, there was no way in which they would agree to the signature of any n.l.m. appearing on the same page with that of any participating state. Since then, the Palestine Liberation Organization has further enhanced its international status and has now been accepted as a full member of the United Nations Commission for Western Asia.[27]

While this conflict about the participation and signature of the national liberation movements caused heated debate, it was nothing compared with the arguments relating to the status of a national liberation struggle. The solution to this problem would control whether such a conflict fell within the purview of Protocol I as an international armed conflict, or remained a non-international conflict governed by Protocol II. In this context one should consider the number of United Nations resolutions that have been passed in praise of and supporting wars of national liberation, condemning colonialism, and invoking international aid for those engaged in the search for self-determination even though this might seem to mean disregarding some of the obligations in Article 2 of the Charter, ultimately denying that the definition of aggression adopted by the General Assembly[28]

> could in any way prejudice the right to self-determination, freedom, and inde-
> pendence, as derived from the Charter, of peoples forcibly deprived of that right
> and referred to in the Declaration on Principles of International Law concerning
> Friendly Relations and Cooperation among States in accordance with the Charter
> of the United Nations,[29] particularly peoples under colonial and racist regimes or
> other forms of alien domination; nor the right of these peoples to struggle to that
> end and to seek and receive support, in accordance with the principles of the
> Charter and in conformity with the above-mentioned Declaration.

With this in mind it is perhaps not surprising that the countries of the third world, who in fact possessed the majority of votes at the Conference, sought to secure recognition that such armed conflicts would in future be considered as international conflicts governed by the international law of armed conflict. In view of the realities of world politics this endeavour bore fruit and was accepted by consensus, albeit after much debate.

In accordance with traditional international law, "war is a contention between two or more States through their armed forces, for the purpose of overpowering each other and imposing such conditions of peace as the victor pleases."[30] Moreover, by Article 1 of the Hague Regulations,[31] for any unit to be subject to or enjoy the protection of the laws of

---

[27]*The Times* (London), July 23, 1977.
[28]G. A. Res. 3314 (XXIX), December 24, 1974, Art. 7.
[29]G. A. Res. 2625 (XXV), October 24, 1970.
[30]2 Oppenheim, *International Law* (1906; unchanged in Lauterpacht ed., 1952), s. 54.
[31]Annexed to Hague Convention IV respecting the Laws and Customs of War on Land, 1907 (Scott, *The Hague Conventions and Declarations of 1899 and 1907* (1908), 100, Schindler/Toman, 57.

war it must be commanded by a superior responsible for the acts of his subordinates, have a fixed distinctive emblem recognizable at a distance, carry arms openly, and conduct operations in accordance with the laws and customs of war. By Article 1 of Protocol I, however, an international armed conflict is defined as including "armed conflicts in which peoples are fighting against colonial domination and alien occupation and against racist régimes in the exercise of their right of self-determination, as enshrined in the Charter of the United Nations and the Declaration on Principles of International Law concerning Friendly Relations and Cooperation among States in accordance with the Charter of the United Nations." While the Protocol thus elevates the Declaration on Friendly Relations into a binding statement of treaty law, it makes no attempt to define what is meant by "colonial domination, alien occupation, racist régime or self-determination," regardless of the fact that these terms may have acquired a particular meaning in the practice of the United Nations. The Geneva Conference on Humanitarian Law in Armed Conflict was not held under the auspices of the United Nations; many of its participants were not members of the United Nations; the invitations to attend were sent out by the government of Switzerland; and the working drafts were prepared by a non-governmental organization, the International Committee of the Red Cross, not in any way associated with the United Nations. Moreover, in practice, many a body engaged in hostilities against an unpopular establishment or seeking the reins of power after the withdrawal of a colonial authority has claimed the right to describe itself as a national liberation movement seeking self-determination. Such was the case, for example, in the civil war between Nigeria and "Biafra," the conflict between the rival parties in Angola, and the hostilities between Ethiopia and its border peoples. None of these, however, has been recognized as an international conflict, even though some foreign element may have been involved.

It becomes necessary, therefore, to examine the interplay between this first article of Protocol I and the parallel article of Protocol II. According to the latter, a non-international conflict is one not covered by Article 1 of the first Protocol,

> and which takes place in the territory of a High Contracting Party between its armed forces and dissident armed forces or other organized armed groups which, under responsible command, exercise such control over a part of its territory as to enable them to carry out sustained and concerted military operations and to implement this Protocol [which] shall not apply to situations of internal disturbances and tensions, such as riots, isolated and sporadic acts of violence and other acts of a similar nature, as not being armed conflicts.

While it is perfectly reasonable to exclude incidents such as those that occurred during the Chicago Democratic Convention or at Kent State, this definition is so framed as to require a level of military organization and sophistication that ensures its application only in the traditional type of civil war. Since a government in power, particularly one that may represent a minority ethnic group, is unlikely to agree that it is governing inconsistently with the principles of self-determination, especially if it has been elected by virtue of a balloting qualification enacted by itself, it is going to necessitate difficult exercises in classification to decide when a Protocol II situation differs from or becomes a Protocol I situation, especially when there is no local regional organization claiming the right to declare what is an authentic national liberation movement.

Obviously, once it was decided that n.l.m.s could wage an international armed conflict and be protected by international law, it became necessary to examine the definition of combatants to ensure that the members of such movements would, when captured, be treated as prisoners of war and not subject to trial as traitors or rebels under the established criminal law. Article 43 of Protocol I defines armed forces and appears to be in accordance with the traditional view, in that it requires a responsible command answerable to a party to the conflict, "even if that party is represented by a government or an authority not recognized by an adverse party," which would frequently be the case in a war of national liberation and is the case in the present Middle Eastern situation. Moreover, the forces in question must be subject to an internal disciplinary system which is to enforce compliance with the rules of armed conflict. Reflecting the position of guerilla movements during World War II, it is provided that if paramilitary or armed law enforcement agencies are incorporated into the armed forces, the adverse party must be so informed. The legal development in this article relates to the unrecognized entity, especially as it goes on to provide that all members of the armed forces are combatants, that is to say, "they have the right to participate directly in hostilities." According to Article 44 any captured combatant is "a prisoner of war," and, subject to certain limitations, although combatants are obliged to comply with the rules of international law, violation of such rules "shall not deprive a combatant of his right to be a combatant or . . . of his right to be a prisoner of war." The limitations just referred to are intended to protect the civilian population, a matter which is now perhaps more difficult than previously, since members of n.l.m.s frequently wear the same clothing as the population among whom they operate and seek protection. Reflecting the old law and its requirement of distinguishing marks for combatants, the article obliges combatants

> to distinguish themselves from the civilian population while they are engaged in an attack or in a military operation preparatory to an attack. Recognizing, however, that there are situations in armed conflicts where, owing to the nature of the hostilities an armed combatant cannot so distinguish himself, he shall retain his status as a combatant, provided that, in such situations, he carries his arms openly (a) during each military engagement, and (b) during such time as he is visible to the adversary while he is engaged in a military deployment preceding the launching of an attack in which he is to participate.

Presumably, the laying of an ambush or an attack from the rear by individuals in civilian clothing would be protected. What is not clear is whether the "visibility" referred to means by way of the naked eye or with the assistance of optical aids. The article goes on to state that "acts which comply with [these] requirements . . . shall not be considered as perfidious within the meaning of Article 37, paragraph 1 (c)," which expressly states that "the feigning of civilian, non-combtant status" constitutes perfidy. It would appear, therefore, that a member of a regular armed force would not enjoy the same protection as the members of the n.l.m. against whom he might be operating, for he is clearly required to wear a uniform or otherwise clearly distinguish himself, a point which is emphasized by paragraph 7 of the Article. This article, therefore, breaks with the traditions of humanitarian law and of the law of war as such. These have always been regarded as operating universally, reciprocally,[32] and without any limitation of a discriminatory character[33]—as is recognized by the Protocol itself in other contexts.[34]

Article 44 also provides that a combatant who does not satisfy the limiting conditions just expounded "shall forfeit his right to be a prisoner of war, but he shall, nevertheless,

---

[32]See, e.g., Schwarzenberger, *The Frontiers of International Law* 32 (1962).

[33]See, e.g., Lauterpacht, "Rules of Warfare in an Unlawful War," in Lipsky, *Law and Politics in the World Community* 89, 92-3 (1953).

[34]E.g., Arts. 9 (wounded and sick), 70 (relief for civilian population), 73 (refugees and stateless persons), 75 (fundamental guarantees for those in hands of adverse party).

be given protections equivalent in all respects to those given to prisoners of war." Moreover, if such a "combatant" is captured while not engaged in an attack or in preparations therefor, he "shall not forfeit his rights to be a combatant and a prisoner of war by virtue of his prior activities." The Protocol makes no attempt to explain how the captor is to decide this particular point, nor how the captive will prove his status. In fact, by Article 45, if he claims such status and any doubt arises whether he is so entitled, "he shall continue to have such status and, therefore, to be protected . . . until such time as his status has been determined by a competent tribunal." If he is not held as a prisoner of war and is charged by his captors with an offence arising out of the hostilities, he has the right to claim such status before a judicial tribunal, and the decision as to status should, if possible, be made before any trial on the substantive charges, for if he is so entitled the act with which he has been charged may lose its criminality. Unless the trial takes place *in camera*, this judicial determination as to status shall be made in the presence of the representative of the protecting power. The provision is thus wider than that in Article 4 of the Third Geneva Convention of 1949, in that it calls for the presence of the protecting power, and while that Convention extended to nationals of the captor if they were part of the forces of another party to the Convention,[35] it did not extend to members of an armed force carrying out warlike acts while in civilian clothes.[36] It has also been held by an Israeli court that the Convention would not apply to members of an organized movement, even though in a recognizable uniform, if that movement did not constitute an organ or part of the forces of a state.[37] The new Protocol, on the other hand, applies equally to members of such groups provided they are waging a war of national liberation.

A further apparent concession to n.l.m.s is found in Article 77. Experience has shown that in the past these movements have frequently recruited juveniles into their ranks, perhaps relying on the reluctance of regular forces to fire upon children. The Protocol attempts to stop this practice. Article 77 forbids the enrolment or recruitment of children under fifteen, but provides that if such children do take part in the conflict and are captured they will, nevertheless, enjoy in addition to their rights as prisoners of war the privileges that the Article affords to children. Further, regardless of any crime in relation to the conflict committed by such a wrongfully enlisted juvenile, even though it be a grave breach, he cannot be executed if under the age of eighteen when the crime was committed. In this, his position is better than that of women. By Article 76 they are protected against indecencies, but if they have committed offences relating to the conflict the party holding them is entitled to pronounce the death sentence, though it is to endeavour not to. If the sentence is pronounced, then if the woman is pregnant or is a mother with a dependent infant, she may not be executed. This prohibition may well raise problems for those countries that still have mandatory death sentences for certain offences and that regard a prolonged delay before execution as non-humanitarian. It may also mean that dependent children will be taken away from their mothers and placed in care, thus permitting execution of the woman concerned.

Another issue which reflects the concerns and influence of the newly independent states and third world countries generally is the position of mercenaries. In history, mercenaries have played a respectable role in war,[38] while Vattel went so far as to imply that there was almost a duty upon a sovereign to allow his nationals to serve in foreign armies:[39]

[35]See *Public Prosecutor* v. *Koi*, [1968] A.C. 829.
[36]*Mohamed Ali* v. *Public Prosecutor*, [1968] 3 All E.R. 488.
[37]*Military Prosecutor* v. *Omar Mahmud Kassem* (1969), 42 I.L.R. 470.
[38]See, e.g., Mockler, *The Mercenaries* (1969), ch. 1-6; Bayley, *Mercenaries for the Crimea* (1977).
[39]*Le Droit des Gens ou Principes de la Loi Naturelle* (1758), Liv. III, ch. 2, s. 13 (Carnegie tr., 1916, 239-40, italics added).

Mercenary soldiers are foreigners who voluntarily enter into the service of a State for a stipulated pay. As they are not subjects of the sovereign they owe him no service in that capacity, and consequently *the pay he offers them is the motive of their service.* . . . The question has been much discussed whether the profession of a mercenary soldier be legitimate or not, whether individuals may, for money or other rewards, engage as soldiers in the service of a foreign prince? The question does not seem to me very difficult of solution. Those who enter into such contracts without the express or implied consent of their sovereign are wanting in their duty as citizens. But when the sovereign leaves them at liberty to follow their inclination for the profession of arms, they become free in that respect. Now, every free man may join whatever society pleases him best and seems most to his advantage, and may make common cause with it and take up its quarrels. He becomes in some measure, at least for a time, a citizen of the State into whose service he enters. . . . *Such mercenary soldiers, by learning the art of war, will render themselves capable of serving their country, if ever it has need of them.* . . . Can the sovereign properly allow his subjects to serve foreign powers indiscriminately as mercenaries? He can, and for this simple reason—that *in this way his subjects learn an art the knowledge of which is both useful and necessary.* The tranquility, the profound peace which Switzerland has so long enjoyed in the midst of wars which have agitated Europe, would soon become disastrous to her if her citizens did not enter the service of foreign princes and thereby train themselves in the art of war and keep alive their martial spirit.

While Vattel emphasizes the significance of payment as an incentive, he does recognize that the mercenary may "make common cause and take up the quarrels" of the state he serves. This would therefore extend his comments on the legality of such service to those who enlist for ideological reasons as in the case of the International Brigade in Spain,[40] or Jordan's Arab Legion, the Gurkha regiments in the British Indian Army or the French Foreign Legion, although these were recognized parts of state forces, the Eagle Squadron, volunteers in Israel, and the like, even though they would undoubtedly receive pay for their services. However, his comments would probably not extend to those who aided the Biafrans in Nigeria or fought on the losing side after Angola secured its independence and the local factions fought for supremacy. In view of the rôle played by white mercenaries and ideological volunteers in Biafra, the Congo, and Angola, accompanied in developed countries by a fairly wide rejection, particularly by the youth, of professional soldiery, especially soldiers of fortune, it was perhaps not surprising that active steps were taken to suppress such activities. Where some countries are concerned, legislation relating to foreign enlistment was applicable, but often this only related to enlistment on behalf of a recognized state or opposed to a government with which the particular country was at peace. Allegations of terrorism and other atrocities by white mercenaries in Angola resulted in the trial and execution of some who were captured and a proposed international convention to declare mercenarism, defined as being service on behalf of colonialism against national liberation, a capital offence.

At Geneva the issue was fully debated, and Article 45, while not making mercenarism *per se* a crime, declares that "a mercenary shall not have the right to be a combatant or a prisoner of war," thus placing him in the position of one who unlawfully takes up arms and who may therefore be tried for illegal belligerency. The concept no longer directly reflects the prejudices of the third world for it is no longer a requirement of the definition that the service be on behalf of a colonial or imperialist power. By Article 47 a mercenary is specially recruited locally or abroad; he must take a direct part in the

---

[40]One author, at least (Mockler, *op. cit.*, 17), regards its members as being in the same position as the historical mercenary.

hostilities—thus, advisers would not be so defined; he must be motivated "essentially" for the desire of private gain and be promised payment in excess of that received by members of the armed forces holding similar rank or performing similar functions; he must be an alien or a non-resident of the territory controlled by the party to the conflict enlisting him; he must not be a member of the armed forces of such a party—which would imply that all he need do is enlist in the regular forces rather than a mercenary unit or, if such a body of men is involved, the party to the conflict should embody them in its armed forces; *and* he must not have been sent by a state not involved in the conflict on official duty as a member of its armed forces. Thus any troops going from, for example, Cuba to Angola or Ethiopia would be outside the definition.

A problem arose in so far as Rhodesia was concerned. Since there had been no recognition of the colony of Southern Rhodesia as an independent state, there could be no Rhodesian nationality. The white Rhodesians could not be regarded as nationals of the entity on whose behalf they fought, while it may well be argued that since general conscription applied they had all been recruited specially either locally or abroad. Does this mean that it would have been possible for the Patriotic Front to argue that all members of the self-styled Rhodesian armed forces were in fact mercenaries, or would they have been saved by virtue of their being residents—at least some of them—of territory under the control of a party to the conflict, especially as it is clear that they were not motivated essentially by the desire for reward? The issue was further complicated by the decision of the World Council of Churches calling on member churches "to urge their government to treat enlistment in the armed forces of the illegal Rhodesian regime as a criminal offence, to punish offenders accordingly, and to outlaw any recruitment for this purpose."[41]

Even before the Protocol had been opened for signature, some states made it clear that they are taking the condemnation of mercenaries extremely seriously. Thus, under the Australian Crimes (Foreign Incursions and Recruitment) Bill, 1977, it will be an offence to recruit or advertise, facilitate or promote recruitment of another to serve with the armed forces of a foreign country. The Bill prohibits persons from preparing for, or engaging in, incursions into foreign countries, but does not prohibit enlistment of mercenaries outside Australia. It will still be possible, therefore, for an Australian to recruit if he is outside his own country and presumably to enlist while abroad. Moreover, it remains to be seen whether the term "country" will be understood widely enough to include recruitment on behalf of a national liberation movement, an entity seeking to secure recognition as such, or a government engaged in an armed conflict undertaken in the name of national liberation and self-determination.

There is one other major innovation in Protocol I which reflects the significance of the countries of the third world. As is well known, these countries have to a great extent been responsible for the shift in the United Nations from concern with the rights of man to the rights of people, though it is perhaps difficult to ascertain exactly what this last word means. Their campaign reached its culmination in 1973 when the General Assembly adopted its International Convention on the Suppression and Punishment of the Crime of Apartheid,[42] which came into force in July 1976. It was perhaps not surprising, therefore, that when the Geneva Conference was deliberating what new offences should be added to the Geneva Conventions list of grave offences, carrying with them susceptibility to universal jurisdiction and perhaps imposing a liability upon all signatories of the

---

[41]*The Times* (London), August 6, 1977.
[42]Res. 3068 (XXVIII), November 30, 1973 (adopted by 91-4 [Portugal, South Africa, U.K., U.S.A.], with 26 abstentions).

Protocol to prosecute and punish, the third world should have insisted upon the inclusion of this offence in the Protocol. A number of delegations pointed out that customary law, the Geneva Conventions, and the Protocol all forbade adverse or discriminatory treatment within the confines of humanitarian law, maintaining that there was therefore no need specifically to provide for apartheid. In addition, they contended that the "offence" was difficult to define and the drafting of an indictment would be almost impossible. The partisans replied that, since the adoption of the Apartheid Convention, and in accordance with common knowledge, everyone was aware of the fact that apartheid referred to the policy of separation imposed by the white régimes in Southern Africa. Thus, under Article 85, it is now a grave breach of international humanitarian law as prescribed by the Protocol and as such a war crime, wilfully to commit "practices of apartheid and other inhuman and degrading practices involving outrages upon personal dignity, based on racial discrimination." Even if it be accepted that one knows what is meant by apartheid, it may be difficult to decide what are the "practices of apartheid." It will be even more difficult and open to subjective determination to decide what are other "inhuman and degrading practices involving outrages upon personal dignity, based on racial discrimination." Would this include, for example, the Japanese practice of parading European prisoners of war through the streets of occupied Singapore? The thought of drafting an indictment charging this grave breach boggles the imagination, especially as it can be argued that every supporter of the government of South Africa is wilfully indulging in "practices of apartheid."

There was one matter on which the third world countries, this time under the leadership of Mexico, were unable to carry the day, primarily due to the opposition of both the western group and the Soviet bloc and most of its socialist allies. It would have been incongruous to hold a conference to update or develop the humanitarian law of armed conflict, if no attempt were made to deal with the problems inherent in weapon development. In accordance with the law *durante bello*, "the right of belligerents to adopt means of injuring the enemy is not unlimited,"[43] and this prohibition is repeated in the Protocol, which forbids methods and means of warfare "of a nature to cause superfluous injury or unnecessary suffering . . . [or] which are intended, or may be expected to cause widespread, long-term and severe damage to the natural environment."[44] As to the substantive definition of such weapons, a special *ad hoc* committee was established to examine the problem with a view to further action, for it was considered that this problem was not really one to be dealt with in a protocol amending and developing the Geneva law. Nevertheless, third world countries in particular were anxious to have prohibitions written in or, at least, to secure the establishment of a standing organ able to examine new weapons and to declare them illegal. It was contended by the opponents of this proposal that such measures would impinge upon and perhaps foreclose the efforts of the *ad hoc* committee and possibly even interfere with general disarmament discussions. *In fine*, a resolution was adopted advocating furthur study and review, but not imposing any obligation of the kind sought.

While the Protocol does not deal with specific weapons, it does have a number of provisions expressly concerned with means and methods of warfare in a somewhat general fashion. The nearest to a ban on particular weapons is to be found in Article 36 of the Protocol stipulating that, when studying, developing, acquiring, or adopting any new weapon, a party is obliged to determine whether its employment would ever be

[43]Hague Regulations, Art. 22.
[44]Art. 35.

prohibited by the Protocol or any other rule of international law. There is no indication of what is to happen if the result of the study should prove positive. Presumably, it is considered sufficient to imply that in such a case the development, acquisition, or adoption would not take place, since, if it did, the party concerned would be in breach of international law, which is based on the principles of good faith and *pacta sunt servanda*.[45]

Although the traditional law has forbidden perfidy, there has been no clear indication of what falls within its purview. Article 37 attempts to fill this gap, while at the same time preserving the old distinction between perfidious acts and legitimate ruses. Acts are perfidious if they invite "the confidence of an adversary to lead him to believe that he is entitled to, or is obliged to accord, protection under the rules of international law applicable in armed conflict, with intent to betray that confidence." Ruses, on the other hand, are merely intended to mislead the adverse party so as "to induce him to act recklessly," and they remain lawful so long as they do not infringe any rule of law and "do not invite [his] confidence with respect to protection" under the law of armed conflict. While the use of camouflage and decoys constitute legitimate ruses, the feigning of civilian, non-combatant status amounts to perfidy, although as has been seen this may not be true when members of n.l.m.s are involved. It is equally perfidious to feign incapacitation by wounds or to pretend an intent to surrender or negotiate a truce. It is similarly forbidden to seek protected status by false use of signs or emblems of United Nations forces or of those of a non-party to the conflict, and this latter ban is reiterated in Article 39, especially when engaged in military operations. These provisions, however, do not affect the traditional law relating to espionage or the use of flags in armed conflict at sea. While it is not perfidy, it is forbidden by Article 38 to make improper use of the red cross, red crescent, red lion and sun, or any other protected emblem, such as that pertaining to cultural property,[46] and Article 85 includes as a grave breach the perfidious use of any such emblem. In this connection it is perhaps worth mentioning that, for some time now, problems have arisen with regard to the three 'Red Cross' emblems. For religious reasons,[47] Israel has insisted upon using the Red Shield of David as its emblem, but protected status for this was denied at Geneva in 1949 by one vote, and since then the Arab states, receiving third world support, have consistently prevented any recognition being afforded to this sign. However, ever since the Middle East war began the sign has, for the most part, been recognized by Israel's adversaries, and it has recently been included as a protected medical service symbol in a training document issued by the United States Department of the Army.[48] Despite possible contentions, therefore, that the Red Shield of David has acquired recognition as a protected emblem under customary law, the Israel government has still considered that it should be placed on a treaty basis, especially as its Red Shield Society cannot be a member of the League of Red Cross Societies so long as its emblem remains unrecognized. In view of the counter-

[45]See, e.g., Cheng, *General Principles of Law* 105-60 (1953); Herczegh, *General Principles of International Law and the International Legal Order* 30, 47-9 (1969); Kelsen, *Principles of International Law* 447 (Tucker ed., 1966); Lauterpacht, "The Definition and Nature of International Law," 1 *Collected Works* 5, 47 (1970); "Règles générales du droit de la paix," 62 *Hague Recueil* 99 (1937), reprinted in 1 *Collected Works* 193, 210 (1970); Schwarzenberger, "The Fundamental Principles of International Law," 87 *Hague Recueil* 195, 290-326 (1955); Tunkin, *Theory of International Law* 86, 218-24 (1974).

[46]"A shield, pointed below, per saltire blue and white (a shield consisting of a royal-blue square, one of the angles of which forms the point of the shield, and of a royal-blue triangle above the square, the space on either side being taken up by a white triangle)," Hague Convention for the Protection of Cultural Property in the Event of Armed Conflict, 1954, Art. 16, Schindler/Toman, 661.

[47]See, e.g., Rosenne, "The Red Cross, Red Crescent, Red Lion and Sun and the Red Shield of David," 5 *Israel Y.B. on Human Rights* 9 (1975); Bugnion, *The Emblem of the Red Cross* (1977).

[48]"Your Conduct in Combat under the Law of War," T.R.A.D.O.C. Pam 27-1 (1974), 9.

argument that there should be no proliferation of signs,[49] Libya and Norway in 1977 proposed a resolution calling for consideration of an entirely new emblem to replace the three now recognized. This proposal failed to secure the necessary two-thirds majority, the socialist states voting with those opposing. Though the Israel emblem is in fact used, it might well be possible to argue that its false use is not forbidden by Article 38. However, at the 1976 session, a Canadian proposal to condemn as perfidy the wrongful use of any emblem, though unprotected and unrecognized, which was habitually used in an armed conflict to secure protection for those using it, was overwhelmingly defeated, it being alleged that this would amount to indirect recognition of the Israeli emblem.

One of the issues most clearly affecting humanitarian law during actual conduct of hostilities is the treatment meted out to those *hors de combat*. Article 49 expressly forbids any order to deny quarter or any threat that hostilities will be conducted on that basis. Quarter is, of course, important to those who have become *hors de combat*, and Article 41 defines this as being in the power of an adverse party, having clearly expressed an intention to surrender, or having been rendered incapacitated by wounds or sickness to an extent that the person in question is incapable of defending himself, provided that he abstains from any hostile act and does not attempt to escape. Moreover, if persons have fallen into the adverse party's hands under conditions which prevent their evacuation in accordance with the terms of the Third Geneva Convention, "they shall be released and all feasible precautions shall be taken to ensure their safety." Apparently, they are to be released in this fashion without giving any parole and even if it is known that they will return to active combat duties with the minimum of delay. According to the 1923 Rules of Air Warfare,[50] "when an aircraft has been disabled, the occupants when endeavouring to escape by means of a parachute must not be attacked in the course of their descent." Although these Rules have never been ratified, they are important "as an authoritative attempt to clarify and formulate rules of law governing the use of aircraft in war,"[51] and "to a great extent, they correspond to the customary rules and general principles underlying the conventions on the law of war on land and at sea."[52] While this may be so, in both world wars the practice was not always in accordance with such a "principle,"[53] and the Italian War Regulations of 1938, having forbidden fire upon airmen whose machines had crashed, expressly permitted such hostile action against those descending in parachutes.[54] Now the matter has been placed beyond doubt. By Article 42 no person parachuting from an aircraft in distress may be attacked during his descent, and if he lands in the territory of an adverse party, unless it is clear that he is engaged in a hostile act, he must be given an opportunity to surrender before being attacked. This protection does not extend to airborne troops. Nothing, however, is said about airborne agents, spies, or saboteurs, who may have been compelled to bale out before reaching their destinations. This article was subject to much opposition, especially on behalf of the Arab countries, who unsuccessfully sought to include an amendment authorizing attack if the parachutist appeared to be descending behind his own lines.

When discussing the status of national liberation movements reference was made to the definition of combatants and their right to be treated as prisoners of war on capture. By Article 45 a presumption that he is a prisoner of war is created on behalf of any person

[49]This is a somewhat artificial argument since, in addition to the three emblems, recognized signs now exist for cultural objects, civil defence, and dangerous forces.
[50]Schindler/Toman, 147.
[51]2 Oppenheim, *op. cit. supra* note 30 (1952 ed.), at 519.
[52]*Loc. cit., supra* note 50.
[53]See, e.g., Spaight, *Air Power and War Rights* 155-64 (1947).
[54]Arts. 35(3), 38 resp. (2 Oppenheim, *op. cit. supra* note 30, at 521, n. 5).

who has taken part in hostilities and who falls into the hands of the adverse party. Should it transpire that he is not entitled to enjoy such status, he is nevertheless entitled to the fundamental guarantees provided by Article 75 on behalf of all persons held by an adverse party. These fundamental guarantees, which are to be enjoyed by all without any distinction based upon race, colour, sex, language, religion or belief, political or other opinion, national or social origin, wealth, birth or other status, or other similar criteria, may be regarded as the basic minimum conditions of humanitarian law in armed conflict. Moreover, each party is to respect the person, honour, convictions, and religious practices of all such persons. It is not obvious from the Protocol what is meant by "convictions," for it was made clear during the Conference that this refers to something wider than beliefs of a religious nature. The Article places an absolute ban on (a) violence to the life, health, physical, or mental well-being of persons, in particular murder, torture, physical or mental, corporal punishment or mutilation; (b) outrages upon personal dignity, especially humiliating and degrading treatment, enforced prostitution and any form of indecent assault; (c) hostage-taking; (d) collective punishments; and (e) the threat to commit any of these. The Article then goes on to define the conditions under which such persons may stand trial, reflecting the basic concepts of the western rule of law and of fair trial. Here, war criminals are placed in a better position than are mercenaries, for there is no provision to guarantee the latter a fair trial or any standard of treatment. When the Soviet Union and its allies ratified the Third Geneva Convention on Prisoners of War they added a reservation to the effect that Article 85, which extends the benefits of the Convention to all prisoners of war prosecuted by the detaining power for acts committed before capture, did not apply to those "convicted in accordance with the principles of the Nuremberg trial, for war crimes and crimes against humanity, it being understood that persons convicted of such crimes must be subject to the conditions obtaining in the [detaining] country for those who undergo their punishment."[55]

By Article 75 of the Protocol

> in order to avoid any doubt concerning the prosecution and trial of persons accused of war crimes or crimes against humanity, the following principles shall apply: (a) persons who are accused of such crimes should be submitted for the purpose of prosecution and trial in accordance with the applicable rules of international law; and (b) any such persons who do not benefit from more favourable treatment under the Conventions or this Protocol shall be accorded the treatment provided by this Article, whether or not the crimes of which they are accused constitute grave breaches of the Convention or of this Protocol.

As we have seen, grave breaches constitute war crimes. This provision may not be as protective as might be assumed, for there is no provision in the Protocol forbidding reservations to any particular article. It was generally accepted at the Conference that the traditional law concerning reservations to treaties would apply, namely, that a ratifying party could add such reservations as it pleased, subject, perhaps, to the interpretation adopted by the World Court in its opinion on *Reservations to the Genocide Convention*,[56] as modified by Article 19(c) of the Vienna Convention on Treaties,[57] that is to say so long as the reservation is not incompatible with the purpose of the treaty. Since the purpose of the Protocol is to promote humanitarian law and to extend its protection to all those falling into the hands of an adverse party, it might be possible to argue that for those

[55]See, e.g., Schindler/Toman, 517.
[56][1949] I.C.J. 15, 21.
[57]1969—8, I.L.M. 679.

states ratifying the Vienna Convention any such reservation would be illegal. It should be mentioned, however, that as of December 31, 1983 none of the socialist states which had made this reservation to the 1949 Convention had ratified Vienna.

In addition to prisoners of war, military personnel who are *hors de combat* are the wounded, sick, and shipwrecked, the traditional categories on whose behalf the International Committee of the Red Cross has exercised its humanitarian tasks. Apart from containing a number of technical articles with regard to the identification of, for example, medical establishments and transports, or the use of identification lights by medical aircraft, and the conditions under which such aircraft may operate, the Protocol develops the law relating to the rights and protection of the wounded and sick beyond the point at which it was left by the 1949 conventions. Perhaps the most important provision is to be found in Article 10 which, in addition to postulating that they be protected and respected, provides that they are to be treated humanely and to receive, "to the fullest extent practicable and with the least possible delay," the medical care they require, and such treatment is always to be without discrimination other than for purely medical reasons. By Article 11 they are protected from medical experimentation, even though they consent thereto, and may not be subjected to "any medical procedure which is not indicated by the state of health of the person concerned and is not consistent with generally accepted medical standards" which would be applied to the nationals of the party responsible for the procedures in question, such nationals not being deprived of their liberty in any way. An exception is allowed for blood transfusions and skin transplants provided they are given absolutely voluntarily and only for therapeutic purposes. Deviations from these restrictive provisions constitute grave breaches of the Protocol.

In view of some recent experiences with regard to medical personnel in civil disturbances, it is interesting to note that Article 16 forbids punishment of any medical personnel for acting in a manner consistent with medical ethics, regardless of the status of the patient. Such personnel may not be required to carry out any acts incompatible with medical ethics or the medical rules designed to protect the wounded and sick or those contained in the Conventions and the Protocol. This may well raise problems for the medical officer who is told to stand by when the military officials of his own state are pursuing policies with regard to the wounded and sick which are inconsistent with such medical standards. The Protocol is not of great assistance to the medical officer who may have attended enemy personnel and is required to give information concerning their whereabouts or those who have protected them. Article 16 provides that medical officers cannot be compelled to give information to the adverse party or their own party if such information might prove harmful to the patient or his family. This problem may be of major significance during a war of national liberation, especially as the immunity is limited in the case of the medical officer's own party by the limiting statement "except as required by the law" of that party. In so far as the shipwrecked are concerned it is sufficient to refer to the definition, which is perhaps wider than might be expected. The term covers all persons, whether military or civilian, in peril at sea or in other waters as a "result of misfortune affecting them or the vessel or aircraft carrying them and who refrain from any act of hostility," and they continue to be so described and protected as such so long as they continue to refrain from hostilities and until they acquire another status under the Conventions or Protocol.

One of the problems that has proved an obstacle to the re-establishment of relations between the United States and Vietnam has concerned the missing and the dead. This matter is now covered by the Protocol, "prompted mainly by the right of families to know the fate of their relations." Article 33 imposes an obligation upon the parties to a conflict, "as soon as circumstances permit, and at the latest from the end of active hostilities," to search for such missing persons as are notified to them by the adverse party. Provision is made for the recording and imparting of information concerning all those who have been detained for more than two weeks, or have died during detention. The Protocol also expresses the hope that, even during hostilities, arrangements might be made between the parties whereby search teams might be able to operate on the battlefield, receiving proper respect and protection while carrying out their duties. Similar provisions are made for notifying, maintaining, and respecting the places of interment of the dead and regulating the return of bodies or exhumation and reburial.

A further hindrance to normal United States-Vietnam relations concerns American aid to the rebuilding of that country. This too has its legacy in the Protocol. As the result of a Vietnamese initiative, Article 91 requires payment of compensation by any party to the conflict violating the Conventions or Protocol, if the case demands—whatever that may mean. The party concerned is also made responsible for all acts committed by members of its armed forces, including, presumably, a single act of looting.

Another technical development to be found in the Protocol relates to the protection of civil defence personnel, who are given a special protective emblem.[58] This protection may, in certain circumstances, even extend to military personnel deputed to such service. Differences are likely to arise between countries that regard the civil defence units as part and parcel of their armed forces and those that do not. In so far as military civil defence personnel are concerned, however, they only remain protected by the Protocol as long as they are employed exclusively for such purposes.

Another new class of protected persons is described in Article 79. The developments in the field of news-gathering, and the large number of deaths suffered in post-1945 hostilities by journalists who are not war correspondents in the technical sense of that term[59] caused some concern, particularly in France, which suffered a number of such casualties during the Vietnam war. Following a French initiative, the United Nations called upon the Conference to consider whether such persons should be specially protected. The French had originally desired a special United Nations Convention, but the matter is dealt with in Article 79. Since journalists or television technicians who are not accredited war correspondents "engaged in dangerous professional missions in areas of armed conflict" may well be mistaken for spies, it is now provided that such persons shall be considered as civilians and entitled to the protection accorded to the latter, provided, of course, they do nothing incompatible with civilian status. To ensure their proper protection they may carry an identity card issued by the government of nationality or residence, or of the state in which the news medium employing them is located. A journalist need not, therefore, have any relation to the parties to the conflict, although the authority in whose area his dangerous mission is being conducted would almost certainly be aware of his presence.

From the point of view of the ordinary person's understanding of humanitarianism in armed conflict, perhaps the greatest innovations in the Protocol relate to civilians and to civilian property. While debate may continue as to the value or otherwise of a neutron bomb which apparently kills while leaving buildings and property intact, the Protocol has sought to protect the civilian population, objects that are of civilian and non-military significance, and installations that, if destroyed, would release forces inimical to civilian

---

[58]See Schultz, *Civil Defence in International Law* (1977, issued under auspices of Danish National Civil Defence and Emergency Planning Directorate).

[59]See Hague Regulations, Art. 13, and Geneva Convention III, 1949, Art. 4, giving war correspondents prisoner of war status. See also note 10 above.

or ecological welfare. Reflecting a traditional and perhaps an even out-of-date concept of warfare, Article 48 lays down a basic rule that the parties to a conflict must at all times distinguish between combatants and civilians and between civilian and military objectives, directing their operations only against the latter. It has already been indicated that these distinctions will be difficult to maintain in armed conflicts involving n.l.m.s, and may be equally difficult to acknowledge in time of total war. As long ago as 1947, drawing upon the experience of Britain in World War II, H. A. Smith contended that since it would appear that "modern war cannot be carried on with anything less than the combined effort of the whole nation, we must accept the consequences of our choice. We cannot boast, as we have done, that every man and woman in the country is now mobilised for war service, and at the same time claim for them the immunity of non-combatants."[60] Nevertheless, the Protocol continues to maintain the distinction and appears, moreover, to ignore the fact that *in extremis* a party whose territory has been occupied may be prepared to sacrifice both civilians and property in the name of survival. Article 49 imposes the same restrictions upon attacks directed against the national territory of a party under the control of an adverse party.

Reiterating a customary rule, Article 51 forbids attacks against the civilian population or against individuals, as well as any act or threat of violence the purpose of which is to spread terror among that population. The article also forbids indiscriminate attacks, which are defined as including those that employ a method or means of combat which cannot be directed at a specific military objective, or the effects of which cannot be limited so that military objectives and civilians or civilian objects would suffer alike. In addition it proscribes attacks that treat

> as a single military objective a number of clearly separated and distinct military objectives located in a city, town, village or other area containing a similar concentration of civilians or civilian objects, or which may be expected to cause incidental loss of civilian life, injury to civilians, damage to civilian objects, or a combination thereof, which would be excessive in relation to the concrete and direct military advantage anticipated.

So worded, this could be interpreted as a complete ban on aerial attack, other than on troops in the field. It is perhaps not surprising that France, for example, indicated unwillingness to accept this ban, since it might well inhibit a party's inherent right of self-preservation. While the civilian population is thus protected, parties are forbidden to move the population in such a way as to seek to shield, seek immunity for, or impede military operations. This would mean that if a party breaches its obligations concerning its duty to protect civilians and to preserve the distinction between military and civilian objectives, so that the adverse party will not attack them, such breach removes the protection from the innocent civilians who, according to the article, cannot be attacked by way of reprisal.

The definition of a civilian object is excessively simple, namely, any object which does not by its "nature, location, purpose or use make an effective contribution to military action and whose total or partial destruction, capture or neutralisation, in the circumstances ruling at the time, offers a definite military advantage," and, in case of doubt whether an object normally used for civilian purposes is being used in the above fashion, its innocence shall be presumed. Closely related to this is Article 53, which forbids acts of hostility against "the historic monuments, works of art or places of worship which

[60]*The Crisis in the Law of Nations* 77, (1947).

constitute the cultural or spiritual heritage of peoples," a concept which is almost impossible of objective definition, especially as, unlike the Hague Convention for the Protection of Cultural Property in the Event of Armed Conflict,[61] no provision exists whereby registration or other means of notifying the adverse party of the identification of such objects is provided. In fact, an attempt to introduce a provision for interchange of such information between opponents was frustrated, partly it would appear because the Arab nations were of opinion that this might enable Israel to secure implied recognition. However, by Article 85 an attack on such a place only constitutes a grave breach if a special arrangement for its protection exists.

Conscious perhaps of the experience of ecological warfare in Vietnam, Article 54 prohibits starvation of civilians as a method of warfare as well as attacks against crops, drinking water installations, irrigation works, and the like, which are indispensable to the survival of the civilian population. Even if such objects are used in direct support of the military, action against them that may be expected to leave the civilian population with such inadequate food or water as to cause its starvation or its removal is not permitted. While a party is permitted to act against such objects in defence of its territory against invasion, this is only true with regard to territory under its control, so that no such derogation is permitted in respect of that part of the territory under enemy occupation. The Protocol also requires care to be taken to protect the natural environment against long-term and severe damage, and Article 55 prohibits methods or means of warfare that are intended or may be expected to cause such damage to the natural environment as to prejudice the health and survival of the civilian population. In view of the fact that the major powers are continuing their research programs relating to environment modification and weapons that are known to be likely to affect the environment, it is of interest to bear in mind that this article expressly forbids attacks against the natural environment by way of reprisal. Similar protection is provided for works and installations containing dangerous forces, namely, dams, dykes, and nuclear electrical generating installations, even when they are military objectives, if the attack may cause the relase of dangerous forces with consequent severe loss to the civilian population. Moreover, military objectives within the vicinity of such installations may not be attacked if this might cause the release of dangerous forces from such installations. While the parties are enjoined to avoid locating military objectives in the vicinity of such installations, they are permitted to erect military installations for the sole purpose of defending those protected works from unlawful attack. This, of course, raises the historic argument as to the non-military character of a defended place. Who is to decide that action taken by such a defence installation was purely protective and taken with justifiable grounds for anticipating an unlawful attack; and who is to deny the contention of the attacked party that it had no intention of attacking the installation in question, so that the alleged act of defence was in fact one of military offence?

This type of difficulty has always faced the commander in the field, but it is far more pressing since there is now more specific definition of protected areas, more of them are placed outside the area of attack, and more violations of the protecting Articles are made grave breaches by Article 85. With this in mind, the draftsmen introduced Article 82, which makes it incumbent upon the parties to the Protocol "at all times to ensure that legal advisers are available, when necessary, to advise military commanders at the appropriate level on the application of the Conventions and this Protocol and on the appropriate instruction to be given to the armed forces on this subject." While the presence

---

[61]1954, *loc. cit., supra* note 46. The definition in the Convention is far wider.

of such an adviser may well cause an officer to hesitate before launching an attack and, if he is tried for war crimes or grave breaches, inhibit a plea that he was acting on superior orders and was unaware of the illegality of the act involved,[62] a number of serious problems remain.[63] There is the problem of the training of such legal advisers; there is the need to instil in officers and men alike a new respect for the international law of armed conflict even though compliance therewith might appear to interfere with the immediate military advantage; further difficulties will arise in view of differing approaches to, at least, the customary law of war, as well as differences as to what the likely effect of a particular means or method of attack will be; and there will also be hierarchic problems as between the adviser and the commander to whom he is attached. The situation has perhaps not been rendered any easier by the refusal of the Conference to include an article receiving Canadian support that would have defined the nature of superior orders.[64] On the other hand, Article 86 imposes penal or disciplinary responsibility upon a commander who knew or ought to have known that a subordinate was likely to commit or had already committed a breach, if he failed to take all feasible measures within his power to prevent or repress that breach. To some extent, this article reflects the position of the Japanese General Yamashita after World War II,[65] as does Article 87, which requires the commander to ensure that his troops obey the law and are aware of their obligations under the Conventions and the Protocol—an undertaking in which, hopefully, the legal adviser will be sufficiently competent to participate. However, to some extent this need may be mitigated if the parties to the Protocol carry out their obligation under Article 83 concerning dissemination, in time of peace as in armed conflict, among their military personnel and the civilian population.

While much may be gained by providing legal advisers for commanders and proclaiming their liability for the acts of subordinates, it is equally necessary to define some of the offences that are to be considered as grave breaches, in addition to those referred to in the Conventions concerning injury to the human person and unlawful and wanton destruction of property unjustified by military necessity.[66] In the first place, the Protocol extends the Convention concept to cover all those given a protected status by the Protocol, while Article 11, as has been seen, makes medical abuse a grave breach. Article 85, in addition to condemning practices of apartheid, also condemns as grave breaches the launching of unlawful attacks against the civilian population, installations containing dangerous forces, non-defended or demilitarized areas, persons *hors de combat*, or the perfidious use of recognized protected emblems. The Article then adds the transfer by an occupying authority of parts of its own civilian population into occupied territory or the transfer of the local population within or outside this territory. This elevates a breach of Article 49 of Convention IV into a grave breach and, in so far as Israeli settlements in occupied areas of Jordan or Syria are concerned, would include such settlements. As to territory occupied by either of these or by Egypt in breach of the terms of the United Nations partition resolution,[67] this might not be the case, especially in view of the Israeli contention that no territory that was formerly part of, presumably biblical, Israel can be regarded as occupied.

---

[62]See Green, *Superior Orders in National and International Law* (1976).

[63]See e.g., "The Role of Legal Advisers in the Armed Forces," ch. IV *infra*.

[64]See, e.g., Dinstein, *The Defence of "Obedience to Superior Orders" in International Law* (1965), Green, *op. cit. supra* note 62, and Keijzer, *Military Obedience*, 1978.

[65]*Re Yamashita* (1946), 13 Ann. Dig. 255 and 327 U.S. 1. See also Reel, *The Case of General Yamashita* (1949); see also ch. X *infra*.

[66]Conv. I, Art. 50, II, Art. 51, III, Art. 130, IV, Art. 147.

[67]Res 181 (II), November 29, 1947.

As a means of avoiding the kinds of problem that arose after the Korean war, it is now a grave breach unjustifiably to delay the repatriation of prisoners of war or of civilians, or to deprive any protected person of the rights of a fair and regular trial. In view of the differing interpretations of unjustifiable delay or of a fair and regular trial, despite the terms of Article 75, it is likely that those responsible for drafting indictments are going to be severely taxed. Their task will not be rendered easier by the knowledge that it is also a grave breach to make objects that are part of the cultural heritage of peoples the subject of attack. It remains to be seen whether a neutral state will be prepared to try a person within its jurisdiction accused by a belligerent of having unlawfully attacked an object regarded by that belligerent as part of the cultural heritage of its people or even of mankind, whether or not the object has been made the subject of some special protective arrangement.

Since it is so clear that the approach to these articles is likely to be highly subjective, some means of control and supervision is necessary. In the past, belligerents have depended upon the watchfulness of protecting powers and have used the International Committee of the Red Cross as an intermediary. Unfortunately, it became clear at Geneva that many of the third world states regard the latter with some suspicion and are much more likely to depend upon some other humanitarian organization either of its own or belonging to some friendly state. In practice it is often difficult to secure agreement among parties to a conflict on the identity of protecting powers and there is often a tendency to regard states fulfilling such tasks as unfriendly. Throughout the Protocol, therefore, national "red cross" bodies are placed in parallel with other unidentified humanitarian organizations whenever reference is made to the International Committee.

Article 5 has attempted to deal with the protecting power problem. Parties are required to designate protecting powers from the beginning of a conflict, but if this has not been done, or if the power designated has not been accepted by the adverse party, the International Committee or some other impartial humanitarian organization—if such there be—is to offer its good offices in seeking to reach agreement, and failing such may offer itself to serve as a substitute. Any such offer is to be accepted, although the functioning of the substitute is subject to the consent of the parties to the conflict.

The Geneva Conventions provided for a rudimentary method of determining whether they were being observed. While the protecting power or the International Committee has always been able to act on its own, the Conventions provided for an enquiry procedure to be set up, by agreement of the parties, to investigate alleged violations.[68] There was, however, no procedure outlined in the event of their failing to agree. As was demonstrated by the advisory opinion on *Interpretation of the Peace Treaties*,[69] should one of the parties prove adamant little or nothing can be done. At Geneva, therefore, an attempt, which received broad Canadian support, was made to establish a compulsory standing enquiry procedure for such purposes. Due largely to the determined opposition of the socialist states, who contended that any form of compulsory and automatic enquiry procedure was completely incompatible with national sovereignty, the idea of a permanent body with compulsory powers of investigation and acting on its own initiative was rejected. Instead, Article 90 comprises a complicated procedure for the establishment of an International Fact-Finding Commission. As a party alleged to have committed a breach is unlikely to prove willing to allow the Commission to operate within its own territory, provision has been made for parties to the Protocol to make a declaration

[68]I—52, II—53, III—132, IV—149.
[69][1950] *I.C.J.* 65, 211.

accepting the authority of the Commission *ipso facto* and without special consent. However, as with the Optional Clause under Article 36 of the Statute of the World Court, such an obligation only works on the basis of reciprocity. Further, the Commission has no power to judge. Its sole function is to enquire into any facts alleged to constitute a grave breach or other serious violation of the Conventions or the Protocol, and to facilitate through its good offices "the restoration of an attitude of respect" therefor. In view of the inevitable time delays that are likely to ensue, particularly if an inspection *in situ* is necessary and has been agreed to, it is likely that many of the facts into which the Commission is supposed to enquire will have disappeared long before the Commission gets under way or reaches the area in question.

These comments have been directed to what may be regarded as some of the more salient and often innovative features of Protocol I, and it has not been considered necessary to enter into excessive detail as to the protection of civilians or the special rights of women or young persons, or some of the technical provisions concerning medical transports, civil defence, or relief. Enough has been said to make it clear that many of the parties to the Geneva Conference may have difficulty in accepting the Protocol as it stands and will only do so subject to varying reservations, particularly to those provisions that may be considered to be more political than humanitarian in character. On the other hand, it may well be that the political situation of the modern world is such that states will find it embarrassing and perhaps even diplomatically impossible to make such reservations. The Protocol came into effect upon the deposit of only two instruments of ratification, but it will depend upon the good faith of the parties for effectiveness. One can only look with despair upon statements of the kind made by President Mobutu of Zaire, a country that co-operated fully at Geneva, when he accused Angola, Cuba, and the Soviet Union of assisting ex-Katangan gendarmes in their invasion of Shaba.[70] He stated that he was using pigmy troops "who specialize in the use of poisoned arrows. With these arrows we are sure of destroying the enemy, whereas with bullets there are always survivors, and, in a state of war, the Red Cross intervenes. After the poison arrows are used, we send in the commandos to pursue the aggressors." There are of course loopholes in any system. It must be hoped that states will not go out of their way to find such loopholes.

Though Protocol II is the more historic of the documents to come from the Geneva Humanitarian Law Conference, in that it is the first treaty laying down legal regulations for the conduct of non-international conflict, it is nevertheless possible to deal with it fairly shortly. Its aim is to reduce the bitterness and extreme violence that normally accompany such conflicts, but attempts to do this can easily be destroyed on the rock of sovereignty and the right of a government to preserve itself. Once it has become certain that affairs within a state have deteriorated to the point that a non-international conflict exists, the provisions of Protocol II come into effect. As with Protocol I two ratifications are required, so that technically if only one state has ratified, and that is the state affected by a non-international conflict, the authorities would be able to argue that the Protocol did not apply and that they remained free to conduct their affairs as they pleased. If the Protocol does apply, it does so without any adverse distinction, a principle which is of extreme importance in a type of conflict that may arise between groups of different "race, colour, sex, language, religion or belief, political or other opinion, national or social origin, wealth, birth, or other status," and, in case anything has been omitted, "any other similar criteria." From the point of view of the persons involved the most

[70]*The Times* (London), April 22, 1977.

important articles are probably 5 and 6. Article 7 seeks to preserve the traditional cleavage between civilians and combatants, a differentiation that is hardly realistic in a conflict on the level of a civil war. However, this latter article provides that the civilian population and individual civilians are to enjoy general protection against the dangers arising from military operations, and must not be the object of attack, nor subjected to acts or threats of violence intended to spread terror. For this article to have meaning, both governments and those opposed to them will have to revise their entire philosophy of conducting non-international conflicts, for, in the past, terror against the civilian population has been an inevitable part of the armoury of government and rebels alike.

Article 5 lays down the minimum conditions for the treatment of those who have been deprived of their liberty for reasons related to the conflict. The detaining party is required to provide them with food, drinking water, and safeguards regarding health, hygiene, and protection against the weather to the same extent as the local civilian population. Similarly, if they are required to work, their conditions and safeguards shall be the same as those of the local population. One might ask whether this means equal rates of pay and the right to organize, even though such organization may have political overtones. Persons detained are entitled to practise their religion and to receive spiritual assistance from religious personnel if requested and where appropriate. In view of the political and frequently antiestablishment stance adopted by, for example, the World Council of Churches or, in the case of Latin America, some worker priests, this may often be regarded as inappropriate in a non-international conflict. The article goes on to define the terms of detention to bring them as close as possible to those required during an international conflict. Similarly, Article 6 seeks to reproduce, so far as they are relevant, the fundamental guarantees of Article 75 of Protocol I, laying down the procedures for trial on the basis of individual and not group responsibility. It postulates the presumption of innocence, rejects trials *in absentia*, and forbids attempts to compel anyone to testify against himself or to confess—a provision which runs counter to many modern internment practices. Like Protocol I, the Article forbids the pronouncement of the death sentence upon juveniles under eighteen and its execution in the case of pregnant women or the mothers of young children. The change of wording from "dependent" to "young" is not believed to possess any significance.

A vital innovation from the point of view of humanitarian law in non-international conflicts is introduced by the last paragraph of Article 7. History has shown time and time again that ruthlessness in civil war is the order of the day, with slaughter and extermination of opponents a common occurrence, both sides seeking to rival each other but in fact merely setting off a circular process of increasing massacres. The Protocol seeks to mitigate this horror and at the same time to build up some measure of good will for the future. An attempt, supported by Canada, to include a provision to postpone all executions until after hostilities had ceased, in the hope that time would heal and the new authority would realize the value of restraint, was rejected. However, it was agreed that the authorities in power should endeavour to grant the broadest possible amnesty to those who had participated in the conflict or had been detained in any way by reason thereof. Even though it was accepted that the power to grant amnesty was part of the sovereign rights of a government, and though it was hoped that the authorities would themselves realize the value of granting amnesty, it was nevertheless considered helpful to express this desire in an international instrument.

To a limited and far less technical extent, Protocol II reproduces the protective provisions of Protocol I with regard to medical care of the wounded, sick, and shipwrecked, as well as for their protection against pillage and ill treatment. It provides, too, for the search, protection, and interment of the dead. Medical and religious personnel are protected and cannot be punished for ministering to any person requiring their services, nor can they be compelled to carry out any acts incompatible with their professional ethics. However, information that medical personnel may acquire concerning persons under their care is protected only to the extent provided by national law. The same is true of their right not to impart information relating to such persons. By introducing the limiting pressures of national law, the Protocol makes it possible for any authority to remove the protection of medical personnel attending the adverse party. Reflecting the new concerns with cultural objects and with the environment, Articles 14 to 16 seek to place outside the scope of military activity historic monuments, works of art, and places of worship "which constitute the cultural or spiritual heritage of peoples," objects indispensable to the survival of the civilian population, and works and installations containing dangerous forces. It is true that hope may exist that neither a government nor a rebel force will seek to destroy its people's future, but realism dictates that an ideology about to be defeated may decide that defeat and *Götterdämmerung* are synonyms, and it is perhaps doubtful that, except in the rarest cases, a treaty provision will in fact impose restraints.

Protocol II makes provision for allowing national relief societies to operate, but, reflecting some of the problems that arose during the Biafra operations in Nigeria, relief activities from outside on behalf of civilians are permitted only if undertaken with the consent of the party to the Protocol, if they are of an exclusively humanitarian and impartial nature, and if they are conducted without any adverse distinction. This consent requirement indicates how strong, even today, is the belief in national independence and unrestricted sovereignty. This adherence to sovereignty was evidenced perhaps more clearly than at any other time when the Conference rejected an effort to write into the Protocol an obligation to disseminate its principles by education. Article 19 merely states that the Protocol shall be disseminated as widely as possible. Countries which might be described as "non-international-conflict-prone" rejected any provision that might be construed as obliging them to teach those who in the future may take up arms against the state their rights in the case of resort to such action.

An infringement of sovereignty that was accepted is found in Article 17. In many recent non-international conflicts the authorities in power have resorted to measures of resettlement in order to deprive the rebels of local support and supplies. Protocol II states that the displacement of the civilian population shall not be ordered for reasons related to the conflict unless the security of the civilians involved or imperative military reasons so demand. Since this Protocol contains no enforcement provisions and makes no reference to the punishment of breaches, it must be presumed that the decision as to "imperative military reasons" will be made by the local commander and that his decision will be final. The Article also provides that civilians shall not be compelled to leave their own territory for any reason connected with the conflict. If this is not to be construed as contradicting the earlier provision, it must mean that no individual civilian can be compelled to leave the territory under the control of either the government or the rebels, as the case may be, or may be expelled into the territory of a neighbouring state and that in this case the provision cannot be ignored on the basis of imperative military necessity.

Protocol I deals with situations which may involve an entity that is not a state, while Protocol II can only operate in the case of conflicts involving non-state entities. By Article 96 of the former, the authority representing such an entity, that is to say the n.l.m., may deposit with the Swiss government a unilateral declaration invoking the Protocol for the conflict. As a result the Conventions and the Protocol become binding upon the authority in question, which thereby assumes all the rights and obligations of any High Contracting Party. However, it may be that the "colonial" power against which the n.l.m. is fighting has not ratified the Protocol—neither South Africa nor "Rhodesia" participated in the Geneva Conference—and in that case the legal situation would remain as before, with the n.l.m. only bound to other parties to the Protocol. Perhaps surprisingly, Protocol II makes no provision for any type of accession or acceptance of its terms by the rebel authorities. This reflects the determination of governments, especially those of third world states, not to accept any treaty provision that would impliedly place their opponents on an equal basis, so the Protocol makes no reference to parties to the conflict, tending to refer rather to the rights of the persons affected than to the obligations of those who may be in power. This is in accordance with Article 3, which reaffirms the "responsibility" of a government, "by all legitimate means, to maintain or re-establish law and order in the State or to defend [its] national unity and territorial integrity," while clearly stating that the existence of the Protocol is no basis to justify any direct or indirect intervention by outsiders, not even if the rebels have established a form of government or the government, having ratified the Protocol, indulges in widespread massacres in disregard thereof. To some extent, this clear affirmation of governmental "responsibility" appears to negate the entire Protocol.

If the Protocols are observed, it cannot be denied that they contribute a major development in the progress and application of humanitarian law in armed conflict. However, it is equally undeniable that many states among those more prone to being affected by international than non-international conflicts are likely to find that they can only accept Protocol I with varying reservations, particularly with regard to some of the political provisions or to some of those imposing limitations on military action that might affect their right of self-preservation. On the other hand, as these states are often least likely to be involved in non-international conflicts, they may be among the first to ratify Protocol II. Contrariwise, states that are more likely to be affected by non-international conflicts, that is those states where such hostilities appear to be endemic or part of the way of life, may be extremely unwilling to ratify Protocol II. Even though this Protocol lacks a supervisory system, it seeks to limit their freedom of action in dealing with civil wars affecting their continued existence in their present governmental form. At first blush, they might be the more willing to accept Protocol I, especially in view of its recognition of the importance of self-determination and national liberation. On the other hand, many of these states are themselves confronted with tribal peoples already asserting their right to "self-determination," and receiving encouragement from neighbours who are opposed to the existing government. This type of situation would militate against ratification by even these states, who might well fall back on the argument that they cannot be expected to ratify Protocol I if it has not been ratified by the greater powers, or if the latter have added reservations which virtually destroy all the provisions inserted to satisfy the political demands of the developing countries. Finally, it is perhaps worth mentioning as a possible indication for the future that, when the Protocols were opened for signature in December 1977, while Canada and most western powers were among the signatories, France and the German Federal Republic failed to sign, as did Israel which, perhaps not surprisingly in view of its attitude towards the Palestine Liberation Organization, had also refused to sign the Final Act.

Since this was written, the Protocols have come into force, having received the necessary number of ratifications. The majority of states ratifying have come from the Third World, although Austria, Denmark, Finland, Norway, Sweden and Switzerland from the Western world have ratified, as have Cuba, the Lao People's Democratic Republic and

Vietnam from the Communist bloc. Yugoslavia, too, has ratified. As yet (July 1984) no major power, with the exception of the Chinese People's Republic, has done so. However, it would appear from statements made in a variety of countries that the preponderant view is that much of Protocol I, at least, is expressive of customary international law in view of the number of countries supporting the various proposals during the drafting Conference.[71]

---

[71]See, e.g., Murray, "The 1977 Protocols and Conflict in South Africa," 33 *I.C.L.Q.* 1984, 462, discussing *S.* v. *Sagarius and Others* [1983] 1 S.A. 833(S.W.) and *S.* v. *Mogoerane and Others* (1982, unreported, Transvaal Provincial Division).

II

The Man in the Field and the Maxim
Ignorantia Juris Non Excusat

War crimes trials, whether conducted by tribunals established under international agreement, like that at Nuremberg,[1] or under municipal law, like that which rendered the decision regarding the *Llandovery Castle*,[2] as well as trials under national military law, like that of Lieutenant Calley,[3] inevitably raise a multitude of legal problems. Among the most important of these is the knowledge of the accused. Too often, insufficient attention is paid to this, even though the inevitable defence of superior orders and the reaction to it of the tribunal concerned[4] to a very great extent are based on this factor, since success or otherwise of the plea depends on whether or not the act ordered was palpably or manifestly illegal, which obviously depends on the accused's knowledge of what is in fact lawful. If the writer's experience on joining the British Army during the Second World War is anything to go by, the extent of the knowledge of the law of the ordinary soldier stems rather from his own resources than those of the military establishment. While he was told that, as a prisoner of war, the Geneva Convention of 1929[5] merely required him to give his name, number and rank, he was never given any instruction as to the rights of enemy personnel, his duties towards them or the nature of illegal weapons or acts of war. Moreover, it would appear that in some armies the situation has probably not changed too radically. Thus, in one of the courts martial arising out of the operations of United States personnel during the Vietnam War it was held that even though the acts perpetrated by the accused were in keeping with the training received

---

[1]The London Charter, 8 Aug. 1945, 82 UNTS 280 (Schindler/Toman, 823.
[2](1921) HMSO Cmd. 450 (Cameron, *The Peleus Trial* (1948), App. IX).
[3]*U.S.* v. *Calley* (1973) 46 C.M.R. 1131, 48 C.M.R. 19; *Calley* v. *Callaway* (1974) 382F Supp. 650, (1975) 519 Fed. Rep. (2d) 184 (Goldstein and others, *The My Lai Massacre and its Cover-Up: Beyond the Reach of Law?* (1976), 475-573).
[4]See, e.g., Dinstein, *The Defence of 'Obedience to Superior Orders' in International Law* (1965); Green, *Superior Orders in National and International Law* (1976); Keijzer, *Military Obedience*, 1978.
[5]Art. 5, 118 LNTS 343 (Schindler/Toman, 271).

during basic training, this would not provide a defence if the order concerned was palpably illegal on its face.[6]

It is difficult to expect the ordinary soldier to know what orders he is permitted and required to obey, or the officer what orders he is allowed to give, without in either case running the risk of trial for breach of the law of war, if he does not know what that law is. While it may be true that most systems of criminal law postulate the maxim *ignorantia juris quod quisque tenetur scire, neminem excusat,*[7] it must not be forgotten that those who live within a national system of law may be presumed to accept the national ethic and to be aware of the nature and basic principles of their country's criminal code, or at least know where to find them. This is hardly the case in so far as international law is concerned. This is a highly sophisticated system parts of which are controversial, and this is particularly true of that part of it which relates to the law of war. After all, the soldier understands that his task is to kill his enemy, that the aim of his country is to subdue that enemy, and it may seem somewhat strange to him that while his act and the purpose for which it is done are both lawful, nevertheless he is only allowed to carry out this act in a particular way and in accordance with certain rules, which rules are often abstruse, complex in form and certainly difficult to find. However, if Protocol I Additional to the Geneva Conventions of 12 August 1949, and relating to the Protection of Victims of International Armed Conflicts, 1977,[8] receives general acceptance both the man and the officer may be a little better off from this point of view in any future war. By Article 82 legal advisers are supposed to be attached to service units,[9] while Article 83 imposes duties of teaching and dissemination upon the Contracting Parties, and this service is supposed to extend to the civilian population as well as the armed forces.

In the meantime, it is important to examine the extent to which states are already obliged to inform their armed forces of the law of war and to refer, if possible, to the steps and methods which have been or ought to be taken to this end.

In looking at this problem it must be borne in mind that international law is made up of treaties, customary law and, nowadays to an increasing extent, judicial decisions. Also, unlike municipal law, international law is, in theory at least, universally applicable and the law of one country's courts in this field has as much validity as that of any other country. As it was so aptly put by Vattel:[10]

> Since men are by nature equal, and their individual rights and obligations the same, as coming equally from nature, Nations, which are composed of men and may be regarded as so many free persons living together in a state of nature, are by nature equal and hold from nature the same obligations and the same rights. *Strength or weakness, in this case, counts for nothing. A dwarf is as much a man as a giant is; a small Republic is no less a sovereign State than the most powerful Kingdom.*

It becomes necessary, therefore, to examine where this equally applicable law is to be found and the extent to which it imposes an obligation upon its subjects to ensure that it is made known to their nationals. With treaties the situation is relatively straightfor-

---

[6]*U.S.* v. *Keenan* (1969) 39 C.M.R. 108.

[7]"Ignorance of the law, which every man is bound to know, excuses no man" (see Selden, *Table Talk* (1689), "Law"; 4 Blackstone, *Commentaries on the Laws of England,* ch. 2, s. V. (10th ed., 1787, 27).

[8]Schindler/Toman, 555.

[9]See "The Role of Legal Advisers in the Armed Forces," ch. IV *infra.*

[10]*Le Droit des Gens ou Principes de la Loi Naturelle* (1758), Bk. I, Intro., s. 18 (Carnegie tr., 1916, vol. 3, p. 7—italics added).

ward. All that is required is to determine which are the relevant documents and then to examine the terms of those treaties. Frequently, to a very great extent these treaties are simply codifications of customary law and, in so far as they are not themselves law-creative, the only obligation that rests upon non-parties is to be derived from that customary law. To the extent that this is so it may be argued that even states which are not parties to any particular treaty will, nevertheless, be bound perhaps even by its very terminology in so far as that treaty is merely a codification of customary law. The members of a non-party's armed forces would be bound by this customary law,[11] and it is in their interest that they be informed as to its content.

For the most part, it has been generally said that the law of war is to be found in the Hague Conventions of 1907 as amended by the various Red Cross Geneva Conventions of 1929 and 1949.[12] However, even the Hague Conventions themselves refer to 'the laws and customs of war' and at times do not spell out in excessive detail what even the treaty law entails. Thus, all that Hague Convention IV[13] with respect to the laws and customs of war on land says about penalties for violations of the Regulations attached thereto is to be found in Article 3:

> A belligerent party which violates the provisions of the said Regulations shall, if the case demands, be liable to pay compensation. It shall be responsible for all acts committed by persons forming part of its armed forces.

There is no provision for personal liability or for punishment of the soldier who actually commits the violation. The only basis on which such individuals can therefore be tried is either their own municipal law which would not, of course, extend to any enemy, or customary international law, just as non-military personnel who indulge in warlike acts are similarly liable as war criminals under the same customary law. In the first edition of his *International Law*[14] Oppenheim says

> according to a generally recognized customary rule of International Law hostile acts on the part of private individuals are not acts of legitimate warfare, and the offenders can be treated and punished as war criminals. Even those writers who object to the term "criminals" do not deny that such hostile acts by private individuals, in contradistinction to hostile acts by members of the armed forces, may be severely punished. The controversy whether or not such acts may be styled "crimes" is again only one of terminology; materially the rule is not at all controverted.

Although, in this passage Oppenheim apparently excludes from his concept of war crimes "hostile acts by members of the armed forces," he points out that "belligerents have not an unlimited right as to the means they adopt for injuring the enemy,"[15] and comments[16] that

> the roots of the present Laws of War are to be traced back to practices of belligerents

---

[11]See, e.g., in relation to the law of maritime warfare comments by Sir Samuel Evans in *The Möwe* (1915) P. 1, 12; see, also, *The Blonde* (1922) 1 A.C. 313; and more generally, the *Nuremberg Judgement* (1946) Cmd. 6964, p. 65 (41 *Am. J. Int'l Law* (1947), 172, 248-9).

[12]See Schindler/Toman.

[13]*Ibid.*, 57.

[14]Vol. 2 (1906), 63.

[15]*Ibid.*, 114 (citing Art. 22 of Hague Regulations of 1899, Schindler/Toman, 76).

[16]*Ibid.*, 74.

which arose and grew gradually during the latter part of the Middle Ages. The unsparing cruelty of the war practices during the greater part of the Middle Ages began gradually to be modified through the influence of Christianity and chivalry.

At this juncture it might be useful to draw attention to the 1474 trial of Peter Hagenbach at Breisach.[17] As Governor for the Duke of Burgundy Hagenbach established a

regime of arbitrariness and terror (which) extended to murder, rape, illegal taxation and wanton confiscation of private property, and the victims of his depredations included inhabitants of neighbouring territories as well as Swiss merchants on their way to and from the Frankfurt fair.

After Hagenbach's capture, the Archduke of Austria, as sovereign of Breisach, set up a tribunal of 28 judges from the Allied towns, and at his trial the accused pleaded that everything that he had done had been on the orders of his master, but the prosecution alleged that he had "trampled under foot the laws of God and man." The tribunal was of opinion that to accept such a defence would be contrary to the laws of God and, since the crimes were established beyond doubt, sentenced Hagenbach to death. In many ways the charge with its reference to the laws of God and of man seems like a predecessor of the provision of the Treaty of Versailles aimed at bringing the Kaiser to trial:[18]

The Allied and Associated Powers publicly arraign William II of Hohenzollern, formerly German Emperor, for a supreme offence against international morality and the sanctity of treaties . . .
In its decision the tribunal will be guided by the highest motives of international policy, with a view to vindicating the solemn obligations of international undertakings and the validity of international morality.

While the Treaty called for the establishment of a specially established international tribunal, it did not specify the law which this tribunal would apply and by which the offences were to be judged. A somewhat similar hiatus is apparent in the Treaty provision[19] concerning the trial by military tribunals of "persons accused of having committed acts in violation of the laws and customs of war," who if found guilty are to "be sentenced to punishments laid down by law." While the Treaty does not indicate what law it has in mind, the Reichsgericht which delivered the *Llandovery Castle* judgment[20] was clearly aware that it was operating in accordance with international law:

. . . The firing on the boats was an offence against the law of nations. . . . Any violation of the law of nations in warfare is . . . a punishable offence, so far as, in general, a penalty is attached to the deed. The killing of enemies in war is in accordance with the law of the State that makes war. . . , only in so far as such killing is in accordance with the conditions and limitations imposed by the Law of Nations. The fact that his deed is a violation of International Law must be well known to the doer, apart from acts of carelessness, in which careless ignorance is a sufficient excuse. In examining the existence of this knowledge, the ambiguity of many of the rules of International Law, as well as the actual circumstances of the case, must be borne in mind, because in wartime decisions of great importance have frequently to be made on very insufficient material. This consideration, how-

---

[17]Schwarzenberger, *International Law*, vol. 2, *The Law of Armed Conflict* (1968) ch. 39.
[18](1919) Art. 227 (112 B.F.S.P. 1; 13 *Am. J. Int'l Law* (1919), Supp.).
[19]Art. 228.
[20]*Loc. cit.*, n. 2 above.

ever, cannot be applied to the case at present before the Court. The rule of International Law, which is here involved [regarding the sinking of the hospital ship and the firing on the boats of the survivors], is simple and universally known. No possible doubt can exist with regard to the question of its applicability. The Court must in this instance affirm [the commander's] guilt of killing contrary to International Law . . .

Perhaps the earliest codification of the law of war was that prepared by Professor Lieber of Columbia University, during the American Civil War and promulgated by President Lincoln in 1863[21]. This reflects what was generally understood by the European states as constituting the law at the time and clearly provides for the trial and punishment of a variety of specified offences committed by troops against the inhabitants of invaded territory, but it makes no reference to the need to ensure that members of the United States armed forces are made aware of what they may and what they may not do, although by and large the offences listed are those which would be found in any national penal code. The first call for recognition of the need to inform the armed forces of the rules of war is to be found in the *Oxford Manual* prepared by the Institute of International Law at its Oxford meeting in 1880.[22] In the Preface the Institute states why it has drawn up its statement of the laws of war on land:

> By so doing, it believes it is rendering a service to military men themselves. In fact so long as the demands of opinion remain indeterminate, belligerents are exposed to painful uncertainty and endless accusations. A positive set of rules, on the contrary, if they are judicious, serves the interests of belligerents and is far from hindering them, since by preventing the unchaining of passion and savage instincts—which battle always awakens, as much as it awakens courage and manly virtues—it strengthens the discipline which is the strength of armies; it also ennobles their patriotic mission in the eyes of the soldiers by keeping them within the limits of respect due to the rights of humanity. But in order to attain this end it is not sufficient for sovereigns to promulgate new laws. It is essential, too, that they make these laws known among all people, so that when a war is declared, the men called upon to take up arms to defend the causes of the belligerent States, may be thoroughly impregnated with the special rights and duties attached to the execution of such a command. The Institute, with a view to assisting the authorities in accomplishing this part of their task, has given its work a popular form, attaching thereto statements of the reasons therefor, from which the text of a law may be easily secured when desired.

While the text of the *Oxford Manual* seems to satisfy the expressed desire of achieving a 'popular form', it must not be overlooked that the ordinary person, civilian or military, was unlikely to seek this document out. Furthermore, while the Institute might have been composed of the most eminent international lawyers of the day, it must be borne in mind that it was, as it is now, an unofficial learned society whose proposals possessed no binding force and could only aim at providing suggestions which, if acceptable to governments, would be enacted into law, either by way of statute or by treaty. It would appear that, despite the expressed desire of the Institute, little was done to make the contents of the *Manual* known to the members of the armed forces. Even when countries

[21]U.S. Adjutant General's Office, General Orders No. 100 (Schindler/Toman, 3). There were, however, codes of military discipline promulgated by Richard II in 1383, and Henry V in 1415, as well as a Swiss *Sempacherbriff* in 1393, and a number of similar codes in 16th century France. All of these "married" international law and all were published and made known to the troops. See Gardot, "Le Droit de la Guerre dans l'Oeuvre des Capitanes Français du XVIe Siècle," 72 *Hague Recueil* 1948, 397, 467-73.

[22]Schindler/Toman, 35.

started issuing *Manuals of Military Law* with sections devoted to the law of war, these manuals were not issued to the troops or even all officers, and in many cases non-officers were actively discouraged from seeking access to them.

To some extent the *voeu* of the Institute did have an effect. In Hague Convention II of 1899[23] it was clearly provided in Article 1 that

> The High Contracting Parties shall issue instructions to their armed land forces which shall be in conformity with the 'Regulations respecting the laws and customs of war on land' annexed to the present Convention

and the same provision was repeated in the IVth Convention of 1907,[24] respecting the law of warfare on land.

The only other Hague Convention to deal with dissemination is No. X of 1907[25] for the Adaptation to Maritime Warfare of the Principles of the Geneva Convention of 1864[26] which related to the amelioration of conditions of the wounded and sick or armies in the field. In its form, however, it differed from the wording in Convention IV and appeared to lay more emphasis on the knowledge of those who were to be protected than of those whose conduct was restricted:

> The Signatory Powers shall take the necessary measures for bringing the provisions of the present Convention to the knowledge of their naval forces, and especially of the members entitled thereunder to immunity, and for making them known to the public.

Although other Conventions agreed at the Hague dealt with such issues as the rights of neutrals and naval bombardment, the signatories apparently did not consider it necessary to include a provision seeking to ensure that the rules and prohibitions were made known to the personnel who were most directly affected and upon whose conduct it was necessary to rely to ensure compliance.

Perhaps even more surprising is the silence in this matter of the Rules regarding Air Warfare[27] drafted by the Commission of Jurists called for by the 1922 Conference of Washington. While it is true that these Rules were never adopted and so have no legal significance as such, they cannot be cavalierly ignored, for, "to a great extent, they correspond to the customary rules and general principles underlying the conventions on the law of war on land and at sea."[28] While the Rules go into great detail as to what may not be done in aerial warfare, the members of the Commission apparently did not consider it necessary for the states which might adopt these Rules to undertake any commitment to make them known to their respective air forces. Equally strange is the silence of the Draft Convention for the Protection of Civilians against New Engines of War drawn up by the International Law Association at Amsterdam in 1938.[29]

In what has now come to be described as humanitarian law in armed conflict, the International Committee of the Red Cross has consistently endeavoured to ensure that treaties relating to the wounded and sick or prisoners of war contain provisions obligating

---

[23]Scott, *The Hague Conventions and Declarations of 1899 and 1907* (1918), 100 (Schindler/Toman, 57).
[24]*Ibid.*
[25]Art. 20, Scott, *op. cit.*, 163 (Schindler/Toman, 245).
[26]I Am J. Int'l Law (1907), Supp. 90 (Schindler/Toman, 213).
[27]1923, 17 *Am. J. Int'l Law* (1923), Supp. 245 (Schindler/Toman, 147).j
[28]*Ibid.*, 139; see, also, 2 Oppenheim, *International Law* (7th ed., 1952), 519; Spaight, *Air Power and War Rights* (1947) 42-3.
[29]I.L.A., *Report of 40th Conference*, 40 (Schindler/Toman, 163).

the parties to inform their personnel of the commitments involved. Article 27 of the 1929 Convention of the Amelioration of the Condition of the Wounded and Sick in Armies in the Field[30] is reminiscent of Hague Convention X. This reads

> The High Contracting Parties shall take the necessary steps to instruct their troops, and in particular the personnel protected, in the provisions of the present Convention, and to bring them to the notice of the civil population.

A somewhat similar concern with the interest of those protected is to be found in the 1929 Prisoners of War Convention,[31] for by Article 84 the text of this Convention is to be posted, "whenever possible, in the native language of the prisoners of war, in places where it may be consulted by all the prisoners." It even has to be communicated, when so requested, to prisoners "who are unable to inform themselves of the text posted." Presumably, it is anticipated that those responsible for the prisoners of war will be sufficiently acquainted with the terms of the Convention by such posting—that is, if they can read the language of the prisoners—for there is no obligation on the parties to make the terms known to their own personnel.

A somewhat new departure is to be found in the revised texts of the Geneva Conventions of 1949 which resulted from the desire of the International Committee of the Red Cross to bring the 1929 texts up to date, taking into consideration the experiences learned during the Second World War. Article 47 of the Convention on Wounded and Sick in the Field,[32] and Article 48 of that on Wounded, Sick and Shipwrecked Members of Armed Forces at Sea[33] are much wider than their precursors, reflecting recognition of the fact that modern armies are frequently conscript in character and their personnel should, to the extent that that is possible, be aware of their obligations before enlistment, and certainly before the outbreak of hostilities:

> The High Contracting Parties undertake, in time of peace as in time of war, to disseminate the text of the present Convention as widely as possible in their respective countries, and, in particular, to include the study thereof in their programmes of military and, if possible, civil instruction, so that the principles thereof may become known to the entire population, in particular to the armed fighting forces, the medical personnel and the chaplains.

The 1949 Conventions on Prisoners of War[34] and the Treatment of Civilian Persons in Time of War[35] take due account of their specialist character:

> Art. 127, Ps W—The High Contracting Parties undertake, in time of peace as in time of war, to disseminate the text of the present Convention as widely as possible in their respective countries, and, in particular, to include the study thereof in their programmes of military and, if possible, civil instruction, so that the principles thereof may become known to all their armed forces and to the entire population.
>
> Any military or other authorities, who in time of war assume responsibilities in respect of prisoners of war, must possess the text of the Convention and be specially instructed as to its provisions.

[30]5 Hudson, *International Legislation* (1936), 1 (Schindler/Toman, 257).
[31]5 ibid., 20 (Schindler/Toman, 271).
[32]75 UNTS 31 (Schindler/Toman, 305).
[33]*Ibid.*, 85 (333).
[34]*Ibid.*, 135 (355).
[35]*Ibid.*, 287 (427).

The High Contracting Parties are bound to enact any legislation necessary to give penal effect to the Convention and, by Article 128,

> shall communicate to one another through the Swiss Federal Council and, during hostilities, through the Protecting Powers, the official translations of the present Convention, as well as the laws and regulations which they may adopt to ensure the application thereof.

The 1929 provision with regard to the posting of the Convention has been extended so that all regulations and orders must be in a language that the prisoners can understand.

The first paragraph of Article 144 of the Civilians Convention is in the same terms as Article 127 of the Prisoners of War Convention, but it proceeds

> Any civilian, military, police or other authorities, who in time of war assume responsibilities in respect of protected persons, must possess the text of the Convention and be specially instructed as to its provisions,

and the same requirement respecting intercommunication of legislation appears in Article 145.

At the present time there has been some widening of the concept of non-military objectives and a treaty now exists for the Protection of Cultural Property in the Event of Armed Conflict.[36] It cannot be denied that in the past the military have not been over-scrupulous in respecting cultural property and at times occupying forces have not hesitated to destroy monuments in the territory of their enemy. Moreover, even in peacetime states have on occasion considered that modernization is perhaps more important than the preservation of those national cultural monuments which might constitute part of "the cultural heritage of every people." Cultural property is defined as

> a) movable or immovable property of great importance to the cultural heritage of every people, such as monuments or architecture, art or history, whether religious or secular; archeological sites; groups of buildings which, as a whole, are of historical or artistic interest; works of art; manuscripts; books and other objects of artistic, historical or archeological interest; as well as scientific collections and important collections of books or archives or of reproductions of the property defined above;
> b) buildings whose main and effective purpose is to preserve or exhibit the movable cultural property defined in sub-paragraph (a) such as museums, large libraries and depositories of archives, and refuges intended to shelter, in the event of armed conflict, the movable cultural property defined in sub-paragraph (a);
> c) centres containing a large amount of cultural property as defined in sub-paragraphs (a) and (b) to be known as 'centres containing monuments'.

This definition is so comprehensive and yet so vague that it is clear some measures of dissemination to inform the military and others concerned will be absolutely vital if the Convention is to have any meaning, especially as troops engaged in actual operations are unlikely to view as protected an article regarded by the enemy or a neutral as having significant cultural significance and enjoying immunity, if respect for such an object or group of them might interfere with the success of the operation or involve its cancellation.

---

[36]1954, 249 *UNTS* 240 (Schindler/Toman, 661); see, also, Williams, *The International and National Protection of Movable Cultural Property* (1978), 15-51; and Protocol I, Art. 53.

The draftsmen seem to have been aware of this danger and of the need to inform troops of their obligations. There are two provisions relating to the dessemination which to some extent are repetitive:

> Art. 7—The High Contracting Parties undertake to introduce in time of peace into their military regulations or instructions such provisions as may ensure observance of the present Convention, and to foster in the members of their armed forces a spirit for the culture and cultural property of all peoples. The High Contracting Parties undertake to plan or establish in peacetime, within their armed forces, services or specialist personnel whose purposes will be to secure respect for cultural property and to co-operate with civilian authorities responsible for safeguarding it.
>
> Art. 25—The High Contracting Parties undertake, in time of peace as in time of armed conflict, to disseminate the text of the present Convention and the Regulations for its execution as widely as possible in their respective countries. They undertake, in particular, to include the study thereof in their programmes of military and, if possible, civilian training, so that its principles are made known to the whole population, especially the armed forces and personnel engaged in the protection of cultural property.

It is obvious that the only way such 'property of great importance to the cultural heritage of every people' can be protected without the items becoming so numerous and trivial as to be ridiculous—for every person's idea of what constitutes such property from the point of view of, for example, art is likely to be highly subjective—will be by the compilation of agreed lists that will be available to the armies in the field. Such lists are envisaged, but later experience suggests that these may perhaps not be available by the time armed conflict begins and, as became clear during debate at the 1976 session of the Diplomatic Conference on Humanitarian Law in Armed Conflict, it can easily happen that one belligerent is so determined not to recognize its adversary, that it will not even agree to the compilation of such lists if it means that cooperation is in any way necessary with what is now known as the 'adverse party' rather than the 'enemy'. Nevertheless, Article 53 of Protocol I prohibits the commission of

> any acts of hostility directed against the historic monuments, works of art or places of worship which constitute the cultural or spiritual heritage of peoples

but it gives no hint as to how the man in the field is to be informed of their identity. Since the Article is prefaced by the statement that it is adopted "without prejudice to the provisions of the (1954) Hague Convention for the Protection of Cultural Property in the Event of Armed Conflict," it must be presumed that the draftsmen of the Protocol were satisfied with the identification process embodied in that Convention. Article 6 of the Convention requires cultural property to "bear a distinctive emblem so as to facilitate its recognition," and by Article 16

> the distinctive emblem . . . shall take the form of a shield, pointed below, per saltire blue and white (a shield consisting of a royal-blue square, one of the angles of which forms the point of the shield, and of a royal-blue triangle above the square, the space on either side being taken up by a white triangle). The emblem shall be used alone, or repeated three times in a triangular formation (one shield below) . . .

Clearly, military personnel will have to receive instruction as to the nature of this emblem, as well as all other emblems now recognized as conferring protection, but neither the

Convention nor the Protocol indicates how they are to be made aware of these emblems. Presumably, the general provision for dissemination embodied in the Protocol is regarded as sufficient. Cynics might be excused if they regard such provisions as somewhat idealist and completely out of tune with the realities of active warfare. Their cynicism will not be reduced by the further provision in Article 17 of the Convention that

> the distinctive emblem may not be placed on any immovable cultural property unless at the same time there is displayed an authorization duly dated and signed by the competent authority of the High Contracting Party.

This will necessitate further instruction to the man in the field as to who the 'competent authority' of the enemy for this purpose is—and is it to be expected that operations are to cease while some member of an attacking force examines the immovable cultural object to ascertain whether it has the correct certificate affixed?

In the years since the Second World War most of the armed conflicts which have occurred have been non-international, so that generally speaking there have been no rules of international law, with the possible exception of the minimal rules of humanity as outlined in common Article 3 of the 1949 Geneva Conventions, applicable, for states have traditionally relied upon the argument that civil wars and the like are matters of domestic jurisdiction with which the rest of the world has no concern. And this principle is confirmed by Article 2 (7) of the Charter of the United Nations unless there is a threat to international peace.[37] However, an early effort at bringing civil war situations within the purview of international law is to be found in the Nyon Agreement of 1937[38] aimed at suppressing unlawful submarine attacks upon merchant ships trading with ports under the control of, primarily, the Spanish Government. By Article 1

> The participating Powers will instruct their naval forces to take the action indicated in paragraphs II and III below with a view to the protection of all merchant ships not belonging to either of the conflicting Spanish parties.

While it may be argued by the purist that this is not really directed at imparting rules of humanitarian behaviour to the citizens or military personnel of any contracting party, in the sense that they may need to know the law in order to defend themselves, it is nevertheless an instance of an international obligation that requires states parties to the agreement to inform their personnel of the new law that has been created and which they would be required to observe and carry through.

It became clear in Korea and Vietnam that the law of war as it had been drawn up at The Hague and Geneva was now out of date. For one thing, there was no provision with regard, for example, to environment protection, and when the International Committee of the Red Cross drew up its draft proposals for amendments to the 1949 law to be presented to a diplomatic conference on humanitarian law in armed conflict, it decided to take the opportunity, in so far as it could, to bring the traditional law up to date, as well as to attempt to extend at least the basic principles of humanitarian law to non-international conflicts too. This is not the place to discuss the proposals embodied in the

---

[37]"Nothing contained in the present Charter shall authorize the United Nations to intervene in matters which are essentially within the domestic jurisdiction of any state or shall require the Members to submit such matters to settlement under the present Charter, but this provision shall not prejudice the application of enforcement measures under Chapter VII [with respect to threats to the peace, breaches of the peace and acts of aggression]."

[38]181 *LNTS* 137 (Schindler/Toman, 799).

two Protocols intended to be additions to the Geneva Conventions and aimed at achieving this end.[39] We are concerned solely with the problem of dissemination and enlightenment of those likely to be called upon to give effect to the new rules, whether they be described as part of the law of war or as rules of humanitarian law. Before looking at the provisions of the Protocols it should be pointed out that it matters little what conventions say or require, if the states which are parties to them do not ensure that their military personnel are in fact sufficiently aware of their provisions and understand what is required of them as not to be likely to breach their provisions.

The operations in Korea and Vietnam and the United States courts martial arising therefrom[40] indicate that there was something gravely lacking in the education being given to United States armed forces, and perhaps indicating that not enough emphasis was being imparted to officers to indicate that the United States accepted the view expressed in Article 22 of the Hague Regulations that "the right of belligerents to adopt means of injuring the enemy is not unlimited", even though this article is reprinted in the United States Department of the Army Field Manual on the Law of Land Warfare,[41] accompanied by the comment

> The means employed [in injuring the enemy] are definitely restricted by international declarations and conventions and by the laws and usages of war.

It is perhaps because of what happened in these two theatres that the United States military authorities thereafter issued a variety of pamphlets on the teaching of the law of war to the armed forces.[42] However inadequate these might be,[43] they show a determination to make some effort to ensure that American troops have at least some knowledge of what they may and may not do during armed conflict. As a result, where they are concerned there may now be some validity in upholding the authority of the *ignorantia juris* maxim.

Among the new departures in Protocol I is a provision concerning the protection of journalists.[44] This aims at giving journalists who are not accredited war correspondents some protection by means of an identity card to ensure that when captured they are treated as civilians. Obviously, members of the armed forces will have to be aware of the nature of this card and know that any attempt by them to use such an identity certificate would amount to a breach of the law of war. In fact the British Government has now ceased the practice in Northern Ireland of having soldiers in civilian clothing passing themselves off as regular journalists, thus indulging in a form of 'perfidy', while at the same time endangering true journalists entitled to such cards and the civilian status concomitant therewith.[45]

Similar measures of instruction will be necessary in view of the new provisions con-

---

[39]See, e.g., "The New Law of Armed Conflict," ch. I *supra*.

[40]See, e.g., "Superior Orders and the Reasonable Man," ch. III *infra*; *Superior Orders in National and International Law* (1976), 126 *et seq.*

[41]Dept. of the Army, FM27-10 (1956), para. 33.

[42]Dept. of the Army, 27-200, "The Law of Land Warfare—A Self-Instructional Text" (1972); ASubjScd 27-1 (1970), "The Geneva Conventions of 1949 and Hague Convention No. IV of 1907" (2-hour lecture course).

[43]For criticisms see Green, "Aftermath of Vietnam: War Law and the Soldier," 4 Falk, *The Vietnam War and International Law—The Concluding Phase* (1976), 147, 168 *et seq.*).

[44]Art. 79.

[45]See Green, letter on "Journalists in Battle Areas," *The Times* (London), 1 Mar. 1976; see, for action likely to endanger such journalists, report by Robert Fisk, "Times correspondent riding shotgun with Soviet Army," *The Times*, 21 Jan. 1980.

cerning the protection of civil defence personnel,[46] who are now protected by a distinctive emblem comprising a blue equilateral triangle on an orange background. Moreover civilian defence personnel, like journalists, and medical and religious personnel, are required to carry a distinctive identity card. The truly educated soldier anxious not to deny immunity to any protected person or object will have to carry a booklet of his own listing all the distinctive emblems and reproducing the relevant identity cards. Failure to do this may well lead to a charge of breaches of the law of war, to which it will now be impossible for him to plead ignorance of the law. While the national authorities may have carried out their obligations to teach the new law, it can hardly be expected that the ordinary man in the field will be able to remember the shape and colour of every distinctive emblem, or the particulars which he would find on a properly issued identity card.

Protocol I imposes an obligation to disseminate the Geneva law as amended. By article 83

> the High Contracting Parties undertake, in time of peace as in time of armed conflict, to disseminate the Conventions and the Protocol as widely as possible in their respective countries and, in particular, to include the study thereof in their programmes of military instruction and to encourage the study thereof by the civilian population, so that those instruments may become known to the armed forces and to the civilian population. Any military or civilian authorities who, in time of armed conflict, assume responsibilities in respect of the application of the Conventions and this Protocol shall be fully acquainted with the text thereof.

Since it may well happen that this has been inadequately done, or since issues may arise which lead the troops to question whether particular orders or activities comply with the Geneva law, and as in time of total war there may be insufficient time to impart such instruction before conscripts are sent into action, Article 82 attempts to fill this potential hiatus:

> The High Contracting Parties at all times, and the Parties to the conflict in time of armed conflict, shall ensure that legal advisers are available, when necessary, to advise military commanders at the appropriate level on the application of the Conventions and this Protocol and on the appropriate instruction to be given to the armed forces on this subject.

A number of points arise in connection with these proposals. In the first place, Article 82 implies that some of the officers attached to the judge advocate division of a military force should be knowledgeable in at least that part of the law of war that may be described as humanitarian law. Such a requirement would almost certainly necessitate a revision of the training afforded by the relevant military services and perhaps also the placing of a greater emphasis on the international law of war with particular reference to the principles of humanitarian law in armed conflict. The reason that states are only required to 'encourage' civilian study of these principles is to be found in the constitutional difficulties confronting some federal states where education is not within the central government's competence, and also to preserve the position in those countries where independence is demanded by such educational authorities as universities in so far as their curricula and teaching programmes are concerned. There can be little doubt that, even if these provisions are conscientiously carried out, military commanders will have to recognize that, while their function may be to conduct hostilities with a view to the early defeat

---

[46]Ch. VI.

of the enemy, regulation of the conduct of the men in their command so as to ensure compliance with the law and its restrictions is a fundamental obligation, as well as a policy matter of importance to national dignity. If this occurs, there are likely to be less transgressions of the law and certainly fewer opportunities for those accused of breaches to plead ignorance in their defence. However, there is inherent in the provisions the assumption that proper educational programmes, at least of the military, conducted by properly qualified persons will be instituted.

Some countries have taken their obligation in regard to educating their armed forces seriously and have introduced courses in the law of armed conflict. Unfortunately, the courses in question tend to be rather short[47] and many commanding officers consider them to be of less significance than the other matters included in the normal training programme. The result is that, too often, instruction is delegated to an unqualified officer or regarded by the troops to whom it is directed as a matter of humour. This draws attention to activities already commenced in cooperation with the International Committee of the Red Cross by the Institut Henri Dunant in Geneva. Under the direction of Professor Pictet, who is also Vice President of the International Committee of the Red Cross, the Institut has introduced a number of courses on humanitarian law in armed conflict which have already been attended by members of the armed forces from various countries, as well as by graduate students. In addition, the Institut is anxious to organize seminars for interested parties and on a regional basis, and is receiving encouragement and cooperation particularly from some of the developing countries. Where developed countries are concerned, difficulties are encountered in view of historical backgrounds and a desire to follow their own tradition. The International Institute of Humanitarian Law at San Remo also runs such courses. It is to be hoped that in both cases care is taken that idealism and belief in the principles of humanitarian law do not prejudice the awareness of the instructors as to the realities of war. If they ignore these and elevate the principles of Geneva to too high a level, rather than achieving their object of instruction to ensure respect for the law, they may induce an attitude of disbelief and cynicism.

Problems of a somewhat different kind arise concerning Protocol II[48] which deals with non-international armed conflicts. In so far as the regular armed forces are concerned, their position is already governed by the provisions in Protocol I just referred to, although it could easily be argued that since Protocol I only deals with international conflicts, any education in relation thereto is completely irrelevant for non-international conflicts. Specific steps must therefore be taken to ensure that no such escape from the obligation to observe humanitarian law is possible. In the event of a non-international conflict, however, one of the contestants is likely to be recruited primarily from civilians, as well as dissident members of the armed forces. If the Protocol is to have any meaning and come into operation immediately upon the conflict becoming sufficiently serious to be considered an armed conflict rather than a riot or a minor insurrection, it will be necessary for the civilian population to be educated in the basic principles of humanitarian law as part of the country's ordinary educational programme and regardless of the likelihood of any conflict arising. However, any attempt to postulate an international obligation requiring states to educate their subjects as to their rights and duties in time of civil war or other non-international armed conflict may easily be construed as an attempt to interfere in the domestic jurisdiction of a state. Further, it smacks of encouragement to dissidents to resort to armed conflict, secure in the knowledge that the government is subject to

---

[47]See, e.g., Introduction, n 19, p. xxi *supra*.
[48]Schindler/Toman, 619.

restrictions on its freedom in restoring order and re-establishing its authority, having already taught those who are now opposed to the government exactly what rights they will be entitled to, and which might limit the normal operation of the criminal law, should they decide to resort to armed force. In fact, at Geneva this proposal met with opposition from some Latin American countries, where it might be thought that their past history suggests a real likelihood of non-international conflict breaking out with the resultant creation of a Protocol II situation. A further objection was raised by the Soviet Union which contended that any obligation to educate its civilian population along such lines would be contrary to the prohibition contained in the Law on the Defence of Peace[49] which forbids war propaganda in whatever form it is carried out, arguing further that such education would also be contrary to the Soviet commitment to educate for peaceful purposes. In view of these reservations, it is perhaps not surprising that although instruction of the civilian population as to the law regulating civil conflict is of prime importance, all that appears in Protocol II is the simple statement

The Protocol shall be disseminated as widely as possible.[50]

leaving it to each state to decide on the identification of those to whom the dissemination should be directed and the manner in which this should be done.

As originally drafted, and in fact accepted in Committee, the commitments for dissemination were somewhat more effective, and included an obligation[51]

> to disseminate the present Protocol as widely as possible in time of peace, so that it may become known to the armed forces and to the civilian population.
> In time of armed conflict, the Parties to the conflict shall take appropriate measures to bring the provisions of the present Protocol to the knowledge of their military and civilian agents and persons subject to their control.

While one may sympathize with a government which finds it objectionable to accept an obligation to educate its people as to their rights against the government should they decide to resort to armed force to overthrow that government, this unaccepted provision appears reasonable. The anti-government forces will not be a party to the Protocol which is only open for signature or accession by parties to the Geneva Conventions, and is thus only available to states. It would seem, therefore, that unless this anti-government contestant makes a statement accepting the obligations of the Protocol, there would have been imposed upon the government a unilateral obligation as to its operations for re-establishing its authority and, moreover, a requirement to inform the military and the civilians supporting it of their duties to observe the provisions of the Protocol, even though their opponents were not so doing. On the other hand, it might be argued that by becoming a party a state accepts the obligations for all its citizens, so that during a non-international conflict even its opponents would be, in law at least, still bound by the state's international undertakings. This one-sidedness of burdens might have proved in practice, therefore, more apparent than real. What is perhaps of more significance than the rather narrow obligation that the Protocol imposes upon parties is the absence of any provision like that in Protocol I relating to the teaching of Protocol II in military curricula. The reason for this lacuna lies in the fact that some countries were unwilling, in relation

---

[49]21 Mar. 1951, c. Tunkin, *Theory of International Law* (1974), 85-6.
[50]Art. 19.
[51]I.C.R.C. Doc., D/1388/1 b (1976).

to a non-international conflict, to accept directions as to the precise method by which their armed forces were to be informed of their obligations under Protocol II, especially as this Protocol is intended to limit the freedom of action of the contestants in such a conflict, including the rights normally accruing to state forces in upholding state authority during an armed confrontation.

There can be little doubt that if the states parties to the Geneva Conventions and the two amending Protocols, particularly Protocol I, take their obligations regarding dissemination seriously, and in fact introduce proper educational programmes[52], there would be more realization by both the armed forces and the civilian population that there is in fact a real law of war carrying as much risk of punishment in the event of its breach, as is the case with national criminal law. At the same time, no member of the field forces would be able to contend, if charged with a breach of the law, that not only was he unaware of the existence of any particular rule, but that no attempt had ever been made to enlighten him. Moreover, military commanders would have to rethink their attitudes to the whole conspectus of the law of war and give it its due and proper place in military training. In so far as the civilian population is concerned, if the obligations are to be fully carried out, both as regards Protocol I and in any real sense for Protocol II, there would be a need for governments to rethink the nature of their educational programmes, despite the possibility that schools and pacifists among the teaching staffs might offer real objections. In fact, in spite of tradition, there would have to be some measure of cooperation between civilian education authorities and the military. Since this would almost certainly be rejected in many countries, use might have to be made of the personnel of the national Red Cross Society. But this too would often mean a rethinking of the entire approach and philosophy of such Society. For the main part, the members of the national Society are concerned with internal medical auxiliary aid programmes and the offer of assistance in the event of national and sometimes international catastrophes, but they are hardly concerned with problems of armed conflict or the law relating thereto. Perhaps, if they were able to enlist qualified persons, and this again raises the problem of cooperation with the military or at least of the legal branch, this would be reasonable. Otherwise, it must be remembered that the international law of peace and war, as well as the principles of humanitarian law, is highly technical and the terms of treaties are often ambiguous if not actually obtuse. For unqualified persons to attempt to educate others as to their meaning may be just as dangerous as the absence of any education at all.

While in the past it might have been possible for any state to argue that while common sense dictated that it should educate its troops in the law of war, the legal obligation so to do was somewhat nebulous and rather in the nature of a pious hope. Now, however, the obligation is clearly laid down. What may still be necessary is the establishment of some observation centre or clearing house which might be able to oversee and advise whether this is being carried into effect in a reasonable manner such that ordinary soldiers may understand, while a bare minimum may be presumed as equally accepted by all services regardless of arm or nationality. To some extent this is being attempted by the Henri Dunant Institut, while the International Committee of the Red Cross may be expected to continue to issue pamphlets outlining the basic minima of obligations in the field of humanitarian law. These educational activities, combined with the obligation in the Conventions to report to the International Committee which, presumably, is entitled to comment on such reports, may be the beginning of a new era of education of both the military and the civilian populations in that part of international criminal law which is

[52]This is already being done in the Canadian forces, see Introduction, n. 19 above.

concerned with breaches of the principles of international humanitarian law in time of armed conflict. Should this be the case, we would see the dawn of an era in which it was true of the man in the field during combat, as it is for the civilian charged with a criminal offence, that *ignorantia juris non excusat*. At the same time we would be doing no more than reverting to the situation that existed during the sixteenth century when there existed in Piedmont a military school which taught the laws of war and of discipline.[53]

[53]See Gardot, *loc. cit.*, 465-6.

III

Superior Orders and the Reasonable Man

Recent allegations concerning a "massacre" of Vietnamese by United States forces in the Song My area of Vietnam, together with disclosures of a similar event during British anti-guerrilla operations in Malaya, have drawn renewed attention to the problem of the behaviour of troops in war, and the extent to which they may be expected to obey the laws of war. This is not the place to examine the philosophical aspect of whether there are or can be any rules of war, particularly if one of the belligerents is waging an "illegal" or "criminal" war, or is not recognized as a state so that the operations do not technically qualify as a war in the traditional sense. The *Kawasaki* case[1] demonstrates that "war" may exist, even though neither the parties nor third states recognize the operations as such. It is also clear, at least since the Geneva Conventions of 1949,[2] that laws regarding the humane treatment of wounded and sick prisoners of war and civilians in occupied territory operate even in armed conflicts not of an international character,[3] as well as those which only one party regards as a war, or if only one is party to the Conventions, or if territory is occupied and no resistance met.[4]

Since the laws of war apply to all such hostilities, members of the armed forces accused of breaking these laws are likely to be tried by court martial or a war crimes tribunal. In the case of members of one's own forces, there is no need to charge war crimes; every army is subject to its own system of law and normally has a penal code based on its ordinary municipal law. Troops are under the jurisdiction of their national command and there is no need to seek any extraordinary ground to establish jurisdiction over them. With members of another armed force, be it allied or enemy, this basis for jurisdiction

---

[1]*Kawasaki Kisen Kabushiki Kaisha of Kobe* v. *Bantham S.S. Co.* [1939] 2 K.B. 544.
[2]Schindler/Toman, I-305, II-333, III-355, IV-427; see also Protocols I-551, II-619.
[3]Art. 3 of each Convention.
[4]Art. 2 of each Convention.

does not exist and some special authority has to be found. This is provided by international law which permits those—including neutrals[5]—into whose hands offenders against the laws of war may fall to try them for the alleged breaches of the law, and the Oradour trial in France, when the trial for war crimes of French traitors was severed from that of their German colleagues, illustrates the type of problem that may well arise because of the conflict of jurisdictions.[6]

Invariably in these trials the accused contends that as a member of the armed forces he is obliged to obey the orders of his superiors, and he frequently seeks to evade personal responsibility on the ground that whatever act he is alleged to have committed was performed as the result of an order, so that, if criminal liability lies against anybody, it is against the authority who issued the order. In the trials that followed the Second World War, the order-issuing authority was frequently alleged to have been Hitler or some other of his senior dignitaries who were either dead or whose whereabouts were unknown; if the plea served to provide the factual actor with a defence, it would have been impossible to proceed against anyone. However, it must not be thought that the plea is to be found only in connection with offences committed by military personnel. Thus it is provided by the Norwegian Penal Code that "in cases where a superior cannot be punished for a misdemeanour committed by somebody in his service, the subordinate can always be held responsible, even if the penal provision, according to its wording alone, is directed against the superior."[7]

In civilian life the position of hierarchic authority that exists in the armed services is not frequently come across, but accused persons have been known to put forward the plea of obedience in an ordinary criminal process, and this was particularly true in the earlier days of colonial rule. They have also alleged that some other person exercised such coercion, compulsion or duress upon them that they were obliged to act as they did, but had not done so as free agents. Before examining the problem from the point of view of military or international law, it is useful to refer to the position in municipal criminal law, for members of the armed forces do not normally lose their liability under that law merely by virtue of having joined the forces; some of the Penal Codes make express reference to the problem.

According to the German Penal Code, "no act constitutes an offence if its perpetrator was compelled so to act by *irresistible force* or by a threat entailing an *immediate and otherwise not avertible danger* to his own or one of his family member's body or life."[8] The 1916 Criminal Code of Lagos, East and West Nigeria provides that "a person is not criminally responsible for an act or omission if he does or omits to do the act . . . (2) in obedience to the order of a competent authority which he is bound by law to obey, unless the order is *manifestly unlawful* . . . but this protection does not extend to an act or omission which would constitute an offence punishable with death, or an offence of which grievous harm to the person of another, or an intention to cause such harm, is an element. . . . *Whether*

[5]Thus, the 1949 Conventions, at least where "grave breaches" are concerned, require each High Contracting Party to seek out those, regardless of nationality, alleged to have committed or ordered such breaches, and try them before local courts or transfer them for trial to another High Contracting Party "concerned," provided the latter has made out a prima facie case (Art. 49, 50, 129, 146). See Canada's Geneva Conventions Act, 1964 (S.C. 1965, c. 44), s.3, and "Unit Guide to the Geneva Conventions," 1949, CFP 318(4), para. 702 (2), which states that "Canada, or any other nation bound by the Conventions including the enemy, may capture and try any person who commits or orders to be committed any of the acts defined as grave breaches of the Convention." See also Cowles, "Universality of Jurisdiction over War Crimes," 33 *Calif. L. Rev.* 177 (1945).
[6]*The Times* (London), Jan. 2, 13, 14, 16, 17, 19-21, 29-31, Feb. 4, 9-14, 19, 20 and 23, 1953.
[7]1902/61, s.41 (Andenaes ed., 1961, at 28).
[8]1871/1961, s.52 (Mueller ed., 1961, at 41, italics added).

an order is or is not *manifestly unlawful is a question of law*."[9] The Colombian Penal Code recognizes the liability of both the actor and the superior ordering the action, but provides for mitigation of punishment: "An act is justified when committed pursuant to . . . an obligatory command of a competent authority. . . . [T]he person causing another to act shall be liable. . . . Anyone performing an act under [such] circumstances who *exceeds the limits imposed by law*, [or] by the authorities . . . shall be subject to a [reduced] punishment. In cases specially favorable for the accused, the sentence may be suspended."[10] The Turkish Criminal Code is in somewhat similar terms: "No punishment shall be imposed if the perpetrator acted (1) in order to execute . . . an order given by a responsible authority, execution of which is the perpetrator's duty; . . . *if the order issued is contrary to law*, the *punishment* for the felony resulting from the violation of the law, *shall be suffered by the person who has issued the order. Whoever* while performing [such] an act . . . , *surpasses the limit prescribed either by law*, by competent authority, *or by necessity, shall be punished* in accordance with a specified scale of reduced penalties."[11]

The Canadian Criminal Code puts the issue of obedience in juxtaposition with that of coercion. By section 15, "[N]o person shall be convicted of an offence in respect of an act or omission in obedience to the laws for the time being made and enforced by persons in *de facto* possession of the sovereign power in and over the place where the act or omission occurs." It would appear from this wording that there could be no reproduction of the trials of the regicides in Canada,[12] and the immunity extends to acts done in obedience to "public functionaries holding office thereunder."[13] As to the problem of duress, section 17 provides that "[A] person who commits an offence under compulsion *by threats of immediate death or grievous bodily harm from a person who is present when the offence is committed* is *excused* for committing the offence *if he believes that the threats will be carried out* and if he is not a party to a conspiracy or association whereby he is subject to compulsion, but this section does not apply where the offence that is committed is treason, murder, piracy, attempted murder, assisting in rape, forcible abduction, robbery, causing bodily harm or arson." Thus in *Dunbar* v. *R.*[14] the appellant contended that he had been compelled by threats to his life to act as chauffeur for a robbery during which murder was committed; it was held that his choice to participate in the undertaking made him a party to the unlawful common undertaking, and that since murder had been committed the compulsion would not excuse him, even though he was not present at the actual killing. As to the defence of superior orders, this was put forward in *R.* v. *Laroche* when a municipal treasurer pleaded that she had paid moneys to the mayor on his instructions, in the honest belief that he was entitled to receive them; the majority of the Supreme Court was of opinion "that there could be no honesty or honest opinion of right in these transactions."[15]

Broadly speaking, the position of a member of the Canadian armed forces is identical with that of a civilian under municipal law. By section 125 of the National Defence Act all civil defences are available to an accused serviceman appearing before a military tribunal, and by QR&O 103.03 the terms of section 17 of the Criminal Code on compulsion are spelled out. By QR&O, Chapter 19, "every officer and man shall obey the orders of officers and men who are senior to him . . . [but i]f an officer or man is given an order

---

[9] S.32 (Brett and McLean ed., 1963, at 482, italics added).
[10] 1936, ss.25,26,27 (Eder ed., 1967, at 21, italics added).
[11] 1926/64, ss.49,50 (Gürelli ed., 1965, at 28).
[12] See references to *Axtell* and *Cooke, infra* notes 33, 34.
[13] Constantineau on *De Facto Doctrine, c. Martin's Criminal Code,* 1955, at 55.
[14] [1936] 4 D.L.R. 737. See also *R.* v. *Farduto* (1913), 10 D.L.R. 669.
[15] [1964] S.C.R. 667, 673.

that he considers to be in conflict with the *National Defence Act*, QR&O, or general or particular orders binding on him, he shall point out the conflict orally, or in writing if the order does not require immediate obedience, to the superior by whom the order was given. If the superior still directs him to obey the order, he shall do so."[16] Queen's Regulations and Orders do not indicate what his position will be if he carries out the order and it transpires that it was in fact illegal. The only guidance that is given is to be found in section 74 of the National Defence Act which demands obedience to "lawful commands." QR&O 103.16(J) stipulates that the command must be lawful, and gives as an example that a man would be justified in refusing to sign a receipt for pay if he considered it incorrect, even though he were ordered to sign. Presumably, if it is not lawful for him to be ordered to sign such a receipt, it would not be lawful for him to be ordered to commit a war crime and, if he obeyed that order, then presumably he would be liable. Some evidence for this contention may be derived from *Fitch* v. *The Queen* in which Cameron J. pointed out that the order must "be one relating to a military duty. For example, a command given by an officer to a man to perform some domestic office not relating to military duty is not a command within the meaning of this section."[17] A man would be placed upon the horns of a dilemma if he were called upon to decide whether an order given him by an officer constituted a lawful requisition or unlawful looting.

The last Penal Code to which reference need be made is that of India. By section 76 there is no offence if the act were done "by a person who is, or who by reason of a mistake of fact and not by reason of a mistake of law in good faith believes himself to be bound by law to do it." Commenting on this, Ratanlal points out that nothing but fear of instant death would constitute a defence for a policeman who tortured anyone on the orders of his superior, and he cites two nineteenth century cases as illustrative of his argument.[18] In *Gurdit Singh* the court considered the case of a naik and two men who had fired on a mob that was threatening them, and held that "they must be taken to have known that the naik was wrong in law in firing upon the mob, and that they were not bound to obey his illegal order."[19] A year earlier, a police officer who committed a wrongful act under the order of his superior officer had been held liable "as his mistake of law in supposing himself authorised cannot be accepted as a good defence though it may be a ground for mitigation of punishment."[20]

There seems to be little doubt that the Indian Penal Code was based on the principles that had evolved in England since the early days of the common law, and which later were adopted by the United States. The present situation in these two countries is easily stated. According to Halsbury:

> . . . No duress . . . excuses the taking of an innocent life. . . . [E]vidence of threats and violence to the accused may rebut the presumption that the accused intended the probable consequences of his act, and, where the offence is proved by the proof of the doing of an act, it seems that a plea of duress may be set up, not to show that no offence has been committed but to excuse from punishment. . . . The mere fact that a person does a criminal act in *obedience to the order of a duly constituted superior does not excuse the person who does the act from criminal liability,* but the fact that a person does an act in obedience to a superior whom he is bound to obey, *may exclude the inference of malice or wrongful intention* which might otherwise follow

[16]QR&O 19.015, 19.02.
[17](1954) 1 C.M.A.R. 249,251.
[18]*Law of Crimes,* 1966, at 138.
[19]P.R. No. 16 of 1883.
[20]*Nga Myat Tha* (1882) S.J.L.B. 164.

from the act. . . . Soldiers and airmen are amenable to the criminal law to the same extent as other subjects. . . . *Obedience to superior orders is not in itself a defence to a criminal charge.*[21]

This is in accord with the earliest Mutiny Act of 1688 and is supported by Stephen and by Dicey. The former states:

[Soldiers] are bound to execute any *lawful* order which they may receive from their military superior. . . . Probably . . . the order of a military superior would justify his inferiors in executing any orders for giving which they might *fairly suppose* their superior officer to have good reasons. . . . The doctrine that a soldier is bound under all circumstances whatever to obey his superior officer would be fatal to military discipline itself [for example, an order to shoot the Commanding Officer or to desert]. . . . [I]t is not less *monstrous to suppose that superior orders would justify a soldier in the massacre* of unoffending civilians in time of peace, or in the exercise of inhuman cruelties, such as the slaughter of women and children, during a rebellion. . . . [A] soldier should be *protected by orders* for which *he might reasonably believe his officer to have good grounds.*[22]

This would appear to impose upon a soldier the virtually impossible task of having to decide, when faced with an order that might not be lawful, whether in his view the officer had good grounds for issuance. Dicey does not go so far:

When a soldier is put on trial on a charge of crime, *obedience to superior orders* is not of itself a defence. . . . A soldier is *bound to obey any lawful order* which he receives from his military superior. But *a soldier cannot any more than a civilian avoid responsibility* for breach of the law *by pleading* that he broke the law in *bona fide obedience to the orders.* . . . [His] position is in theory and may be in practice a difficult one. He may . . . be liable to be shot by a Court-martial if he disobeys an order, and to be hanged by a judge and jury if he obeys it. . . . The hardship of a soldier's position resulting from this inconvenience is much diminished by the power of the Crown to nullify the effect of an unjust conviction by means of a pardon.[23] While, however, a soldier runs no substantial risk of punishment for obedience to *orders which a man of common sense may honestly believe to involve no breach of law,* he . . . cannot avoid liability on the ground of obedience to superior orders for any act *which a man of ordinary sense must have known to be a crime.*[24]

Dicey's rejection of superior orders not only applies to members of the armed forces, but reaches to the ministerial level: "The Minister or servant of the Crown who . . . takes part in giving expression to the Royal will is legally responsible for the act in which he is concerned, and he cannot get rid of his liability by pleading that he acted in obedience to royal orders. Now supposing that the act done is illegal, the Minister concerned in it becomes at once liable to criminal or civil proceedings in a Court of Law."[25]

The position in the United States is almost identical. According to the *Corpus Juris Secundum*[26] "except in the case of homicide, an act which would otherwise constitute a crime may be excused when committed under duress or compulsion which is present, imminent and impending and which produces a well grounded apprehension of death

---

[21]3rd (Simonds) ed., vol. 10, ss.539,541,1169 (italics added).
[22]1 *History of the Criminal Law* 204-06 (1883) (italics added).
[23]See *R. v. Thomas* (1816), 4 M. & S. 441 (MS Bayley J.). Dicey points out that the Attorney-General could enter a *nolle prosequi.*
[24]*The Law of the Constitution* 298-99, 302 (8th ed., 1915) (italics added).
[25]*Ibid.,* 322-23.
[26]Vol. 22, "Criminal Law," ss.43,39.

or serious bodily harm if the act is not done. . . . As a general rule, a person who, while acting under the authority or direction of a superior, performs a criminal act is responsible therefor," and this is true even if the actor is the officer of a corporation, an agent or a servant. "The rules of law as to the liability of a soldier for the execution of the orders of his superiors are the same in criminal as in civil cases; thus he is not criminally liable for the execution of a lawful order, or one which is *fair and lawful on its face; but an order illegal on its face is no justification* for the commission of a crime."[27] These statements are fully backed up in the doctrinal writings in words that reflect the same attitudes as do those of Stephen and Dicey. According to Wharton:

> [W]here a person relies on a command of legal authority as a defense, it is essential that the command be a lawful one, which he was required to obey. . . . An order which is illegal in itself, and not justified by the rules and usages of war [here applied as much to the operations of the National Guard or armed forces in the case of internal disturbance as to war in the international sense] or which is, in substance, *clearly illegal*, so that *a man of ordinary sense and understanding would know* as soon as he heard the order read or given *that it was illegal*, will afford no protection for a homicide. . . . Moreover, if it is not part of the soldier's military duty to kill the particular victim, his act in so doing is criminal as though he were a private citizen. When an act committed by a soldier is a crime, even when done pursuant to military orders, the fact that he was ordered to commit the crime by his military superior is not a defense.[28]

As to the possibility of conflicts between the two systems of jurisprudence, "Recognition of the peculiar necessity of discipline in the military service and of the position in which the subordinate may find himself through no fault of his own, in the event that commands of his superiors clash with the civil authority, has led courts in well-considered cases to regard obedience to a military order as a justification for conduct which would otherwise give rise to civil or criminal liability, unless the order is *so palpably unlawful that a reasonable man in the position of the person obeying it would perceive its unlawful quality*."[29] Perhaps the most comprehensive doctrinal statement of the United States position, and one that has been adopted by the courts[30], is by Hare:

> The question is . . . had the accused *reasonable cause for believing in the necessity* of the act which is impugned, and in determining this point a soldier or member of the *posse comitatus* may obviously take the orders of the person in command into view as proceeding from one who is better able to judge and well informed; and, if the circumstances are such that the command may be justifiable, he should not be held guilty for declining to decide that it is wrong with the responsibility incident to disobedience, *unless the case is so plain as not to admit of a reasonable doubt*. A soldier consequently runs little risk in obeying any order *which a man of common sense so placed would regard as warranted by the circumstances*.[31]

The quotations from Wharton and Hare raise the problem of what is meant by the "reasonable man" in this context. However, before considering this or the relevance of the defence of superior orders to war crimes *per se*, it may be useful to look at some of the judicial applications of the doctrine outlined above. Perhaps the earliest cases in the

[27]C.J.S., vol. 6, "Army and Navy," s.37 (2) (italics added).
[28]1 *Criminal Law and Procedure*, 257-58, s.118 (1957 ed.) (italics added).
[29]135 ALR Annot. 10,37 (italics added).
[30]See, for example, *Commonwealth, ex rel. Wadsworth* v. *Shortall* (1903), 55 Atl. 952, 956.
[31]Hare, *Constitutional Law*, 920 (1889) (italics added).

United Kingdom were those concerning the regicides after the Restoration, when it was held that obedience to the Commonwealth did not extend to an accused the protection of the Act of 1494,[32] whereby obedience to a king de facto who was not also de jure king did not after a restoration render his adherents liable for treason. In *Cooke's* case the former Chief Justice of Ireland was tried for his part in the proceedings against the King in that he presented the indictment and demanded judgment against him; his plea that "they were not my words, but their words that commanded me" was rejected, for "you know by a printed authority, that where a settled court, a true court is, if that court meddle with that which is not in their cognizance, it is purely void; the minister that obeys them is punishable; if it be treasonable matter, it is treason; if murder, it is mur- der. . . . [If the Common Pleas sentence a man to death when it should be the King's Bench,] it is murder in the Executioner. . . . You speak of a court: 1 It was not a court: 2 No courts whatsoever could have any power over a king in a coercive way, as to his person. . . . [T]he acting by colour of that pretended authority was so far from any extenuation, that it was an aggravation of the thing."[33] In this case there was constant reference to the fact that the accused was learned in the law and would therefore know what the position really was. In *Axtell*[34] there was no such basis for argument, for the accused was merely the guard commander at the execution, who "justified that all he did was as a soldier, by the command of his superiour officer, whom he must obey or die. It was resolved that was no excuse, for his superiour was a traitor, and all that joyned him in that *act* were traitors, and did by that approve the treason; and where the command is traiterous, there the obedience to that command is also traiterous." The court took the line that even a common soldier must have known that it was an act of treason to participate in any way in the execution of one's king.

The reasoning in *Axtell* appears to have provided the basis of the argument by the Advocate General of India during one of the Indian National Army Trials. The defence had contended that the acts of the accused were legal within the terms of the "Indian National Army Act" and so excepted from the Indian Penal Code and the Indian Army Act, to be met by this argument:

> [A]n act of treason cannot give any sort of rights nor can it exempt a person from criminal responsibility for the subsequent acts. Even if an act is done under a command, where the command is traitorous, obedience to that command is also traitorous. It is submitted that the accused cannot in law seek to justify what they did as having been done under the authority of the I.N.A. Act. No authority purporting to be given under that Act can be recognised by this court or indeed any court of this country. The assumption of any such authority was illegal from the beginning. Any tribunal or authority purporting to be established under that Act would be in repudiation of the allegiance which is inherent in a court of the country. Those who instituted or took part in the proceedings were themselves liable to be punished for offences against the State. All orders under the I.N.A. Act or by any tribunal or authority purporting to be established by it are without sanction. They cannot protect the persons who made such orders or acted upon them.[35]

It has been said above that a servant cannot plead in his defence that he was acting

---

[32]11 Hen. VII, c.1.

[33](1660), 5 St.Tr. 1077,1113,1115. See also *War Crimes (Preventive Murder) (Germany) case* (1960), 32 I.L.R. 563.

[34](1661) Kelyng 13, 84 E.R. 1060.

[35]See Green, "The Indian National Army Trials," 11 Mod. L.R. 47, 53-54 (1948). See also *Hindustan Times*, Nov. 6, 1945.

under the orders of his master. Nevertheless, in *Kidd's Case*, Ward L.C.B. pointed out "It is true, a servant is not bound to obey his master but in lawful things, which [three of the accused] say they thought this was, and that they knew not to the contrary, but that their masters acted according to the King's commission,"[36] and the jury found them not guilty of piracy. This decision should be compared with *R. v. James* in which workers were charged with having unlawfully stopped up the airway to a colliery neighbouring that of their master, having been ordered by him so to do. It was there held that:

> If a master told his servant to shoot a man, *he would know that was an order he ought to disobey.* . . . If a man claims a right which he knows not to exist, and he tells his servants to exercise it, and they do so acting *bona fide*, I am of opinion that that is not a felony in them, even if in so doing they obstruct the airway of a mine [contrary to 7 & 8, Geo. IV, c.30]. . . . If these men acted *bona fide* in obedience to the orders of a superior, conceiving that he had the right which he claimed, they are not within this Act of Parliament. But if either of these men *knew that it was a malicious act on the part of his master,* I think then that he would be guilty of the offence charged.[37]

Another case concerning non-military personnel in which superior orders were important is *R. v. Trainer* charging manslaughter against the driver and fireman of a railway train; Willes J. said there:

> [H]e should hold that in a criminal case an inferior officer must be held justified in obeying the directions of a superior, *not obviously improper or contrary to law*—that is, if an inferior officer acted honestly upon what he might *not unreasonably* deem to be the effect of the orders of his superior, he would not be guilty of culpable negligence, those orders *not appearing to him*, at the time, improper or contrary to law. . . . [T]heir duty was to obey the special instructions issued to them as well as they could, presuming there was *no apparent illegality* in them. . . .[38]

Other cases considered by the English courts have referred to orders issued to military personnel, and the guiding statement, which has also been adopted in the United States, is perhaps that by Lord Mansfield in *Wall v. M'Namara* concerning an allegation of false imprisonment by the Lieutenant-Governor of Gambia:

> In trying the legality of acts done by military officers in the exercise of their duty, particularly beyond the seas, . . . great latitude ought to be allowed, and they ought not to suffer for a slip of form, if their intention appears by the evidence to have been upright; it is the same as when complaints are brought against civil magistrates, such as justices of the peace, for acts done by them in the exercise of their civil duty. There the principal inquiry to be made is, by a Court of Justice, how the heart stood? And if there appears to be nothing wrong there, great latitude will be allowed for misapprehension or mistake. But . . . if the heart is wrong, if cruelty, malice, and oppression, appear to have occasioned or aggravated the . . . injury complained of, they shall not cover themselves with the thin veil of legal forms, nor escape, under the cover of a justification the most technically regular. . . .[39]

Another case of unlawful arrest was decided by Willes J. who remarked "I should probably

---

[36](1701), 14 St. Tr. 147, 185.
[37](1837), 8 C. & P. 131, 132-33; 173 E.R. 429, 430 (italics added).
[38](1864), 4 F. & F. 105, 111-12, 113; 176 E.R. 488, 491, 492 (italics added).
[39](1779), 1 Term Rep. 536; 99 E.R. 1239.

hold that the orders [to arrest another member of the military] are an absolute justification in time of actual war . . . unless the orders were such as could not legally be given. . . . [A]n officer or soldier, acting under the orders of his superior—*not being necessarily or manifestly illegal*—would be justified of his orders."[40] Here Willes J. is referring to such orders as may be lawfully given, and in another case in the same year he referred to this again: "[I]f the military should injure [civilians] in their persons or their property, not even the command of a superior officer will justify a soldier in what he does, unless the command should turn out to be legal, and to be within the limits of the protection given by the Mutiny Act and the Articles of War. It is only by reason of the 88th section [of the Act], . . . that a soldier acting *bona fide*, and in discharge of what he supposes to be his duty, could ever set up as against a citizen not a soldier, the justification of superior command."[41] If such a test were to be the controlling measure, it would be almost impossible for a soldier ever to plead the defence of superior orders, at least when the act has been committed against a civilian. Perhaps a more practical approach was adopted by Howard J. before whom a police officer pleaded guilty to attempting to pervert the course of justice. Acting on instructions the constable had enlarged a hole in a door that he knew was to be inspected by magistrates, and the learned judge ruled that "no order, even if it were given by any superior officer, to do what you attempted to do, can possibly excuse you trying to do it."[42]

The attitude of the United States courts seems to have been a little more realistic and therefore more lenient than that of the English courts. In so far as the acts of servants in compliance with the orders of their masters are concerned, the leading case is *Giugni v. U.S.*, in which a sea captain pleaded that he was obeying the orders of his government; Woodbury, Circuit Judge, held that "[i]t requires no citation of authorities to support the proposition that an employee is not immune from punishment for his criminal acts for the reason that those acts were done on his employer's orders."[43] The other cases to be mentioned all refer to acts of the military, and relate to both civil and criminal liability. As to his civil liability, one of the earliest cases is *Mitchell* v. *Harmony*, which was an action for trespass arising from seizure of property in Mexico; Chief Justice Taney held that "the order given was to do an illegal act; to commit a trespass upon the property of another; and can afford no justification to the person by whom it was executed. . . . And upon principle, . . . it can never be maintained that a military officer can justify himself for doing an unlawful act, by producing the order of his superior. *The order may palliate, but it cannot justify*."[44] In an action arising from the arrest of a suspected "night rider," Carroll J. recognized that "It may be and doubtless is true that, looking at the matter from a military standpoint, the order to act as Franks did was *not such an unreasonable command as that a soldier of common sense* would feel authorized to refuse to obey. But . . . conduct like this is such an intolerable invasion of private rights, . . . that we cannot consent that all military orders, however reasonable they may appear, will afford protection in the civil or criminal courts of the state."[45]

The divergence between the military and the civilian approach to the same issue was discussed by the Supreme Court in *U.S. ex rel. Toth* v. *Quarles*,[46] which arose from the arrest in the United States of a member of the air force after he had been demobilized

---

[40]*Keighley* v. *Bell* (1866), 4 F. & F. 763, 790; 176 E.R. 781, 793 (italics added).
[41]*Dawkes* v. *Lord Rokeby* (1866), 4 F. & F. 806, 831; 176 E.R. 800, 811.
[42]*The Times*, December 15, 1962.
[43](1942), 127 F.2d 786, 791.
[44](1851), 13 How. 115, 137 (italics added).
[45]*Franks* v. *Smith* (1911), 134 S.W. 484, 490-91 (italics added).
[46](1955), 350 U.S. 11, 18.

for a murder he was alleged to have committed while serving in Korea, to which in accordance with the Uniform Code of Military Justice[47] he had been returned to stand trial by court martial. The Court held this was an unconstitutional invasion of the rights of a civilian even though it meant, in the absence of Congressional legislation conferring jurisdiction on the municipal courts in such circumstances, that the accused went free and untried. Speaking for the majority, Mr. Justice Black recognized that "It is true that military personnel because of their training and experience may be especially competent to try soldiers for infractions of military rules. Such training is no doubt particularly important where an offense charged against a soldier is purely military, such as diso-bedience of an order, leaving post, etc.," but civilians are entitled to trial by jury, and "juries may reach completely different conclusions than would be reached by specialists in any single field, including specialists in the military field." That the special military knowledge of officers may be important in judicial proceedings has been recognized by Canadian military law and its significance was construed in *Chenoweth* v. *R.*[48] and *Hryhoriw* v. *R.*[49] This fact is of importance, as will be seen below, in construing the significance of "reasonableness" in a military context.

Just as they have recognized the fact that special knowledge may be important in relation to military circumstances, so have the courts recognized the dilemma in which a serviceman may find himself when confronted with an order which may be unlawful. The law has been well set out in *McCall* v. *McDowell*:

> Except in a plain case of excess of authority, where at first blush it is *apparent and palpable to the commonest understanding* that the order is illegal, I cannot but think that the law should excuse the military subordinate when acting in obedience to the orders of his commander. Otherwise he is placed in the dangerous dilemma of being liable in damages to third persons for obedience to an order, or to the loss of his commission and disgrace for disobedience thereto. . . . The first duty of a soldier is obedience, and without this there can be neither discipline nor efficiency in an army. . . . True, cases can be imagined where the order is *so palpably atrocious as well as illegal that one can instinctively feel that it ought not to be obeyed*, by whomever given. . . . Between an order plainly legal and one palpably otherwise—particularly in time of war—there is a wide middle ground, where the ultimate legality and propriety of orders depends or may depend upon circumstances and conditions of which it cannot be expected that the inferior is informed or advised. In such cases, justice to the subordinate demands . . . that the order of the superior should protect the inferior; leaving the responsibility to rest where it properly belongs—upon the officer who gave the command.[50]

References to the duty of a soldier to obey orders and the limitations imposed by the criminal law upon the ordinary man have been referred to in other cases. Thus in *Riggs* v. *State* it was held that "an order illegal in itself, and not justifiable by the rules and usages of war, so that *a man of ordinary understanding* would know, when he heard it read or given, that the order was illegal, would afford the private no protection for a crime under such order; but an order given by an officer to his private which *does not expressly and clearly show on its face, or on the body thereof its own illegality*, the soldier would be bound to obey, and such order would be a protection to him."[51] Arising out of a soldier's supposed duty to prevent an escape and "in obedience to what he believed to be his

[47]1950, 64 Stat. 109.
[48](1954) 1 C.M.A.R. 253.
[49]*Ibid.*, 277.
[50](1867), 1 Abb. 212, 218; 15 Fed. Cas. 1235, 1240-1 (italics added).
[51](1866), 91 Am. Dec. 272 (italics added).

duty," Brown J. said in *U.S* v. *Clark*: "I have no doubt [as to the position of] acts of a subordinate officer performed in compliance with his supposed duty as a soldier; and unless the act were *manifestly beyond the scope of his authority, or . . .* were such *that a man of ordinary sense and understanding* would know that it was illegal, that it would be a protection to him, if he acted in good faith and without malice. As there is no reason in this case to suppose that Clark was not doing what he conceived to be his duty, and the act was *not so clearly illegal that a reasonable man* might not suppose it to be legal,"[52] and since there was no malice, Brown was discharged. Here is an attempt to apply what Lord Mansfield called the test of the heart, military duty, and the concept of ordinariness, and presumably if the order were "manifestly" beyond the authority of the officer giving it then "a man of ordinary sense and understanding would know it was illegal."

Two other cases involving homicide in response to orders are of interest. The accusation in *U.S.* v. *Carr* arose from the suppression of a mutiny, and the court held:

[A] soldier is bound to obey only the lawful orders of his superiors. If he receives an order to do an unlawful act, he is bound neither by his duty nor his oath to do it. . . . [A]n order from an officer to shoot another for disrespectful words merely would, if obeyed, be murder both in the officer and soldier. . . . Place yourselves in the position of the prisoner at the time of the homicide. Inquire whether at the moment he fired . . ., with his surroundings at the time, *he had reasonable ground to believe, and did believe,* that the killing or serious wounding was necessary. . . . If he had reasonable ground so to believe then the killing was not unlawful. But if . . . the mutinous conduct . . . had ceased, and it so appeared to the prisoner, or if he could reasonably have suppressed the disorder without the resort to such violent means as the killing of the deceased, and it would *so have appeared to a reasonable man under the circumstances,* the killing was unlawful. But . . . the law will not require an officer charged with the order and discipline of a camp or fort to weigh with scrupulous nicety the amount of force necessary to suppress disorders. The exercise of *a reasonable* discretion is all that is necessary.[53]

The reasoning in *Carr* together with the quotation from Hare[54] were cited with approval in *Commonwealth, ex rel. Wadsworth* v. *Shortall* which concerned homicide by a member of the National Guard during a coal strike. He had received orders "to shoot, and shoot to kill" anyone approaching a particular house and not stopping when challenged. Mitchell J. said that in the instant case "there was no ground for doubt as to the legality of the order to shoot . . . he . . . acted only on his orders when the situation appeared to call for action under them."[55]

Before leaving the American municipal decisions, reference might be made to two recent cases in which orders were pleaded, although the courts held that the situations with which they were dealing were not really military in character. An army convoy was proceeding along the road with orders not to break convoy, under threat of prosecution. One of the trucks crossed the traffic lights and was involved in a collision. Qua J. recognized that "Failure of instant obedience leads to military punishment, which may be severe. . . . [However, a]n order to keep the convoy together even if that involved continuing in the face of a red light, although illegal, *cannot . . .* under circumstances not here in dispute, *be deemed palpably and obviously illegal* to a private soldier in the position of the plaintiff," but such an order would not excuse reckless or negligent driving.[56] The

---

[52](1887), 31 Fed. 710, 717 (italics added).
[53](1872), 1 Woods, 480 (italics added).
[54]*Op. cit. supra* note 31.
[55](1903), 55 Atl. 952, 957.
[56]*Neu* v. *McCarthy* (1941), 33 N.E. 2d 570, 573-74 (italics added).

remaining case must be the most amazing in which the plea of superior orders has ever been put forward. In *State* v. *Roy* the appellant had been convicted of assault with intent to commit rape, and appealed on the ground that he was a private soldier obeying the orders of his sergeant. It is perhaps not surprising that Denny J. felt "The contention has no merit. The duty of a subordinate to obey a superior officer, while one is subject to military law, has reference only to lawful commands of such superior officer, in matters relating to military duty. And there is certainly nothing on this record to indicate that either of these defendants were engaged in any activity relating to military duties on the night in question."[57]

It would appear that in the view of municipal courts in the United States, a soldier may plead superior orders as a justification for his actions, provided the order was lawful or he had reasonable ground to believe in the circumstances that it was so, unless the order was so "palpably" outrageous that "a reasonable man of ordinary understanding" would have been repelled at the idea of committing the act ordered.

Having considered the problem from the point of view of the civilian courts, it is now time to see what military law and the international law of crimes have to say where this defence is concerned. The earliest case on record appears to be the trial of Peter of Hagenbach in 1474.[58] Hagenbach had been appointed *Landvogt* (Governor) of the Upper Rhine by Charles, Duke of Burgundy, and had sought to secure the submission of the populace to his master by a policy of what would today probably be described as crimes against humanity. On his capture, the Archduke of Austria, on whose territory he had been seized, ordered his trial by a tribunal consisting of judges appointed by the Allied towns. For the Archduke it was contended that Hagenbach had "trampled under foot the laws of God and man," but his counsel contended that "Sir Peter von Hagenbach does not recognise any other judge and master but the Duke of Burgundy from whom he had received his commission and his orders. He had no right to question the orders which he was obliged to carry out, and it was his duty to obey. Is it not known that soldiers owe absolute obedience to their superiors? Does anyone believe that the Duke's *Landvogt* could have remonstrated with his master or have refused to carry out the Duke's orders? Had not the Duke by his presence subsequently confirmed and ratified all that had been done in his name?" The tribunal rejected the defence and Hagenbach was executed.

The next case which is important from the point of view of the development of the doctrine of superior orders in time of war is the *Wirz Trial*,[59] arising from the atrocities committed against Federal prisoners of war at Andersonville during the American Civil War. Since this was a military trial, there was no judgment delivered, but as the court found Wirz guilty of the charges against him it must be presumed that the judges accepted the views expressed by the Judge Advocate:

> With what detestation must civilized nations regard that government whose con-
> duct has been such as characterized this pretended confederacy. *An ordinary com-*
> *prehension of natural right, the faintest desire to act on principles of common justice,* would
> have dictated some humane action, would have extorted from some official a rec-
> ognition of international rules of conduct. . . . [I]t was not . . . ignorance of the
> law; it was the *intrinsic wickedness* of a few desperate leaders, seconded by mercenary
> and *heartless monsters*, of whom the prisoner before you is a fair type. . . . It is

---

[57](1951), 64 S.E. 2d 840, 841.
[58]See 2 Schwarzenberger, *International Law*, "The Law of Armed Conflict," ch. 39, at 462-66 (1968) (Schwarzenberger first discussed this case in *Manchester Guardian*, September 24, 1946).
[59]H.R. Exec. Doc. No. 23, 40th Cong., 2d Sess., 764, 773, 774, 802 (italics added).

urged that during all this time [the accused] was acting under General Winder's orders. . . . A superior officer cannot order a subordinate to do an illegal act, and if a subordinate obey such an order and disastrous consequences result, both the superior and the subordinate must answer for it. General Winder could no more command the prisoner to violate the laws of war than could the prisoner do so without orders. The conclusion is plain, that where such orders exist both are guilty. . . . Strongly as it may strike you that strict justice would require the punishment of the arch-conspirator himself . . . you cannot stop the course of justice or refuse to brand [the accused's] guilt as the law and evidence direct. . . . Nothing can ever separate them. . . . [The accused] executed the bloody work with an industry which was almost superhuman and with a merriment which would have shamed a demon. . . . There could be no collision where the subaltern was only anxious to surpass an incomparable superior. . . . If the accused still answer that, admitting the facts charged, he did these things in the exercise of authority lawfully conferred upon him, and that what he did was necessary to the discipline and safety of the prisoners, I answer him in the language of Lord Mansfield [in *Wall v. M'Namara*].[60]

The case which is nowadays normally cited as being the point of departure for any analysis of the defence of superior orders is the South African case of *Reg.* v. *Smith*; in delivering judgment, Solomon J. declared that "it is monstrous to suppose that a soldier would be protected where the order is *grossly* illegal. [But that he] is responsible if he obeys an order not strictly legal . . . is an extreme proposition which the Court cannot accept. . . . [E]specially in time of war immediate obedience . . . is required. . . . I think it is a safe rule to lay down that if a soldier *honestly believes* he is doing his duty in obeying . . . and the orders are *not so manifestly illegal* that he . . . ought to have known they were unlawful, [he] will be protected by the orders. . . ."[61]

The problem became of major significance during the war crimes trials that followed the First World War. By Article 228 of the Treaty of Versailles Germany recognized the right of the Allied Powers to try alleged war criminals by military tribunals and undertook to hand over such persons to stand trial, while by Article 229 it was provided that trials would be held by the Power against whose nationals the crimes were alleged to have been committed. It was subsequently agreed, however, that the German *Reichsgericht* (Supreme Court of the Empire) at Leipzig should be the court before which such accused would appear. By section 47 (2) of the German Military Penal Code, 1882, while the subordinate is bound to obey the orders of his superior, he would be punishable as an accomplice to a criminal act if he knew that the order concerned an act which was criminal by either civil or military law—and this was still the German law at the end of the Second World War. The scope of section 47 was discussed at Leipzig in two cases involving the destruction of hospital ships. The *Dover Castle* was torpedoed and the commander of the U-boat involved pleaded that he had acted on Admiralty orders issued in the belief that hospital ships, contrary to the law of war, were being used for military purposes.[62] He was acquitted, since "it is a military principle that the subordinate is bound to obey the rules of his superiors. . . . When the execution of a service order involves an offence against the criminal law, the superior giving the order is alone responsible. . . . The Admiralty Staff was the highest service authority over the accused. He was in duty bound to obey their orders in service matters. So far as he did that, he was free from criminal responsibility." The tribunal was of opinion that in the circumstances of the case the

[60](1779), 1 Term Rep. 536 (see *supra* note 39).
[61](1900), 17 S.C. 561 (Cape of Good Hope) (italics added). See also *R.* v. *Werner*, [1947] 2 S.A.L.R. 828.
[62](1921) Cmd. 1450 at 42; 2 Ann. Dig. 429.

accused was entitled to believe that the orders concerning foreign hospital ships were not contrary to international law, but were reprisals.

Only six weeks later, the *Reichsgericht* showed that the defence was not as extensive as might have appeared from the *Dover Castle* decision. The accused in the *Llandovery Castle*[63] were alleged to have opened fire on the survivors of the torpedoed hospital ship causing grave loss of life, and pleaded the orders of the U-boat commander. On this occasion, the court said:

> [N]o importance is to be attached to the statements put forward by the defence, that the enemies of Germany were making improper use of hospital ships for military purposes, and that they had repeatedly fired on German lifeboats and shipwrecked people. . . . Whether this belief was founded on fact or not, is of less importance as affecting the case before the court, than the established fact that the *Llandovery Castle* at the time was not carrying any cargo or troops prohibited [under the Hague Convention on Naval Warfare (Convention X). The killing of the survivors was homicide under the German Penal Code, and was also] an offence against the law of nations. . . . Any violation of the law of nations in warfare is . . . a punishable offence, so far as, in general, a penalty is attached to the deed. The killing of enemies in war is in accordance with the will of the State that makes war (whose laws as to the legality or illegality on the question of killing are decisive), only in so far as such killing is in accordance with the conditions and limitations imposed by the law of nations. The fact that his deed is a violation of International Law must be *well-known* to the doer. . . . The rule of International Law, which is here involved, is *simple and universally known*. No possible doubt can exist with regard to the question of its applicability. . . . [The] order does not free the accused from guilt. . . . [A]ccording to para. 47 of the Military Penal Code . . . the subordinate obeying [an] order [involving a violation of the law] is liable to punishment, if it was *known* to him that the order of the superior involved the infringement of civil or military law. . . . It is certainly to be urged in favour of the military subordinates that they are under no obligation to question the order of their superior officer, and they can count upon its legality. But no such confidence can be held to exist, if such an order is *universally known to everybody, including also the accused*, to be *without any doubt whatsoever* against the law. As naval officers by profession [the accused] were *well aware* . . . that one is not legally authorized to kill defenceless people. They well knew that this was the case here. . . . They should, therefore, have refused to obey. As they did not do so, they must be punished.

The court rejected the idea that the orders might have been enforced by violence, pointing out that in such circumstances the order would have been impossible of achievement, but recognized that to "have refused to obey the order . . . would have required a specially high degree of resolution. A refusal to obey the commander of a submarine would have been something so unusual that it is humanly possible to understand that the accused could not bring themselves to disobey. That certainly does not make them innocent. . . . They had acquired the habit of obedience to military authority and could not rid themselves of it. This justifies the recognition of mitigating circumstances in determining the punishment. . . . The killing of defenceless shipwrecked people is an act in the *highest degree contrary to ethical principles*. . . ."

In some war crimes trials the defence is put forward, only to be rejected on the ground that no such order was in fact given. In the *Crusius* case it was alleged that accused had been ordered to shoot prisoners of war; the Leipzig Court found that the alleged remark related only to wounded enemies suddenly resuming hostilities, and "Such an order, if

---

[63](1921) Cmd. 1450, at 45; 2 Ann. Dig. 436 (italics added). Both these decisions are reproduced in Cameron, *The Peleus Trial* (1948), App. X, IX resp.

it were issued, would not have been contrary to international principles, for the protection afforded by the regulations for land warfare does not extend to such wounded who take up arms again and renew the fight. Such men have by so doing forfeited the claim for mercy granted to them by the laws of warfare. On the other hand, an order of the nature maintained by the accused Crusius would have had *absolutely no* justification."[64]

Despite the decision in *Smith* and the *Llandovery Castle*, and the provision in the German Military Penal Code, the principle was not generally accepted that superior orders provided no defence to a charge of war crimes, merely serving to mitigate the punishment. The first edition of Oppenheim's *International Law* stated that "in case members of forces commit violations ordered by their commanders, the members cannot be punished, for the commanders alone are responsible, and the latter may, therefore, be punished as war criminals on their capture by the enemy."[65] A similar statement appears in the 1914 edition of the British *Manual of Military Law*,[66] but this is perhaps not surprising in view of the fact that Oppenheim was joint author of the section of the *Manual* on the "Law and Usages of Warfare on Land." The United States *Rules of Land Warfare* were based on the British *Manual*, and a similar provision is to be found in the 1940 edition.[67] The first edition of Oppenheim published after the First World War appeared with the statement unchanged, although Roxburgh as editor added a note that "the contrary is sometimes asserted . . . [but] the law cannot require an individual to be punished for an act which he was compelled by law to commit,"[68] and even in the fourth edition McNair seems to consider the statement to be consistent with customary law.[69] The first mention that is made of the *Llandovery Castle* in Oppenheim is to be found in the first edition prepared by Lauterpacht.[70] There is a simple reference to the decision in a footnote, but it is not regarded as having had any effect on what the editor regards as the traditional rule.

A fundamental change is to be found in the editions of 1940 and 1944, both of which were prepared by Lauterpacht. The entire paragraph has been rewritten to read:

> The fact that a rule of warfare has been violated in pursuance of an order of the belligerent Government or of an individual belligerent commander does not deprive the act in question of its character as a war crime; neither does it, in principle, confer upon the perpetrator immunity from punishment by the injured belligerent. . . . Undoubtedly, a Court confronted with the plea of superior orders adduced in justification of a war crime is bound to take into consideration the fact that obedience to military orders *not obviously unlawful*, is the duty of every member of the armed forces and that the latter cannot, in conditions of war discipline, be expected to weigh scrupulously the legal merits of the order received. . . . However, . . . the question is governed by the major principle that members of the armed forces are bound to obey lawful orders only and that they cannot therefore escape liability if, in obedience to a command, they commit acts which both violate *unchallenged rules of warfare and outrage the general sentiment of humanity.*[71]

This statement of the law is supported by a reference to the decision in the *Llandovery Castle*. Lauterpacht appears to justify his departure from previous editions, including his

[64](1921), 2 Ann. Dig. 438, note *b*.
[65]Vol. 2, S. 253 (1906).
[66]Para. 443 (the 1929 ed. is to the same effect).
[67]1914, Art. 366; 1940, Art. 345.
[68]1921, S. 253, at 342, n. 3.
[69]1926, S. 253, at 410, n. 2.
[70]1935, S. 253, at 452, n. 1.
[71]1944, S. 253, at 452-53 (italics added), and 453, n. 2 (the same statement appears in the 7th ed., 1952, the last edited by Lauterpacht).

own, by stating that "a different view has occasionally been adopted in military manuals and by writers, but it is difficult to regard it as expressing a sound legal principle."[72] In explanation of the reference to "writers," he comments: "n.2. See, e.g., § 253 of the previous editions of this volume. . . . However, the great majority of writers is in favour of the view advanced in the text."

It was not only the leading English textbook on international law that was amended in this way after the outbreak of the Second World War. The British *Manual* statement was also changed, and the wording that Lauterpacht had introduced into Oppenheim was adopted *expressis verbis*.[73] Seven months later a similar amendment was made to the United States Field Service Manual to the effect that "individuals and organizations who violate the *accepted laws and customs of war* may be punished therefor,"[74] but superior orders "may be taken into consideration in determining culpability, either by way of defense or in mitigation of punishment."

The French authorities, too, felt that a restatement of the law on this subject was necessary. During the First World War the writers differed as to the availability of the defence to Germans accused of war crimes, with the majority rejecting the defence, and "In every case where the plea of superior command was invoked the courts made short shrift of it and if the evidence established the guilt of the accused he was condemned, even when he produced conclusive proof that he acted under orders."[75] Article 327 of the *Code Pénal* provides that "no crime or delict is committed when the homicide . . . was ordered by law or by legal authority," but the Ordinance concerning the Prosecution of War Criminals removes this defence regarding "Laws, decrees or regulations issued by the enemy authorities, orders or permits issued by these authorities . . . which are or have been subordinated to them . . . , but can only, in suitable cases, be pleaded as an extenuating or exculpating circumstance."[76]

Other Allied countries tended to introduce similar legislation, frequently after their liberation, in order to make it clear that in trials before their military courts no accused would be able to avoid responsibility on the plea that he was acting under orders, especially as it was so easy to cite as the superior responsible some officer who was either dead or untraceable.[77] The practice of the tribunals established after 1945 illustrates the way in which the defence has developed in modern times, and for our purpose it is only necessary to draw attention to a relatively small selection of the trials that took place.

There is a general tendency to assume that the Nuremberg Judgment[78] is the only one that needs citing in connection with war crimes, but there were already a number of decisions in which the defence of superior orders had been considered before that judgment was rendered. Of those in Europe perhaps the most important was the *Peleus* case (1945),[79] the first of the trials to be held. Apart from the fact that the vessel was a merchant ship, the facts were almost identical with those in the *Llandovery Castle*, and on this occasion one officer successfully refused to obey the order to fire on survivors, although he subsequently did so. As to the defence, the Judge Advocate said:

---

[72]*Ibid.*, 453.
[73]Amendment 34, April 1944 (text reproduced in Cameron, *op cit. supra* note 63, at 150).
[74]Change No. 1, November 15, 1944 (italics added—*ibid.*, 152).
[75]2 Garner, *International Law and the World War*, 487 (1920).
[76]3 UN War Crimes Commission, *Law Reports of Trials of War Criminals* 93, 96.
[77]For some of these laws, see *ibid.*, vol. 5, at 20-23; for the Soviet position, see Greenspan, *The Modern Law of Land Warfare*, 491 (1959).
[78]1946, H.M.S.O., Cmd. 6964; 41 *Am. J. Int'l L.* 172 (1947).
[79]Cameron, *op cit. supra* note 63, at 128-29 (for an abbreviated text, see 13 Ann. Dig. 248, *sub. nom. In re Eck*—italics added).

[T]he duty to obey is limited to the observance of orders which are lawful. There can be no duty to obey that which is not a lawful order. . . . The fact that a rule of warfare has been violated in pursuance of an order of a belligerent government, or of an individual belligerent commander, does not deprive the act in question of its character as a war crime, neither does it confer upon the perpetrator immunity from punishment by the injured belligerent. Undoubtedly a Court confronted with a plea of superior orders adduced in justification of a war crime is bound to take into consideration the fact that obedience of military orders *not obviously unlawful* is a duty of every member of the Armed Forces, and that the latter cannot in conditions of war discipline be expected to weigh scrupulously the legal merits of the order received. The question, however, is governed by the major consideration that members of the Armed Forces are bound to obey *lawful orders only*, and that they cannot therefore escape liability if in obedience to a command they commit acts which both *violate unchallenged rules of warfare and outrage the general sentiment of humanity*. It is quite obvious that no sailor and no soldier can carry with him a library of International Law, or have immediate access to a professor in that subject who can tell him whether or not a particular command is a lawful one. . . . [I]s it not fairly obvious to you that if in fact the carrying out of [the] command involved the killing of these helpless survivors, it was not a lawful command, and that it must have been *obvious to the most rudimentary intelligence that it was not a lawful command*, and that those who did that shooting are not to be excused for doing it upon the ground of superior orders? . . .

Among the other trials held before the Nuremberg Judgment was delivered, that concerning the atrocities at Jaluit Atoll and known as the *Masuda* case[80] is of interest. One of the defence counsel was an officer in the Japanese Navy and drew attention to the absolute discipline and obedience expected in the Japanese forces, citing the Imperial Rescript which states that "Subordinates should have the idea that the orders from their superiors are nothing but the orders personally from His Majesty the Emperor," and he contended that it was impossible to apply "the liberal and individualistic ideas which rule usual societies unmodified to this totalistic and absolutistic military society." The accused were sentenced to death, the Judge Advocate having accepted the statement from an earlier [unnamed] case that "An order *illegal in itself* and *not justified by the rules and usages of war*, or in its substance *clearly illegal, so that a man of ordinary sense and understanding would know* as soon as he heard the order read or given that it was illegal, will afford no protection for a homicide, provided the act with which he may be charged has all the ingredients in it which may be necessary to constitute the same crime in law." A somewhat similar view was taken by the Canadian Military Court which tried *Holzer* at Aurich, Germany.[81] The accused was charged with killing a Canadian prisoner of war and the Judge Advocate quoted Lauterpacht's statement from Oppenheim, and asserted that the *Llandovery Castle* had clearly established that "The defence of superior orders would afford no defence if the act was *manifestly and indisputably contrary to international law* as for instance the killing of unarmed enemies." He also applied the common law test with regard to the validity of a defence based on coercion or duress.

The British court in the *Buck* case[82] recognized that certain basic facts had to be recognized. As the Judge Advocate said, "What did each of these accused know about the rights of a prisoner of war? . . . The Court may well think that the men are not lawyers: they may not have heard either of the Hague Convention or the Geneva Convention; they may not have seen any book of military law upon the subject; but the Court has to

---

[80](1945), 1 *War Crimes Reports* 71, 74 (italics added). In fact, Rear Admiral Masuda committed suicide before the trial opened and a *nolle prosequi* was entered in his case.
[81](1946), 5 *ibid.*, 15 (italics added).
[82](1946), 13 Ann. Dig. 293-94 (italics added).

consider whether men who are serving either as soldiers or in proximity to soldiers know as a matter of the *general facts of military life* whether a prisoner of war has certain rights . . . [including], when captured [the right to] security for his person. . . . The position under international law is that it is contrary to rules of international law to murder a prisoner. . . ." He then cited Oppenheim with approval and expressed the view that a man would be guilty of a war crime in pursuance of an order if "the order was *obviously unlawful*, if the accused knew that the order was unlawful, or if he *ought to have known it to be unlawful* had he considered the circumstances in which it had been given." The same British Military Court held only a month later that no one had to obey an unlawful order, and that it was no defence to argue that German law would not consider an order to kill in the circumstances of the case as unlawful, provided, said the Judge Advocate, that the Court was satisfied that "the order was *one which could not have been tolerated in any place where a system of justice was used.* . . ."[83]

In so far as the Nuremberg Tribunal was concerned, it had no option but to reject the defence of superior orders, for this was clearly provided by its Charter of establishment. The Tribunal dealt with the defence somewhat shortly:

> [I]ndividuals have international duties which transcend the national obligations of obedience imposed by the individual State. He who violates the laws of war cannot obtain immunity while acting in pursuance of the authority of the State if the State in authorising action moves outside its competence under international law. . . . That a soldier was ordered to kill or torture in violation of the international law of war has never been recognised as a defence to such acts of brutality, though . . . the order may be urged in mitigation of the punishment. The true test, which is found in varying degrees in the criminal law of most nations is not the existence of the order, but whether *moral choice* was in fact possible. . . . Superior orders . . . cannot be considered in mitigation where *crimes as shocking* and extensive have been *committed consciously, ruthlessly and without military excuse or justification.* . . . Participation in such crimes as these has never been required of any soldier and he cannot now shield himself behind a mythical requirement of soldierly obedience at all costs as his excuse for commission of these crimes. . . . [In fact,] many of these men have made a mockery of the soldier's oath of obedience to military orders. When it suits their defence they say they had to obey; when confronted with Hitler's brutal crimes, which are shown to have been within their general knowledge, they say they disobeyed. The truth is they actively participated in all these crimes, or sat silent and acquiescent, witnessing the commission of crimes on a scale larger and more shocking than the world has ever had the misfortune to know.[84]

Of the trials that took place in the years immediately following Nuremberg perhaps those of the United States Military Tribunals sitting at Nuremberg are the most important, and many of them are more concerned with public knowledge and understanding than the International Military Tribunal's concept of "moral choice." Thus, in *Re Milch* the tribunal pointed out:

> [V]ery soon [after the accused joined the Nazi Party in 1933] he must have realized that he had joined a band of villains whose programme contemplated every crime in the calendar. The Nazi code was not a secret. It was published and proclaimed by the Party leaders. . . . The *humblest citizens* of Germany *knew* that *the iniquitous doctrines* of the Party were *being implemented by ruthless acts of persecution and terrorism which occurred in public view.* . . . The defendant did not live in a vacuum. He was

---

[83]*Rohde Case* (1946), 5 *War Crimes Reports*, 54, 58 (italics added).
[84]*Op. cit supra* note 78, at 42, 83, 92, 118; 221, 271-72, 283, 316 resp. (italics added).

not blind or deaf. Long before 1939; long before his military loyalty was called into play; long before the door to withdrawal was closed, he could have seen the bloody handwriting on the wall, for murder and enslavement of his own countrymen was there written in blazing symbols. But he had taken on the crimson mantle of the Party. . . . Others with more courage and higher principles and with more loyalty to the ancient German ideals rebelled and withdrew. . . . The defendant had his opportunity to join those who refused to do the evil bidding of an evil master, but he cast it aside. . . . By accepting such attractive and lucrative posts under a head whose power they knew to be unlimited, they ratify in advance his every act, good or bad. They cannot say at the beginning, "The Führer's decisions are final; we will have no voice in them; it is not for us to reason why; his will is law", and then, when the Führer decrees . . . barbarous inhumanities . . . to attempt to exculpate themselves by saying, "Oh, we were never in favour of *those* things". . . .[85]

Field Marshal Milch's case is typical of those involving senior officers, as became clear in the *High Command Trial* itself; the Tribunal there rejected the plea, saying:

All of the defendants in this case held official positions in the armed forces of the Third Reich. Hitler from 1938 on was Commander-in-Chief of the Armed Forces and was the Supreme Civil and Military Authority in the Third Reich, whose personal decrees had the force and effect of law. Under such circumstances to recognise as a defence . . . that a defendant acted pursuant to the order of his government or of a superior would be in practical effect to say that all the guilt charged . . . was the guilt of Hitler alone because he alone possessed the law-making power of the State and the supreme authority to issue civil and military directives. To recognise such a contention would be to recognise an absurdity. . . . The rejection of the defence of superior orders . . . would follow of necessity from our holding that the acts . . . are criminal . . . because they then were crimes under International Common Law. International Common Law must be superior to and, where it conflicts with, take precedence over National Law or directives issued by any governmental authority. A directive to violate International Common Law is therefore void and can afford no protection to one who violates such law in reliance on such a directive. . . . The defendants . . . who received *obviously criminal orders* were placed in a difficult position but servile compliance with orders *clearly criminal* for fear of some disadvantage or punishment not immediately threatened cannot be recognised as a defence. To establish the defence of coercion or necessity in the face of danger there must be a showing of circumstances such that a *reasonable man* would apprehend that he was in such imminent physical peril as to deprive him of freedom to choose the right and refrain from the wrong. . . . [Moreover,] . . . an article by Goebbels . . . contained the following correct statement of the law: "It is not provided in any military law that a soldier in the case of a *despicable crime* is exempt from punishment because he passes the responsibility to his superior, especially if the orders of the latter are in *evident contradiction to all human morality and every international usage of warfare.*" . . . Within certain limitations, [a soldier] has the right to assume that the orders of his superiors and the State which he serves and which are issued to him are in conformity with International Law. Many of the defendants here were field commanders. . . . Their legal facilities were limited. They were soldiers—not lawyers. Military commanders in the field with far reaching military responsibilities cannot be charged under International Law with criminal participation in issuing orders which are not obviously criminal or which they are not shown to have known to be criminal under International Law. Such a commander cannot be expected to draw fine distinctions as to legality in connection with orders issued by his superiors. He has the right to presume, in the absence of specific knowledge to the contrary, that the legality of such orders has been properly determined before their issuance. He cannot be held criminally responsible for a mere error of judgment as to disputable legal questions.[86] It is

---

[85](1947), 7 *War Crimes Reports*, 27, 41-42 (italics added).
[86]Cp. comments of Lord Mansfield in *Wall* v. *M'Namara*, *supra* note 39.

therefore considered that to find a field commander criminally responsible for the transmittal of such an order, he must have passed the order to the chain of command and the order must be one that is *criminal upon its face*, or one which he is shown to have known was criminal.[87]

In the *Hostages Trial* the issue was complicated by reason of the fact that the defence made use of the earlier statements of Oppenheim and the military *Manuals*; according to the court:

[T]he rule that superior order is not a defence to a criminal act is a rule of fundamental criminal justice that has been adopted by civilized nations extensively. . . . [T]he municipal law of civilised nations generally sustained the principle at the time the alleged criminal acts were committed. This being true, it properly may be declared as an applicable rule of International Law. . . . Implicit obedience to orders of superior officers is almost indispensable to every military system. But this implies obedience to *lawful orders only*. If the act done pursuant to a superior's order be murder, the production of the order will not make it any less so. It *may mitigate but it cannot justify* the crime. . . . [I]f the illegality of the order was not known to the inferior and he could not *reasonably* have been expected to know of its illegality, no wrongful intent necessary to the commission of a crime exists and the inferior will be protected. But the general rule is that members of the armed forces are bound to obey only the *lawful orders* of their commanding officers and they cannot escape criminal liability by obeying a command which violates International Law and *outrages fundamental concepts of justice*. . . . The defence relies heavily upon the writings of Prof. L. Oppenheim to sustain their position. It is true that he advocated this principle throughout his writings. As a co-author of the *British Manual of Military Law*, he incorporated the principle there. It seems also to have found its way into the United States *Rules of Land Warfare* (1940). We think Professor Oppenheim espoused a decidedly minority view. . . . [His] statement completely overlooks the fact that an illegal order is in no sense of the word a valid law which one is obliged to obey. The fact that the British and American armies may have adopted it for the regulation of their own armies as a matter of policy, does not have the effect of enthroning it as a rule of International Law. They are neither legislative nor judicial pronouncements. They are not competent for any purpose in determining whether a *fundamental principle of justice has been accepted by civilized nations generally*. It is possible, however, that such regulations, as they bear upon a question of custom and practice in the conduct of war, might have evidentiary value, particularly if the applicable portions had been put into general practice. It will be observed that the determination whether a custom or practice exists, is a question of fact. Whether a fundamental principle of justice has been accepted is a question of judicial or legislative declaration. In determining the former, military regulations may play an important role but, in the latter, they do not constitute an authoritative precedent. Those who hold to the view that superior order is a complete defence to an International Law crime, base it largely on a conflict in the articles of war promulgated by several leading nations. While we are of opinion that army regulations are not a competent source of International Law where a fundamental rule of justice is concerned, we submit that the conflict in any event does not sustain the position claimed for it. . . . If the Court finds that the army regulations of some members of the family of nations provide that superior orders is a complete defence and that the army regulations of other nations express a contrary view, the Court would be obliged to hold . . . that general acceptance or consent was lacking among the family of nations. Inasmuch as a substantial conflict exists among the nations whether superior order is a defence to a criminal charge, it could only result in a further finding that the basis does not exist for declaring superior order to be a defence to an International Law crime. But . . . army regulations are not a competent source of International Law when a fundamental rule of justice is concerned.

---

[87]*In re Von Leeb* (1948), 12 *ibid.*, 1, 71-74 (italics added).

This leaves the way clear for the Court to affirmatively declare that superior order is not a defence to an International Law crime if it finds that the principle involved is a fundamental rule of justice and for that reason has found general acceptance. International Law has never approved the defensive plea of superior order as a mandatory bar to the prosecution of war criminals. This defensive plea is not available to the defendants . . . , although . . . it may be considered in mitigation of punishment. . . .[88]

It is perhaps unfortunate that the tribunal did not take the opportunity to point out that by both English and American criminal law the defence was strictly limited and far more restrictive than would appear from the *Manuals*. Moreover, as is pointed out in the 1956 edition of the American *Army Field Manual—Law of Land Warfare*, "those provisions of the Manual which are neither statutes nor the text of treaties to which the United States is a party should not be considered binding upon courts and tribunals applying the law of war,"[89] for military *Manuals* are just like textbooks merely for guidance as to what the law is. If they are not in accordance with established law, tribunals will disregard them. If it is felt that such statements represent the law and are adopted, it is the acceptance by the court and not the statement in the *Manual* or the textbook which is declaratory of the law. Furthermore, while it may be generally true that *lex specialis derogat generali*, the World Court has shown[90] that this is not an inevitable principle, and where the *lex specialis* itself purports to apply the *lex generalis* as does Anglo-American military law it is by no means improper that, when it is found that the *lex specialis* is incompatible with the *lex generalis*, the former is amended to bring it into line.

Of all the decisions of the American tribunals dealing with the defence, perhaps that in the *Einsatzgruppen Trial*[91] is the most comprehensive; there the tribunal said:

> [T]he obedience of a soldier is not the obedience of an automaton. A soldier is a reasoning agent. He does not respond, and is not expected to respond, like a piece of machinery. It is a fallacy of widespread consumption that a soldier is required to do everything his superior officer orders him to do [e.g., shoot a superior]. . . . [A]n order to require obedience must relate to military duty.[92] . . . And what the superior officer may not militarily demand of his subordinate, the subordinate is not required to do. Even if the order refers to a military subject it must be one which the superior is authorised under the circumstances to give. The subordinate is bound to obey only the lawful orders of his superior and if he accepts a criminal order and executes it with a malice of his own, he may not plead Superior Orders in mitigation of his defense. If the nature of the ordered act is *manifestly beyond the scope* of the superior's authority, the subordinate may not plead ignorance of the criminality of the order. If one claims duress in the execution of an illegal order it must be shown that the harm caused by obeying the illegal order is not disproportionately greater than the harm which would result from not obeying the illegal order. It would not be an adequate excuse . . . if a subordinate, under orders, killed a person known to be innocent, because by not obeying it he himself would risk a few days of confinement. Nor if one acts under duress, may he, without culpability, commit the illegal act once the duress ceases. . . .

---

[88]*In re List* (1948), 15 *Ann. Dig.* 632, 649-52 (italics added).
[89]FM27-10, para. 1. See also, Garner, *op cit.*, n. 75 above, vol. 1, at 12; who describes such *Manuals* as "for the guidance of military and naval forces . . . [which] may, of course, be altered by the government which issues them, except in so far as the obligatory character of their rules is established by international law."
[90]*Rights of Minorities in Upper Silesia (Minority Schools)*, P.C.I.J. Ser. A, No. 15, at 31, 33 (1928); *Ambatielos case* (Prelim. Obj.), (1952) I.C.J. Rep. 28, 42.
[91]*In re Ohlendorf* (1948), 15 *Ann. Dig.* 656, 665-68 (italics added).
[92]Cp. *State v. Roy, supra* note 57.

After citing the Nuremberg Judgment, the tribunal referred to German military codes going back to that of Prussia, 1845, which provided for punishment if the subordinate knew the order "related to an act which is *obviously aimed at a crime*" and finished its survey by referring to the German author Schwinge who wrote in 1940: "Hence, in military life, just as in other fields, the principle of absolute, i.e., blind obedience, does not exist." It then continued:

> Yet, one of the most generally quoted statements on this subject is that a German soldier must obey orders though the heavens fall. The statement has become legendary. The facts prove that it is a myth. . . . To plead Superior Orders one must show an *excusable ignorance of their illegality*. . . . What S.S. man could say that he was unaware of the attitude of Hitler towards Jewry? . . . But it is stated that in military law even if the subordinate realizes that the act he is called upon to perform is a crime, he may not refuse its execution without incurring serious consequences, and that this, therefore, constitutes duress. . . . [T]here is no law which requires that an innocent man must forfeit his life or suffer serious harm in order to avoid committing a crime which he condemns. The threat, however, must be *imminent, real and inevitable*. . . . The test to be applied is whether the subordinate acted under coercion or whether he himself approved of the principle involved in the order. If the second proposition be true, the plea of Superior Orders fails. The doer may not plead innocence to a criminal act ordered by his superior if he is in accord with the principle and intent of the superior. Where the will of the doer merges with the will of the superior in the execution of the illegal act, the doer may not plead duress under Superior Orders. If the mental and moral capacities of the superior and subordinate are pooled in the planning and execution of an illegal act, the subordinate may not subsequently protest that he was forced into the performance of an illegal undertaking. Superior means superior in capacity and power to force a certain act. It does not mean superiority only in rank. . . . If the cognizance of the doer has been such, prior to the receipt of the illegal order, that the order is *obviously but one further logical step in the development of a program which he knew to be illegal in its very inception*, he may not excuse himself from responsibility for an illegal act which could have been *foreseen by the application of the simple law of cause and effect*. . . . One who embarks on a criminal enterprise of *obvious magnitude* is *expected to anticipate* what the enterprise will logically lead to. In order successfully to plead the defense of Superior Orders the opposition of the doer must be constant. It is not enough that he mentally rebel at the time the order is received. If at any time after receiving the order he acquiesces in its illegal character, the defense of Superior Orders is closed to him.[93]

The American tribunals were not alone in their attitude. In *Müller's Case* the Belgian Court of Cassation agreed that the defence would not lie when the order " 'should be disobeyed in view of its *manifest violation of a superior principle of humanity*' . . . [and its] *'flagrantly illegal character . . . universally recognised* as being contrary to law'."[94]

Since the termination of war crimes trials by Allied tribunals, there had been little opportunity for comment upon the defence of superior orders other than from German and Israeli tribunals, until United States courts martial began hearings in Korea and Vietnam. The new Bundeswehr was founded in 1956 and a year later a new military criminal law—*Wehrstrafgesetz*—was introduced concerning the rights of a soldier in peacetime, and expressly recognizing his right to disobey an order he believes to be criminal. Under the new law, an order can be disobeyed when it would lead to the commission

---

[93]See, however, *Peleus Trial, supra* note 63, re accused Lenz, and debate initiated by Lord Cork and Orrery in House of Lords, April 25, 1950.

[94]*Auditeur-Général près la Cour Militaire* v. *Müller* (1949), 16 *Ann. Dig.* 400, 402 (italics added).

of a crime or misdemeanour; if the subordinate nevertheless carries out the order, he incurs no guilt if he does not know, and it is not *apparent* to him that a crime or misdemeanour is thereby committed.[95] This reminds one of the position in Canada, although there is no provision made for the manner in which the subordinate is to record his doubts and apparently compliance after indicating those doubts would not be considered sufficient to ground a defence.[96] As regards trials arising out of the war, German courts have been faced with the usual plea of compliance with orders. In the *Burmeister Case* the accused stated that he did not think about his orders, assuming that since it was wartime and they came from the highest quarters, they must have been alright. The Bonn Court rejected the plea of obedience to orders since the accused had supported the Nazi "death machine" and "had been *clearly aware* that the extermination of Jews was a crime."[97] In a later case the court took the line that the accused were entitled to the benefit of the doubt to an extent sufficient to reduce murder charges to manslaughter findings.[98] The verdict is not easy to accept, even though one might agree with the judge that there were "little fishes sitting in the dock, while the sharks swim around free"; it is difficult to see how nurses participating in the euthanasia programme who had injected fatal doses on instructions from doctors could possibly be unaware of the illegality of their actions or of their abuse of the patients' trust. A more dignified attitude was adopted by Alfred Rapp, a former S.S. commander of an extermination camp; he stated that "what has happened is so frightful that I neither can nor will ask for lenience" and declined to plead obedience to orders, although he maintained that it had been impossible for anyone to go against them.[99] This does not tally with evidence given at the S.S. cavalry trial at Frankfurt, at which Dr. H. G. Seraphim, a historian, stated that not one case was known of an S.S. man being punished for refusing to take part in mass executions, although there were countless examples of refusal to obey such orders receiving little or no attention; he agreed, however, that it probably required more than a little courage to refuse to obey.[100]

One of the most famous war crimes trials of recent years was that of Adolf Eichmann,[101] who insisted that everything he did was in accordance with superior orders. The District Court pointed out that for the defence to succeed necessitated considering whether the orders were "*manifestly unlawful*" and held that whether this was in fact the case was a question of law to be decided by the court by objective tests. Their task was facilitated, however, by Eichmann's own statement "that I see in this murder, in the extermination of Jews, one of the gravest crimes in the history of humanity . . . I already realised at the time that this solution by the use of force was something unlawful, something terrible. . . ." The Supreme Court repeated that the orders were "*manifestly unlawful . . . contrary to the basic ideas of law and justice*," and pointed out that Eichmann "performed the order of extermination at all times *con amore*, with full zeal and devotion to the task." In fact, as the District Court made clear, its decision was in line with that of the Israeli District Military Court and Court of Appeal in *Chief Military Prosecutor* v.

---

[95]*The Times*, February 8, 1957.
[96]See *supra* note 16.
[97]*The Times*, December 12, 1962, April 1, 1963.
[98]*Ibid.*, March 13, 1965.
[99]*Ibid.*, March 19, 1965.
[100]*Ibid.*, April 7, 1964. See also evidence of Dr. Adelaide Hurtval in *Dehring* v. *Uris* [1964] 2 W.L.R. 1298 for an example of a prisoner successfully refusing to take part in medical experiments (Hall and Williams, *Auschwitz in England*, 1965).
[101]*A.G., Israel* v. *Eichmann* (1961/62), 36 I.L.R. 5 (District Court), 277 (Supreme Court), 257-58, 314-15, 318 (italics added).

Melinki,[102] a trial of Israeli military personnel arising out of their actions at Kafr Kassem in 1956. In the District Court Judge Halevy, one of the members of the court trying Eichmann, said:

> [T]he distinguishing mark of a "manifestly unlawful order" should fly like a black flag above the order given, as a warning saying "Prohibited". Not formal unlawfulness, hidden or half-hidden, nor unlawfulness discernible only by the eyes of legal experts, is important here, but *a flagrant and manifest breach of the law, definite and necessary unlawfulness appearing on the face of the order itself, the clearly criminal character of the acts ordered to be done, unlawfulness piercing the eye and revolting the heart, be the eye not blind nor the heart stony and corrupt*—that is the measure of "manifest unlawfulness" required to release a soldier from the duty of obedience upon him and make him criminally responsible for his acts.

The Court of Appeal put it in slightly less dramatic terms, "calling in aid the *feeling of lawfulness* which lies hidden deep *within the conscience of every human as such*, even if not conversant with the law books."

In view of the experience gained after the Second World War and as if determined to avoid being faced with similar contentions concerning superior orders again, including, as in the *Einsatzgruppen* case, allegations of *ex post facto* legislation, the British and American governments issued new military *Manuals* in which the references to superior orders are fully in accord with modern practice. According to the 1951 edition of the British *Manual of Military Law*,[103] physical force removes the stigma of criminality, as does, generally speaking, threats, "moral force," violence not amounting to physical compulsion, hunger or danger to life or property. As to superior orders, it provides that if an order is "manifestly illegal, [a person] is under a legal duty to refuse to carry out the order and if he does carry it out he will be criminally responsible for what he does in doing so." It goes on to say that even if the order relates to an act which is illegal, but not manifestly so, the subordinate actor will not be excused, although it may give rise to a defence on other grounds, such as reducing a charge of culpable negligence. That part of the *Manual* which deals with "The Law of War on Land"[104] clearly states that "obedience to the order of a government or of a superior, whether military or civil, or to a national law or regulation, affords no defence to a charge of committing a war crime but may be considered in mitigation of punishment." It also provides that no criminal responsibility lies in the face of physical compulsion against his will, or if his own life is in danger, unless the act involves the taking of innocent life. Otherwise threats are no defence, but may again mitigate punishment, as would compulsion arising from hunger or immediate danger to life or property. This latter does not concern itself with physical compulsion by a third party. The American *Field Manual* on "The Law of Land Warfare"[105] likewise makes no reference to manifest illegality, although it does say that armies are only obliged to obey "lawful orders." In so far as the law of war has been violated as the result of an order, the order does not "constitute a defense in the trial of an accused individual, unless he did not know and *could not reasonably have been expected to know* that the act ordered was unlawful," but even then the order may result in punishment being mitigated.

It was probably not expected that the first test of the present American approach to

---

[102](1958) cited *Eichmann, ibid.*, 256-57 (italics added).
[103]Part I, ch. V, s. 23.
[104]Part III, paras. 627-30.
[105]FM27-10, 1956, para. 509.

superior orders would be experienced against American troops alleged to have committed crimes against an enemy in an undeclared war. But this is the situation as a result of the wars in Korea and Vietnam. The uproar in the public media concerning the Song My (My Lai) atrocities has implied that the United States authorities have been unaware of the methods of unlawful warfare engaged in by their forces or have sought to "hush up" any cases of which they may have learned. In fact, this is far from being the case and long before this *cause célèbre* became known, American courts martial in operation areas were trying United States personnel for what, if they had been committed by the enemy or an ally—although the tendency has been to leave the allied authorities to try their own if they so wish—would have been treated as war crimes. In 1966 an accused charged with the premeditated murder of a Vietnamese was sentenced to 35 years, and in the course of its judgment the tribunal said that "the issuance or execution of an order to kill under the circumstances of this case is unjustifiable under the laws of this nation, the principles of international law, or the laws of land warfare. Such an order would have been beyond the scope of authority for a superior to give and would have been *palpably unlawful*."[106] In an effort to define "palpable unlawfulness," reference might be made to Winthrop's *Military Law and Precedents*,[107] which indicates what is regarded as an illegal order in words that have been accepted by courts martial: ". . . but to justify an inferior in disobeying an order as illegal, the case must be an extreme one and the illegality not doubtful. The order must be clearly repugnant to some specific statute, to the law or usage of military service, or to the general law of the land, the unlawfulness of the command must thus be a fact, and, in view of the authority of military orders emanating from official superiors, the onus of establishing this fact will, in all cases—except where the order is palpably illegal upon its face—devolve upon the defense and clear and convincing evidence will be required to rebut the presumption."[108] This statement forms the basis for the relevant paragraph of the *Manual for Courts Martial* that, "to justify from a military point of view a military inferior in disobeying the order of a superior, the order must be one requiring something to be done which is palpably a breach of law and a crime or injury to a third person, or is of a serious character (not involving unimportant consequences only) and if done would not be susceptible of being righted. An order requiring the performance of a military duty or act can not be disobeyed with impunity unless it has one of these characteristics."[109] However, it must be borne in mind that "an order requiring the performance of a military duty or act is presumed to be lawful and is disobeyed at the peril of the subordinate."[110]

Many of the American cases refer to the allegedly unlawful killing of prisoners or suspected enemy sympathizers and the guiding rules are to be found in the *Manual for Courts Martial* which provides as follows:

[A] homicide committed in the proper performance of a legal duty is justifiable. Thus . . . killing to prevent the escape of a prisoner if no other apparent means are adequate, killing an enemy in battle and killing to prevent the commission of an offense attempted by force or surprise . . . are cases of justifiable homicide. The general rule is that the acts of a subordinate, done in good faith in compliance with his supposed duty or orders, are justifiable. This justification does not exist, however, when those acts are manifestly beyond the scope of his authority, or the *order*

---

[106]*U.S.* v. *Schultz* (1966, court martial; 1968 Review Board) 39 *C.M.R.* 133, 136 (italics added).
[107]2d ed., 1920, at 575.
[108]See, for example, *U.S.* v. *Ciesielski* (1968), 39 *C.M.R.* 839, 850.
[109]1951, para. 416.
[110]*Ibid.*, para. 1969B. See *U.S.* v. *Trani* (1952), 3 *C.M.R.* 27.

is such that a man of ordinary sense and understanding would know it to be illegal, or the subordinate wilfully or through negligence does acts endangering the lives of innocent parties in the discharge of his duty to prevent escape or effect an arrest.[111]

The significance of these rules was examined in *U.S.* v. *Kinder*[112] arising from the killing of a Korean civilian, whom the evidence did not disclose as an enemy, ally, intended saboteur or thief, and who was in custody and not resisting, violent or attempting to escape or commit any offence. The order to shoot the prisoner was apparently given to scare other locals from entering the prohibited area in which he had been arrested and to boost the morale of the troops. After the killing the officer returned a false report of the circumstances, as did the accused on the instructions of the officer concerned. The accused was found guilty and sentenced to life imprisonment, which was reduced by the confirming officer to two years,[113] a sentence approved by the Board of Review. The accused testified that his officer had stated

> . . . that any orders that he gave were definitely not to be questioned in any way . . . and . . . he fully understood he was to obey the orders of Lieut. Schreiber no matter what they were. He knew it would have been wrong to shoot the Korean without an order. He thought Lieut. Schreiber had the authority to order the Korean shot. At the time he did not know the difference between a legal and an illegal order and thought that any order Lieut. Schreiber gave him was legal. He thought the order to shoot the Korean was legal. . . . He would not have thought an order to kill another American was illegal but he would not have obeyed it. . . . He did not know what Lieut. Schreiber would have done to him if he had not obeyed but he does not believe he would have had him shot. He had not heard of anyone being shot for an offense without getting a trial. . . .

The Board of Review found that "neither the laws of our nation, federal or military, nor the laws and usages of war as recognized by our nation and its allies, justify the issuance of an order by the accused's superior officer to kill the victim under the circumstances shown. . . . [T]he superior officer issuing the order was fully aware of its illegality . . . and maliciously and corruptly issued the unlawful order. . . ." The Board then examined a number of military and civil precedents, embracing most of the cases analyzed earlier in connection with the position under United States law, and concluded:

> [No justification will lie if the homicide is the result of an order] manifestly beyond the scope of the superior officer's authority and . . . *so obviously and palpably unlawful as to admit of no reasonable doubt on the part of a man of ordinary sense and understanding.* . . . [I]n the context of the evidence, the conclusion is inescapable that the accused was aware of the criminal nature of the order, not only from the palpably illegal nature of the order itself, but from the surreptitious circumstances under which it was necessary to execute it. . . . Of controlling significance . . . is the *manifest and unmistakable illegality* of the order. . . . Human life being regarded as sacred, moral, religious and civil law proscriptions against its taking existing throughout our society, we view the order as commanding an act so *obviously beyond the scope of authority* of the superior officer and *so palpably illegal on its face as to admit of no doubt of its unlawfulness to a man of ordinary sense and understanding.* The distance from the battle line and other circumstances . . . cannot be reasonably considered as furnishing any basis to *a man of ordinary sense and understanding* to assume that

[111]Para. 197 (italics added).
[112](1954), 14 *C.M.R.* 742, 763, 770, 773-75, 776, 781 (italics added).
[113]In a Saigon (Vietnam) case in 1970, when the court discovered that the mandatory sentence for the crime of which the accused was found guilty was life imprisonment, it found him guilty of a different offence carrying a lesser penalty.

the laws and usages of war . . . would justify the killing. In our view no rational being of the accused's age [20], formal education [grade 11], and military experience [two years] could have . . . considered the order lawful. Where one obeys an order to kill . . . for the apparent reason of making [the] death an example to others, the evidence must be strong indeed to raise a doubt that the slayer was not aware of the illegality of the order. . . . The inference of fact is compelling . . . that the accused complied with the palpably unlawful order fully aware of its unlawful character. . . . [As to the contention] that the accused was mistaken in law as to the legality of the order of his superior officer, the defense fails for a prerequisite of such defense is that the mistake of law was an honest and reasonable one and . . . the evidence . . . justifies the inference that the accused was aware of the illegality of the order.

The Board rejected the argument that the accused mistakenly believed that all orders must be obeyed, and cited the *Einsatzgruppen Case*[114] to show

. . . that a soldier or airman is not an automaton but a "reasoning agent" who is under a duty to exercise judgment in obeying the orders of a superior officer to the extent, that where such orders are manifestly beyond the scope of the issuing officer's authority and are *so palpably illegal on their face that a man of ordinary sense and understanding would know them to be illegal,* then the fact of obedience to the order of a superior officer will not protect a soldier for acts committed pursuant to such illegal orders. . . . [Further,] where an airman is fully aware of the existence of a conspiracy between his superior officer and another to accomplish an unlawful purpose and in compliance with a palpably illegal order, the unlawful nature of which he is aware, commits an overt act to effect the object of the conspiracy, the necessary criminal intent is present and he has become a co-conspirator and cannot claim obedience to orders of a superior officer to prevent his conviction of conspiracy. . . .[115]

In *Kinder*, there was evidence to show that the superior officer had made it clear that all his orders were to be obeyed, but this did not avail the accused. In one of the Vietnam cases,[116] also involving a charge of unpremeditated murder in compliance with orders, there was evidence to show that the actions taken were "in line with training received from the Marine Corps," but the Board of Review held, confirming the court martial's decision and Law Officer's summation, that "Marine Corps training" would not constitute a defence:

[T]he acts of a Marine done in good faith and without malice, in compliance with the orders of a superior . . . [are] justifiable, unless such acts are manifestly beyond the scope of his authority and such that *a man of ordinary sense and understanding* would know them to be illegal. Therefore, if you find beyond a reasonable doubt that the accused under the circumstances of his age and military experience could not have honestly believed the order issued . . . "to be legal under the laws of war", then the killing of the alleged victim was without justification. A Marine is a reasoning agent, who is under a duty to exercise judgment in obeying orders to the extent that when such orders are manifestly beyond the scope of the authority of the one issuing the order, and were *palpably illegal upon their face,* then the act of obedience to such orders will not justify acts pursuant to such illegal orders.

---

[114]See *supra* note 91.
[115]The Board agreed that if the order had been *lawful,* the accused could not have been found guilty of conspiracy: *U.S.* v. *Saglietto* (1941), 41 *F. Supp.* 21. For the trial of the officer issuing the order to Kinder, see *U.S.* v. *Schreiber* (1955), 18 *C.M.R.* 226, and see *supra* note 46.
[116]*U.S.* v. *Keenan* (1969), 39 *C.M.R.* 108, 117 (italics added).

The last case to which reference need be made here, and which expressly relied upon the *Kinder* decision, is *U.S.* v. *Griffen*.[117] Again a prisoner was shot on the orders of a superior officer; some time earlier all the members of the slayer's platoon had been killed or wounded in the same general area, and the slayer felt that the platoon's security might have been endangered if the prisoner were kept. The Review Board pointed out that "the killing of a docile prisoner taken during military operations is not justifiable homicide." It accepted as good law the view of the *Manual* that "the act of a subordinate, done in good faith in compliance with the supposed order of a superior, is not justifiable when the order is such that *a man of ordinary sense and understanding would know it to be illegal* . . . [and] it is difficult to conceive of a military situation in which the order of a superior would be more patently wrong. Accordingly, we view the order as commanding an act so obviously beyond the scope of authority of the superior officer and *so palpably illegal on its face as to admit of no doubt of its unlawfulness to a man of ordinary sense and understanding.*"

It is clear from these cases that the courts have tended to measure "palpable illegality" by the "man of ordinary sense and understanding," although in both *Kinder* and *Keenan* reference was made to the understanding of the accused, given his age, education and military experience. This is similar to the Canadian stand[118] and the decisions in *Cooke* and the *War Crimes (Preventive Murder) (Germany) case*,[119] in both of which the court paid attention to the fact that the accused were legally qualified. This raises the fundamental issue whether "the man of ordinary sense and understanding" is the proper agent for measuring the "palpable unlawfulness" of a military order. As was brought out in some of the United States courts martial, the circumstances may be such (for example, the act may be committed well behind the lines) that there is no real military necessity for it, and in such a situation the measure of the order may well be that of "the man on the Clapham omnibus." This would probably apply to most offences committed against prisoners of war once they had been removed from the scene of capture. It would also probably apply to the cases alleged to have occurred in Vietnam of prisoners being dropped from helicopters *pour encourager les autres*, a practice which was expressly condemned in *Kinder*.

But there are offences which are of such a kind and occur in circumstances so closely connected with operations that it is probably unfair to measure them by any standard other than that of the "reasonable soldier," and it may even be unfair to judge them by persons other than those possessed of military experience. It is true that there have been attempts made in the United States, as a result of the experience gained by a large civilian conscripted army, to bring the military within normal civil jurisdiction,[120] but the Supreme Court has shown its awareness of the possibility of a civilian tribunal reaching a decision very different from that of a tribunal made up of military specialists.[121] It may even be questioned whether a military code, manual or directions to courts martial drafted by lawyers, newly qualified or not, who carry military ranks merely because they serve in the Judge Advocate's or Defence Departments, but who have no idea of the realities of service life particularly in action, are the proper persons to be responsible for preparing these regulations and legislation. Likewise, it may be that permanent courts martial with

[117](1968), 3 *C.M.R.* 586.
[118]See *supra* notes 48 and 49.
[119]See *supra* note 33.
[120]See Johnson, "Unlawful Command Influence: A Question of Balance," 19 *JAG Journal* 1965, at 87.
[121]*U.S. ex rel Toth* v. *Quarles, supra* note 46.

permanent presidents who have achieved senior rank by long service are not the best judges of the actions of young soldiers whose experience of warlike conditions has been gained under conditions that were completely unknown when their judges were serving personnel.

In deciding whether the order was one which a soldier "of ordinary sense and understanding would know to be illegal" on the face of it, justice may well demand that consideration be paid to the general conditions in which the accused found himself, the length of time he had been in action, the nature of the hostilities, the type of enemy confronting him and the methods of warfare employed against him. While some attention must be paid to the casualties borne by the accused's comrades as a result of illegal methods of warfare, care must be taken, as was brought out in *Griffen*, not to allow resentment, hatred, anger or sorrow to overcome even a soldier's reasonable understanding of right and wrong. While one might expect a soldier to be more likely to fire and kill persons awaiting interrogation who appear to be making a break for freedom, as is alleged to have happened in North Malaya in 1948,[122] than might be the case with an escape from civil custody, there is little doubt that even a soldier "of ordinary sense and understanding" would appreciate the "palpable unlawfulness" of an order to enter a village in what is understood to be a "cleared area" and exterminate all life, regardless of age, sex or allegiance, as is alleged to have happened at Song My.

It may not only be necessary to change the concept of reasonableness in so far as superior orders addressed to a military subordinate are concerned. If justice is to be achieved, it may also be necessary to change the law with regard to prejudice in relation to military trials. In the case of Malaya, the British authorities announced that a commission had been set up to investigate the facts and recommend whether proceedings should be instituted. In the meantime, a complete news blackout was imposed. Where Song My was concerned, there had been a veritable trial by news media. The accused, their counsel, potential prosecution witnesses and the command all issued statements, as did those engaged in a Congressional enquiry. The danger was that, even if there were adequate grounds for a trial, and even if the honour of the United States might demand that the matter be fully aired in a judicial fashion with the guilty being made to pay, there was a grave risk that no action could be taken because of prejudice, even though it was assumed that a military court might consist of persons sufficiently honest and aware of military reality to pay attention only to the facts, and to be as capable of closing their minds to extraneous and biased matter as it is presumed a jury is to an improper question.

From the discussion that has taken place about superior orders in both civil and military courts, whether in time of peace or armed conflict, it is clear that, while they may constitute ground for mitigating punishment, these orders cannot be accepted as justifying an illegal act—at least where the act ordered is of such a character that the order is "palpably unlawful." In deciding whether it is so palpable, which is a question of law for the court, it is submitted the standard of measurement cannot be universal, but must depend on whether the accused is a civilian or a serviceman and whether the offence is of a kind that can be considered as being civil in character though committed by a soldier. If the act is essentially military in character and has been committed in war conditions, then the palpability must be looked at from the point of view of the reasonable soldier, and decided by military personnel who are themselves likely to be aware of how the reasonable soldier thinks, reacts and does.

[122]*The Times*, February 4, 1970.

During the Geneva Diplomatic Conference on Reaffirmation and Development of Humanitarian Law applicable in Armed Conflicts attempts were made to secure the inclusion of an article regulating the validity and scope of the defence of superior orders in Protocol I,[123] which dealt with international armed conflict. Unfortunately, although at one time it appeared as if agreement might be possible, the Protocol as adopted is silent on this matter,[124] although it deals with the concomitant of superior orders, namely command responsibility.[125] In view of this silence on the part of the Protocol, one must assume that the customary law on the subject as set out above still prevails.

In order to assist the military man, it is suggested that he should be informed by his national authorities that he is to behave in accordance with the following principles[126]:

    i. Lawful orders issued by superiors to subordinates under their command shall be obeyed by those subordinates.

    ii. There shall be a presumption that all orders issued by superiors to their subordinates are in fact legal.

    iii. If an order obviously entails the commission of a criminal act it shall not be obeyed.

    iv. No subordinate shall be liable to court martial or other disciplinary proceedings for refusing to obey such an order.

    v. Should a subordinate obey such an order, the surrounding circumstances shall be taken into consideration in order to ascertain whether the order may be pleaded in mitigation of punishment. The tribunal shall also examine the personal characteristics, such as age, education and intelligence of the accused, in considering mitigation.

    vi. In assessing whether the order in question obviously involves the commission of a criminal act, the tribunal shall examine whether the order was so obvious to other persons in similar circumstances as the accused, that is to say, not to the reasonable man, but to the reasonable soldier faced with the same factual situation as the accused.

[123]For discussion of the Protocol see ch. I *supra*.

[124]A proposal on superior orders was adopted by Committee I at the 1977 session but it was rejected by the Conference at the 45th Plenary on 30 May 1977, see 3 *Official Records*, 331, 6 *ibid.* 307-9; Bothe, Partsch and Solf, *New Rules for Victims of Armed Conflicts*, 1982, 524.

[125]See Ch. X *infra*.

[126]For full exposition of the issue of superior orders, see Green, *Superior Orders in National and International Law*, 1976; Dinstein, The Defence of *'Obedience to Superior Orders' in International Law*, 1965; Keijzer, *Military Obedience*, 1978.

IV

The Role of Legal Advisers in the Armed Forces

Article 82 of Protocol I Additional to the Geneva Conventions of 12 August 1949, and relating to the protection of victims of international armed conflicts,[1] provides that

> The High Contracting Parties at all times, and the parties to the conflict in time of armed conflict, shall ensure that legal advisers are available, when necessary, to advise military commanders at the appropriate level on the application of the Conventions[2] and this Protocol and on the appropriate instruction to be given to the armed forces on this subject.

This is a new departure in that it lays an obligation upon States to take proper steps to ensure that at least the commanders of their own forces may apprise themselves of the legality of the actions which they contemplate undertaking. At the same time, the commander is obligated to make certain that the men under his command are aware of the law of Geneva, so that they, too, may assess the legality of the actions in which they are required to participate. If one looks at the history of the law of war and of its enforcement, which may to some extent be regarded as an extension of national criminal law into the international sphere, this provision is merely a recognition of practical necessity and the purpose that it aims to achieve is not quite so innovative as might appear, although a treaty requirement to this effect is undoubtedly a new development.

As early as the fifteenth century, at the trial of Peter von Hagenbach[3] at Breisach, it was made clear that commanders are presumed to know the law. Two centuries later, at the trial of the regicides, Cooke,[4] the former Chief Justice of Ireland who presented

---

[1]Schindler/Toman, 551.

[2]*Ibid.*, 305, 333, 355, 427.

[3](1474), Schwarzenberger, 2 *The Law of Armed Conflict*, ch. 39 (1968); Green, *Superior Orders in National and International Law*, 263 (1976).

[4](1660), 5 *St. Tr.* 1077; Green, *supra* note 3, at 24.

the indictment against Charles I, was held to be obviously liable for treason in that, as Chief Justice, he was certainly aware of what constituted a proper court and the limits of that court's jurisdiction. In so far as the law of war is concerned, the trial of *Sawada*[5] by a United States Military Commission sitting in Shanghai illustrates the somewhat more severe line adopted towards an accused who is legally qualified as compared with one who is not.

On the other hand, it must be borne in mind that the majority of members of the armed forces not only are not legally qualified, but frequently know little or nothing of the law of war, whether this relates to their own rights or to the rights of others and the duties that they owe to such others. Thus, in *Re Buck*[6] the Judge Advocate at a British war crimes trial asked

> What did each of these accused know about the rights of a prisoner of war? . . . The Court may well think that the men are not lawyers: they may not have heard either of the Hague Convention or the Geneva Convention; they may not have seen any book of military law upon the subject; but the Court has to consider whether men who are serving either as soldiers or in proximity to soldiers know as a matter of the general facts of military life whether a prisoner of war has certain rights. . . .

Nevertheless one must not overlook the fact that nowadays we have abandoned the principle of unquestioning obedience on the part of the most common soldier, who is no longer to be considered

> an automaton but a reasoning agent who is under the duty to exercise judgment in obeying the orders of a superior officer to the extent that, where such orders are manifestly beyond the scope of the issuing officer's authority and are so palpably illegal on their face that a man of ordinary sense and understanding would know them to be illegal, then the fact of obedience to the order of a superior officer will not protect a soldier for acts pursuant to such illegal orders.[7]

This is not the place to consider how to assess the duties or the understanding of the ordinary soldier,[8] nor is it necessary to examine the law concerning compliance with superior orders, provided, of course, that such orders are lawful.[9] The problem lies in the fact that so much of international law, and particularly of the law of war, is controversial with varying writers asserting conflicting arguments and not all countries accepting the same view of its scope. Thus, it was not until 1975 that the United States, by its ratification of the Geneva gas protocol,[10] accepted that, save in certain very limited and carefully defined circumstances, the use of gas and other deleterious materials was contrary to law. Furthermore, when operating in the field the serviceman, officer and private soldier alike, is more concerned with the need to defeat his enemy than with the niceties of the law, particularly as in such circumstances he has no means of ascertaining what that law is, for it is most unlikely that a qualified international lawyer will be available for consultations, while the necessities of the service will frequently mean that there is no time for such consultations in any case.

---

[5](1946), 5 *War Crimes Reports* 1; Green, *supra* note 3, at 315.
[6](1946), 13 *Ann. Dig.* 292; Green, *supra* note 3, at 286.
[7]*U.S. v. Kinder* (1954), 14 *C.M.R.* 742, 776; Green, *supra* note 3, at 132. *See also In re Ohlendorf (Einsatzgruppen* Trial) (1948), 15 *Ann. Dig.* 656, 665; Green, *supra* note 3, at 312.
[8]See, *e.g.,* "Superior Orders and the Reasonable Man," ch. III *supra.*
[9]For a full discussion of this problem, see Green, *supra* note 3.
[10](1925), 94 *L.N.T.S.* 65; Schindler/Toman, 109.

Too frequently, the ordinary soldier has argued that, since he is bound to obey, since his superiors have greater knowledge of the situation than he has, and since he has been trained to assume that his superiors will only issue orders that are in accord with the law,[11] it goes without comment that he cannot be held liable for acts which he commits that are contrary to the law of war and, if they are, then, he has contended, he is protected by the concept of superior orders. As has already been seen, in so far as an order involves an act that is so "palpably illegal . . . that a man of ordinary sense and understanding would know [it] to be illegal," this defence will not lie. As to officers, there is a wealth of jurisprudence concerning war crimes to illustrate that they, too, will frequently contend that compliance with superior orders suffices to excuse all actions, especially when it is clear, to them at least, that such actions are justifiable on the basis of military necessity. Here, too, the decisions of war crimes tribunals amply illustrate the futility of such contentions. In addition, it is easy to argue that, while the ordinary person is aware that in so far as his national criminal law is concerned *ignorantia juris quod quisque tenetur scire, neminem excusat*,[12] this cannot be true of the international law of war, for those who live within a national system of law may be presumed to accept the national ethic and to be aware of the nature and basic principles of their country's criminal code, or at least know where to find them, while international law is a highly sophisticated system, much of which is controversial and, from the point of view of the layman, shrouded in mystery.

To some extent, even before the adoption of Article 82, attempts had been made to ensure that members of the armed forces would be made aware of the contents of the treaty rules of war by imposing obligations with regard to their dissemination.[13] A number of States have issued manuals of military law outlining the obligations imposed by the laws of war upon their respective armed forces. However, such manuals are only intended

> for the guidance of military and naval forces . . . [and] may, of course, be altered by the government which issues them, except in so far as the obligatory character of their rules is established by international law.[14]

On a more official level, the *United States Army Field Manual—Law of Land Warfare*[15] expressly states

> those provisions of the *Manual* which are neither statutes nor the text of treaties to which the United States is a party should not be considered binding upon courts and tribunals applying the law of war.

Perhaps the true status of such manuals is best seen in the comments of the United States military tribunal in *Re List (The Hostages Trial)*:[16]

> The fact that the British and American armies may have adopted [Oppenheim's views on the validity of superior orders as a defence to a war crimes charge] for the regulation of their own armies as a matter of policy does not have the effect of enthroning it as a rule of International Law. . . . Army regulations are not a

[11]See, *e.g.*, U.S. Army "Lesson Plan" on teaching "The Geneva Conventions of 1949 and Hague Convention IV of 1907," Dept. of the Army, ASubjScd 27-1 (8 Oct., 1970).
[12]See Selden, *Table Talk*, "Law," (1689); Blackstone, 4 *Commentaries on the Laws of England*, ch. 2, s. 5 (1769); see also ch. II, *supra*.
[13]See, *e.g.*, Green, "Humanitarian Law and the Man in the Field," 14 *Can. Y.B. Int'l L.* 96 (1976).
[14]Garner, 1 *International Law and the World War*, 12 (1920).
[15]FM 27-10, para. 1.
[16](1948), 8 *War Crimes Reports* 34; Green, *supra* note 3, at 308.

competent source of International Law. They are neither legislative nor judicial pronouncements. They are not competent for any purpose in determining whether a fundamental principle of justice has been accepted by civilized nations generally. It is possible, however, that such regulations, as they bear upon a question of custom and practice in the conduct of war, might have evidentiary value, particularly if the applicable portions had been put into general practice. . . . Determination, whether a custom or practice exists, is a question of fact. Whether a fundamental principle of justice has been accepted is a question of judicial or legislative declaration. In determining the former, military regulations may play an important role but, in the latter, they do not constitute an authoritative precedent.

Some armed forces have attempted to go further in assisting those of their personnel who may feel that they have received an order which involves conduct contrary to the laws of war. Among these, perhaps the most important is the United States. While recognizing that it "takes courage" to question a superior as to the legality of the order that has been given, a soldier who considers that he has received an illegal order is advised to report this fact:[17]

> Usually, the soldier will report any known or suspected violations of the law of war through his chain of command. . . . Most commanders have established reporting procedures by local regulations and directives which require prompt, initial reports through the chain of command. Failure to comply with these regulations and directives may subject you to prosecution under the Uniform Code of Military Justice.
> While a soldier should normally report through his chain of command, you may hesitate to do so if someone in the chain above you was involved in the alleged crime, or if for some other reason you feel that such channels should not be effective. At such times, there are other officers to whom you can report or with whom you may properly discuss any possible violations of the laws of war. . . .
> . . . You may also discuss the problem with a Judge Advocate, a military lawyer who knows the law of war and how it applies. Many soldiers prefer to discuss problems with the Chaplain, and this is an accepted way to report violations of the law of war.

This directive deals with the dilemma of the soldier after receiving an order to commit an illegal act. While its purpose and aim may be highly laudable, it is submitted that its content is somewhat unrealistic. As it points out, it takes a great deal of courage to question and report a senior officer alleged to have given an illegal order. Further, it is highly questionable whether many of the members of the Judge Advocate's Department of any army are really acquainted with the rules of international law or are able to say whether a particular order is likely to result in a breach of the law of war. This is even more true of members of the chaplaincy. Finally, it is extremely doubtful whether such a legally qualified officer will be present in the field when the ordinary soldier receives an order which places him in such a dilemma. Moreover, the role of the Judge Advocate, at least in those forces organized in a fashion similar to those of the United Kingdom, tends to be somewhat restricted. His role is more related to the organisation and supervision of military discipline by way of courts martial, although he is also regarded as legal adviser to the forces and, at lower echelons, frequently serves the ordinary serviceman as would a solicitor in civil life. While it is true that some members of the Judge Advocate General's staff may have some knowledge of international law of war, it prob-

[17]*Supra* note 11; Green, "Aftermath of Vietnam: War Law and the Soldier," in Falk, 4 *The Vietnam War and International Law*, 147 (1976) [reproduced in Green, *Law and Society* 397, 424 (1975)].

ably goes too far to describe Judge Advocates as such as "military lawyers who know the law of war and how it applies."

The Protocol has made the problem even more urgent than it ever was. The scope of legal regulation has been greatly widened, affecting both the law of The Hague and of Geneva. In so far as the former is concerned, a wealth of new regulations has been introduced concerning means and methods of warfare, declaring certain objects, which might in the past have been regarded as legitimate military objectives, as no longer within the realm of attack. At the same time, on the level of Geneva humanitarian law, efforts have been made to clarify and extend the rights of medical personnel, and to define more precisely their units and transports which are now rendered immune from attack. Equally, special provision has been made with regard to chaplains and civil defence personnel. Again, vastly extending the scope of the Fourth Geneva Convention, the Protocol has enlarged the protection and respect to which civilians and civilian objects are now legally entitled. On all these issues, the commander in the field, as well as the commandant of a prisoner of war camp, will require to be far more acquainted with the rules of law than might have been considered necessary before 1977. Throughout the Protocol there is to be found a desire to increase the scope of humanitarian law in armed conflict. The draftsmen were, however, aware of the pressures and doubts of the military mind, and realised that it would always be necessary to seek to harmonise these humanitarian ideals with the realities of military necessity. The commander in the field is far too prone to be aware of the latter and may not necessarily agree that humanitarianism is something with which he need to be too concerned. He might also feel that a critic's view of humanitarian law is somewhat partisan or subjective and the result of a lack of knowledge of military realities. The presence of a legal adviser, properly trained and knowledgeable, is likely to help to reduce the imbalance between humanitarian law and *raison de guerre*.

The decision to require legal advisers to be made available to advise military commanders on the application of the law of Geneva could in practice remove some of the difficulties that have been outlined above, while it is clear that their purpose would differ from that normally fulfilled by Judge Advocates at the present time. Moreover, it is hardly likely that the type of official envisaged in Article 82 would be able to fulfill the tasks outlined in the United States "Lesson Plan," nor perhaps should he.

Much could be made of the language in which Article 82 has been expressed, but it is not the purpose here to consider whether this is compulsive or hortatory. In accordance with the normal assumptions of treaty law, it is being presumed that the parties will act on the basis of good faith,[18] so that any State ratifying the Protocol will, in fact, proceed with the appointment of the adviser in question. Similarly, it is not considered necessary to enter into any discussion of problems which may be faced by those States in which there is an armed forces ombudsman, or where some of the personnel may be organised in trade unions. Nor is it considered necessary, for the purposes of this paper, to examine the situation that exists when there is a recognised procedure for protest whereby the individual receiving an order which he deems to be illegal may seek some form of protection when the superior issuing the order persists in maintaining it despite the subordinate's protest.[19]

---

[18]See, *e.g.*, Cheng, *General Principles of Law*, 105-60 (1953); Herczegh, *General Principles of International Law and the International Legal Order*, 30, 34-39 (1969); Kelsen, *Principles of International Law*, 447 (Tucker ed., 1966); Lauterpacht, "The Definition and Nature of International Law," 1 *Collected Papers* 5, 47 (1970); "Règles générales du droit de la paix," 62 *Hague Recueil* 99 (1937); Schwarzenberger, "The Fundamental Principles of International Law," 87 *Hague Recueil* 195, 290-326 (1955); Tunkin, *Theory of International Law* 86, 218-24 (1974).

[19]See, *e.g.*, *re* U.S.A. and Imperial Ethiopia, Green, *supra* note 3, at 253-54, 209.

Before considering the practical implications of Article 82, it may be as well to point out that, while showing a sense of realism, the Article reflects the non-reciprocity which has almost become a feature of Protocol I.[20] The Protocol has redefined international armed conflict to include wars of national liberation.[21] However, since national liberation movements are not States, they cannot become High Contracting Parties, although by Article 96(3) they are able to make declaration whereby they assume the same rights and obligations as High Contracting Parties. Since this will only occur when they are recognised as national liberation movements engaged in an armed conflict seeking self-determination, it is only as a party to the conflict that they are required to appoint the requisite legal advisers. Nothing is said in the Protocol as to where these are to be found, how they are to be trained or what their status is to be. Is it to be assumed that lawyers—military lawyers trained in the international law of armed conflict—will always be found in the ranks of a national liberation movement? What if none is available? Is the military commander of a national liberation movement to be in a better position than that of a State force because he does not have available to him the legal advice which may temper his conduct and save him from breaches of the law?

Let it be assumed for the sake of argument that States have carried out their obligations under Article 82 and legal advisers have in fact been appointed. Does this necessarily mean that the number of breaches of the laws of war will decrease? In the first place, since the military officer considers that his first task is to overcome the enemy and achieve his immediate objective with minimum losses, there is little doubt that a determined military commander will almost invariably place the needs of his operation before all else, and it may well be that some commander will treat the views of his adviser in the same cavalier fashion as Keitel did those of Canaris relating to the ill-treatment of Soviet prisoners of war.[22] Canaris stated:

> The Geneva Convention for the treatment of prisoners of war [of 1929] is not binding in the relationship between Germany and the U.S.S.R. Therefore only the principles of General International Law on the treatment of prisoners of war apply. Since the eighteenth century, these have gradually been established along the lines that war captivity is neither revenge nor punishment, but solely protective custody, the only purpose of which is to prevent the prisoners of war from further participation in the war. This principle was developed in accordance with the view held by all armies that it is contrary to military tradition to kill or injure helpless people. . . . The decrees for the treatment of Soviet prisoners of war enclosed are based on a fundamentally different viewpoint.

Although Keitel testified that he "really agreed" with Canaris,[23] he nevertheless made a note on the memorandum:

> The objections arise from the military concept of chivalrous warfare. This is the destruction of an ideology. Therefore I approve and back the measure.[24]

Clearly, if in future, a commander were so to disregard the advice given him by his legal adviser, advice which, in the words of the Nuremberg judgment, "correctly stated the legal position," it would merely mean that such a commander would have absolutely no

---

[20]See, "The New Law of Armed Conflict," ch. I *supra*.
[21]Art. 1, see discussion *supra* note 20.
[22]H.M.S.O., *Trial of German Major War Criminals*, (1956), Part 22, Judgment, 452.
[23]*Ibid.*, 492.
[24]*Ibid.*, 453.

basis on which to rest his defence when faced with a charge alleging war crimes or grave breaches of the Convention or Protocol. The legal adviser, on the other hand, would have recourse to any protest procedure that may be available.

Moreover, it has to be remembered that controversy rages as to the exact scope of the rules of war, particularly in so far as they have not been embodied in treaties but are claimed to be part of general or customary international law. This divergence is well illustrated by examination of the comments on superior orders to be found in the various editions of Oppenheim's *International Law* and in the British and American *Manuals* based thereon,[25] or in the comments on chemical weapons to be found in Hyde's *International Law chiefly as Interpreted and Applied by the United States*[26] as compared with the views of Major-General Cramer, United States Judge Advocate General in 1945,[27] and of the General Counsel of the Department of Defence during the 1971 hearings of the Senate Committee on Foreign Relations concerning ratification of the Geneva Protocol[28] and the subsequent statement issued concomitant with ratification.[29] What will be the position, therefore, if the legal adviser gives advice which is in accordance with his own country's views of the customary law of war but does not coincide with the view of the enemy in whose hands the commander who has acted in accordance with that advice might find himself? Would the commander be able to plead that he has acted in accordance with that advice, honestly though mistakenly believing it to be correct? Would the legal adviser in question be liable to stand trial in accordance with the *ignorantia juris* maxim or the principle that he who holds himself out as an expert must show the expertise of an expert, bearing in mind that the legally qualified accused in *Sawada*[30] was more severely punished than his non-qualified co-accused?

Another problem that may arise relates to the hierarchic relationship as between the commander and his legal adviser. Difficulties may well be encountered when the latter is junior to the commander and seeks to advise him that the action which he proposes taking is contrary to the law and, if pursued, will render the commander liable to criminal charges which, if the action amounts to a grave breach, should be instituted by the legal adviser himself. Clearly, it will be necessary for the parties to the Protocol to instil into their armed forces an entirely new approach to the law. This, of course, is incumbent upon them anyway in accordance with Article 83 relating to dissemination:

> The High Contracting Parties undertake, in times of peace as in time of armed conflict, to disseminate the Conventions and this Protocol as widely as possible. . . , and to include the study thereof in their programmes of military instruction. . . , so that these instruments may become known to the armed forces. . . .

In fact, Article 82 must remain a somewhat empty obligation if Article 83 is not obeyed. It might even be possible to argue that the responsibility for supervising the study of the Conventions and Protocol should rest upon the legal adviser. This, of course, will depend on the structure of particular armies and is probably only feasible in time of peace, for in time of war any legal adviser attached to a serving unit would probably be fully employed in watching the acts of the commanding officer on a day-to-day basis—that is to say, if such advisers were actually deployed in the field. It would be necessary not

[25]See Green, *supra* note 3, at 265-75.
[26]Vol. 3, 1818-22 (1947).
[27]Reprinted in 10 *I.L.M.* 1304 (1971).
[28]*Ibid.*, 1300.
[29]69 *Am. Int'l L.* 403-5 (1975); *U.S. Digest* 857-60 (1975).
[30]See note 5 *supra*.

only to instil into the forces a new respect for the law, but also to emphasise to commanders that their legal advisers have a special role to play and that their advice must be heeded, regardless of rank. To ignore such advice will entail criminal liability, and the legal adviser must be protected from any possible victimisation or disciplinary or other proceedings arising from the unpopular nature of his advice or the determination with which he seeks to press it.

Article 82 merely requires legal advisers to be made available to military commanders "at the appropriate level." It is apparently open to each party to the Protocol to decide for itself at what level they shall be made available. This is particularly so in view of the fact that the Protocol makes no attempt to define commander and in accordance with military hierarchy it may be contended that even the lowest non-commissioned officer is a commander *vis-à-vis* the men below him. There can be no doubt, of course, that, for the purpose of Article 82, a commander is, normally at least, an officer in the field or one capable of giving orders which lead to military operations. This means that at some stage or other determination must be made of the level of the command at which it becomes necessary to accredit legal advisers. To leave this to individual States is likely to result in great confusion, and in the possibility that when and if trials take place the accused commander will be provided with a legitimate defence on the basis that the illegality of the act in question was by no means clear; that he honestly thought that it was legal, and his high command did not consider it necessary for a legal adviser to be allocated to him. To prevent this possibility, consideration will have to be given to some further international agreement laying down the level of command at which the appointment of advisers is necessary. In so far as an alliance like NATO is concerned, this may be relatively simple. If, however, hostilities involving rival ideologies and interpretations of the law were to take place, the matter could become serious.

Some countries, the Federal German Republic, for example, have had legal advisers of the kind envisaged here for some time. In West Germany they are specially selected and trained lawyers who retain their civilian status and are attached to military commands in peace-time and accompany the commander to whom they are attached on field exercises. In this way hierarchic difficulties are avoided, and it is hoped that a special relationship of trust is created between the commander and his adviser, with the latter regarded by his commander as an administrative specialist to whom he must pay proper attention, while remaining personally responsible for all military decisions which may be made. In the event of hostilities, the status of the adviser changes. He will then be put into uniform and given a rank so that he receives combatant and, if necessary, prisoner of war status. While problems of rank may inevitably arise, it is hoped that prior training and the relationship already created will mitigate any difficulties and prevent the commander looking upon his adviser as an interloping civilian in uniform. In The Netherlands, on the other hand, the practice is to take serving field officers of at least ten years standing and send them to the university to pursue courses in war law, after which they are posted to commands as military legal advisers.

In contrast to this, in armed forces which would be instituting a relatively new concept and in which, traditionally, the legal officer is a member of the armed forces, it might suffice, in view of the different and specialist type of work involved, to create a new division in the Judge Advocate's Department where military lawyers, either those already serving or specially recruited, could be trained in the law of war, bearing in mind in their training, also, that they require, if their advice is to receive due attention in operations, more than basic military training. These officers could then be posted to fulfil the tasks of legal advisers as provided for in Article 82. If properly trained, and if separated from their colleagues in the Judge Advocate's Department, they should also be able to satisfy the teaching demands of Article 83, especially as they are not likely, in peace-time, to be fully employed in their advisory work. In so far as their training is concerned, some of the courses organised at present for this purpose by the International Institute of Humanitarian Law might well be useful.[31]

Not only is the Protocol silent as to the level of command involved, but there is no indication of the type of training that the legal advisers should be given or the type of person who should be selected.

While it may be relatively easy for United Nations forces or those of allied nations, particularly, perhaps, those belonging to regional organisations, to coordinate on this matter, the problem is more complex when there is no common training or service as between the armed forces of various nations. This may be met, in the case of NATO, the United Nations or regional alliances by instituting common programmes. However, it must not be ignored that States are jealous of their sovereignty and regard the training of their armed forces as a matter of domestic jurisdiction, concerning which they are not likely to be open to interference. Once again, therefore, confusion is likely to ensue owing to varying conceptions of what the law is, different interpretations of what the recognised law means, dissimilar methods of training and unequal levels of education. Clearly, the most useful solution to these problems would be the adoption of an international agreement laying down standards of training and perhaps involving the drafting of an acceptable manual. This, however, is probably an idealistic solution unlikely to achievement at the present time. Failing this, it might be helpful if, for example, the International Committee of the Red Cross or the San Remo International Institute of Humanitarian Law were to issue such training manuals in the hope that they might be acceptable by the parties to the Protocol, at least as guides to help in preparing their own courses. Even more useful would be the organization of training courses by either of these bodies open to members of the legal branches of the armed forces of parties to the Protocol, enrolment being limited on the basis of minimal qualification and perhaps minimum rank. This, however, would mean that the instructors would have to be chosen with extreme care, perhaps solely from neutral countries, while the programmes that they use and the commentaries on which they base themselves might have to be approved by the authorities of the services from which the students are enrolled.

Perhaps more practical at the present moment, and recognising the prejudices and reservations of States, is to express the hope that the parties to the Protocol will themselves institute proper training programmes making full use of the resources at their disposal. This means that they should be prepared to support the introduction of courses in war law at universities and law schools, and the authorities running such institutions should not be averse to accepting advice and assistance from such sources without putting forward specious arguments relating to academic independence. The authorities must also be prepared to resist the complaints that will inevitably be made by idealistic pacifists and their bemused followers of every age-group. On the other hand, it cannot be regarded as sufficient basis for helping in the running of such courses that a person is a member of a national Red Cross society who may have read the Conventions and the Protocol.

War law is a highly technical subject, whether in its offensive or its humanitarian aspect. Those who purport to deal with it must themselves be specialists in the field. The courses that they teach must be carefully prepared. After all, the legal advisers who

---

[31]See "1er Cours International sur le Droit de la Guerre pour Officiers, Sanremo (16-23 Juin 1976)," 16 *Revue de Droit Pénal Militaire et de Droit de la Guerre* (special issue, 1977).

are the products of their training will be responsible for ensuring that the commanders to whom they are attached observe the provisions of the Conventions and the Protocol. While they may not be able to prevent wars, they are required to seek maintenance of the rule of law when war takes place. On their advice depend the prestige and honour of their country together, often, with the freedom and very life of the commanders whom they have been posted to advise.

V

Human Rights and the Law of Armed Conflict

At first sight it might seem somewhat incongruous to consider human rights, law and armed conflict as being in any way related. Since the Nuremberg Judgment's approach to aggressive war, there has been a tendency to regard armed conflict as a clear rejection of legal processes, while the majority of people would argue that war has been rendered illegal by the adoption of the Charter of the United·Nations. Moreover, the experiences of the Second World War, together with evidence of what has happened in the various armed conflicts that have taken place since 1945 in Korea, Vietnam, Africa and elsewhere, suggest that in time of conflict, whether international or non-international, human rights are among the earliest casualties. However, since time immemorial attempts have been made to control the horrors of war and to maintain that even in such situations man must comply with certain overriding principles, whether they be described as the law of God, of chivalry or of humanity. Further, even in classical times there was some measure of recognition that when conflicts occurred, there were still some people who might be considered as outside the scope of the activity and entitled to protection. In fact, if one seeks to define the meaning of human rights in relation to armed conflict, one has to realise that this concept is wider than is normally assumed. When talking of human rights in this context, one refers to the rights of the individual combatants, of those like the wounded and sick or prisoners who are *hors de combat*, of those who attend to the needs of the latter, and of the rights of civilians. In fact, it is perhaps better to regard the problem of respect for human rights in this relationship as being part of what is often described as humanitarian law.

According to the leading Western military manuals[1] of the law of armed conflict, in

---

[1]H.M.S.O., *British Manual of Military Law*, Part III: The Law of Land Warfare 1-2 (W.O. Code No. 12333, 1958); U.S. Dept. of Army, *Field Manual: The Law of Land Warfare* 3 (FM 27-10, 1956); see also Dept. of Army, Pamphlet 27-161-2, 2 *International Law* 15-16 (1962).

accordance with the Hague Regulations of 1907,[2] this law is based on rules of chivalry, humanity and necessity, concepts which are not easy to define. It is no easier, though, to find a universal definition of human rights, and the wording of the Preamble to the Hague Convention No. IV, 1907, on the Law and Customs of War on Land is not really any clearer:

> Animated by the desire to serve . . . the interests of humanity and the ever progressive needs of civilization . . . the inhabitants of the belligerents remain under the protection and the rule of the principles of the law of nations, as they result from the usages established among civilized peoples, from the laws of humanity, and the dictates of the public conscience.

By and large, it may be said that what we now know as the modern law of armed conflict is to be found in the Hague Conventions of 1907, commonly known as the Hague Law, and the Geneva Conventions of 1949, as amended by the two Additional Protocols of 1977, and known jointly as the Geneva Law. To some extent, the Hague Law is really concerned with humanizing armed conflict and introducing proposals for the protection of those who are *hors de combat*, although Protocol I of 1977 relating to International Armed Conflict, which deals to a limited extent with means and methods, may in fact weaken the protection of the victims of war by doing so. Prior to the adoption of these Conventions, there were isolated agreements from the latter part of the nineteenth century on which dealt with the law in a piecemeal fashion, and there were also various rules and principles which had become accepted as part of customary law, as is made clear by the Preamble to Hague Convention IV; some reference to these may be of value.

It is perhaps as well to commence with the situation in feudal times, when the modern state system was beginning to develop and armed conflict was becoming a type of contest played according to rules. At that time, however, such rules as there were remained uncodified, but were generally accepted by knights as rules of chivalrous conduct to be observed among themselves. In fact, in both England and France there were courts of chivalry to ensure that the rules were observed, and commanders were wont to try offenders against these rules, regardless of the nationality of the offender or of his victim. There was, in other words, something similar to a rule of law prevailing among the orders of knighthood. Thus in 1370, at the siege of Limoges, where the English commander had given an order that no quarter was to be given to captives, three French knights who had been captured appealed to John of Gaunt and the Earl of Cambridge, saying, "My lords, we are yours: you have vanquished us. Act therefore to the law of arms", and they were spared and treated as prisoners.[3] Again, in 1474, at Breisach, the Allied Cities established a tribunal to try Peter of Hagenbach for offences against the laws of God and of man, in that while administering occupied territories he had indulged in looting, pillage, rapine, murder, attacks upon civilians and against neutral merchants. His plea that he had been complying with the orders of his prince was rejected on the ground that he must have known of the inhuman character of those orders and his acts, and he was executed.[4]

Over the course of the next two centuries, princes began to lay down rules governing the conduct of their forces and imposing duties of humanity with regard to the treatment of civilians. These obligations related to the basic need to sustain life in an agricultural

---

[2] "The right of belligerents to adopt means of injuring the enemy is not unlimited," Art. 22 (in Schindler/Toman, 63, 76; reaffirmed in Protocol I, 1977, Art. 35(1), *ibid.*, 551.
[3] Keen, *The Laws of War in the Middle Ages*, 1 (1965).
[4] Schwarzenberger, *International Law*, vol. 2: *Armed Conflict*, Ch. 39 (1968).

society, a provision which did not become generally accepted until the second half of our own century. Thus, Maximilian II decreed that

> none shall thieve any plough or mill or baking oven or any thing which serves the needs of the community whether it be from friend or foe, nor shall he without consent damage or break these things, nor shall he willingly cause wine or grain or flour to leak away or to spoil or to come to any harm, on pain of corporal punishment.[5]

Again, in 1690 it was laid down that "he who would dare in foreign countries to set ablaze or demolish hospitals or schools or baking ovens or to despoil a smithy or ploughs or farm implements in a township or hamlet shall be punished as a bloody villain."[6] Gustavus Adolphus in 1631 was more general in his orders and prohibited plundering by his army and imposed severe punishments for non-compliance, while during the Seven Years War Friedrich of Saxony informed his forces that

> among other things, there is a special prohibition against any kind of unruly behaviour, robbery, plundering, theft, arson, and similar acts of ruthlessness, on pain of death or severe corporal punishment. Particular care shall be taken to avoid any damage to wooded areas, homes, fields and gardens, fruit, fruit trees, barns and all property belonging to the estate owners and farmers.[7]

Things had advanced so far by the seventeenth century that one finds Shakespeare having Fluellen say in *Henry V*: "Kill the poys and the luggage! 'tis expressly against the law of arms."[8] Similarly by the English Laws and Ordinances of Warre, 1639, which regulated the behaviour of the army, there were forbidden, among other things, marauding of the countryside, individual acts against the enemy without authorisation from a superior, private taking or keeping of booty, or the private detention of a prisoner,[9] which meant that the latter was unlikely to be subjected to private vengeance or death or cruelty in the absence of a ransom. Although there were no clear rules regarding the safety of women, children and other non-combatants, especially if a city had only been taken after a siege, the clergy tended to be respected, while many a commander issued orders to his troops to spare the lives of the women, the young and the old.

While these developments for the more humane treatment of civilians were taking place, there was also a growing belief in the need to care for those who were *hors de combat* by reason of wounds.[10] By the middle of the sixteenth century it was fairly well established that doctors could not be taken prisoner,[11] while during the siege of 1552-53 François de Guise was summoning medical aid "to succour the abandoned wounded soldiers of the enemy and to make arrangements for their transport back to their army,"[12] provisions which we find repeated in the Geneva Law of today. Only a century passed before tentative arrangements were made for the mutual recognition and reciprocal care of the wounded in the field.

---

[5]*Artikel auf Teutsche Landsknechte*, Art. 53.
[6]*Churfürstlich Brandenburgisches Kriegsrecht*, Art. 59 (1690). Both of these quotations come from *Corpus Iuris Militaris Kriegsrecht und Artikels Brieffe* (Johann Friedrich Schukzen ed. 1693).
[7]*Kriegsvölkerrecht—Leitfaden für den Unterricht* (The International Law of Warfare, Instructional Guidelines) Part 7, para. 3 (German Forces Publication ZDv 15/10, 1961).
[8]Act 4, Scene 7.
[9]Clode, 1 *Military Forces of the Crown*, App. VI (1869).
[10]*See*, "War Law and the Medical Profession," ch. VI *infra*.
[11]Belli, *De Re Militari et Bello Tractatus*, Part VII, Ch. III, 34 (1563) (Carnegie tr. 1936, p. 187).
[12]Butler and Maccoby, *The Development of International Law*, 187, n. 28 (1928).

In 1679 a convention was signed between the Elector of Brandenburg, for the League of Augsburg, and the Count of Asfield, who commanded the French forces [providing] for a mutual respect towards both hospitals and wounded. . . . [A] convention [of] 1743 between Lord Stair on behalf of the Pragmatic army and the Marshal Noailles for the French during the Dettingen campaign bound both sides to treat hospitals and wounded with consideration. Noailles, when he thought that his operations might cause alarm to the inmates at the hospitals at Tachenheim, went so far as to send word that they should rest tranquil as they would not be disturbed. A fuller, and more highly developed type of agreement, was that signed at L'Ecluse in 1759 by the Marshal de Brail, who commanded the French, and Major General Conway the British general officer commanding. The hospital staff, chaplains, doctors, surgeons and apothecaries were not . . . to be taken prisoners; and, if they should happen to be apprehended within the lines of the enemy, they were to be sent back immediately. The wounded of the enemy who should fall into the hands of their opponents were to be cared for, and their food and medicine should in due course be paid for. They were not to be made prisoner and might stay in hospital safely under guard. Surgeons and servants might be sent to them under the general's passports. Finally, on their discharge, they were themselves to travel under the same authority and were to travel by the shortest route.[13]

There therefore seem to have been repeated efforts made to achieve some recognition for human rights, at least insofar as the sick and wounded were concerned, and along lines which are accepted in the Red Cross agreements of today, but it must not be thought that the situation had yet hardened sufficiently for these principles to be applied automatically. During the revolutionary wars, General Moreau proposed to Krug, the Austrian commander, that

the roads leading to hospitals [should] be marked by special signs [to] indicate the presence of wounded in the vicinity. Troops were to avoid these roads wherever possible or, in passing along them, were to abstain from disturbing noises. Hospitals were to remain the property of the belligerent even after he had evacuated the country. The belligerent in occupation was, under proper security, to furnish or requisition materials for the hospitals. Those soldiers who recovered were to be allowed to rejoin their former units. When it was decided to evacuate the entire hospital, the occupying belligerent was to provide an escort for the convoy of the waggons.[14]

In view of the ideological character of the conflict, it is perhaps not surprising that Krug rejected these proposals, in much the same way as there was fairly little respect shown for the ordinary humanitarian rules of war on the Eastern front during the Second World War.

It must not be thought that these apparently humanitarian arrangements were solely the result of the philanthropic sentiments of the commanders involved. To have to provide for and maintain the enemy's wounded could be expensive, so while "philanthropy forbade the abandonment of the enemy wounded, good policy required that the main burden of their nursing should still be thrown on the enemy,"[15] and the best way to do this, and at the same time to increase the burdens of the enemy, was to arrange for repatriation of the wounded. Some of these problems would not arise if there were some general, as distinct from bilateral, international agreement for dealing with the wounded, and in 1764

[13]*Ibid.*, 149-50.
[14]*Ibid.*, 150.
[15]*Ibid.*

Chamousset . . . referred with regret to the thousands of lives which had been sacrificed when, as a result of military operations, the forced and hurried evacuation of hospitals had become necessary in order to save the wounded from falling into the enemy's hands. Péyrilhe in 1780 proposed international recognition of the principle that the wounded should not be made prisoners of war and should not enter into the balance of exchanges.[16]

But it was not until after the experiences of Florence Nightingale in the Crimea and the publication of Henri Dunant's *Souvenir de Solferino* in 1862, following his experiences at the battle of that name three years earlier, that an attempt was made to give effect to these earlier ideas, and shortly thereafter the first Geneva Convention on the Red Cross was adopted, introducing, as a matter of universal international law, recognition for the human rights of the sick and wounded, as well as for those who attended them.

During the American Civil War, the first attempt to codify the law of armed conflict in a manner that would regulate the means of conduct while seeking to preserve respect for human rights was undertaken by Professor Lieber, whose Code received official promulgation by order of President Lincoln. For the first time a government issued instructions to its army relating to its conduct in the field, which purported to be expressive of generally accepted practice, and on which it was in fact based. Apart from dealing with such matters as martial law and the treatment of deserters, the Lieber Code also concerned itself with the proper treatment of prisoners of war and the wounded, as well as the behaviour of an army of occupation and the need to maintain the rule of law insofar as that was compatible with military necessity. From the point of view of what we now know as human rights, it prescribed, among other things, that

military necessity does not admit of cruelty—that is, the infliction of suffering for the sake of suffering or for revenge . . . the unarmed citizen is to be spared in person, property, and honor as much as the exigencies of war will admit. . . . protection of the inoffensive citizen of the hostile country is the rule . . . The United States acknowledge and protect, in hostile countries occupied by them, religion and morality; strictly private property; the persons of the inhabitants, especially those of women: and the sacredness of domestic relations. Offenses to the contrary shall be rigorously punished. . . . Slavery . . . exists according to municipal or local law only. The law of nature and nations has never acknowledged it. . . . Fugitives escaping from a country in which they were slaves, villains, or serfs, into another country, have, for centuries past, been held free . . . , even though the municipal law of the country in which the slave had taken refuge acknowledged slavery within its own dominions. Therefore, in a war between the United States and a belligerent which admits of slavery, if a person held in bondage by that belligerent be captured by or come . . . under the protection of the military forces of the United States, such person is immediately entitled to the rights and privileges of a freeman. To return such person into slavery would amount to enslaving a free person, and neither the United States nor any officer under their authority can enslave any human being. *Moreover, a person so made free by the law of war is under the shield of the law of nations*, and the former owner or State can have, by the law of postliminy,[17] no belligerent lien or claim of service. All wanton violence committed against persons in the invaded country, . . . all robbery . . . or sacking, even after taking a place by main force, *all rape, wounding, maiming or killing of such inhabitants, are*

[16]*Ibid.*, 150-51. These principles are recognised to this day and are to be found in the Geneva Conventions of 1949 (Wounded and Sick, Wounded, Sick and Shipwrecked, and Prisoners of War, Schindler/Toman, 305, 333, 355 resp. and Protocol I, 551.
[17]The rule whereby a man who has been taken prisoner resumes his former legal status on liberation.

prohibited under the penalty of death . . . Crimes punishable by all penal codes, *such as arson, murder, maiming, assaults, highway robbery, theft, burglary, fraud, forgery, and rape,* if committed by an American soldier in a hostile country against its inhabitants, are not only punishable as at home, but in all cases in which death is not inflicted, the severer punishment shall be preferred.[18]

While the Lieber Code was generally recognised by most nations as being expressive of the law of war and of limits imposed by it, it was not adopted by any other country. Nevertheless, it formed the basis of the Final Protocol of the Brussels Conference called in 1874 by Czar Alexander II, which produced a Project of an International Declaration concerning the Laws and Customs of War.[19] This was primarily concerned with *jus in bello* as between the armies, affirming the customary rule that "the laws of war do not recognize in belligerents an unlimited power in the adoption of means of injuring the enemy", and indicating some of the activities, such as a refusal to give quarter, which were expressly forbidden. It also provided that since "prisoners of war are lawful and disarmed enemies . . . they must be humanely treated". Perhaps more important from the point of view of the preservation of human rights in time of armed conflict, the Project laid down that "family honour and rights, and the lives and property of persons, as well as their religious convictions and their practice, must be respected".

Equally important, perhaps, from the point of view of the development of humanitarian law in armed conflict, is the *Oxford Manual,* adopted by the Institute of International Law in 1880. The *Manual* reaffirmed the rules of the Lieber Code and the Brussels Project as regards the conduct of the belligerent forces *inter sese,* but it also laid down that, for example, spies are entitled to a proper judicial hearing, that

> It is forbidden to maltreat inoffensive populations. Family honour and rights, the lives of individuals, as well as their religious convictions and practice, must be respected. Private property, whether belonging to individuals or corporations, must be respected . . . Offenders against the laws of war are liable to the punishments specified in the penal law.[20]

It is clear that to some extent the *Manual* was reiterating what appeared in the Brussels Project. Although the latter was signed by only fifteen States and was not ratified, its importance lies in the fact that it, together with the *Oxford Manual,* provided the basis on which the Hague Convention of 1899 concerning warfare on land rested. This Convention itself is no longer of significance, for it was revised at the Second Hague Peace Conference of 1907, where a number of Conventions concerning various aspects of warfare, and largely directed to limiting its extremities, were adopted. Of them all, the most significant is Convention IV respecting the Laws and Customs of War on Land,[21] the Regulations annexed to which still constitute the most fundamental postulation of the laws of war that we have, especially with regard to the means and methods of warfare. Many of the provisions which may be considered to be concerned with the maintenance of human rights at large, however, are now to be found in more modern documents.

While developments were taking place concerning the regulation of hostile activities between the armed forces and directed to the protection of non-combatants, more detailed

[18]Promulgated as General Orders No. 100, 24 April 1863. Lieber Instructions, Arts. 16, 22, 37, 42, 43, 44, 47 (Schindler/Toman, 3 ff., emphasis added).
[19]Schindler/Toman, 27.
[20]Arts. 7, 49, 54, 84 (*ibid.* 35 ff.). The Institute is an independent scientific association of the most respected jurists in international law.
[21]*Ibid.,* 57.

regulations were drafted and adopted with regard to the treatment of the wounded and sick, as well as the shipwrecked. Broadly speaking, it was the intention of all such agreements that those who were *hors de combat* by virtue of the conflict and were no longer able to take an active part in hostilities should be treated with humanity and protected from the rigours and dangers inherent in active warfare. Moreover, provision was made for the care of such persons and the immunity from attack of those responsible for their treatment.[22] In addition, the Geneva Conventions of 1864 and 1868 were drawn up in the knowledge that the International Committee of the Red Cross was available to assist in caring for the sick and wounded, with the presence of this neutral body likely to ensure respect for the provisions of the Conventions.[23]

In view of the fundamental importance of the Hague Regulations, it is proper that their significance in regard to human rights be examined. From this point of view, perhaps the most important provision of the Regulations, and one that underlies the whole of the law of armed conflict, is the assertion that belligerents do not possess unlimited discretion as to the means they may employ for injuring the enemy, and the concomitant provisions that they may not harm one who has laid down his arms or "employ arms, projectiles, or material calculated to cause unnecessary suffering". The significance for the individual of this latter provision is modified somewhat, since the concept of "unnecessariness" refers not to the suffering actually endured by the individual, but to suffering which is beyond that essential for the achievement of the purpose for which it has been inflicted, that is to say, suffering which goes beyond the mere disabling of the victim. It is for this reason that the Regulations repeat what had been established in feudal times—that quarter must not be denied to those willing to lay down their arms. Closely related to this ban on unnecssary suffering is Declaration IV, 3, adopted at the 1899 Hague Conference,[24] which forbade any use of the "Dum-Dum Bullet", that is to say, bullets which expand or flatten easily on impact with the human body. From the point of view of placing a person *hors de combat*, an ordinary bullet suffices. One that flattens or expands on impact causes injury gratuitous and unnecessary to this purpose.

It is only in an incidental fashion, and if one interprets the concept in the broadest sense, that one is able to say that, apart from the relations between the armed forces, the Hague Regulations dealt with human rights. (While at the time of the adoption of the Universal Declaration of Human Rights in 1948 concern seemed to centre on the rights of the individual as a person, a point has now been reached where human rights seems to cover every idea that may be likely to make man's life comfortable or full. As a result, one now talks of social, cultural, political, economic and environmental rights, regarding them all as interrelated and constituting the sum total of human rights.) Insofar as cultural rights were concerned, the Hague Regulations required those responsible for conducting sieges or bombardments to take "all necessary steps . . . to spare, as far as possible, buildings dedicated to religion, art, science, or charitable purposes, [and] historic monuments", and imposed a duty upon the besieged "to indicate the presence of such buildings or places by distinctive and visible signs, which [were to] be notified to the enemy beforehand". The rights of civilians were only taken into consideration in the section of the Regulations dealing with military authority over the territory of the enemy. In the first place, an occupant was required to take all steps in his power to preserve

[22]See *supra* note 10, n. 11.
[23]In view of later developments, and the manner in which these Conventions have become, together with the Convention on the protection of civilians, part of the overall humanitarian law of armed conflict, discussion of their present relevance is postponed to a later point in this paper.
[24]Schindler/Toman, 103.

public order and safety. In addition, he was forbidden to force the population to provide information concerning its own nation's army or defences, and he was similarly forbidden to compel the inhabitants to swear allegiance to him. At the same time, "family honour and rights, the lives of persons, and private property, as well as religious convictions and practices" were to be respected, and private property was to be immune from confiscation. In order to preserve the economic stability of the civilian population in occupied territory, the occupying authority was required to assess taxes and other imposts in accordance with the law of the true sovereign, and his right to go beyond this was limited to the needs of the army or of the administration of the territory. The occupant's right to take requisitions was limited and he was only permitted to seize state property. Perhaps among the most important of the human rights of the population to be respected was that of individual liability for wrongdoings, so that "no general penalty, pecuniary or otherwise, [was to] be inflicted upon the population on account of the acts of individuals for which they cannot be regarded as jointly and severally responsible".

Of the other Conventions adopted at the Hague in 1907, perhaps the only one that is important from the point of view of the preservation of human rights is Convention No. IX concerning Bombardment by Naval Forces.[25] The Convention appears to be almost self-contradictory. It clearly declares that "the bombardment by naval forces of undefended ports, towns, villages, dwellings, or buildings is forbidden", but states that if a naval force sought to requisition money or supplies for its immediate use and this requisition was refused, then even an undefended place might be subjected to bombardment. However, such a bombardment would only be lawful if due notice had been given, which would have enabled the civilian population to depart. As with Convention No. IV, this Convention too provides for the protection of cultural establishments. It also provides that whenever a bombardment is decided upon, regardless of the reason, "if the military situation permits, the commander of the attacking force, before commencing the bombardment, must do his utmost to warn the authorities". Not only is it clear that military discretion was regarded as more important than the preservation of human values, but Convention IX, as Convention IV, also contains an all-participation clause. That is to say, not only does the general rule of treaty law apply so that only the parties to the treaty are bound, but the Conventions would not apply in any war if any of the belligerents, however small or insignificant or nominal its participation, were not a party to the particular Convention involved. In such cases, whatever human right is preserved by the Convention, it would only be protected to the extent that a belligerent commander was prepared of his own good grace to recognise its importance.

After the end of the First World War, there was little development in the law of armed conflict that might be considered as being concerned with human rights. In 1922, by the Treaty of Washington,[26] submarines were forbidden from attacking merchant vessels unless the crew and passengers had first been placed in safety, and by the Treaty of London of 1930, it was pointed out that

> For this purpose the ship's boats are not regarded as a place of safety unless the safety of the passengers and crew is assured, in the existing sea and weather conditions, by the proximity of land, or the presence of another vessel which is in a position to take them on board.[27]

[25]*Ibid.*, 723.
[26]*Ibid.*, 789.
[27]*Ibid.*, 793.

This restriction on naval warfare applied equally to surface vessels and submarines, and, if fully observed, would virtually prevent any attack upon a merchant vessel by a submarine. It is perhaps of interest to point out that, in its Judgment, while the Nuremberg Tribunal confirmed the illegality of unrestricted naval warfare directed against merchant shipping,[28] which automatically meant ignoring the right to life of survivors, it nevertheless refused to condemn Dönitz[29] or Raeder[30] for their orders to the German fleet, because of the similar orders issued on behalf of the Allies.[31] Once again, military necessity prevailed over respect for human rights.

The use of aircraft and the introduction of aerial bombardment during the First World War drew attention to lacunae in the law of armed conflict, for all that had come out of the Hague Peace Conferences of 1899 and 1907 was a Declaration[32] forbidding the launching of projectiles from balloons. In 1923, therefore, a Commission of Jurists drew up the Hague Rules of Air Warfare.[33] Even though these were never adopted by States, they are important since the general view was that they were expressive of customary law. From the point of view of human rights, although the use of incendiary or explosive projectiles by or against aircraft was not forbidden, "aerial bombardment for the purpose of terrorizing the civilian population, of destroying or damaging private property not of military character, or of injuring non-combatants [was] prohibited." In fact, only bombardment of military objectives was considered lawful, and if a lawful objective could not be attacked without the indiscriminate bombardment of the civilian population, no aerial bombardment was to take place. On the other hand, "in the immediate neighbourhood of the operations of the land forces, the bombardment of cities, towns, villages, dwellings or buildings is legitimate provided that there exists a reasonable presumption that the military concentration is sufficiently important to justify such bombardment, having regard to the danger thus causd to the civilian population." While it was recognised that the rights of civilians might have to give way to military necessity, the draftsmen of the Rules seem to have been far more concerned about preserving cultural monuments and went so far as to provide for the establishment of security zones around such installations. Perhaps the most significant provision of the Hague Air Rules in relation to human rights was the provision that the occupants of a disabled aircraft seeking to escape by parachute were immune from attack during their descent. (This rule only achieved treaty recognition in 1977, in Article 42 of Protocol I.) Despite the numerous instances of this and the other Rules being disregarded, it should not be overlooked that in both World Wars, and particularly during the First World War, the old rules of chivalry involving some measure of respect for human rights were often observed between the airmen themselves.[34]

Of more significance than the Hague Rules was the Geneva Protocol of 1925,[35] which prohibited the use of asphyxiating, poisonous or other gases and of bacteriological methods of warfare. Although the majority of writers maintained, in view of the large number of States that ratified this, that the use of gas as a weapon was contrary to customary law, the United States refused to accept this view until 1975,[36] and even then reserved the right, as so many others had done, to use it in retaliation. Moreover, the United

---

[28]Cmd. No. 6964, at 108 (1946).
[29]*Ibid.*, 109.
[30]*Ibid.*, 112.
[31]*Ibid.*, 109. In the Far East, Nimitz declared unrestricted U.S. submarine warfare against Japan from the moment hostilities began (*id.*).
[32]Schindler/Toman, 141.
[33]*Ibid.*, 147; see Arts. 22, 24(4).
[34]See *e.g.*, Spaight, *Air Power and War Rights* 20-21, 109-120 (1947).
[35]Schindler/Toman, 109.
[36]*Ibid.*, 119; see, also, Presidential statement 14 I.L.M. 299.

States refused to agree that this type of warfare could not be used if civilians were employed to screen attacks or to control rioting prisoners of war, and even claimed that it remained legal for the purpose of clearing a field of fire. The general view today, however, is that gas is forbidden, certainly against civilians, and almost certainly against troops. While it may be true that at least the use of pre-1945 gases as a weapon was somewhat uncertain in view of weather vagaries, there seems to be little doubt that the ban on this weapon stems from humanitarian rather than militarily utilitarian motives.[37]

Some may argue that the greatest contribution in the treaty field to the preservation of human rights was the Pact of Paris (Kellogg-Briand Pact) adopted in 1928.[38] By this Pact, war as an instrument of national policy was declared foresworn, although there were sufficient reservations from leading powers in connection with their claim to a right of self-defence to render the ban somewhat artificial. Moreover, the definition of self-defence was based on auto-interpretation, so that in some cases it was so extensive as to almost run counter to the Pact. Thus, Great Britain maintained that the Pact did not prevent military action on behalf of British Empire interests in the Mediterranean area, and particularly in the vicinity of the Suez Canal.[39] If one accepts the interpretation of the Pact adopted by the Nuremberg Tribunal,[40] aggressive war was rendered a crime, and since all States are assumed to be law-abiding and purport to be such, a strong blow would have been struck for the human right to life. Reality indicates, however, that this is far from being the case. In fact, even the declaration by the United Nations that aggression is a crime[41] expressly excludes from this ban armed conflicts alleged to be fought on behalf of a national liberation movement seeking to overthrow imperialist, neo-colonialist and racist régimes. Since self-determination has been elevated to the level of the first and principal of all human rights by the two international Covenants in this field,[42] one can only presume that the right to self-government takes precedence over the right to life.

Perhaps the first major indication that there was a new approach to the importance of protecting human rights in time of conflict, at least the rights of the general population as distinct from those of the fighting forces, appeared in the various statements made on behalf of the United Nations during the Second World War. These pronouncements, while often criticised as propounding principles of law *de novo* and *ex post facto*, in many ways suggested a reassertion of the principles which underlay the prosecution of Hagenbach at Breisach and found their legal expression in the London Charter,[43] which set up the International Military Tribunal at Nuremberg. Apart from the condemnation of aggressive war as a crime, this condemned such traditional war crimes as murder, deportation to slave labour and plunder of property. The London Charter also specified crimes against humanity, namely murder, extermination, enslavement, deportation, and other inhuman acts committed against any civilian population, or persecution on political, racial or religious grounds, provided that such crimes were in execution of or in connexion with any crime within the jurisdiction of the Tribunal, regardless of whether they were legal by the domestic law or not. By tying the offence to matters already within the

[37]Re U.S. experiments, *see Globe and Mail* (Toronto), 25 February 1980.
[38]94 *L.N.T.S.* 57.
[39]See e.g., Wheeler-Bennett, *Documents on International Affairs, 1928*, 1-14 (1929); Toynbee, *Survey of International Affairs, 1928*, 10-26, 36-47 (1929).
[40]Cmd. No. 6964, at 38-42 (1946).
[41]113 *I.L.M.* 710 (1974); 14 *ibid.* 588 (1975).
[42]Int'l Covenant on Civil and Political Rights, Int'l Covenant on Economic, Social and Cultural Rights, 1966 (6 *I.L.M.* 368, 360 (1967), Art. 1 in each case).
[43]1945. Schindler/Toman, 823.

jurisdiction of the Tribunal, the Charter tended to reduce the scope of the offence, and in its Judgment the Tribunal virtually ruled that, at least insofar as it was concerned, a crime against humanity would in fact have to amount to a war crime.[44] When, at the instruction of the General Assembly of the United Nations,[45] the International Law Commission drew up its statement of Principles of International Law Recognized in the Charter of the Nuremberg Tribunal and in the Judgment of the Tribunal, it confirmed that crimes against humanity were to all intents and purposes war crimes under another name; for, having listed what it considered to amount to such crimes, the Commission stated that this was the case only "when such acts are done or such persecutions are carried on in execution of or in connexion with any crime against peace or any war crime."[46]

The great United Nations manifestos on human rights, namely, the Universal Declaration[47] and the two international Convenants,[48] may be ignored for our purpose, since they do not deal in any way with the problem of armed conflict, although there is the possibility of derogation in favour of public order and the general welfare in a democratic society,[49] and it might perhaps be argued that these are indeed threatened in time of armed conflict. In the European Convention on Human Rights[50] this becomes much clearer, for by Article 16 derogations are permitted in times of declared public emergency. The European Court of Human Rights in its Judgement in the *Anglo-Irish* case[51] took the line that the decision as to whether a public emergency existed or not was one which should be left to the country concerned, a view which is to be found also in the Canadian War Measures Act.[52]

From the point of view of the modern law of armed conflict, the most important documents to be considered when examining the reality of human rights during war are the 1949 Geneva Conventions[53] and the Protocols supplementary thereto of 1977.[54] The first three of the 1949 Conventions relate almost exclusively to the rights of service personnel, and those who for the main part might be described as camp followers. Broadly speaking, the aim is to ensure the protection of life and limb of those who have been rendered *hors de combat* by wounds, sickness, shipwreck or capture. Apart from provisions concerning the health, welfare, feeding and medical treatment of these individuals, the Conventions also lay down that they must not be subjected to torture, nor made the object of reprisals; that women must be specially respected and protected; that all those in enemy hands must be protected from ignominy, attack or ridicule; and that in the event of there being need to subject such persons to punishment, this may only be done after a proper trial, by a proper judicial tribunal, applying what may be described as those principles of the rule of law which are respected in modern Western societies.[55] In addition, the Conventions provide that no person in enemy hands may be subjected

[44]Cmd. No. 6964, at 65 (1946); see also, Schwelb, "Crimes Against Humanity," 23 *Brit. Y. B. Int'l Law* 178, 205 (1946).
[45]G.A. Res. 95(I), 11 December 1946 (Schindler/Toman, 833).
[46]Schindler/Toman, 835.
[47]G.A. Res. 217A (III), 10 December 1948.
[48]*Supra* note 42.
[49]See, e.g., Green, "Derogation of Human Rights in Emergencies," 16 *Can. Y. B. Int'l Law* 92, 102-104 (1978).
[50]1950. 213 *U.N.T.S.* 222.
[51]1978. 17 *I.L.M.* 680, 707-709 (1978); 58 *I.L.R.* 188.
[52]7 *R.S.C.* 1970, c. W-2.
[53]*Supra* note 16.
[54]Schindler/Toman, Pr. I (int'l armed conflicts) 551, Pr. II (non-int'l armed conflicts) 619.
[55]To specify the relevant articles of the various Conventions involved would almost necessitate a listing of most of the provisions of the documents in question.

to biological experimentation, nor wilfully left without medical attention or exposed to contagion or infection.[56] Moreover, reflecting the new understanding of the universal application of human rights and their protection, it is expressly declared that there may be no priority in treatment other than on medical grounds, and there must be no "adverse distinction founded on sex, race, nationality, religion, political opinions, or any other similar criteria." To a great extent, it may be said that these Conventions merely amount to a codification and reaffirmation of what had long been recognised as law concerning the sick, wounded and shipwrecked, brought up to date in the light of the experience of the Second World War and the war crimes committed between 1939 and 1945, and written in language which reflected the new concern with the international protection of human rights. On one level, each of the Conventions went beyond these traditional ideas. In what has come to be known as Common Article 3, they introduced the minima of humanitarian consideration into non-international conflicts. They made these protective elements applicable not only to combatants who might be captured, and who in a non-international conflict would often, because of the ideological hatreds engendered, require special protection, but extended the protection even to civilians. All persons falling into the hands of the adverse party[57] are to be protected, again without any adverse distinction, against

> violence to life and person, in particular murder of all kinds, mutilation, cruel treatment and torture;
> taking of hostages;
> outrages upon personal dignity, in particular, humiliating and degrading treatment;
> the passing of sentences and the carrying out of executions without previous judgment pronounced by a regularly constituted court affording all the judicial guarantees which are recognized as indispensable by civilized peoples.

In addition, the wounded and sick—even those belonging to rebel formations or, equally, government personnel in rebel hands—are to be collected and cared for.

The greatest departure made by the Geneva Law of 1949 and which may be regarded as a manifesto of human rights for civilians during armed conflict is the Fourth Convention Relative to the Protection of Civilians. During the Second World War, as became particularly clear in the evidence presented at the war crimes trials, those whose human rights were most likely to be trampled upon in wartime were civilians—not those subjected to bombing, but those who found themselves in enemy hands and who, unlike the wounded, sick and shipwrecked, lacked any Protecting Power authorised to supervise and protest the conduct they received. The Convention extends to all those in the hands of a party to a conflict, so that it covers both enemy and neutral subjects; but they are only protected if their home State is a party to the Convention, and neutrals are only protected if their home State is not diplomatically represented with the occupying authority. Failing this, the only protection they may enjoy is that provided by customary law. While the presence of a Protecting Power offers some opportunity for ensuring that the human rights of those protected are indeed respected, of more importance is the substance of the rights which are available for protection. Insofar as medical rights are concerned, the Convention is really little more than an adaptation of the provisions in the other Geneva Conventions relating to the sick and wounded of the armed forces. The Fourth Convention makes it clear, however, that no medical officer attending a

---

[56]For a general discussion of these provisions, see *supra* note 10.
[57]This is the way the Conventions and the Protocols almost invariably refer to the enemy.

civilian, regardless of the nationality of that civilian—and there must be no adverse discrimination by the doctors or the Occupying Power—can be punished for the services he renders.

The purpose of the Fourth Convention was to prevent a repetition of the situation resulting from the Nazi occupation of Europe during the Second World War, when nationals of the occupied territories were subjected by their countries' enemy to every form of indignity and cruelty known to man. The Convention's provisions are intended to ensure that civilian nationals of a party to a conflict falling into the hands of an enemy, whether in the territory of that enemy or in territory occupied by him, preserve their dignity as human beings and, to the extent possible in view of the war situation, retain and enjoy those rights which are normally considered as belonging to human beings, regardless of race, nationality, sex, political belief, or any other special characteristic.

Apart from providing for proper medical care for civilians caught in a war situation, the Fourth Convention details the arrangements that should be made to look after or-phaned children and those who have become separated from their families, including requirements for their education in a fashion that will preserve their cultural and linguistic identity, thus preventing any repetition of the Nazi processes of cultural genocide. Other Nazi practices that were to be forbidden in the future include a ban on both physical and mental coercion against civilians, especially if this is in an effort to secure information from them. Perhaps more important is the provision that the taking of hostages, which had been practised throughout occupied Europe, is forbidden, as is the imposition of collective punishments. For the future, occupying authorities were bound to recognise the principle of individual responsibility, while such inhuman practices as corporal pun-ishment, torture, mutilation and medical experimentation are all forbidden. If these provisions are indeed followed in a future armed conflict, the activities that were asso-ciated with the Nazi concentration camps and the Holocaust will become matters of the past. It must not be overlooked, however, that in many of the conflicts that have taken place since 1949, be they in Indo-China or in Africa, the depth of ideological hatred has been such that while the parties have paid lip-service to the Convention[58] and even acceded thereto, the practice has been far from what the Convention requires.[59]

While the Civilians Convention contains detailed provisions regarding repatriation and internment, and provides for the sustenance of all non-nationals finding themselves in the hands of the occupant, it also forbids the occupant from changing the local law or seeking to punish the inhabitants for what it, the occupant, regards as crimes committed against itself before the occupation commenced. At the same time, it seeks to guarantee that persons tried for offences against the occupant will receive a fair trial in accordance with the rule of law and, to make sure that this is in fact the case, a representative of the Protecting Power is entitled to be present at any trial for an offence carrying a sentence of death or two years' imprisonment or more. A problem arises with regard to the execution of a death sentence. In order to allow full opportunity for appeal and requests for clemency, the Convention provides that no death sentence may be carried out until six months have elapsed, and if it is considered necessary for security reasons to shorten this period, the Protecting Power must be informed and given an opportunity to make representations. There are some countries, however—Pakistan, for example—where to

---

[58]E.g., in January 1980, the Soviet puppet government in Afghanistan announced its respect for the Geneva Conventions and its intention to allow Red Cross representatives to visit political and security prisoners, as well as persons captured during the fighting.

[59]E.g., the reports of refugees from Vietnam and Kampuchea indicate that policies of near genocide are being pursued.

suspend execution of a death sentence is considered to increase the anguish associated with the penalty, and these countries seek to fulfil the appellate processes as speedily as possible. The likelihood of a six months delay is thus unreal in such countries. Here there is a possible conflict between differing views of humanitarian principles.

The war crimes trials after the Second World War indicated that the worst atrocities were not committed at the front or against prisoners, but were rather those which were perpetrated against helpless civilians. Forced labour of enemy civilians brought into Germany proper was responsible for innumerable deaths, with the occupant often transferring his own population as settlers into places that the forced labourers had left. This accomplished a dual purpose: it removed enemy civilians to assist in the German war effort, while at the same time providing for an ultimate take-over or subversion of enemy territory. These practices are now forbidden and rank among those grave breaches of the Convention which render the perpetrators liable to punishment not only by their own country, but by any country into whose hands they fall. Moreover, the parties to the Convention have undertaken to search for any persons accused of such offences and alleged to be in their territory, and, if they themselves are unwilling to institute proceedings against them, they are obligated to hand them over to any party to the Convention which has made out a *prima facie* case. Perhaps the simplest way of indicating the nature of the human rights which the Convention seeks to protect is by reproducing the text of Article 147 defining grave breaches (Article 148 forbids any agreement between parties which would seek to grant absolution in respect of such breaches):

> wilful killing, torture or inhuman treatment, including biological experiments, wilfully causing great suffering or serious injury to body or health, unlawful deportation or transfer or unlawful confinement of a protected person, compelling a protected person to serve in the forces of a hostile Power, or wilfully depriving a protected person of the rights of fair and regular trial prescribed in the present Convention, taking of hostages and extensive destruction and appropriation of property, not justified by military necessity and carried out unlawfully and wantonly.

It would be naive to imagine that the mere postulation of rights in a treaty is in any way a guarantee that these rights will in fact be enjoyed. The Convention purports to achieve compliance by providing for its own dissemination by way of inclusion in military, and hopefully, civilian, programmes of instruction, on the assumption that knowledge of what rights are guaranteed by law will result in a wider observance of those rights.[60] At the same time, it is hoped that the presence of representatives of the International Committee of the Red Cross and of the Protecting Power will work in the same direction, because of the publicity that will result from their reports. Moreover, the Convention even provides for the possibility of joint enquiries being instituted by the parties to examine any alleged violation, so that "once the violation has been established, the parties to the conflict shall put an end to it and shall repress it with the least possible delay."[61] It must be remembered, however, that the Civilians Convention only protects non-nationals in the hands of an Occupying Power. Despite all the talk about the importance of human rights, and despite the knowledge of what happened, for example, to German dissidents and "undesirables" during the Second World War, nationals only enjoy the limited protection afforded them by other international agreements on the preservation of human rights to which their home State may be a party. Such international

---

[60]See e.g., "The Man in the Field and the Maxim *Ignorantia Juris Non Excusat*," ch. II *supra*.
[61]Similar provisions appear in the four Geneva Conventions.

agreements, however, as noted, allow for derogations in time of emergency, and the question whether an emergency warrants derogations tends to be a matter of auto-interpretation.[62]

When public opinion, and later the United Nations, became interested in the preservation of human rights, the emphasis was upon the rights of the individual, so much so that the usual manner to describe such rights was by reference to the rights of man. This emphasis has gradually shifted to the rights of groups and of peoples, with the individual becoming of somewhat less significance. In addition, to some extent the concept of what constitutes human rights has changed. Today, the idea has developed into what might be described as the rights necessary to enable people to enjoy a full and happy life in the widest possible sense. While the law of war has always recognised an immunity for places of worship, as well as for those, like schools, clearly intended for civilian non-combatant use, nowadays the protection of such inanimate objects has been much extended, so as to protect those objects which are considered as essential if the role that culture has to play in this connexion is recognised.

With this end in view, in 1954 the Hague Convention on the Protection of Cultural Property in the Event of Armed Conflict was drawn up. The parties,

> convinced that damage to cultural property belonging to any people whatsoever means damage to the cultural heritage of all mankind, since each people makes its own contribution to the culture of the world [, affirm] that the preservation of the cultural heritage is of great importance for all peoples of the world and that it is important that this heritage should receive international protection.[63]

In spite of this broad statement implying that each people's cultural heritage is part of the cultural heritage of mankind, the definition in the Convention tends to be a little more selective, and it is quite feasible that the properties protected by it are only those whose significance for the world's culture, as distinct from a merely chauvinistic approach, is virtually self-evident:

> movable or immovable property of great importance to the cultural heritage of every people, such as monuments of architecture, art or history, whether religious or secular; archaeological sites; groups of buildings which, as a whole, are of historical or artistic interest; works of art; manuscripts, books and other objects of artistic, historical or archaeological interest; as well as scientific collections and important collections of books or archives or of reproductions of [such] property [, together with] buildings whose main and effective purpose is to preserve or exhibit the movable cultural property [so] defined . . . such as museums, large libraries and depositories of archives, and refuges intended to shelter, in the event of armed conflict, [this] movable cultural property.[64]

In the event of armed conflict, such cultural property is to be marked with an identity emblem defined in the Convention, and is to be immune from attack. Presumably, this mark will have to be large enough to be recognised from a distance, or else a commander wishing to launch an attack will be required to send a scout to ascertain whether the proper mark is affixed or not. As a further step to preventing cultural genocide, a Protocol attached to the Convention forbids the exportation of cultural property from occupied territory and enjoins the parties after the conflict to return any such property wrongly exported.

---

[62]*Supra* note 49.
[63]Schindler/Toman, 661.
[64]*Ibid.*, Art. 1.

Since 1945, most conflicts which have occurred have been of a non-international character, in the sense that two or more sovereign States have not confronted each other, at least not directly, even though they may have fought through surrogates or on behalf of a surrogate. This has meant that the individuals engaged in these conflicts have, for the main part, been unprotected. International law has traditionally regarded conflicts within a territory and only involving a government and its citizens—however the latter might choose to describe themselves—as being within the government's domestic jurisdiction and outside the scope of the law of armed conflict. The only protection offered such nationals by the Geneva Conventions has been through the medium of Article 3 common to all four Conventions, and this article has of course not operated to protect nationals held or captured by their own country in an international conflict. When the International Committee of the Red Cross decided to recommend the updating of the 1949 Conventions, it took the opportunity to try and fill this lacuna. It did so in a way that would appeal to and would reflect the views of the majority of the States in the world, most of which were born either after 1945 or 1949, during the retreat from colonialism and empire.

The first session of the Geneva Conference on Humanitarian Law in Armed Conflict took place in 1974, and the only article that was approved dealt not with what would normally be described as human rights, but with extending human rights into a field which would not normally be protected by international law. The participants found it possible to differentiate among conflicts between governments and their peoples. As the result of Article 1 of Protocol I, international conflicts now include those "in which peoples are fighting against colonial domination and alien occupation and against racist régimes in the exercise of their right of self-determination."[65] This means that at least some wars which would traditionally have been regarded as civil are now within the purview of international law. The participants are therefore protected by the rules of the law of war and enjoy such human rights as are granted to the forces in the field and those *hors de combat* under the Geneva Conventions, and presumably under such customary rules of law as are to be found in the Hague Regulations.

Another important feature of Protocol I is that, for the first time since the Hague Conference of 1907, an attempt has been made to make the methods and means of warfare subject to recognition of the human rights of non-combatants. For those accepting the Protocol, it is now prohibited to employ means and methods of combat which may be expected to cause widespread, long term and severe damage to the natural environment. Attacks which are likely to cause excessive injury to civilians or damage to civilian objects, as compared to the concrete and direct military objective anticipated, are described as indiscriminate and forbidden. In fact, if it becomes apparent that this is likely to be the case, the attack in question must be suspended or cancelled. The starvation of civilians as a method of warfare is forbidden, and objects, such as foodstuffs, livestock, drinking water installations and the like, which are indispensable to the survival of the civilian population are immune from attack. The same immunity attaches to works and installations containing dangerous forces, that is to say, dams, dykes and nuclear electrical generating stations, if the forces released by an attack on such installations are likely to cause severe losses among the civilian population. It is, of course, far too early to project how successful these bans will be should it become apparent to a commander in any future war that observance of the rules will, in his view, unduly hamper the success of his operation. However, by Article 85, the launching of such an attack might well make the commander in question liable to trial for a grave breach of the Protocol.

[65]*Supra* note 2.

As regards the rights more generally considered as being human rights, Protocol I provides special protection for women and children. Surprisingly, in view of its recognition of modern trends, while specifically protecting women from rape, the Protocol makes no special provision for the formal protection of men, though it does forbid any form of indecent assault against protected persons. The Protocol is supplementary to the Geneva Conventions, so that all the protection afforded by them remains in place, and it is made clear that forbidden acts are proscribed for both military and civilian personnel. It is expressly stated that

> The following acts are and shall remain prohibited at any time and in any place whatsoever, whether committed by civilians or by military agents:
> (a) violence to the life, health, or physical or mental well-being of persons, in particular: (i) murder; (ii) torture of all kinds, whether physical or mental; (iii) corporal punishment; and (iv) mutilation;
> (b) outrages upon personal dignity, in particular humiliating and degrading treatment, enforced prostitution and any form of indecent assault;
> (c) the taking of hostages;
> (d) collective punishments; and
> (e) threats to commit any of the foregoing acts.[66]

The Article stipulating this goes on to provide for a proper trial fully in accordance with the "generally recognized principles of regular judicial procedure." As if to make assurance doubly sure, this Article appears under the rubric of fundamental guarantees, as part of the section of the Protocol devoted to the treatment of persons in the power of a party to the conflict, thus indicating that they are valid in one's own, as well as in occupied, territory and applicable to one's own nationals, as well as to those belonging to the adverse party. Moreover, it states *expressis verbis* that these guarantees are additional "to other applicable rules . . . relating to the protection of fundamental human rights during international armed conflict."[67] The general applicability of these rules to all persons in the power of a party to the conflict and at all times is emphasised by the provision that persons accused of war crimes or crimes against humanity are to be tried in accordance with the applicable rules of international law, even if they are accused of grave breaches of the Conventions or the Protocol.

Prisoners of war, the wounded and sick are in the direct power of their captors and are therefore in need of special protection, for they are the most obvious objects of attack. The medical experiments at Auschwitz and the accusations that have been made with regard to the taking of blood from enemy captives for the use of one's own personnel have resulted in a need to spell out in some detail what medical rights now exist. In addition to specifying that medical treatment shall be in accordance with the needs of the patient and generally accepted medical standards, it is, "in particular, prohibited to carry out on . . . persons [who are in the power of the adverse party, or who are interned, detained or otherwise deprived of liberty as a result of an international armed conflict], even with their consent: (a) physical mutilations; (b) medical or scientific experiments; (c) removal of tissue or organs for transplantation", unless required for the benefit of the patient.[68] Blood for transfusion and skin for grafting may be given, so long as they are given voluntarily and without any inducement or coercion, and only for therapeutic

[66]*Ibid.*, Art. 75(2).
[67]*Ibid.*, Art. 72.
[68]*Ibid.*, Art. 11.

purposes, and so long as a proper register of all such donations is maintained and available at all times for inspection by the Protecting Power. In view of the ban on other transplants, it would appear that a captive could not even consent, for example, to a kidney transplant carried out for the benefit of his own brother.

It has already been indicated that, insofar as the law of armed conflict is concerned, much reliance is placed on the threat of condign punishment as the means for ensuring respect for the human rights laid down by that law. Protocol I goes further than the Geneva Conventions and widens the scope of grave breaches that are now liable to such punishment, and concerning which the parties have undertaken to cooperate with each other in connexion with criminal proceedings and in regard to extradition. There is also envisaged, when sufficient ratifications are received and on an optional basis, the establishment of an International Fact-Finding Commission which will be able to look into any facts alleged to be a grave breach and to facilitate, through its good offices, the restoration of an attitude of respect for the Conventions and the Protocol. At various places, the Protocol provides that the breach of certain specific articles amounts to a grave breach, and Article 85 adds a number which are relevant from the point of view of human rights: transfer of parts of its own population by the Occupying Power into occupied territory and deportation or transfer of parts of the population of the occupied territory; unjustifiable delay of repatriation of prisoners of war or civilians; practices of *apartheid* (as understood by the United Nations resolutions on this subject and the Convention declaring *apartheid* a crime against humanity,[69] that is to say, only when committed by the white population of Southern Africa, although the provision also refers to "other inhuman and degrading practices involving outrages upon personal dignity, based on racial discrimination"); intentional attack upon "clearly-recognized historic monuments, works of art or places of worship which constitute the cultural or spiritual heritage of peoples and to which special protection has been given by special arrangement;" and depriving protected persons of the rights of fair and regular trial.

On the face of it, therefore, the Geneva Conventions together with Protocol I would appear to guarantee to those who are *hors de combat*, whatever the reason and whatever their status, those rights which are now considered to be fundamental to all people by virtue of their being human.

Since Protocol I concerns itself only with international armed conflicts, the International Committee of the Red Cross sought, through the medium of Protocol II,[70] to extend some protection to those involved in a civil war not amounting to a war of national liberation for the achievement of self-determination. The provisions of Protocol II are similar to those in Protocol I, although somewhat modified, with regard to objects essential to the sustenance of the civilian population, like foodstuffs; the protection of cultural monuments; the general protection of the civilian population from the effects of conflict; and the treatment of the sick and wounded, although the right of medical persons to treat, for example, the rebels is limited by the provisions of national law. More important from the point of view of the protection of human rights is Part II of the Protocol dealing with humane treatment. It lays down that all who are not actively engaged in the conflict are entitled to respect for their honour, person, convictions and religious practices and must be treated humanely and without any adverse distinction. It is prohibited to order that there shall be no survivors, while murder, mutilation, torture, corporal punishment, violence to the life, health and physical or mental well-being of persons are forbidden.

[69]G.A. Res. 2106 (XX), 21 December 1965. Convention, 1973, 13 *I.L.M.* 50 (1974).
[70]*Supra* note 54.

Also prohibited are collective punishments, the taking of hostages, acts of terrorism, humiliating and degrading treatment, including rape, enforced prostitution and indecent assault, together with slavery and the slave trade. Children must be properly cared for, and none under the age of fifteen should be recruited. Persons who are detained for any reason must be treated with humanity, and their medical and other needs must be guaranteed. In addition, persons charged with offences related to the conflict are entitled to a proper and fair trial, and no one under the age of eighteen, regardless of whether his crime amounted to a war crime, may be executed, nor shall a death sentence be carried out on pregnant women or mothers of small children—a ruling which exceeds that of many national systems which only suspend execution until after confinement. Perhaps most important from the point of view of rehabilitating the society affected by the conflict is the provision that at the end of the hostilities the authorities shall endeavour to proclaim the broadest possible amnesty for those involved in the conflict.

As with the Conventions and Protocol I, respect depends upon those called upon to carry these obligations into effect. In the case of Protocol II there is nothing concerning breaches, supervision or punishment. There is not even an obligation upon the parties to make the contents of the Protocol known to their people so that they may be aware of their obligations and rights should a non-international conflict ensue. All that is provided is that "the Protocol shall be disseminated as widely as possible." The reason for this hiatus is the unwillingness of what may be described as civil-war-prone countries to educate their nationals as to their rights, should those nationals decide to seek to overthrow the régime.

It cannot be denied that in time of conflict one is likely to hear arguments to the effect that military necessity is all-powerful and overrides any considerations which limit military freedom of action. It must be remembered, however, that the laws of war have developed in the light of experience and that, in so far as modern conventions are concerned, military personnel have participated in the drafting. This means that any limitations upon military action have been drawn up with knowledge of what constitutes military necessity. In fact, "all the laws of war . . . are an outcome of a realistic compromise between humanitarian considerations, on the one hand, and the arguments of military necessity, on the other. It is arguable that the Geneva Conventions [of 1949 as extended by the Protocols of 1977] reflect the tilting of the scales in favor of humanitarian consideration, whereas in other instances (principally, the Hague Conventions [of 1907]) there is a more balanced equilibrium between such considerations and the demands of military necessity. . . . [It must be remembered, however, that l]egal norms do not acquire a humanitarian nature simply because they are incorporated in one series of conventions rather than another. Their character must be determined by substance and not by purely technical criteria."[71] Cynics, nevertheless, might rightly assert that there seems little purpose in providing for respect for human rights in the law of armed conflict, for when a conflict erupts, it is because the rule of law has broken down between the parties. There is no point, in such circumstances, in relying on the international agreements relative to human rights for, as we have seen, in emergency these are subject to derogations. However, unlike the international agreements relative to the preservation of human rights in peacetime, the law of armed conflict lays down penal measures for those who offend gravely against human rights. It would appear, therefore, that paradoxical though it may seem, there is more chance for the effective enforcement of human rights and

---

[71]Dinstein, "Human Rights in Armed Conflict: International Humanitarian Law," in Meron, *Human Rights in International Law*, vol. II, 1984, 345, 346.

punishment for offences against them in time of armed conflict than there is during peace.

VI

War Law and the Medical Profession

The regimen I adopt shall be for the benefit of my patients according to my ability and judgment and not for their hurt or any wrong. I will give no deadly drug to any. . . . Whatsoever house I enter, there will I go for the benefit of the sick, refraining from all wrongdoing or corruption. . . . Whatsoever things I see or hear concerning the life of men, and my attendance upon the sick or even apart from them, which ought not to be noised abroad, I will keep silence thereon, counting such things to be as sacred secrets. (Hippocratic Oath)

It was reported in July 1979 that Dr. Luisa Mistrali-Guidotti, a missionary doctor serving in Zimbabwe-Rhodesia, had been shot and killed by government troops while making her rounds in her "familiar" ambulance car near Mtoko. She had previously been threatened with arrest for attending to wounded guerrillas.[1] Except for the fact that she had been killed, rather than taken prisoner and mistreated or tortured, her case had much in common with that of Dr. Sheila Cassidy, who in 1976 had been imprisoned and tortured for her services to Allende supporters during the Chilean revolution. Incidents such as these serve to emphasize that the medical profession is as much prone to the risks of armed conflict as is everybody else. But they also draw attention to the question whether that profession is entitled to any special rights, or subject to any special obligations, over and above those applicable to others.

In biblical times there was little need to provide for the rights of medical personnel, for wars waged then at the instruction of God were frequently accompanied by the complete extermination of the enemy, so that a medical service, other than for the care of the Israelites, would have been redundant.[2] The situation was not very different in ancient Greece and Rome, for, generally speaking, the "barbarians" were treated as

---

[1] *The Citizen* (Ottawa), July 14, 1979.
[2] See, e.g., Exodus 32: 27-28; Numbers 21: 3, 35; 31: 7, 17; Deuteronomy 2: 34; 3: 16; 13: 15; Joshua 6: 21.

beyond any protection. During the Crusades, religious hatreds tended to lead to the complete destruction of the enemy, although by the twelfth century the Knights of the Order of St. John of Jerusalem had established a hospital in Jerusalem for the care of the sick as well as for injured Crusaders, and by the sixteenth century they had established themselves as the Sovereign Order of Malta and are now described as members of the Sovereign and Military Order of the Hospitallers St. John of Jerusalem, called the Order of Malta, largely devoted to the care of the sick and wounded. In fact, members of the Order were known as Knights Hospitallers.

By the fourteenth century, writers were beginning to assert that doctors, who were often in clerical orders, enjoyed a special immunity, and Bartolus maintained that their persons might not be seized, while a century later Belli in his *De Re Militari et Bello Tractatus*[3] used this as a basis for his own comments on the role of doctors during war: "persons of doctors may not be seized, and they may not be haled to court or otherwise harassed; consequently attendants may not search them for carrying of arms." While other classical writers did not, for the main part, consider it necessary to comment upon the role of doctors, by the time of Louis XIV careful attention was being given to the need to provide for the care of the wounded, and by a decree of 1708 there was established a permanent medical service "à la suite des armées et dans les places de guerre."[4] Prior to this, any medical services provided for the wounded depended upon the predilections of individual commanders, many of whom had their own personal physicians attached to their staffs. This is perhaps not surprising in view of the fact that commanders were invariably responsible for raising their own units, for their sustenance and their care. Even before Louis XIV had established his medical service, the regiments of Gustavus Adolphus had four surgeons, while the Armada was accompanied by medical personnel, although these tended their own. At this time, the sixteenth century, there was still some sense of chivalry among the military commanders of Europe, and the great French surgeon Ambroise Paré was summoned to Metz by François de Guise during the seige of 1552-53 "to succour the abandoned wounded soldiers of the enemy and to make arrangements for their transport back to their army."[5] A century later the first tentative arrangements were being made for the reciprocal care of wounded in the field, and

in 1679 a convention was signed between the Elector of Brandenburg, for the league of Augsburg, and the Count of Asfield, who commanded the French forces. It provided for a mutual respect towards both hospitals and wounded. . . . [The] convention made, in June 1743, between Lord Stair on behalf of the Pragmatic army and the Marshal Noailles for the French during the Dettingen campaign bound both sides to treat hospitals and wounded with consideration. Noailles, when he felt that his operations might cause alarm to the inmates of the hospitals at Techenheim, went so far as to send word that they should rest tranquil as they would not be disturbed. A fuller, and more highly developed, type of agreement was that signed at L'Ecluse in 1759 by the Marshal de Brail, who commanded the French, and Major-General Conway, the British general officer commanding. The hospital staff, chaplains, doctors, surgeons and apothecaries were not . . . to be taken prisoners; and, if they should happen to be apprehended within the lines of the enemy, they were to be sent back immediately. The wounded of the enemy who should fall into the hands of their opponents were to be cared for, and their food and medicines should in due course be paid for. They were not to be made prisoner and might stay in hospital safely under guard. Surgeons and servants might be sent to them under the general's passports. Finally, on their discharge, they were

[3]1563, Part VII, Ch. III, 34 (Carnegie tr., 1936, 187).
[4]Butler and Maccoby, *The Development of International Law*, 134 (1928).
[5]*Ibid.*, 187, note 28.

themselves to travel under the same authority and were to travel by the shortest route.[6]

During the revolutionary wars, attempts were made to protect the hospitals and virtually to insulate them from military operations. Thus, at the initiative of the French military surgeon Percy, General Moreau proposed to the Austrian commander, Krug, that

> the roads leading to hospitals [should] be marked by special signs which would indicate the presence of wounded in the vicinity. Troops were to avoid these roads wherever possible or in passing along them were to abstain from disturbing noises. Hospitals were to remain the property of the belligerent even after he had evacuated the country. The belligerent in occupation was, under proper security, to furnish or requisition materials for the hospitals. Those soldiers who recovered were to be allowed to rejoin their former units. When it was decided to evacuate the entire hospital, the occupying belligerent was to provide an escort for the convoy of the waggons.[7]

These proposals were, however, rejected by the Austrians, perhaps a decision that should have been expected in view of the ideological character of the conflict.

While there can be no doubt that in the seventeenth and eighteenth centuries there was still some sense of philanthropy which is perhaps not always visible today, there was equally an appreciation that the presence of the enemy's wounded was both an embarrassment and expensive. As a result, commanders were relatively liberal in making arrangements for the evacuation of the wounded, accompanied by medical personnel when possible. "Philanthropy forbade the abandonment of the enemy wounded, but good policy required that the main burden of their nursing should still be thrown on the enemy."[8] These philanthropic and economic considerations would both be served if there was some international convention dealing with the matter, so that it would no longer be necessary to rely on *ad hoc* bilateral arrangements between commanders in the field. In 1764, "Chamousset . . . referred with regret to the thousands of lives which had been sacrificed when, as a result of military operations, the forced and hurried evacuation of hospitals had become necessary in order to save the wounded from falling into the enemy's hands. Péyrilhe in 1780 proposed international recognition of the principle that the wounded should not be made prisoners of war and should not enter into the balance of exchanges."[9] These endeavours were given a fillip by the experiences of Florence Nightingale, who had taken her nurses to the Crimea in 1854, and particularly by the reactions of Henri Dunant, who had been present at the Battle of Solferino in northern Italy in 1859, and whose *Souvenir de Solferino*, published in 1862, was the immediate occasion for the Swiss interest which led to the establishment of the Red Cross movement only a year later. By this time, in fact, it seems to have been generally accepted that the property of hospitals and hospitals themselves could not be seized during war, while officers of the enemy's medical staff, his apothecaries, nurses, and servants were not to be treated as prisoners of war "unless the commander has reasons to retain them," and all captured wounded enemy personnel were considered to be entitled to medical treatment according to the ability of the medical staff.[10] If enemy medical personnel were

---

[6]*Ibid.*, 149-50.
[7]*Ibid.*, 150.
[8]*Ibid.*
[9]*Ibid.*, 150-51.
[10]Lieber Code, promulgated by President Lincoln as General Orders No. 100, April 24, 1863 (Schindler/Toman, 3).

held, they were entitled to stay with their captured comrades and to treat them. Otherwise, they were entitled to receive medical aid from their captors.

The status of the medical profession during war has never been looked at independently, but has always been considered from a functional point of view, that is to say in regard to the need to protect the wounded. Any rights they have received have, therefore, been granted not to doctors as individuals, but as medical personnel and only in that capacity. A doctor who fulfils some other function, even though he be embodied in the armed forces as a medical practitioner, will be looked at from the point of view of his office and not his titular role. Thus, when Lt. Col. Logandan of the Indian Medical Service, who became Governor of the "liberated" Andaman and Nicobar Islands under Japanese supervision during World War II, surrendered to the British authorities, he was held pending investigation for waging war against the Crown, which would not have been the case had he served the Indian National Army as a medical officer.[11] Similarly, in view of the political role he played, Dr. Che Guevara would at no time have been able to claim any of the rights normally attached to a physician during armed conflict.

As an immediate consequence of Dunant's *Solferino* pamphlet, an international conference was organized in Geneva in 1863[12] which resolved to establish national committees to assist the Army Medical Services in time of war and if the need should arise, and to use as their special emblem the Swiss colours reversed, that is to say a red cross on a white background, with an International Committee of the Red Cross situated at Geneva with the task of co-ordinating the activities of the national committees. The Conference was more concerned with the role of the proposed national committees than with the rights or status of medical personnel. It did, however, recommend that "in time of war the belligerents should proclaim the neutrality of ambulances and military hospitals, and that neutrality should likewise be recognized, fully and absolutely, in respect of official medical personnel, voluntary medical personnel, inhabitants of the country who go to the relief of the wounded, and the wounded themselves."

Following this initiative and at the urging of the Geneva Committee, the Swiss government called an international conference in Geneva in 1864, from which there came the first Convention for the Amelioration of the Wounded in Armies in the Field.[13] The majority of the substantive articles of this Convention related to the medical services and their equipment:

> Article 1. Ambulances and military hospitals shall be recognized as neutral, and as such, protected and respected by the belligerents as long as they accommodate wounded and sick.
> Neutrality shall end if the said ambulances or hospitals should be held by a military force. [This, of necessity, must be understood to mean if the establishment is taken over by the military or used for its non-medical purposes.]
> Article 2. Hospital and ambulance personnel, including the quartermaster's staff, the medical, administrative and transport services, and the chaplains, shall have the benefit of the same neutrality when on duty, and while there remain any wounded to be brought in or assisted.
> Article 3. The persons designated in the preceding Article may, even after enemy occupation, continue to discharge their function in the hospital or ambulance with which they serve, or may withdraw to rejoin the units to which they belong.
> When in these circumstances they cease from their functions, such persons shall be delivered to the enemy outposts by the occupying forces.

[11]See Green, "The Indian National Army Trials," 11 *Mod. Law Rev.* 47 (1948).
[12]Schindler/Toman, 209.
[13]*Ibid.*, 213.

Article 4. The material of military hospitals being subject to the laws of war, the persons attached to such hospitals may take with them, on withdrawing, only the articles which are their personal property.

Ambulances, on the contrary, under similar circumstances, shall retain their equipment.

Article 5. Inhabitants of the country who bring help to the wounded shall be respected and shall remain free. Generals of the belligerent Powers shall make it their duty to notify the inhabitants of the appeal made to their humanity, and of the neutrality which humane conduct will confer.

The presence of any wounded combatant receiving shelter and care in a house shall ensure its protection. An inhabitant who has given shelter to the wounded shall be exempted from billeting and from a portion of such war contributions as may be levied.

Article 6. Wounded or sick combatants, to whatever nationality they may belong, shall be collected and cared for. . . .

What is of particular interest in these articles is that, while hospitals were considered to be subject to the laws of war and so liable to remain in enemy hands as equipped establishments, the medical service was treated as a body of privileged civilians. Not only were they not to be treated as prisoners, but, unlike the rest of the civilian population, in the event of enemy occupation they were to be allowed to return to their own units. The combined effect of Articles 5 and 6 is to make clear, on the one hand, that the benefits of the Convention were to be afforded to all wounded on a basis of strict impartiality, so that even enemy personnel would be protected. Moreover, it is equally clear that any civilian assisting a wounded soldier, albeit an enemy, could not be regarded as in breach of the law, and if he himself were an enemy subject he would be entitled to be treated as if he were a neutral, in the sense that he would become immune from any special burdens, such as an obligation to billet troops, that might fall upon the rest of the population. Clearly, what is provided for ordinary private civilians would be equally true for local civilian doctors. If the hostilities during which Doctors Mistrali-Guidotti and Cassidy were fulfilling their professional obligations had been international conflicts at the end of the nineteenth century, they would have been protected and immune from any sort of ill treatment, for both Chile and Great Britain, of which Rhodesia in 1979 was still legally a colony, were parties to the 1864 Convention.

The 1864 Convention only applied to warfare on land and it was soon realized that some similar protection should be made available in the event of maritime warfare. A further conference was convened in Geneva in 1868 which drafted additional articles for this purpose[14] and extended protection to ships conveying the wounded to hospital ships, while the medical staff of the latter were to receive the same immunity as their confrères in land warfare. In order to ensure the protection of hospital ships, these were to fly, together with their national flag, the white flag with the red cross, and were to be certified as such by their own naval authority and under whose control they would be. Unfortunately, none of the participants at the conference ratified this Convention, although the belligerents in both the Franco-German War of 1870-71 and the Spanish-American War of 1898 undertook to observe its provisions. Almost immediately after the latter war, the First Hague Peace Conference met at The Hague in 1899, and adopted a convention,[15] which soon received over forty ratifications, for the adaptation to maritime warfare of the principles of the 1864 Geneva Convention. Before looking at the substance of this convention, it is worth mentioning that this is the only medical convention which was

[14]*Ibid.*, 217.
[15]Convention III (*ibid.*, 221).

drawn up as a result of a conference not convened by the Swiss Federal Government in response to the pressures of the International Committee of the Red Cross.

For the main part the Convention was concerned with hospital ships, both those belonging to the state as well as those operating on behalf of private groups of recognized relief societies. Military hospital ships, defined as those "constructed or assigned by States specially and solely for the purpose of assisting the wounded, sick or shipwrecked, and the names of which shall have been communicated to the belligerent Powers at the beginning or during the course of hostilities, and in any case before they are employed, shall be respected and cannot be captured while hostilities last. . . ."[16] Insofar as private ships were made available for this purpose, they were likewise "to be respected and exempt from capture," so long as they were certified as such and the hostile power was informed. All military hospital ships were to be painted white, with a horizontal green band about a metre and a half in breadth, while in the case of private hospital ships the band was to be red.

The Convention provided that these ships were to afford relief to the wounded, sick, and shipwrecked of belligerents, regardless of nationality, thus confirming the general liability and right of the medical profession to provide their services to all, including the enemy. However, certain military considerations were recognized as important. While governments undertook not to use these ships for any military purpose, the ships

> must not in any way hamper the movements of the combatants. During and after an engagement they will act at their own risk and peril. The belligerents will have the right to control and visit them; they can refuse to help them, order them off, make them take a certain course, and put a commissioner on board; they can even detain them, if important circumstances require it.
>
> As far as possible the belligerents shall inscribe in the sailing papers of the hospital ships the orders they give them.[17]

Whatever rights these provisions confer upon belligerents, including the right to visit and search in order to ascertain that they are in fact what they purport to be, and including confirmation of the fact that what might be described as the principle *volenti non fit injuria*[18] was to apply, in the sense that, if they entered a battle area, they assumed the risks of all within the area, it remains clear that hospital ships were immune from intentional attack, and outside a battle area were to be fully respected.

Insofar as the personnel staffing hospital ships were concerned, the Convention was silent, since, the ships being immune from capture or attack, their personnel were equally outside the range of hostilities. However, the Convention recognized that medical personnel might well be carried on board other vessels, which might be legitimate targets of maritime warfare. As to these,

> the religious, medical or hospital staff of any captured ship is inviolable, and its members cannot be made prisoners of war. On leaving the ship they take with them the objects and surgical instruments which are their own private property.
>
> The staff shall continue to discharge its duties while necessary, and can afterwards leave when the commander-in-chief considers it possible.[19]

---

[16]Art. 1.
[17]Art. 4.
[18]"Intention/consent removes the injury."
[19]Art. 7.

As if to affirm that medical services are part of the concept of humanity and an essential feature of every nation's obligation to observe humanitarian principles, it states that "the belligerents must guarantee to the [medical] staff [of such vessels] that has fallen into their hands the enjoyment of their salaries intact," emphasizing the general interest of all in the practice of medical care on behalf of the wounded and sick. As a result "sailors and soldiers who are taken on board when sick or wounded, to whatever nation they belong, shall be protected and looked after by the captors." These, however, unlike their medical colleagues, become prisoners of war.

For some years after 1864, the International Committee of the Red Cross and the International Conferences of the Red Cross Societies had been investigating the deficiencies of the earlier Convention on the Amelioration of the Condition of the Wounded and Sick in the Field, a review which had been responsible for the Hague Convention on Maritime War just referred to. Now the Red Cross felt it was time to bring that earlier convention up to date and the Swiss government convened a conference for the purpose in 1906 in Geneva. The provisions of the resulting convention[20] are much more detailed with regard to medical establishments, personnel, and matériel than anything that had been agreed earlier and to some extent may be said to reflect more realistically some of the problems that the medical profession would face under combat conditions, including the possibility that their position might be abused even by their own authorities. Thus,

Article 6. Mobile sanitary formations [i.e., those which are intended to accompany armies in the field] and the fixed establishments belonging to the sanitary service shall be protected and respected by belligerents.

Article 7. The protection due to sanitary formations and establishments ceases if they are used to commit acts injurious to the enemy.

Article 8. A sanitary formation or establishment shall not be deprived of the protection accorded by Article 6 by the fact:

1. That the personnel of a formation or establishment is armed and uses its arms in self-defence or in defence of its sick and wounded.

2. That in the absence of armed hospital attendants, the formation is guarded by an armed detachment or by sentinels acting under competent orders.

3. That arms or cartridges, taken from the wounded and not yet turned over to the proper authorities, are found in the formation or establishment.

This is the first treaty acknowledgement that the sick or wounded might in fact be in possession of arms and ammunition when first brought into the care of a medical unit. The provision seeks to ensure that no belligerent will have any ground for ignoring the protection afforded to such persons and to the medical establishments merely by virtue of the presence of such weaponry. At the same time, the provision recognizes that it may be necessary for the medical personnel in whose care the sick and wounded are to defend these persons by military means. So long as the weapons carried by medical personnel, or by guards attached to the hospitals, are used solely to protect such personnel or their patients, the presence of the armour does not invalidate the protection of the personnel and the hospital. However, such arms may not be used for any offensive purpose, and this is indicated by Article 7, even though that article only envisages the abuse of the formations and establishments and makes no reference to personnel.

It is true that Article 9, which introduces the chapter of the Convention on the rights of personnel, states that "the personnel charged exclusively with the removal, transportation, and treatment of the sick and wounded, as well as with the administration of

[20]Schindler/Toman, 235.

sanitary formations and establishments, and the chaplains attached to armies, shall be respected and protected under all circumstances. If they fall into the hands of the enemy they shall not be considered as prisoners of war," and the same provisions apply to the guards attached to such formations. This protection, however, can only subsist so long as the personnel in question are exclusively functioning in a medical or paramedical role. The Convention makes similar provision for the protection of the personnel of volunteer aid societies, be they belligerent or neutral in nationality. By Article 12 the personnel specified in Article 9 as well as those belonging to the relief societies "will continue in the exercise of their functions, under the direction of the enemy, after they have fallen into his power. When their assistance is no longer indispensable they will be sent back to their army or country, within such period and by such route as may accord with military necessity. They will carry with them such effects, instruments, arms, and horses as are their private property."

Here, once again, members of the medical profession are afforded rights which are not granted to any other member of the forces. Normally, it makes no difference whether the arms or mode of transport found in the possession of a captured soldier are his own personal property, or have been supplied by his government. They are all liable to seizure by the authorities of the capturing force. Since war is no longer a personal issue between the individual combatants, and since prisoners are in the care of the enemy authorities and not the soldier capturing them, his possessions too, to the extent that they may be taken from him, are taken over by that authority and not by his captor.[21] Moreover, so long as the medical personnel referred to in the Convention remain in the power of the enemy they are to receive "the same pay and allowances to which persons of the same grade in [their] own army are entitled." By the Hague Regulations prisoners are only paid in this latter form "for work of a similar kind done by soldiers of the national army."

The provisions in the Convention with regard to matériel are equally detailed, but distinctions are drawn between mobile formations and fixed establishments. If the former fall into enemy hands, they are to retain their matériel with their means of transportation and conducting personnel. But "competent military authority shall have the right to employ it in caring for sick and the wounded," and clearly any personnel so employed would be free from any criminal prosecution by their own authorities in respect of such activities. On the return of the personnel to their own lines, they are, to the extent that it is militarily possible, to be accompanied by their matériel. With regard to fixed establishments, however, buildings and matériel remain subject to the laws of war, "but cannot be diverted from their use so long as they are necessary for the sick and wounded." On the other hand, commanders engaged in operations may make use of them in the event of "important military necessity," so long as, "before such use, the sick and wounded who are in them have been provided for." As to the aid societies, their matériel is to be regarded as private property to be respected under all circumstances, although it is subject to the normal rules of belligerent requisition as recognized by the laws and usages of war.[22]

A new departure in the Convention is the recognition of the right to organize convoys to evacuate the sick and wounded, and these are to be treated as if they were mobile sanitary formations. However, Article 17 provides:

[21]Hague Regulations, Art. 4 (Annex to Hague Convention IV respecting the Laws and Customs of War on Land, 1907, *ibid.*, 57).
[22]Requisitions are only permitted for the necessities of the army, may only be demanded on the authority of the commander, and as far as possible must be paid for in ready money, or else a receipt must be given and payment made as soon as possible: *ibid.*, Art. 52.

. . . 1. A belligerent intercepting a convoy may, if required by military necessity, break up such a convoy, charging himself with the sick and wounded whom it contains.

2. In this case the obligation to return the sanitary personnel . . . shall be extended to include the entire military personnel employed, under competent orders, in the transportation and protection of the convoy. The obligation to return the sanitary matériel . . . shall apply to railway trains and vessels intended for interior navigation which have been specifically equipped for evacuation purposes, as well as to the ordinary vehicles, trains, and vessels belonging to the sanitary services. Military vehicles, with their teams [of horses], other than those belonging to the sanitary service, may be captured. . . .

It would appear from this that immunity would not extend to an ordinary railway train or vessel intended for interior navigation unless it had been specially equipped for the purpose of evacuating the sick and wounded. On the other hand, there is nothing to prevent a train or vessel so equipped having the equipment removed and being returned to normal service, even though this might involve the transport of troops or munitions.

Finally, the Convention provided that the Red Cross emblem should be affixed to all personnel, establishments, and matériel used for medical purposes, while the flag "can only be displayed over the sanitary formations and establishments which the convention provides shall be respected, and with the consent of the military authorities. It shall be accompanied by the national flag of the belligerent to whose service the formation or establishment is attached. Sanitary formations which have fallen into the power of the enemy, however, shall fly no other flag than that of the Red Cross so long as they continue in that situation." Equally important was the inclusion of a provision which, in fact, seems to be as much honoured in the breach as in the observance. By Article 23, "the emblem of the red cross on a white ground and the words Red Cross or Geneva Cross may only be used, *whether in time of peace or war*, to protect or designate sanitary formations and establishments, the personnel and matériel protected by the Convention."[23]

Even though the Convention was intended to promote and secure respect for humanitarian principles in time of war, the parties were unable or unwilling to depart from the traditional approach to treaty law, namely that an agreement was only binding upon the parties thereto. In the normal way this would mean that its provisions would not apply between a party and a non-party. In the practice of states at that time, however, the principle was interpreted much more widely in what was known as the general participation concept. By Article 24 the Convention is only binding upon the contracting states in a war between two or more of them. It is not, therefore, binding in any way in the event of a civil war. Moreover, if any of the belligerents in a given war should not be a party to the Convention, then the principles of the Convention would not be binding upon any of them, even though the majority were in fact parties. In practice, insofar as this Convention is concerned, the restriction has not normally been so interpreted. There is a tendency to regard its basic principles as if they were part of customary law.

At the second Hague Peace Conference held the following year, 1907, the powers seemed to have overcome their hesitancies of 1868, and were now willing to accept Convention X for the Adaptation to Maritime Warfare of the Principles of the Geneva Convention of 1906.[24] At the same time, this Convention brought up to date the provisions

---

[23]As will be seen below, the Geneva Conventions of 1929 and 1949 extended the permitted use of the emblem (italics added).
[24]Schindler/Toman, 245.

that were adopted at the 1899 Hague Conference. The first new feature in the 1907 Convention is the recognition of the need to ensure that hospital ships be protected at night as well as by day, and this of course depends on their being readily identifiable. It is therefore provided that if they "wish to ensure by night the freedom from interference to which they are entitled, [they] must, subject to the assent of the belligerent they are accompanying, take the necessary measures to render their special painting sufficiently plain." The parties to the Convention were thus affirming their view that humanitarian principles give way to military necessity. It is unlikely, in practice, that the commander of any war fleet will authorize the hospital ships accompanying him to illuminate themselves at night, thus disclosing his dispositions and strength to any enemy prowler. The parties also seemed to believe that maritime warfare was still, to some extent at least, fought in accordance with earlier techniques. It is unlikely that there will be many hand-to-hand engagements in modern maritime warfare.[25] Nevertheless, the Convention states that "in the case of a fight on board a warship, the sick wards shall be respected and spared as far as possible. The said sick wards and the matériel belonging to them remain subject to the laws of war; they cannot, however, be used for any purpose other than that for which they were originally intended, so long as they are required for the sick and wounded. . . ." But if the capturing commander requires them for other purposes, if the military situation so requires, he may so use them, provided the wounded and sick are properly provided for. The new Convention recognizes that order must be maintained even on board a hospital ship and even, as on land, for defence purposes. In addition, technology had made some progress and this too had to be taken into consideration. As a result, while hospital ships and sick wards lose their protection if used to injure the enemy, "the staff of the said ships and sick wards being armed for maintaining order and for defending the sick and wounded, and the presence of wireless telegraphy on board,[26] is not a sufficient reason for withdrawing protection."

This provision is slightly different from that embodied in the Geneva Convention concerning warfare on land. It will be recalled that the latter permits the arming of medical personnel in self-defence, as well as for the protection of the wounded and sick. Hague Convention X ignores the former. While the Convention recognizes the immunity of hospital ships and sick bays, this immunity is not complete and does not extend fully to the wounded and sick. By Article 12, "any warship belonging to a belligerent may demand that sick, wounded or shipwrecked men on board military hospital ships, hospital ships belonging to relief societies or to private individuals, merchant ships, yachts, or boats, whatever their nationality, should be handed over," and the armed personnel on board would be forbidden from using the weapons that are allowed to them for the defence of their charges in such circumstances. These weapons may only be used if the lives of their charges are endangered, while, by Article 14, "the shipwrecked, wounded or sick of one of the belligerents who fall into the power of the other belligerent are prisoners of war," and accordingly protected in the same way as other prisoners.

As if to emphasize that there is a general responsibility with regard to the safeguarding of the wounded and sick regardless of nationality and regardless of belligerent status, the Convention provides that "after every engagement, the two belligerents, so far as military interests permit, shall take steps to look for the shipwrecked, sick and wounded, and to protect them . . . against pillage and ill-treatment." It should be remembered that this Convention was drawn up before the development of submarine warfare, when the

---

[25]The boarding in Norwegian waters during World War II of the German auxiliary *Altmark* by H.M.S. *Cossack* to release imprisoned merchant seamen was a unique occurrence.
[26]See, however, the case of *The Ophelia*, [1915] p. 129; [1916] 2 A.C. 206.

possibility of picking up survivors is somewhat limited, while in modern conditions, with the development of aerial activity, frequently in response to radio signals, it is unlikely that a belligerent vessel will in fact be able to stay in the vicinity for this purpose. However, as was shown during World War II by the *Graf Spee*, if the attacks are against individual vessels, rather than during an engagement between the belligerents, and depending upon the attitude of the commander, this may in fact happen.

The importance of the Hague and Geneva Conventions here discussed lies in the fact that they were operative during World War I, with both the Central and the Allied and Associated Powers making accusations that the Conventions were being disregarded. Among the chief complaints were those relating to aerial attack upon hospitals, involving, it was maintained, the killing of doctors and nursing staff, as well as the sick and wounded or personnel belonging to both sides. The Allied Powers alleged that the Germans carried out the majority of their bombing attacks by night with the express intention of failing to see the protective emblems carried by hospitals, and it was alleged that they frequently made reconnaissance flights by day in order to facilitate these night attacks. On June 24, 1918 a Canadian hospital behind the British front and occupied as such for some eighteen months was bombed, with doctors, nurses, and patients killed. The hospital roofs bore large Red Cross signs and the building had never been used for military purposes. Moreover, it had been flown over many times during daylight raids.[27] Similarly, on July 15, the United States hospital at Jouy, situated some twenty miles behind the lines in an isolated château, three kilometres from the nearest railway, marked by the recognized signs on its roof, and with a 100-foot cross cut into its lawns, suffered both low and high level attacks on a moonlit night when its indicia must have been clearly visible.[28]

Insofar as the protection of hospitals is concerned, the leading commentator on international law during World War I has said of the Convention that it "merely imposes upon the belligerents an obligation to respect them so far as the necessities of the military situation allow. Each commander must weigh, on the one hand, those necessities and, on the other hand, the imperative demands of suffering humanity and so far as possible spare the places in which the wounded are gathered and the persons who are engaged in caring for them."[29] There can be no doubt that both mistakes and abuses are possible, and this is perhaps particularly true insofar as maritime warfare is concerned, with attacks directed against hospital ships, although if they are properly marked it might be expected that they would be boarded and inspected, in the case of suspected abuse, rather than subjected to attack. This is what occurred with the German vessel *Ophelia*,[30] which had been properly marked and whose certification had been notified to the Allied Powers. This vessel had been boarded and seized by the British and brought in for condemnation as prize. Although fitted as a hospital ship, there was no evidence that she had ever been used for transporting the sick or wounded, her records had been destroyed at the moment of boarding, so there was no evidence of the signals she had been sending, she was equipped, as she was entitled to be, with signalling apparatus, but there was evidence that she had been sending coded messages, while an excess of signalling apparatus and appliances, including 1,260 Verey light signals, was found on board. It was held by the English prize court, and confirmed by the Privy Council on appeal, that she had lost whatever protection and immunity to which she might ever have been entitled.

A large number of hospital ships was sunk, particularly by the Germans and their

[27]*New York Times*, June 26, 1918.
[28]*Ibid.*, July 17, 18, 19, 1918.
[29]Garner, *International Law and the World War*, vol. 1, at 504 (1920).
[30][1915] P. 129; [1916] 2 A.C. 206.

allies, although it has been questioned by at least one authority on the Allied side whether those attacked from the air were deliberate, and were not rather the result of bad sightings, incorrect markings, and sheer propaganda.[31] Be this as it may, in January 1917 the Germans had declared certain sea areas between France and England and in the Mediterranean closed to all allied shipping, alleging that the red cross had been wrongly used and that, as a result, hospital ships found in those areas would be sunk. It will be recalled that specified routes for the use of such ships may be prescribed and that while they may be detained they may on no account be sunk. However, after this announcement, whatever may have been true in the case of aerial attacks, the Germans did in fact sink hospital ships by mine and torpedo. This led to an official protest by the International Committee of the Red Cross:

> in torpedoing ships it [Germany] is not attacking combatants but defenceless beings, wounded or mutilated in war, and women who are devoting themselves to the work of relief and charity. Every hospital ship is provided with the external signs prescribed by conventions, the use of which has been regularly notified to the belligerents, and should be respected by belligerents.[32]

Part of the German defence for attacks against hospital ships lay in the argument that the Allies were in the habit of putting ships on the list of hospital vessels, then taking them off again, and subsequently restoring them to the lists. They also maintained that an unnecessary number had been so registered at the time of the Gallipoli operations. The British reply was to the effect that this practice was not forbidden by the Hague Convention, and that the changes in character were "due to the alteration in the requirements for various classes of tonnage caused by the sinking of ships by submarines, and to changes in the military situation,"[33] It may be questioned whether this is in fact a satisfactory explanation or whether the complaining belligerent has only itself to blame in such circumstances. However, to this it may be answered that, even if the practice is abused, until the attacker ascertains by boarding that the vessel in question is not being used as a hospital ship as it purports to be, it must remain immune from attack. The exchanges between Britain and Germany in this matter resulted in a British decision to cease marking hospital ships with the red cross and to inform Germany that, despite this, German wounded would still be transported in the same vessels as British wounded. To this Germany replied by holding allied prisoners in exposed military objectives,[34] a so-called prophylactic reprisal.

The German authorities also had occasion to protest that the Allied powers were interfering with the supply of hospital matériel directed to enemy countries. Generally speaking, such supplies are not regarded as contraband and liable to seizure, while the allied declaration of blockade excluded hospital supplies, with the exception of rubber goods, including surgical gloves, blankets which could of course be diverted for use by the forces, tubing, and similar articles. The Allies based their policy on the argument that by allowing such supplies into enemy territory it would allow the enemy to release an equivalent amount of domestic stock for such purposes as the manufacture of motor tyres, an obvious contribution to their war effort. Later, the Allies extended the blockade list to cover virtually every item that might be required by enemy hospitals. At the

---

[31]Spaight, *Air Power and War Rights*, 283-85 (1947).
[32]*New York Times*, April 25, 1917.
[33]Cd. 8692 (1917), Correspondence with the German Government regarding the Alleged Misuse of British Hospital Ships, c. Garner, *op cit.* vol. 1, at 510.
[34]*Ibid.*, vol. 1, at 513.

initiative of the American Red Cross Society, the United States Department of State raised the matter with the British and French governments. In July 1916 the latter agreed to permit the Society to ship all types of hospital supplies provided they were directed to the units of the Society operating in enemy territory, and provided that they would be used exclusively by the American Red Cross and destroyed after being once used. However, since such units had been withdrawn from Germany in October 1915 for lack of funds, no such guarantee could be given. In reply, the Germans announced they would no longer allow free passage of hospital supplies to the Allied countries, and their naval forces were instructed to retain all such articles for their own use whenever captured.[35]

As regards the treatment during World War I of medical personnel, shortly after its commencement France accused Germany of taking even surgeons prisoners.[36] The Germans described this as a reprisal for French treatment of the wounded, and on September 18, 1914 the French Minister of War issued a communiqué in which, referring to the obligation resting upon France to give effect to the Geneva Convention, he admonished French medical personnel to treat German wounded with the greatest consideration and threatened to deal severely with those not conforming to the Convention.[37] Implicitly, it would appear therefore that there may have been some truth in the German accusation.

Perhaps the most notorious incident relating to the alleged mistreatment of a member of the medical profession during that war concerns Nurse Edith Cavell.[38] Miss Cavell was an English nursing sister running a hospital in German-occupied Belgium and was allowed by the Germans to continue her medical work. She had, in fact, treated the wounded and sick of both sides with equal care. While so engaged, however, she had assisted some 150 or more British and allied soldiers to escape from Belgium and cross into Holland, which was neutral. She was arrested by the Germans and charged under Article 58 of the German Military Penal Code with war treason[39] in that "with the object of helping a hostile power, or prejudicing the German or allied troops" she guided soldiers to the enemy. She pleaded guilty to having harboured within the medical establishment of which she was the matron, British, French, and Belgian soldiers, supplying them with money and clothes, and aiding them to escape. While so pleading she explained that she regarded it as her duty to enable her countrymen to escape from Belgium, where they were liable to be shot. Her purpose, she said, had not been to conduct them to the lines of Germany's enemies, but merely to get them away. She was tried in accordance with German procedure, which did not measure up to the standards applicable in England or the United States, whose diplomat represented British interests and was not present at the trial as he was entitled to be. She was sentenced to death at 5 p.m. and despite the intercession of the United States and the Spanish ambassador was shot at 2 a.m. It may well be true that she was not guilty of the actual charge against her, for, insofar as those she assisted were able to join the allied forces, it can be argued this was owing to the failure of neutral Holland to prevent their leaving the country for this purpose. It is,

[35]*Ibid.*, vol. 2, at 339-40.
[36]*Ibid.*, vol. 1, at 499, note 1.
[37]*Rev. Gén. de Droit International*, 1915, Docs., 80.
[38]The summary given here is based on Garner, *op. cit. supra* note 29, vol. 2, at 102-5.
[39]War treason may be defined as "hostile acts committed inside the area controlled by the belligerent against whom the acts are directed by persons who do not possess the status of combatants": Greenspan, *The Modern Law of Land Warfare*, 330 (1959). It includes liberating prisoners of war, voluntary supply of money, provision of clothing, etc., to the enemy: Oppenheim, *International Law*, vol. 2, at 575 (1955). According to the British *Manual of Military Law*, Part III, *The Law of Warfare* 183 (1958), "Such acts . . . are offences against the law legitimately proclaimed by the Occupant and may be punished by him with a rigour commensurate with the seriousness of the offence and the requirements of the security of his troops and his administration."

however, somewhat pedantic and naive to suggest that her acts were not in fact part and parcel of this. Much of the protest from the Allies and the United States was directed at the fact that she had trained German nurses, that others charged with similar offences had not been executed, and, perhaps most deplorable of all, that she was a woman. There is nothing in international law that grants to a woman convicted of war treason, or any other offence connected with the war, any right to be treated less severely than a man. The execution of Edith Cavell raised a general outcry and the emotionalism associated therewith is clear from the comment on the case by Professor Garner in his *International Law and the World War*:

> The execution of Miss Cavell revealed Prussian militarism in a very bad light, and while there may be differences of opinion regarding the legal right of a military occupant to execute a woman for such an offence as that which she committed, most fair-minded persons will agree that it was a case of extreme severity accompanied by elements of brutality such as the best sentiment of the civilized world condemns. It was a case in which the rigor of military law might have been tempered by mercy, as was done by the English in similar cases. . . . [The execution] aroused the undying hatred of the English, powerfully stimulated recruiting, and intensified the national determination to avenge what was regarded as a shocking and brutal judicial murder of *an unfortunate woman whose devotion to her own country had caused her to overstep the hard lines set by a military conqueror.* What Thomas Carlyle said of the execution by Napoleon of an old German bookseller may be equally said of the execution of nurse Cavell:
> "I am not sure but he had better have lost his best park of artillery, or had his best regiment drowned in the sea, than shot that poor German bookseller, Palm. It was palpable, murderous injustice which no man, let him paint an inch thick, could make out to be better. It burnt deep into the hearts of men, it and the like of it, suppressed fire flashed in the eyes of men, as they thought of it waiting their day, which day came."[40]

It is interesting to note that, despite the language he uses in this account, and his condemnation of the Germans for the execution, at no time does Garner make the slightest suggestion that what Edith Cavell did was completely inconsistent with her protected status as a nursing sister.

After World War I, and in accordance with an obligation created by the Treaty of Versailles, Germany brought a number of war criminals to trial before the German Reichsgericht sitting at Leipzig. Two of these cases concerned U-boat sinkings of allied hospital ships. Commander Neumann of the U-boat which sank the *Dover Castle*[41] pleaded in his defence that he had complied with German Admiralty instructions, which had been issued in the belief that Allied hospital ships were being used for military purposes. He was acquitted. The court accepted his plea, pointing out that he had not gone beyond his orders and that "it was impossible to give a warning . . . before the torpedo was fired, because [the *Dover Castle*] was escorted by two warships." It pointed out that according to the German Military Penal Code

> a subordinate who acts in conformity with orders is also liable to punishment as an accomplice when he knows that his superiors have ordered him to do acts which involve a civil or military crime or misdemeanour. There has been no case of this here. The memoranda of the German Government about the misuse of enemy Hospital Ships were known to the accused. The facts set out in them he held to

---

[40]Garner, *op. cit.*, vol. 2, at 104-5 (italics added).
[41]1921, H.M.S.O., Cmd. 1450 (reproduced in Cameron, *The Peleus Trial*, App. X (1948).

be conclusive, especially as he had received . . . similar reports from his comrades. He was therefore of the opinion that the measures taken by the German Admiralty against enemy Hospital Ships were not contrary to International Law, but were legitimate reprisals.[42] His conduct clearly shows that this was his conviction. He never made any secret of the sinking of the *Dover Castle*. Not only did he report it to his superiors, but he also admitted it in the present proceedings. It is especially noteworthy that he allowed an English captain, whom he had on board his submarine as prisoner, to observe the approach of the *Dover Castle*. Although this enemy subject thus knew about the sinking of the Hospital Ship, the accused on going ashore gave him a certificate when he asked for one and signed it with his full name, giving his rank in the service. He would not have done this if he had considered that his orders or his execution of them were illegal. The accused accordingly sank the *Dover Castle* in obedience to a service order of his highest superiors, an order which he considered to be binding. He cannot, therefore, be punished for his conduct.

The other trial arose from the sinking of the *Llandovery Castle*,[43] a troop transport until 1916, when she was commissioned as a hospital ship, properly fitted and marked as such, and her name communicated to the enemy powers. Thereafter, she was used exclusively for this purpose. In June 1918 when returning from Canada to England, with a crew of 164, eighty officers and men of the Canadian Medical Corps and eighteen nurses, she was torpedoed in the Atlantic well away from the area declared closed by the Germans. There were only twenty-four survivors, the U-boat having fired on the boats carrying those who escaped from the *Llandovery Castle* after she had been hit. The court described the torpedoing as "inexcusable" and commented adversely on the fact that not only was there no record in the log, but the chart was marked incorrectly to suggest that the U-boat was a long way from the scene of the incident, while the captain imposed an oath of silence on the crew. The accused pleaded superior orders and referred to suggestions of Allied abuses on hospital ships. The court in the course of its judgment said:

> no importance is to be attached to the statements put forward by the defence, that the enemies of Germany were making improper use of hospital ships for military purposes, and that they had repeatedly fired on German lifeboats and shipwrecked people. . . . [T]hroughout the German fleet it was a matter of general belief that improper use of hospital ships was made by the enemy. It must, therefore, be assumed for the benefit of the accused that they also held this belief. Whether this belief was founded on fact or not, is of less importance as affecting the case before the court, than the established fact that the *Llandovery Castle* at the time was not carrying any cargo or troops prohibited under clause 10 of the Hague Convention.

Whether or not the ship was wrongly carrying such forbidden cargo or personnel could, of course, only have been ascertained by boarding and searching her. However, the U-boat commander had said that "he would torpedo a hospital ship, with all its characteristic markings, in the expectation of being able to prove that it was being used for improper purposes. His hope was in vain. In spite of the most minute investigation it was not possible for him to obtain any confirmation of his assumption. . . ." Unfortunately, the commandant had disappeared and the persons accused were charged with firing upon and killing the survivors in their boats. The court rejected their plea of superior orders on the ground that the order in question was "universally known to everybody . . . to

[42]Reprisals are illegal acts taken in response to illegal acts with the intention that the original wrongdoer shall, in response, desist from his illegalities.
[43]*Supra* note 41 (Cameron, App. IX); the statement of fact is taken from the judgment.

be without any doubt whatever against the law." While the court regarded the sinking of the *Llandovery Castle* to be a breach of the law of war, since only the commander could be considered guilty of the torpedoing, no one was punished for sinking this particular hospital ship. The killing of the survivors was illegal not because they were members of the medical services, but because they were shipwrecked survivors.

It is always strange to note that after the end of a war and assertions that the war in question was the last ever to be fought, because a new world order is to be established, it is not long before efforts are being made to bring the law of war more up to date in the light of the lessons learned during the war. Despite the establishment of the League of Nations, the Swiss government in 1929 summoned a conference in Geneva to revise the Red Cross Convention of 1906 and draw up a new one on prisoners of war.[44]

Article 1 of the 1929 Convention makes it clear at the outset that the burden of caring for the sick and wounded, regardless of nationality, is placed fairly and squarely on all belligerents, although the primary responsibility rests, obviously, with the belligerent in whose hands they happen to be:

> Officers and soldiers and other persons officially attached to the armed forces who are wounded or sick shall be respected and protected in all circumstances; they shall be treated humanely and cared for medically, without distinction of nationality, by the belligerent in whose power they may be.
> Nevertheless, the belligerent who is compelled to abandon wounded or sick to the enemy, shall, as far as military exigencies permit, leave them with a portion of his medical personnel and material to help with their treatment.

While the wounded and sick become prisoners of war, this is not the case with the "personnel engaged exclusively in the collection, transport and treatment of the wounded and sick, and in the administration of medical formations and establishments [and] soldiers specially trained to be employed, in case of necessity, as auxiliary nurses or stretcher bearers . . . [who] shall enjoy the same treatment as the permanent medical staff."[45] Moreover, all these persons

> may not be retained after they have fallen into the hands of the enemy [and] in the absence of an agreement to the contrary, they shall be sent back to the belligerent to which they belong as soon as a route for their return shall be open and military considerations permit. Pending their return they shall continue to carry out their duties under the direction of the enemy; they shall preferably be engaged in the care of the wounded and sick of the belligerent to which they belong . . . [and while in enemy hands they shall receive] the same food, the same lodging, the same allowances and the same pay as are granted to the corresponding personnel [in the holding belligerent's own forces].[46]

Unfortunately, it would seem that during World War II these provisions were more honoured in the breach than the observance. By referring to the fact that they should "preferably" care for their own, the Convention acknowledges the realities of human nature. While a doctor may be prepared to treat all and sundry equally, it must be recognized that military personnel will automatically assist their own comrades first.

The 1929 Convention made no provision for hospital ships, but since the 1907 Convention was not abrogated in any way, the latter remained binding in this respect during

---

[44]These Conventions are to be found in Schindler/Toman, 257, 271, resp.
[45]Art. 9.
[46]Art. 12.

the war of 1939-45. The new Convention did, however, recognize the new phenomenon of medical aircraft, which would be protected so long as "they are reserved exclusively for the evacuation of wounded and sick and the transport of medical personnel and material." These aircraft were to be marked with the red cross side by side with their national emblem on both their lower and upper surface. This provision would make it difficult for any aircraft to be used temporarily as an air ambulance, although there would be nothing to prevent local commanders from agreeing between themselves to give immunity to aircraft temporarily fulfilling this function under proper safeguards. While aerial ambulances were to be protected, their freedom of movement was nevertheless somewhat restricted, reflecting perhaps the view that aircraft are always potentially hostile. Thus, "in the absence of special and express permission, flying over the firing line, and over the zone situated in front of clearing or dressing stations, and generally over all enemy territory or territory occupied by the enemy, is prohibited."[47] A regulation of this kind would make it difficult for a medical aircraft to operate during an engagement, and would mean that, for example, helicopters used as during the Korean War to remove casualties from the field would be unprotected. Somewhat similar to the regulations with regard to ships,

> medical aircraft shall obey every summons to land. In the event of a landing thus imposed, or of an involuntary landing in enemy territory and territory occupied by the enemy, the wounded and sick as well as the enemy personnel and material, including the aircraft, shall enjoy the privileges of the present Convention [that is to say, remain protected]. The pilot, mechanics and wireless telegraph operators captured shall be sent back, on condition that they shall be employed until the close of hostilities in the medical service only.[48]

Insofar as the use of the emblem is concerned, the Convention gave legal recognition to the practice of Muslim countries by recognizing in their case the use of the red crescent, and in the case of Iran the red lion and sun, instead of the red cross. It also allowed Voluntary Aid Societies, in accordance with their national legislation, to use the emblem in connection with their humanitarian activities in time of peace, while "as an exceptional measure, and with the express authority of one of the national societies of the Red Cross (Red Crescent, Red Lion and Sun), use may be made of the emblem of the Convention in time of peace to mark the position of aid stations exclusively reserved for the purpose of giving free treatment to the wounded or the sick."[49] The Swiss Arms were similarly protected. As in 1906, the desire was expressed that countries would take legislative measures to prevent the emblem or the terms Red Cross or Geneva Cross from being used for commercial purposes. Members of the Commonwealth, however, appended a reservation so that the legislation in question "may provide that private individuals, associations, firms or companies who have used the Arms of the Swiss Confederation, or marks constituting an imitation, for any lawful purpose before the coming into force of the present Convention shall not be prevented from continuing to use such Arms or marks for the same purpose."[50]

The Convention made no reference to duties of medical personnel as such, nor did it envisage the possibility that such personnel might ignore their proper duties or perform them in a fashion completely incompatible with their professional code. Unfortunately,

[47]Art. 18.
[48]*Ibid.*
[49]Art. 24.
[50]The Canadian reservation is to be found in Schindler/Toman, at 268.

experience in World War II was to show that, at least where members of the German medical corps were concerned, these would prove but vain hopes. Before looking at these aberrations, however, it is well to mention incidents that showed that the attitude towards medical establishments during World War I were still current between 1939 and 1945. As previously, there were instances of the sinking of hospital ships concomitant with the resort to unrestricted submarine warfare almost from the beginning of hostilities. There were also numerous allegations that hospital ships were being attacked from the air, although the leading authority on air warfare has stated that it is "unlikely that the attacks were made deliberately. They were probably due to error and the airmen's ignorance of the identity of the vessels," while in the Mediterranean theatre he suggests that the reflection of the sun off the water often made the identification marks undistinguishable.[51] He also comments that insofar as aerial attacks on hospitals were concerned, "it is almost certain that in no case was the attack deliberate."[52] As to hospitals located in cities this may well be true, regardless of the question of the legality of the bombing of any particular urban area.

What was far more serious in World War II was the behaviour of German medical personnel, although when assessing this it must be borne in mind that the Nazi authorities consciously instituted policies of experimentation and euthanasia against the civilian populations of the occupied territories and those German nationals whom they regarded as being lesser breeds. As regards euthanasia, it is interesting to note what American war crimes tribunals had to say:

> we have no doubt but that Karl Brandt—as he himself testified—is a sincere believer in the administration of euthanasia to persons hopelessly ill, whose lives are burdensome to themselves and an expense to the State or to their families. The abstract proposition of whether or not euthanasia is justified in certain cases of the class referred to, is no concern of this Tribunal. Whether or not a State may validly enact legislation which imposes euthanasia upon certain classes of its citizens, is likewise a question which does not enter into the issues. Assuming that it may do so, the Family of Nations is not obliged to grant recognition to such legislation when it manifestly gives legality to plain murder and torture of defenceless and powerless human beings of other nations. The evidence is conclusive that persons were included in the programme who were non-German nationals.[53]

This was not the only occasion on which an American war crimes tribunal expressed itself in this fashion. In *Re Greifelt*, it said: "It is our view that euthanasia, when carried out under state legislation against citizens of the state only, does not constitute a crime against humanity."[54]

At the Hadamar Sanatorium there was a conscious policy to apply what were understood to be the Führer's instructions to exterminate the mentally sick and those terminally ill with tuberculosis. Some thousands of Germans were dealt with in this way. However, when Polish and Russian nationals arrived, the instruction by the Commandant was that they were to be treated in the same way as the German mentally ill, and some 200 or more were injected with lethal doses of narcotics. Dr. Wahlmann was the only doctor at the Sanatorium and there was no evidence that he had ever examined anybody. However, he was in charge of the pharmacy, requisitioned the necessary drugs, and entered false statements as to the cause of death in his records. Since the defence was

---

[51]Spaight, *op. cit.* at 490, and 491, note 1.
[52]*Ibid.*, 362.
[53]*Re Brandt (The Doctors' Trial)* (1947), cited in *Re Milch* (1947), 7 *Trials of War Criminals* 52.
[54](1948), 13 *ibid.*, 1, at 34.

only able to prove the issue of an "administrative decree" as distinct from a Führerbefehl, and since there was no evidence that any of the Poles or Russians were in fact terminally ill, these defences were rejected. The male nurses who had administered the injections pretending they were for therapeutic reasons were sentenced to death, while Dr. Wahlmann received a life sentence.[55] Today, such policies of extermination directed against classes of nationals would almost certainly fall foul of the Genocide Convention of 1948,[56] and it is perhaps surprising that the Tribunal, in view of the fact that these exterminations were to a great extent part of the German war policy, lacked the courage to condemn them after the war. When faced with an extradition application concerning one of the doctors involved in these and similar activities, the Supreme Court of Ghana showed a much higher sense of humanity.[57]

Intentional killing by doctors has always been regarded as contrary to the true medical ethic and there were war crimes trials dealing with such activities. In the *Natzweiler* case[58] members of the Women's Auxiliary Air Force and the First Aid Nursing Yeomanry who had been operating as radio operators in civilian clothing behind German lines were sentenced to death and to cremation in a trial at which they were not present. Dr. Rohde confessed to administering to them an injection which he knew to be lethal, but which he had told them was against typhus, and there was evidence to suggest that in at least one of the cases the woman was still alive though unconscious when thrown into the furnace. Rohde claimed in his defence that by giving the injection he was performing a service to the women in that they would be in a coma when burned, and so would not feel the pain. He was found guilty and, unlike some other doctors also sentenced to death for war crimes, he was hanged and not shot.

A doctor who was in fact shot was Weisspfennig, the medical officer on board a U-boat which had sunk the merchant ship *Peleus*.[59] As in the case of the *Llandovery Castle* during World War I,[60] the commander of the U-boat stayed after the torpedoing and ordered some of his officers and men to open fire on the boats containing survivors, most of whom were killed. It was explained by the defence that the German U-boat, U-156, had picked up survivors, and though marked with a red cross and identified as such by an allied aircraft this aircraft had returned and attacked the vessel, which had to abandon the survivors in order to dive. It was contended, therefore, that the allies were putting military before humane concerns. A witness from the British Admiralty confirmed this story, which had resulted in a German U-boat Command instruction that

> no attempt of any kind should be made at rescuing members of ships sunk, and this incident includes picking up persons in the water and putting them in lifeboats, righting capsized lifeboats and handing over food and water. Rescue runs counter to the rudimentary demands of warfare for the destruction of enemy ships and crews. . . . Be harsh, having in mind that the enemy takes no regard of women and children in the bombing attacks of the German cities.

---

[55]*Re Klein* (1945) Kintner, *The Hadamar Trial* (1949).

[56]Schindler/Toman, at 171. Art. 2 defines genocide as "acts committed with intent to destroy, in whole or in part, a national, ethnical, racial or religious group, as such," and includes killing and measures intended to prevent births.

[57]*State v. Director of Prisons, ex. p. Schumann*, [1966] G.L.R. 703; 39 I.L.R. 433.

[58]*Re Rohde* (1946), 5 Trials of War Criminals 54; Webb, *The Natzweiler Trial* (1949).

[59]This was the first war crimes trial after the end of the European war: 1945, 1 *ibid.*, 1; Cameron, *The Peleus Trial* (1948). For details of the U-156 incident, see Mallison, *Submarines in General and Limited War*, 84-86 (U.S. Naval War College, *International Law Studies*, vol. 58, 1968).

[60]See *supra* note 43.

This defence was rejected for the commandant, but even if it had been accepted it would not have helped the doctor. He, contrary to the German Naval Instruction and to his knowledge of the duties of a doctor, had been among those who threw grenades at the survivors. His plea that he was obeying superior orders was of no avail, since this was an order which was palpably illegal in the eyes of any medical officer.

One can only assume that the reason for the difference in treatment between the two doctors—one being hanged, a somewhat ignoble treatment for an officer, the other shot, which is regarded as a more dignified death—lies in the fact that, while both clearly disregarded their functions as service doctors, Dr. Rohde had, from the medical point of view, behaved in the more disreputable manner, for his actions were purportedly in the course of his functions as a doctor.

As long ago as the American Civil War, accusations were made of medical experimentation against captured personnel. At no time was it suggested that the practices indulged in by Wirz at Andersonville[61] were anything but a personal aberration, or the result of a consciously directed policy of the Confederate government. During World War II such practices, cultivated to a fine art, were applied in nearly every concentration camp in which nationals of occupied Europe were detained.[62] A number of war crime trials in connection with this policy were held by a variety of allied courts, but it is only necessary to mention a few of the more notable. Perhaps, as a result of Uris's *Q.B. 7*, based on the libel action brought against him by Dehring because of references to the latter's role as a medical experimenter at Auschwitz,[63] the sexual operations are the most widely known. It is also important to note, however, that while Dehring asserted that as a concentration camp prisoner he had no option but to carry out the operations he was ordered to perform, a Norwegian woman doctor in the same camp was successful in declining, comforted Dehring's victims, and lived to give evidence against him.[64]

At the *Doctors' Trial*[65] the whole range of experiments was indicated: (1) limits of human endurance at high altitudes and under high and low pressure; (2) effects of severe chilling and freezing; (3) inducement of malaria and epidemic jaundice; (4) exposure to mustard gas; (5) effectiveness of sulphanilamide on spotted fever and other vaccines; (6) experiments regarding bone, muscle, and nerve regeneration, together with bone transplants from one person to another; (7) experiments to render seawater drinkable; (8) speedy and mass sterilization, castration, and abortion by unorthodox methods; (9) effects of poisons and pharmaceutical preparations on phosphorous burns. In every case where the aim was to ascertain the effect of drugs or a new treatment, the sickness or trauma being treated had been wrongly induced. The only thing that may be said in favour of these experiments is that they were conducted by or under the supervision of doctors. In fact, it was doctors who had the ''honour'' of selecting in the concentration camps those who were considered fit enough to work and those who were to be murdered.[66] Of the gynaecological experiments, Professor Clauberg, who had been personally en-

---

[61]1865 (H.R. Exec. Doc. No. 23, 40th Cong., 2d Sess., 1867-68, vol. 8)—Andersonville was a Confederate P.W. camp under Wirz' command, where thousands of U.S. prisoners died as a result of ill treatment, starvation, and induced disease.

[62]The experiments were taking place in almost every concentration camp; there was effective liaison between the Army Medical Inspectorate and the camp experimenters; the Ravensbruck experiments were reported at the third meeting of the consulting physicians of the Wehrmacht at the Military Medical Academy in Berlin, May 24-26, 1943; and see *Nuremberg Judgment* (H.M.S.O., Cmd. 6964, 64).

[63]Hall and Williams, *Auschwitz in England* (1965).

[64]Dr. Adelaide Hurtval.

[65]*Re Brandt* (1947), cited in *Re Milch* (1947), *supra* note 53, at 49-52.

[66]Evidence re Auschwitz given at Nuremberg, *loc. cit.*, note 62 above.

trusted by Himmler with their organization said that "the experiments could contribute very little to the progress of science."[67] Be that as it may, can anything be said in favour of experiments, however beneficial to mankind they may ultimately prove, when they are carried out without anaesthesia, in unsanitary conditions, without the consent of the guinea pigs, and are performed either upon alien prisoners who should not have been in the camps anyway, for they had done nothing wrong, or upon similarly innocent local nationals victimized as part of an ideological pursuit of genocide?[68]

The American tribunal which conducted the *Doctors' Trial*[69] recognized that medical experiments might be legal and laid down some guiding principles to sustain its view:

> The great weight of the evidence before us is to the effect that certain types of medical experiments on human beings, when kept within reasonably well-defined bounds, conform to the ethics of the medical profession generally. The protagonists of the practice of human experimentations justify their views on the basis that such experiments yield results for the good of society that are unprocurable by other methods or means of study. All agree, however, that certain basic principles must be observed in order to satisfy moral, ethical and legal concepts:
>
> 1. The voluntary consent of the human subject is absolutely essential. This means that the person involved should have legal capacity to give consent; should be so situated as to be able to exercise free power of choice, without the intervention of any element of force, fraud, deceit, duress, overreaching, or other ulterior form of constraint or coercion; and should have sufficient knowledge and comprehension of the elements of the subject matter involved as to enable him to make an understanding and enlightened decision. This latter element requires that before the acceptance of an affirmative decision by the experimental subject there should be made known to him the nature, duration, and purpose of the experiment; the method and means by which it is to be conducted; all inconveniences and hazards reasonably to be expected; and the effects upon his health or person which may possibly come from his participation in the experiment.
>
> The duty and responsibility for ascertaining the quality of the consent rests upon each individual who initiates, directs or engages in the experiment. It is a personal duty and responsibility which may not be delegated to another with impunity.
>
> 2. The experiment should be such as to yield fruitful results for the good of society, unprocurable by other methods or means of study, and not random and unnecessary in nature.
>
> 3. The experiment should be so designed and based on the results of animal experimentation and a knowledge of the natural history of the disease or other problem under study that the anticipated results will justify the performance of the experiment.
>
> 4. The experiment should be so conducted as to avoid all unnecessary physical and mental suffering and injury.
>
> 5. No experiment should be conducted where there is *a priori* reason to believe that death or disabling injury will occur; except, perhaps, in those experiments where the experimental physicians also serve as subjects.
>
> 6. The degree of risk to be taken should never exceed that determined by the humanitarian importance of the problem to be solved by the experiment.
>
> 7. Proper preparations should be made and adequate facilities provided to protect the experimental subject against even remote possibilities of injury, disability, or death.
>
> 8. The experiment should be conducted only by scientifically qualified persons. The highest degree of skill and care should be required through all stages of the experiment of those who conduct or engage in the experiment.

[67]See *Re Hoess* (1947), 7 W.C.T. 11, at 25.
[68]*Supra* note 56.
[69]*Supra* note 65, at 49-50.

9. During the course of the experiment the human subject should be at liberty to bring the experiment to an end if he has reached the physical or mental state where continuation of the experiment seems to him to be impossible.

10. During the course of the experiment the scientist in charge must be prepared to terminate the experiment at any stage, if he has probable cause to believe, in the exercise of the good faith, superior skill and careful judgment required of him that a continuation of the experiment is likely to result in injury, disability, or death to the experimental subject.

Of the ten principles which have been enumerated our judicial concern, of course, is with those requirements which are purely legal in nature—or which at least are so closely and clearly related to matters legal that they assist us in determining criminal culpability and punishment. To go beyond that point would lead us into a field that would be beyond our sphere of competence. However, the point need not be laboured. We find from the evidence that in the medical experiments which have been proven, these ten principles were much more frequently honoured in their breach than in their observance. Many of the concentration camp inmates who were the victims of these atrocities were citizens of countries other than the German Reich. They were non-German nationals, including Jews and "asocial persons," both prisoners of war and civilians, who had been imprisoned and forced to submit to these tortures and barbarities without so much as a semblance of trial. In every single instance appearing in the record, subjects were used who did not consent to the experiments; indeed, as to some of the experiments, it is not even contended by the defendants that the subject occupied the status of volunteers. In no case was the experimental subject at liberty of his own free choice to withdraw from any experiment. In many cases experiments were performed by unqualified persons; were conducted at random for no adequate scientific reason, and under revolting physical conditions. All of the experiments were conducted with unnecessary suffering and injury and but very little, if any, precautions were taken to protect or safeguard the human subjects from the possibilities of injury, disability, or death. In every one of the experiments the subjects experienced extreme pain or torture, and in most of them they suffered permanent injury, mutilation, or death, either as a direct result of the experiments or because of lack of adequate follow-up care.

Obviously all of these experiments involving brutalities, tortures, disabling injury and death were performed in complete disregard to international conventions, the laws and customs of war, the general principles of criminal law as derived from the criminal laws of all civilized nations, and Control Council Law No. 10.[70] Manifestly human experiments under such conditions are contrary to "the principles of the laws of nations as they result from the usages established among civilized peoples, from the laws of humanity, and from the dictates of public conscience."[71]

Among the arguments put forward on behalf of the doctors was the contention that many of the victims of these lethal experiments had already been sentenced to death, so that there was really no further suffering entailed by subjecting them to these medical processes. On this, the Tribunal said:

Another argument presented in briefs of counsel attempts to ground itself upon the debatable proposition that in the broad interest of alleviating human suffering, a State may legally provide for medical experiments to be carried out on prisoners condemned to death without their consent, even though such experiments may involve great suffering or death for the experimental subject. Whatever may be the right of a State with reference to its own citizens, it is certain that such legislation

---

[70]This Law enacted by the Allied Control Council accepted the Principles of the Nuremberg Judgment and was the authority for war crimes trials in Germany, including those conducted by the German government when established.

[71]This is from the Preamble to Hague Convention IV of 1907 and is regarded as the basic source of the law of war.

may not be extended so as to permit the practice upon nationals of other countries who, held in the most abject servitude, are subjected to experiments without their consent and under the most brutal and senseless conditions. . . .

Moreover, assuming for the moment that they had been condemned to death for acts considered hostile to the German forces in the occupied territory of Poland, these persons still were entitled to the protection of the laws of civilized nations. While under certain specific conditions the rules of land warfare may recognize the validity of an execution of spies, war rebels, or other resistance workers, it does not under any circumstances countenance the infliction of death or other punishment by maiming or torture.[72]

There was one case in which a German doctor who had sought to carry out his medical duties but had been prevented from doing so to the full extent because of war conditions, found himself before an allied tribunal.[73] A baby home had been established at Velpke to which the babies of forced foreign labourers were sent. The staff was inadequately trained, but until September 1944 two German doctors had been in the habit of making reasonably regular visits. From then, Dr. Demmerick, a local practitioner, decided on his own initiative to call and attend the babies. Subsequently, owing to the demands of his regular patients, the shortage of doctors, and the disruptions of the war, he ceased doing so, except for the purpose of signing death certificates or when specially summoned. The conditions in the home were deplorable and the deaths numerous because of medical neglect. Despite the fact that he was under no duty to visit the home and regardless of his other obligations, Dr. Demmerick was sentenced to ten years' imprisonment for the war crime of participating in the killings by criminal neglect as a doctor. Perhaps it should be pointed out on his behalf that according to the Geneva Convention of 1929 captured medical personnel should "preferably" be engaged in looking after their own sick and wounded.[74] Apparently, in the eyes of this tribunal this prior obligation did not attach to a free doctor insofar as sick enemy babies were concerned.

Although reference has only been made to crimes by German medical personnel, it should not be thought that the doctors in the forces of the United Nations[75] always behaved in accordance with the rules. The writer received a statement from a doctor with the Royal West African Frontier Force to the effect that, when in Burma, after he had heard of the death in a Japanese prison camp of a friend, a Royal Air Force medical orderly, he stood by for two weeks and watched Japanese wounded die without making any effort to help them. Again, in 1948 Dr. Smith, a captain in the Royal Army Medical Corps, was tried by court martial for ill-treating prisoners of war. The case was not reported as a war crimes trial since Dr. Smith was tried by a British court martial in accordance with the provisions of the British Army Act.[76]

All of these cases serve as warnings to service doctors that their first obligation at all times is to the sick and wounded. Even if they receive orders to take offensive action, these orders must be disregarded. The same is true, perhaps even more true, if the orders are in the medical field and clearly run counter to every principle of medical ethics. If they obey such orders, they run the risk, if captured, of standing trial as war criminals, and to the extent that the orders in question should have been palpably or manifestly unlawful to a doctor, they will not be able to plead superior orders in their defence.[77]

---

[72]At 51-52.
[73]*Re Gerike* (1946) 7 War Crimes Reports 76; Brand, *The Velpke Baby Home Trial* (1950).
[74]Art. 12.
[75]The name of the alliance opposing the Axis Powers during World War II.
[76]*The Times* (London), April 8, 10, 12, 13, 14; May 1, 28, 29; June 1, 17, 1948.
[77]See Green, *Superior Orders in National and International Law* (1976), and ch. III *supra*.

Should they disobey those orders, the military codes of almost all countries in the world will protect them from trial for disobedience. Nor should they think that, if they escape from those seeking to try them, they will necessarily be secure. Professor Schumann had been one of those who had conducted some of the fatal cancer experiments at Auschwitz. He evaded capture by the Allies, and in order to escape standing trial in the German Federal Republic he took up residence in Ghana. In 1966 the German government sought his extradition and Schumann pleaded that all his experiments were political offences in that they were part and parcel of German policy, and as such that he was immune from extradition. The Ghanaian Court of Appeal[78] showed perhaps a much higher respect for human life and dignity than did United States war crimes tribunals when commenting upon euthanasia programs directed against German nationals. Akufo-Addo, C.J., said that "The offence of murder with which [Schumann] is charged is . . . no more of a political character than the offence of, say, robbery with violence . . . committed by a political party activist in a desperate bid to seek means of replenishing the dwindling coffers of his political party."[79] Lassey, J.A., examined the problem in somewhat more detail:

> [I]n the present case . . . the evidence . . . shows that the mass killings complained of are the ordinary crimes against the person known to the municipal laws of the Federal Republic of West Germany, but there is no doubt also that those killings were done in circumstances which were not entirely without some political significance. The . . . offences . . . were committed on the orders of the ruling political party in Germany at the time and they were committed in fulfilment of the political programme or ambitions of the ruling political party . . . prior to and during . . . the Second World War.
>
> . . . In those circumstances is it necessary to widen the scope of meaning of these magic words, "of a political character," if only for reasons of humanity? . . . [I]n order to determine the political character of the particular offence so as to make it not extraditable there must necessarily be present at the time of the commission of the particular crime some element of organized or violent opposition or resistance to the execution of the planned policy of the ruling political party and the offence must be committed in the conflict which might result between the opposing parties. In this context any such offence committed either by the agents of the ruling political party seeking to carry out their principal's orders or by agents of those who dislike or resist the carrying into effect of the particular political policy may be brought under the category of an offence "of a political nature or character" and therefore excusable in extradition proceedings. This . . . should be one of the tests in determining whether in the particular circumstances an offence committed against the municipal laws of a State by a national who has sought asylum or refuge in another State is of a political nature or not.
>
> Merely carrying out wicked orders or plans of a governing political party by State agents against the persons or properties of individuals or groups of individuals who manifestly do not demonstrate any organized violent resistance to the execution of those plans would not stamp the offences committed in such a situation with political character so as to afford the perpetrators an excuse from due prosecution. It is absolutely absurd to me to hold that what is clearly murder in one territory in response to the superior orders of a ruling political party against helpless victims in a lunatic asylum should not lie and the offender [should not be] extradited because it was done in obedience to superior orders of a governing political party.
>
> . . . The offences charged . . . were not committed against the numerous victims in the course of an open conflict or rebellion between the agents of the Nazi Party and the lunatics in Munsungem Institute or the Jews in Auschwitz. These offences are clearly extraditable.[80]

---

[78]*State* v. *Director of Prisons, ex p. Schumann*, [1966] G.L.R. 703; 39 I.L.R. 433.
[79]39 I.L.R. 433, at 439.
[80]*Ibid.*, at 451-52.

As after World War I, so after World War II, but rather more speedily, the International Committee of the Red Cross endeavoured to secure the amendment of the Geneva Conventions dealing with the sick and wounded and prisoners of war. Now, however, there was an added impetus. The fate of the civilian population in occupied Europe at the hands of the Nazis and their allies made it clear that the traditional idea of protecting the direct victims of combat was inadequate, and that some major effort was required to ensure the protection of the civilian population, too, in any future war. As a result, in 1949 at Geneva four new Conventions dealing with the wounded and sick, the wounded, sick and shipwrecked, prisoners of war, and civilians were adopted.[81] These Conventions are to apply in every armed conflict, whether a declared war or not, and in every case of foreign occupation, with the parties undertaking to respect them in all circumstances, and until final repatriation of all those in enemy hands.

Among the issues of particular interest to the medical profession now covered are the adaptation of the Geneva humanitarian provisions to air warfare, provision for the establishment of hospital and safety zones, more specific regulations concerning the repatriation of sick prisoners, and medical protection for civilians in occupied territory. Moreover, for the first time, international treaties provided for the introduction of basic humanitarian principles to be applied during non-international conflicts,[82] including the right to medical treatment for those actively fighting as well as those *hors de combat*, all of whom now enjoy protection from murder of all kinds, mutilation, cruel treatment, and torture. While the Conventions do not say expressly that medical personnel acting during a non-international conflict are to be protected, since the wounded and sick are to be collected and cared for, it must be presumed that members of the medical profession will be entitled to the protection essential to enable them to perform their tasks. Chile and Great Britain, still then sovereign over Rhodesia in the eyes of the world—and there was no suggestion by the administration of either Mr. Ian Smith or Bishop Muzorewa that they did not regard themselves bound by the Geneva Conventions—have both ratified the Conventions, so that Drs. Cassidy and Mistrali-Guidotti were among the personnel protected thereby and entitled to aid the sick and wounded regardless of nationality or political partisanship.

Reflecting the horrors of what took place during World War II, especially as regards Soviet prisoners, the three military Conventions provide that the sick and wounded are to be treated humanely and cared for by the detaining power,

without any adverse distinction founded on sex, race, nationality, religion, political opinions, or any other similar criteria. Any attempts upon their lives, or violence to their persons, shall be strictly prohibited; in particular, they shall not be murdered or exterminated, subjected to torture or to biological experiments; they shall not wilfully be left without medical assistance and care, nor shall conditions exposing them to contagion or infection be created.

Only urgent medical reasons will authorize priority in the order of treatment to be administered. . . .

The Party to the conflict which is compelled to abandon wounded or sick to the enemy shall, as far as military considerations permit, leave them a part of its medical personnel and material to assist in their care.[83]

---

[81]Schindler and Toman, 305, 333, 355, 427 resp.
[82]Art. 3, common to the four Conventions.
[83]Conventions I and II, Art. 12; Convention III, Art. 13.

Further, the persons placed under protection in this way are unable to consent to be treated otherwise. That is to say, they cannot even of their own free will surrender the protection that international law now confers upon them.

It is not necessary here to enter into a general discussion as to the regulations concerning the actual care and treatment to be afforded to prisoners, whether sick or otherwise. The general provision just referred to suffices. In so far as medical units and establishments are concerned, the Conventions affirm what had already been established, while at the same time acknowledging the developments made in technology. As to their personnel, they "shall be free to pursue their duties, as long as the capturing Power has not itself ensured the necessary care of the wounded and sick found in such establishments and units. The responsible authorities shall ensure that the said medical establishments and units are, as far as possible, situated in such a manner that attacks against military objectives cannot imperil their safety."[84] The medical personnel, and those attending them, such as full-time stretcher-bearers, are to be respected and protected so long as they are exclusively employed in their tasks. If captured, they are not to be treated as prisoners of war, and may be retained only so long as "the state of health" of prisoners of war requires this. While so retained, they are to enjoy all the protections that belong to prisoners of war. A provision that would perhaps emphatically indicate how far Edith Cavell went beyond the rights of protected medical personnel and became subject to the captor's law states that "within the framework of the military law and regulations of the Detaining Power, and under the authority of its competent service, they shall continue to carry out, in accordance with their professional ethics, their medical . . . duties on behalf of prisoners of war, preferably those of the armed forces to which they belong."[85] In order to fulfil their professional tasks, they are to be allowed to visit prisoners in labour units or hospitals outside the camp; while in each camp the senior medical officer is to be responsible for organizing the professional activities of retained personnel, and shall receive from the holding medical personnel such facilities as they may require. Although subject to the internal discipline of the camp in which they are held, they cannot be made to perform any work outside their medical duties. As to the personnel whose retention is not required for medical purposes, their departure and return to their own lines is to be arranged as soon as possible.

The means of transport used for medical purposes are entitled to the same protection as mobile medical units, while medical aircraft, defined as those "exclusively employed for the removal of wounded and sick and for the transport of medical personnel and equipment,"[86] are immune from attack while flying at heights, times, and on routes specifically agreed between the belligerents. They must be marked, in addition to their national rondel, with the red cross, crescent, or lion and sun—it remains to be seen how long it will be before the revolutionary Islamic regime in Iran rejects the latter and employs, in company with other Muslim countries, the crescent instead. Medical aircraft must comply with every order to land, but if they do so they, with their occupants, that is to say the wounded and sick as well as their personnel, are entitled to continue their flight. On the other hand, if they make an involuntary landing in enemy or enemy-occupied territory, the wounded and sick together with the crew become prisoners of war, while the medical personnel are to be treated as is always the case when they fall into the hands of the adverse party.

[84]Convention I, Art. 19.
[85]*Ibid.*, Art. 28.
[86]Convention I, Art. 36; II, Art. 39.

Hospital ships shall display the usual emblem on their flags, and will themselves be painted white and display on their sides and on their flat surfaces so "as to afford the greatest possible visibility from the sea and from the air" large dark red crosses. If they wish to be protected at night or in poor visibility, they must "take the necessary measures to render their painting and distinctive emblems sufficiently apparent."[87] The Convention on Wounded, Sick and Shipwrecked still envisions the possibility of a battle on board a ship and provides for the protection of the sick bay. The situation that arose during World War I with respect to allegations against British conversion and reconversion of merchantships at the time of Gallipoli[88] has now been rendered illegal, for "merchant vessels which have been transformed into hospital ships cannot be put to any other use throughout the hostilities,"[89] and there is no exception made for urgent military necessity. Equally, as if reflecting the decision in *The Ophelia*,[90] protection only ceases, and then solely after due warning has been given and ignored after a reasonable time has elapsed, if the ships are "used to commit, outside their humanitarian duties, acts harmful to the enemy . . . [and] in particular, hospital ships may not possess or use a secret code for their wireless or other means of communication."[91]

The four Conventions, again reflecting the experience of World War II, especially in the field of medical experimentation, make provision for the punishment of "grave breaches." These are described as "wilful killing, torture or inhuman treatment, including biological experiments, wilfully causing great suffering or serious injury to body or health."[92] It should be remembered that, as already indicated, the protection conferred by the Conventions cannot be surrendered, even voluntarily, so that the wounded, the sick, the shipwrecked, and protected civilians cannot give their consent to submit to being made medical guinea pigs. The Conventions do not expressly forbid medical personnel from abusing their functions. However, grave breaches of the above character are most likely to be committed by medical personnel or under their supervision, and the Conventions obligate the parties to them to enact the necessary legislation to provide effective penal sanctions for those committing or ordering others to commit such breaches. Moreover, the parties undertake to search for any persons alleged to have committed such crimes and then bring them to trial or to hand them over to some other party which has made out a *prima facie* case.[93] Such obligations exist regardless of the nationality of the offender, so that even neutrals would be similarly bound. This leaves open the question whether, as in the *Schumann* case,[94] extradition processes would still be necessary. The Conventions make no reference to acts committed against one's own nationals, other than what is to be found in common Article 3 regarding a non-international conflict, but it should be borne in mind that the euthanasia and sterilization programs introduced by the Nazis against, for example, German Jews or gypsies, would fall within the ban on genocide as defined by the Genocide Convention of 1948,[95] which has been ratified by the vast majority of members of the United Nations.

[87]Convention II, Art. 43.
[88]See *supra* note 33.
[89]Convention II, Art. 33.
[90]See *supra* note 30.
[91]Convention II, Art. 34.
[92]Convention I, Art. 50; II, 51; III, 130; IV, 147.
[93]Arts. 49, 50, 129, 146, resp.
[94]See *supra* note 78.
[95]Art. 2: ". . . the following acts committed with intent to destroy, in whole or in part, a national, ethnical, racial or religious group, as such: killing members of the group; causing serious bodily or mental harm to members of the group; deliberately inflicting on the group conditions of life calculated to bring about its physical destruction in whole or in part; imposing measures intended to prevent births within the group. . . ." By Art. 1 genocide is a crime at international law whether committed in time of peace or war.

There has been no major war to test the value of the 1949 Conventions, but the experience of Korea and Vietnam showed that there were still deficiencies. In addition, during the conflict between the self-proclaimed Bangladesh and Pakistan, there had been allegations that the latter had subjected captured personnel to blood transfusions on behalf of its own sick and wounded to an extent that the "donors" had died or been reduced to permanent infirmity. This latter conflict raised questions concerning the status of captured personnel in what can only be described as the twilight area between rebellion and war. Moreover, the majority of members of the United Nations had become concerned as to the rights of national liberation movements which might engage in wars of self-determination, and sought to ensure that these conflicts should be regarded as international conflicts protected by the ordinary law. In 1977, at a conference summoned by the Swiss government, two Protocols additional to the Geneva Conventions, and based on drafts prepared by the International Committee of the Red Cross were adopted. Protocol I[96] is concerned with international and Protocol II[97] with non-international armed conflicts. The distinction between the two is highly technical[98] and medical personnel should not concern themselves unduly with the distinction. From a practical point of view they should act as doctors and in accordance with their Hippocratic Oath and medical ethics regardless of the characterization of the conflict. The medical provisions of the two Protocols differ, however.

Protocol I, for the first time, expressly defines what is meant by medical personnel, units, transports, ships, aircraft, and the like. For the purpose of the law of armed conflict we now know that "medical purposes" mean "the search for, collection, transportation, diagnosis or treatment—including first-aid treatment—of the wounded, sick and shipwrecked, or for the prevention of disease," and medical personnel are those assigned by a party to a conflict "exclusively" to these purposes or to the administration of medical units or to the operation or administration of medical transports. Medical transports are any means of transportation assigned exclusively to medical transportation, whether by land, sea, or air.[99] Although it has been made clear since the establishment of Israel that Israel medical units do not use the red cross, crescent, or lion and sun, the Protocol has not remedied the defect of 1949 when the red shield of David failed to secure adoption by only one vote. Technically, therefore, this emblem enjoys no protection, although experience has shown that in practice it does, and the United States has informed its military personnel that in the view of that country it is in fact a recognized and protected emblem.[100] Any medical officer wishing to serve as a doctor with the Israeli forces may argue that, apart from this practical reality, the use of the red shield over thirty years and its acceptance, even by an enemy that denies its validity, have granted it recognition and protection by virtue of customary international law.

The Protocol widens the list of persons who are protected in the sense that there may be no "adverse distinction founded on race, colour, sex, language, religion or belief, political or other opinion, national or social origin, wealth, birth or other status, or on any other similar criteria."[101] For the medical man this means that a patient is a patient, whatever the nationality, creed, opinion, or other characteristic, and the doctor is obliged to treat all equally, regardless of any orders that he may receive to the contrary. Repeating

---

[96]Schindler/Toman, 551.
[97]*Ibid.*, 614.
[98]See, e.g., "The New Law of Armed Conflict," ch. I *supra*.
[99]All these terms are defined in Art. 8.
[100]See Dept. of the Army Training Circular, No. 27-10-1, June 1979. "Selected Problems in the Law of War," 8. A similar pamphlet has been issued by the Federal German Republic.
[101]Art. 9.

the 1949 Convention, the only permitted distinction that may be made among patients is on medical grounds.[102] Would this mean, for example, that had Dr. Demmerick, accused during the *Velpke Baby Home Trial*,[103] been able to prove that his German patients had required his attentions more urgently than the babies, he would not have been convicted? Can it be argued that his first medical obligation was to his regular patients and that they, therefore, were entitled to priority as a medical duty? In other words, would the verdict have been different if the Protocol governed World War II?

As regards the treatment that patients are entitled to and doctors are permitted to give, Article 11 is very specific, and if properly obeyed will result in a discontinuance of at least the most serious abuses of the past. It provides:

1. The physical or mental health and integrity of persons who are in the power of the adverse Party or who are interned, detained or otherwise deprived of liberty as a result of [an international armed conflict] shall not be endangered by any unjustified act or omission. Accordingly, it is *prohibited* to subject the persons described in this Article to *any medical procedure which is not indicated by the state of health* of the person concerned and which is *not consistent with generally accepted medical standards* which would be applied under similar circumstances to persons who are nationals of the Party conducting the procedure and who *are in no way deprived of liberty*.

2. It is, in particular, prohibited to carry out on such persons, *even with their consent*:
a. physical mutilations;
b. medical or scientific experiments;
c. removal of tissue or organs for transplantation, except where these acts are justified in conformity with the conditions provided for in paragraph 1.

3. Exceptions to the prohibition in paragraph 2(c) may be made only in the case of donations of blood for transfusion or of skin for grafting, provided that they are *given voluntarily and without any coercion or inducement*, and then *only for therapeutic purposes*, under conditions consistent with generally *accepted medical standards and controls designed for the benefit of both the donor and the recipient*.

4. *Any wilful act or omission which seriously endangers the physical or mental health or integrity* of any person who is in the power of a Party other than the one on which he depends and which either violates any of the prohibitions in paragraphs 1 and 2 or fails to comply with the requirements of paragraph 3 *shall be a grave breach* of this Protocol.

5. The persons described in paragraph 1 have the *right to refuse* any surgical operation. In case of refusal, medical personnel shall endeavour to obtain a written statement to that effect, signed or acknowledged by the patient.[104]

The Article goes on to provide that full medical records must be kept indicating exactly what treatment has been given, and especially recording every transfusion of blood or donation of skin—a requirement that is particularly important in view of the fact that there is no prohibition upon such blood or skin being given on behalf of personnel belonging to the holding power. However, if two brothers are in enemy hands it would seem neither can consent to a kidney transplant to the other, if this is to be performed by an enemy doctor. All such records are to be available for inspection by the Protecting Power, that is to say, the diplomatic representative accepted by the holding power as representing the interests of the opposing party. It should perhaps be pointed out that paragraph 4 is so worded as to imply that these acts or omissions are not forbidden if

[102]Art. 10.
[103]See *supra* note 73.
[104]Italics added.

carried out against the nationals of the holding power, even though they may be serving in the forces of the adverse party, as was the case with so many German refugees in the British Pioneer Corps during World War II.

As before, medical units and establishments are protected, and in order to prevent their being attacked it is provided that efforts should be made to notify the opposing party of their location, which should be such that attacks against military objectives do not endanger them. But they may not be used in an attempt to shield such objectives from attack.[105] The protection to which medical units are entitled ceases if they are used to commit, outside their humanitarian function, acts harmful to the enemy, but this should only ensue after due warning accompanied by a time limit, which warning has been ignored.[106] There is nothing to be gained here by spelling out the details with regard to transportation and the like, save to mention that there is now some measure of recognition that medical aircraft may have to operate in contact zones and even over territory held by the enemy, and a technical annex has been attached to specify the signals, lights, radio wavelengths, and the like which become important in such circumstances. Needless to say, the Protocol reiterates previous provisions for ordering a medical aircraft to land for the purpose of search and confirmation of status.[107] Now, however, the inspecting party is not allowed to remove the wounded and sick unless the inspection cannot be carried out otherwise. More important, however, if the search confirms the innocence of the aircraft, it must be allowed to leave with its occupants belonging to the adverse party or to neutrals, although any wounded and sick belonging to the inspecting power may of course be retained. If during inspection it is found that the aircraft has been flying without the agreement of the enemy, where such an agreement is required, the aircraft may be seized, but it may only be used thereafter as a medical aircraft.

The provisions of Protocol II concerning medical activities during non-international conflicts are much simpler and briefer than those in Protocol I. Broadly, the sick and wounded are to be respected and protected, and receive humane treatment and the medical care and attention required by their condition.[108] Medical personnel must be respected and granted all available help for the fulfilment of their task, and shall not be compelled to carry out any act incompatible with their humanitarian mission.[109] This proviso is particularly important during a non-international conflict when captured personnel are likely to be subjected to extreme pressure in order to ascertain the whereabouts of others opposing the government forces, and there have been too many instances in the past where medical personnel have co-operated in giving stimulants or have brought persons round from an unconscious state in order to enable an interrogation to continue.

This article opened with reference to two female doctors who were subjected to harassment or other ill treatment because of the assistance they gave to those opposing the establishment during a non-international conflict. If Protocol II comes into force, then, *prima facie*, this will become less likely. Article 10 provides:

> 1. Under no circumstances shall any person be punishable for having carried out medical activities, compatible with medical ethics, regardless of the persons benefiting therefrom.
> 2. Persons engaged in medical activities shall neither be compelled to perform acts or to carry out work contrary to, nor be compelled to refrain from acts required

[105]Art. 12.
[106]Art. 13.
[107]Art. 30.
[108]Art. 7.
[109]Art. 9.

by the rules of medical ethics or other rules designed for the benefit of the wounded and sick, or this Protocol.

3. The professional obligations of persons engaged in medical activities regarding information which they may acquire concerning the wounded and sick under their care shall, *subject to national law*, be respected.

4. *Subject to national law*, no person engaged in medical activities may be penalized in any way for refusing or failing to give information concerning the wounded and sick who are, or have been, under his care.[110]

The phrase italicized indicates that the protection granted to a medical practitioner during a non-international conflict is not as effective as might have been hoped. Assuming a government has no members of the opposing rebel movement in its hands, what it is most likely to want from a doctor is information he will have acquired from his patients. By introducing the reference to national law, the Protocol authorizes the national authority to introduce such penalties, including death, as it may deem desirable. It would seem, therefore, that Protocol II would not have protected either Sheila Cassidy or Luisa Mistrali-Guidotti. Moreover, Protocol II makes no reference to the possibility of breaches, grave or otherwise, nor does it provide for any means of punishment of the authorities or the medical personnel who abuse the medical provisions it contains.

The experience of both world wars and of the conflicts that have taken place since 1945 is evidence of the fact that, whatever Conventions or customary international law may provide, respect for the law as it affects the medical profession during armed conflict, just as it affects any other aspect of war, depends on the good-will of governments and the behaviour of individuals. Insofar as non-international conflicts are concerned, compliance with any desiderata of humanity depends on the depths of ideological hatred and the determination of the government to suppress the opposition whatever the cost—a determination that will invariably be shared by the opposition.

While it is a matter for a doctor's conscience, and one of national as distinct from international law, to decide what instructions he will obey in his behaviour towards his own as distinct from enemy personnel, it may be questioned whether it is compatible with his function as a doctor to refuse to instruct paramedicals of his own force in regard to the treatment of the wounded, because he disapproves of the morality of the war, or because he considers the war itself or acts committed by his own people during it are war crimes. During the Vietnam War, Dr. Levy refused to institute a training program for Special Forces medical aidmen, contending that the war was illegal and that United States personnel were committing war crimes. The comments of his court martial should be noted by all military personnel as emphasizing where political ethics must be considered as giving way to professional medical ethics:

> Refusing to obey an order to commit a war crime is a recognized defence under the Uniform Code of Military Justice. . . . [T]he law officer ruled that although there perhaps occurred instances of needless brutality in the Vietnam War, nevertheless, there was "no evidence that would render this order to train aidmen illegal on the grounds that eventually these men would become engaged in war crimes or in some other way prostitute their medical training by employing it in crimes against humanity." At best, appellant could establish that individual American personnel may have violated the law of war in Vietnam. However, there never was any showing that the medical training appellant was ordered to give had any connection whatsoever with the perpetration of any war crime. Thus, appellant failed to demonstrate how the existence of war crimes committed by individuals

[110]Italics added.

other than those he was ordered to train was relevant to his failure to obey the order. Particularly relevant to this is that he failed to show that Special Forces aidmen as a group engaged systematically in the commission of war crimes by prostituting their medical training.[111]

Perhaps it may be said of a doctor guilty of such conscious acts of omission that he betrayed his mission and ignored his ethics as fully as one who by his acts of commission collaborates with the authorities in certifying that a prisoner, even in peacetime, is fit, for example, to undergo a flogging, or stands by during a flogging to indicate when the safety limit has been reached, and then treats the victim to enable the remainder of the sentence to be carried out. Equally, it can be questioned whether it is in accord with their oath for young doctors to respond to advertisements placed in western newspapers by the justice departments of some Islamic countries seeking surgeons to disarticulate extremities in accordance with Koranic law on the punishment for theft. In wartime, the correct attitude for a doctor is to behave as he would if a completely free agent in peacetime, affording proper treatment to all who appear to require his assistance. Issues of discrimination or whether a conflict is international or non-international are political in character and have nothing to do with his professional activities. As a doctor, his task in war or peace is to treat the sick and wounded. If it be said that by doing so he runs the risk of punishment or death, it might be pointed out that during an epidemic his life is also at risk, but this does not seem to inhibit him.

[111]*Levy* v. *Parker* (1973), 1 *Mil. Law Reporter*, 2130, 2142.

VII

Aerial Considerations in the Law of Armed Conflict

Regardless of the theatre of war that may be involved, the relevant rules of the law of armed conflict are to be found, for the main part, either in the Hague Law or the Geneva Law. The former relates primarily to the rules concerning means and methods and *jus in bello* generally. The Geneva Law, on the other hand, is almost exclusively concerned with what has come to be known as humanitarian law in armed conflict. Both these branches of the law of armed conflict are based on treaty provisions, but there are in addition certain basic principles which have grown through the centuries and are still valid on the basis of customary law.

In so far as air war is concerned, the Hague Law as treaty law plays very little role, but the Geneva Law, concerned as it is with the treatment of prisoners of war as well as the sick, wounded and shipwrecked, is of general application, even if only from the point of view of those who are aerial combatants. To the extent that the Hague Law may comprise principles, for example, the exclusion of weapons that cause unnecessary suffering—and this concept relates not to the subjective reactions of a victim, but suffering which may be said to go beyond that which is essential to render the victim *hors de combat*—or the exemption of non-military objectives from direct attack, that is to say principles which may be considered as being of universal application and stemming from practice, air warfare is as much subject to control as is any other form of warfare.

The Hague Rules, which still form the backbone of the law of war, even though they were annexed to a Convention relating to warfare on land,[1] were drafted in 1899 and then amended and revised in 1907. In view of the technological state of affairs then prevailing, it is perhaps not surprising that, while the two Hague Peace Conferences drew up treaties concerned with warfare on land and at sea, there was no specific treaty dealing with air warfare. The nearest approach to anything of this kind was Declaration

---

[1] Hague Convention IV, 1907, Schindler/Toman, 57.

IV of 1899, replaced by Declaration XIV in 1907.[2] This Declaration prohibited the discharge of projectiles and explosives from balloons or by other new methods of a similar nature. However, it was only effective in a war between states accepting it, and ceased to be operative as soon as a non-party became a belligerent in the particular conflict. This was the only clear rule that existed at the outbreak of World War I, but since it had not been accepted by France, Germany or Austria-Hungary, it was of no binding force during that conflict. This Declaration was to remain valid only until the end of the Third Peace Conference, which never took place.

Before 1914, there was a general belief that aircraft would not be used in direct conflict,[3] but when it became evident that this was not in fact the case, those involved, to a great extent, behaved like feudal knights and there was almost unbelievable evidence of chivalry in their combat conduct.[4] While there was no direct law relating to aerial combat or warfare, it was recognized that the rules of war as applicable in other media were of significance. This may be seen from the decision of the Greco-German Mixed Arbitral Tribunal in *Coenca Bros. v. Germany*,[5] arising from the destruction of private property by the Zeppelin bombing of Salonika, when the city was under allied occupation although Greece was officially neutral. The Tribunal pointed out that, even if the occupation was unlawful,

> Germany's right to defend herself against the Allied occupation of Salonika did not exonerate her from the obligation to observe the rules established by international law. . . .
> The evidence shows that the bombardment of Salonika . . . took place without prior warning by the German authorities, that the attack took place at night, and that the Zeppelin which dropped the bombs was at an altitude of about 3,000 metres. . . .
> It is one of the principles generally recognized by international law that belligerents must, so far as possible, respect the civil population and civilian property. . . .
> The Hague Convention IV of 1907, drawing its inspiration from this principle, has, in Article 26 of the Regulations concerning the laws and customs of warfare on land, clearly laid down that 'the officer in command of an attacking force must, before commencing a bombardment, except in cases of assault, do all in his power to warn the authorities.' . . .
> It is evident that the authors of the Convention intended in this way to accord to the authorities of the threatened town an opportunity either to evade bombardment by offering its capitulation, or to evacuate the civilian population. . . .
> Article 26 only envisaged warfare on land; [but] this Article ought to be regarded as expressing the *opinio communis* on this matter, and there is no reason why the rules adopted for bombardment in land warfare should not apply equally to aerial attacks[6]. . . .
> [Germany] has contended that aerial attack ought to be effected with surprise, and so cannot be announced in advance. . . .
> Even if this allegation . . . were true from the military point of view, it would not follow that aerial bombardments without warning are lawful, but, on the contrary, it would lead to the conclusion that such bombardments are, in general, inadmissible. . . .
> The darkness of the night, the altitude of 3,000 metres, and the fact that, during the occupation, Salonika was not illuminated, made it impossible to aim the bombs

---

[2]*Ibid.*, 141.
[3]Spaight, *Air Power and War Rights* (1924), 130-132.
[4]*Ibid.*, 102-115, 313-323.
[5](1927) 7 Rec. des Décisions des Tribunaux Arbitraux Mixtes, 683.
[6]A somewhat similar rule applies in regard to sea bombardments, see Hague Convention IX, 1907, Schindler/Toman, 723.

with the accuracy required to spare private dwelling-houses and commercial establishments.
. . . [The] bombardment in issue must be considered as contrary to international law. . . .

In view of the approach taken by the Tribunal in the *Coenca* case, there may be some ground for adopting the view that, to the extent that they are generally applicable, the rules in the Hague Regulations may extend to aerial warfare. Thus, the requirement in Article 1 of the Regulations that forces must be under a proper command, carry on their operations in accordance with the laws and customs of war and have a fixed distinctive emblem recognizable at a distance would all apply, although there is little room for the requirement that they carry their arms openly. At the time of the first World War, there was little to distinguish one type of plane from another, in the sense that fighters and bombers then looked somewhat alike. Again, while armies in the field could be distinguished by way of their national uniforms, the same function was fulfilled by the marking of aircraft with distinctive rondels, although, as was made clear by the practice of the Luftwaffe, these did not have to be in national colours; an accepted mark was sufficient. As to compliance with the laws and customs of war, the *Coenca* judgment indicated the applicability of the laws relating to bombardment, but problems arose in connection with disabled aircraft and evacuating pilots. While it might be argued that these could be compared with shipwrecked mariners or others who had laid down their arms, and thus become immune from attacks as *hors de combat*, practice showed that this rule, be it of law or chivalry, was not always observed. Aircrew who did survive evacuation and were captured were, of course, entitled to the same treatment as any other captured combatants and were entitled to prisoner of war status.

The course and the experience of the war made it clear that the adaptation of particular rules from land warfare would not suffice for the future. In view of this, in 1922, the Washington Conference on the Limitation of Armaments appointed a Commission of Experts under the chairmanship of John Bassett Moore. This Commission published in 1923 a draft known as "The Hague Rules of Air Warfare."[7] What must be borne in mind at all times when considering the problem of the rules of aerial warfare, is that the Hague Rules were never embodied in any treaty and are, therefore, not legally binding, other than to the extent that they reflect or express generally accepted rules of customary law. However, they are regarded as "an authoritative attempt to clarify and formulate rules of law governing the use of aircraft in war,"[8] and the latest compilation of the treaties on armed conflict says of them, "to a great extent, they correspond to the customary rules and general principles underlying the conventions on the law of war on land and at sea."[9] Moreover, as recently as 1963, the District Court of Tokyo stated[10] that "students of international law regard them as authoritative on the law of air warfare . . . rules of customary law in view of the fact that these are also found in common in the rules of land and sea warfare." On the other hand, the United States Air Force pamphlet entitled "International Law—the Conduct of Armed Conflict and Air Operations,"[11] even though it frequently draws attention to the compatibility of its statements with the Hague Rules, nevertheless states: "Although the draft Hague Rules have some authority because eminent jurists prepared them, they do not *represent existing customary law as a total code.*"[12]

[7]Schindler/Toman, 147.
[8]Oppenheim-Lauterpacht, *International Law*, Vol. 2, 7th Ed (1952), 519.
[9]Schindler/Toman, op. cit., 147.
[10]*Shimoda* v. *The State (Japan)* (1963) 32 I.L.R. 626, 631 (a full report will be found in 8 *Jap. Ann. Int'l Law* 212.
[11]AFP 110-31 (1976).
[12]At para 5-2c (italics in original).

While the Hague Rules do not, of themselves, amount to or express the law, they have played a role in the development of the law concerning aerial warfare and, as such, cannot be peremptorily dismissed. The Rules attempted to distinguish between military and non-military aircraft, resting on the carrying of papers and distinguishing marks, although it cannot be ignored that the practice of adding formation or private marks as well as painting camouflage designs on aircraft, would often render such distinguishing or national emblems difficult to recognize. In order to prevent acts of perfidy, the Rules forbade the use of false external marks or alteration of marks while in flight, and required states to inform other powers of the authorized marks that their aircraft would carry. While the Rules recognize that aircraft have freedom to fly through air space outside territorial authority, they also confirm that any belligerent or neutral state has authority to regulate or forbid entrance, movement or sojourn of aircraft within its jurisdiction. Further, there is the adaptation of the normal rule of armed conflict law that only combatants may participate in belligerent activities, with the restriction of the exercise of such rights to military aircraft only, and the concomitant requirement that private aircraft are not allowed, when outside their own territorial jurisdiction, to be armed during war. It must be presumed that this would mean that if a private aircraft, carrying arms within its own jurisdiction, took any action other than defensive against an enemy aircraft, its crew would be regarded as unprivileged combatants and punishable as such. In fact, the Rules provide that the crews of military aircraft must be exclusively military and, again adapting the rules of land warfare, postulate that they must individually wear distinctive marks that are easily recognizable at a distance, even if they become separated from their aircraft, which is perhaps a somewhat impractical suggestion. Recognizing that the new medium of travel could have major effects with regard to the care of the wounded, the Rules sought to adapt the Geneva Conventions on this subject to air ambulances. In so far as wounded airmen are concerned, perhaps the most important of the Hague Rules on Air Warfare was the provision that "when an aircraft has been disabled, the occupants when endeavouring to escape by means of a parachute must not be attacked in the course of their descent," in the same way as crew and others abandoning a disabled ship are immune from attack.[13] In so far as the Rules tackled the problem of aerial bombardment, they sought to adapt the general rules to the medium, forbidding attack against non-military objectives or for the purpose of terrorizing the civilian population.

As if to emphasize the difficulty of drafting rules to control aerial warfare, or the impossibility of adapting the ordinary rules applicable in land warfare, the Commission of Experts tackled the problem of aerial espionage, only to produce a somewhat artificial rule. Article 27 of the Rules states:

> Any person on board a belligerent or neutral aircraft is to be deemed a spy only if acting clandestinely or on false pretences he obtains or seeks to obtain, while in the air, information within belligerent jurisdiction or in the zone of operations of a belligerent with the intention of communicating it to the hostile party.

It is perhaps unfortunate that the Rules give no indication as to how one is to distinguish between such "clandestine" activity while in the air from legitimate reconnaissance, or the "transmission during flight of military intelligence for the immediate use of a belligerent," recognized by Article 16 as legitimate hostilities.

In so far as activities against enemy or neutral aircraft are concerned, as well as the

---

[13]See, e.g., *The Llandovery Castle* (1921), H.M.S.O., Cmd. 1450 (Cameron, *The Peleus Trial* (1948), App. IX).

duties owed by belligerent aircraft towards neutral states and vice versa, the Hague Rules of 1923 represent a valiant attempt to adapt the rules of land warfare. It may be said, in fact, that the whole motivation of the Experts was adaptation rather than innovation, and this may well be part of the reason that states were unwilling to accept the Rules as authoritative and binding. Moreover, it was probably too soon after states began to realize or think about the potential value of this arm of warfare for them to accept a statement which purported to regulate the conduct of aerial warfare, before its potential was really appreciated.

Between 1923 and the outbreak of the second World War in 1939, no attempt was made to develop any treaty dealing specifically with air warfare—but then, with the exception of efforts to achieve arms limitation or a ban on such weapons as gas, there was no attempt to deal with the general rules of warfare after 1907. However, in 1929, the Geneva Conventions on the Wounded and Sick[14] and Prisoners of War[15] had been adopted, and these applied to hostilities generally, regardless of the theatre in which they were carried on. The former contained provisions regarding aircraft used for medical purposes, laying down the colour and markings they were to bear, providing for the return of captured crew and granting their medical personnel the same treatment as those belonging to other arms of the service. Unlike other medical transports, recognizing the potential military character of every aircraft, the Convention forbade flight "over the firing line, and over the zone situated in front of clearing or dressing stations, and generally over all enemy territory or territory occupied by the enemy," unless express permission had been granted. The only specific reference to aerial warfare in the Prisoners of War Convention is to be found in Article 1, which expressly stated that "all persons belonging to the armed forces of belligerents who are captured by the enemy in the course of operations of . . . aerial war, subject to such exceptions as the conditions of such capture render inevitable," shall be treated as prisoners of war, while the exceptions so envisaged were to cease as soon as the personnel in question reached a prisoner of war camp.

The second World War made it clear that aircraft could be used in a variety of fashions, including direct support of land forces, the interdiction of enemy activities, reconnaissance, the transport of airborne troops as well as for the airlift of men and supplies, for anti-naval purposes, for the enforcement of a blockade, or, regardless of whether this was legal or not, for the bombardment of the enemy's home territory, heedless of the civilian casualties that might be caused. Even though aerial bombardment during that War often reached the level of indiscriminate attack, regardless of whether military objectives were destroyed or not, and the "blind" weapons used by Germany (such as V_1 and V_2) fall into the same classification from this point of view as the area or saturation bombing indulged in by the Allies, no war crimes charges were brought in respect of such warfare after the conclusion of hostilities. It is true that the Japanese, in accordance with the Enemy Airmen Act and the Formosan Military Law, tried American aircrew for the "unlawful" bombardment of Tokyo and other Japanese cities, but there would appear to have been no legal validity for such charges,[16] and those involved in the trials were subsequently hanged.[17] It should also be noted that Mr. Justice Pal, the Indian member of the International Military Tribunal charged with the trial of the Major Japanese War Criminals at Tokyo, delivered a dissenting judgment primarily because he regarded the

---

[14]Schindler/Toman, 257.

[15]*Ibid.*, 271.

[16]See Judgment of International Mil. Trib. for Far East (1948), Part A, 404-6; see also Spaight, op. cit., (1947 Ed), 58-61.

[17]See e.g., *Re Sawada* (1946), *Re Isayama* (1946), *Re Hisakasu* (1946), 5 *Law Reports of Trials of War Criminals*, 1, 60, 66, resp.

dropping of the atomic bombs on Hiroshima and Nagasaki as at least the equal in terror and criminality as anything with which the Japanese accused were charged.[18] As to war crimes directed against aircrew,[19] there was nothing particularly concerning air warfare in such offences. It was merely that the victims belonged to the air arm.

When the Geneva Conventions came up for review after the second World War in 1949, it was possible to take steps to fill some of the lacunae which had become evident during that war. In so far as air warfare was concerned, it might well be considered that, for the main part, the Conventions were cosmetic in the sense that they made it clear that their provisions applied to those involved in aerial activities. Apart from reiterating that the Conventions on the Wounded and Sick, the Wounded, Sick and Shipwrecked and Prisoners of War[20] applied to all members of the armed forces, their protection was extended to the civil members of military aircraft crews, as well as to the crews of civil aircraft who would not otherwise be entitled to more favourable treatment under other provisions of international law, such as they might, for example, enjoy under the Civilian Convention[21] as civilians in enemy hands. Since the 1949 Conventions were solely concerned with what has been described as humanitarian law during armed conflicts, they have little or no reference to the actual conduct of hostilities. However, in so far as aerial warfare is concerned, Article 12 of the Wounded, Sick and Shipwrecked Convention expressly states that the term "shipwreck" "includes forced landings by sea or from aircraft" and "any attempts upon their (i.e., crew members') lives, or violence to their persons, shall be strictly prohibited." However, they enjoy no more protection than any other shipwrecked persons, so that if they are being picked up by any vessel other than those correctly marked with the Red Cross, or similar insignia, they are not protected, although they would be while still on the water in their own life rafts. Apart from this specific article, the provisions of the 1949 Conventions concerning air warfare were solely of a medical character.

It was not until the adoption in 1977 of Protocol I additional to the Geneva Conventions of 1949[22] that specific attention was paid in treaty law to problems that were peculiar to aerial warfare. The only Article which relates solely to aerial warfare, as distinct from the protection granted to medical aircraft or which apply to all forms of warfare including aerial, is Article 42. For the first time, treaty recognition is given to the provision originally postulated in the 1923 Hague Rules, and it is provided that "no person parachuting from an aircraft in distress may be made the object of attack during his descent." This is so, even though it may be clear that the airman in question is likely to land in his own territory, although once he reaches such territory he would again become the object of legitimate attack like any other member of the armed forces. If, however, he should land in territory under enemy control, he "must be given an opportunity to surrender before being made the object of attack, unless it is apparent that he is engaging in a hostile act," which would include the sending of a radio message to indicate that he had landed and giving his location, or an attempt to destroy his aircraft or its equipment. The Article, however, recognizes that no similar protection can be extended to airborne troops, thus placing a burden on the power that sends them to distinguish clearly between such troops and the aircrew of the aircraft conveying them, as well as a burden upon the defending forces to take every precaution to distinguish, since only the paratroops con-

---

[18]Pal, *International Military Tribunal for the Far East, Dissentient Judgment* (1953).
[19]See, e.g., *Essen Lynching Case (Re Hayer)* (1945) 1 *Law Reports of Trials of War Criminals*, 81; *Re Wielen (Stalag Luft Trial)*, (1947), 11 Ibid, 31.
[20]Schindler/Toman, 305, 333, 355, resp.
[21]Ibid., 427.
[22]Ibid. 551.

stitute legitimate objects of attack. The Protocol also extends the protection granted to shipwrecked airmen, since it provides for their protection so long as they are in peril at sea or in other waters and refrain from any hostile act, and, so long as they so refrain, they remain protected during their rescue and until they acquire some other status. This leaves open the question whether they are still to be considered shipwrecked and protected if they radio their position on the water so that rescue craft may attend them, and suggests that they do not, as before, enjoy such protection only so long as they may be picked up by vessels properly described as hospital craft. This would suggest that there could not, from the point of view of law, be any repetition of the unfortunate *Laconia* incident in 1942.[23] In September of that year, the *Laconia*, a troopship with 1,800 Italian prisoners on board, was sunk by U-156. On learning of this, the U-boat's captain radioed for help in the rescue, provided he was not himself attacked. Doenitz ordered other U-boats to co-operate and Vichy warships were sent to assist. The Royal Navy also sent two ships for this purpose. While the operation was in progress, a United States bomber arrived and saw U-156 on the surface, flying a white flag with a red cross and towing two lifeboats. After staying at the scene for an hour, the aircraft left and contacted its base, and, since no friendly submarines were known to be in the area, it was ordered to attack. It returned and bombed U-156. As a result, Doenitz ordered the abandonment of the rescue, and instructed U-boats to abstain from future rescues. While it would appear that there was a breakdown in communications, especially as the Royal Navy was aware of what was taking place and had despatched vessels to co-operate in search so that a de facto cartel might be said to have been created, it must not be overlooked that, at that date, there was no law which permitted a U-boat or other vessel of war to fly the red cross and enjoy immunity from attack while so doing. Protection would now extend to any vessel while engaged in such operations, for by Art. 18 of the 1949 Convention on the Wounded, Sick and Shipwrecked there is an obligation upon all parties to search for and pick-up survivors after an engagement, and this can only have real meaning if those picking up are protected especially if indicating that they are engaged in such humanitarian activity.

Other provisions in the Protocol which extend the law to cover aerial activities exclusively are those concerning medical aircraft. Now there are clear regulations as to the identification of such aircraft, their radio and light signals, and such other technical matters as are essential if they are to fulfil their tasks in safety. It is also now recognized, in the light of the experience gained in Korea and Vietnam, that medical aircraft will be carrying out their activities in the vicinity of the zone of operations. It is provided, therefore, that when over territory controlled by friendly forces or over seas not under enemy control, such aircraft are free to fly with all the respect due to medical aircraft, even though no agreement to this effect has been worked out with the enemy. However, "for greater safety, a party to the conflict operating its medical aircraft in these areas may notify the adverse party in particular when such aircraft are making flights bringing them within range of surface-to-air weapons systems" of that adverse party. On the other hand, when flying "in and over those parts of the contact zone which are physically controlled by friendly forces and in and over those areas the physical control of which is not clearly established, protection for medical aircraft can be fully effective only by prior agreement between the component military authorities of the parties to the con-

---

[23]A statement of the facts is to be found in Mallison, *Submarines and the Law of Naval Warfare* (1968), 84-5 . . . but he fails to point out that, at that date, the U-boat had no right to fly the Red Cross or receive immunity while engaged in a rescue operation. The Doenitz "no rescue" order is discussed at 137.

flict . . . Although, in the absence of such an agreement, medical aircraft operate at their own risk, they shall nevertheless be respected after they have been recognized as such." In so far as they may be flying over land or sea areas under enemy control, they continue to enjoy protection and respect "provided that prior agreement to such flights has been obtained from the competent authority" of the enemy. If they lack such agreement or deviate from its terms, then they must make every effort to identify themselves and inform the enemy of the circumstances. Once the enemy has recognized the aircraft as a medical aircraft, it must make every effort to give an order to land for inspection, or to take other measures necessary for its own protection, but must, in any case, give the aircraft time to comply with its orders before launching any attack against it. While these requirements would tend to preclude the operation of any order to attack all aircraft at sight, it must be noted that, in the circumstances just referred to, medical aircraft do not, in fact, enjoy the same absolute immunity that is the right of land and sea medical transports. Another restriction placed upon the activities of medical aircraft, as distinct from the general prohibition to indulge in any military or non-medical activities, is the ban, when in contact zones or over territory or water under enemy control, upon any rescue activities on behalf of the wounded, sick or shipwrecked, unless prior agreement has been obtained from the enemy. Air rescue operations directed at picking up airmen who have come down in the water under enemy control or in contact zones, such as the English Channel during the second World War, would no longer be permissible, without the concurrence of the enemy.

Other articles of the Protocol which may be said to relate to air warfare are those which deal with the protection of civilians and civilian objects; which limit the right to bombard; which are concerned with the prevention of excessive incidental non-military losses; which forbid long-term environmental damage or preclude attacks which will release dangerous forces. But all these are directed at hostilities in general. That is to say, whether or not they specifically refer to aerial warfare, those responsible for such activities are as bound as those operating on land or at sea. It may be said, therefore, that these rules, together with any basic principles which operate in time of conflict apply to aerial warfare as they do to hostilities elsewhere. However, Protocol I has not yet been ratified by Canada, the United States, or any leading NATO power—in fact, by mid-July 1984 only six western countries had ratified it—but it is in force, and is the first international document since 1907 which attempts in any way to regulate the means and methods of warfare. In this connection, it should be pointed out that, to some extent, the Protocol reproduces, sometimes in modified and sometimes in extended form, the principles adopted by the Institute of International Law in its Edinburgh Resolution of 1969.[24] While it is true that the Institute possesses no official status so that its Resolutions lack any binding authority, nevertheless, its status is such that its recommendations cannot be dismissed peremptorily—a fact which is demonstrated by the authority and influence of the *Oxford Manual*,[25] promulgated by it in 1880—and one must, therefore, remember that the Resolution purports to codify what were considered to be accepted rules of the customary law of armed conflict. To the extent that this is true, the provisions in the Protocol which are in line with such propositions may be considered expressive of customary law and generally binding.

With this in mind, it is perhaps useful to indicate what may be regarded as the basic principles of the law of armed conflict. Stated simply, while the law of armed conflict is

[24]Schindler/Toman, 201.
[25]*Ibid*, 35.

consistent with the economic and efficient use of force, its aim, nevertheless, is to min-
imize the horrors of the conflict, while not inhibiting the military activities of the parties
in their aim to achieve victory. To this end, military necessity must be balanced against
overriding principles of a humanitarian character, and while the demands of military
necessity are limited by legal and moral, as well as military and political, considerations,
the demands of humanitarianism must be adjusted to those of practical reality. In other
words, if the application of such force would cause injury to non-combatants or civilians,
no more force or greater violence should be used to carry out an operation than is
absolutely necessary in the particular circumstances, but the interests of the civilians
must not outweigh the overall demands of the general operation. The principles of the
law of armed conflict must be applied in a non-discriminatory fashion, and this applies
not only as regards individual victims, but also as between belligerents. This being the
case, the protection of the law of armed conflict extends to all parties to the conflict,
regardless of the origin or legality of the conflict, and regardless of whether the adversary
is to be considered a criminal aggressor.

While it is true that the aim of any conflict is to secure victory, it must constantly be
borne in mind that the means of conducting the conflict are not unrestricted, and must
not involve means likely to cause unnecessary suffering. The concept of unnecessary
suffering is not subjective in the sense that it is measured by the intensity of an injury
suffered by a war victim. It is rather to be measured by relation to the end which is to
be achieved. That is to say, only such suffering should be inflicted as is necessary to
achieve the military objective, by, for example, placing combatants *hors de combat*. With
this end in view, acts of a warlike nature must be directed only against military objects
and objectives, and civilians are exempt from being made the object of direct military
action. Although this is so, it is not a breach of the law of armed conflict if civilians suffer
injury incidental to attack upon a lawful military objective, so long as such incidental
injury is not disproportionate to the military objective which it is sought to achieve.
However, attacks which fail to distinguish between military and civilian personnel, military and civilian objects and military and non-military objectives are forbidden as indiscriminate, although it must be accepted that there is a duty upon the "owner" of such
objects and objectives to take steps necessary to enable the adverse party to make the
necessary distinction. Put simply, the decision whether an objective is legitimate or not
depends upon the contribution an attack on that objective will make to ultimate victory
or the success of the operation of which the attack is part. But with objects normally
devoted to civilian use, such as schools, hospitals or places of worship, if there is any
doubt they are being used for such purposes or being put to military use, they shall
receive the benefit of the doubt and not be subjected to attack.

In deciding whether an objective is or is not an object of legitimate attack, the principle
of proportionality, a principle which is well-established in the customary law of armed
conflict and which seeks to achieve some measures of reasonable connection between
related matters, comes into play. In deciding whether the principle is being respected,
the standard to be applied must operate in good faith and not in accordance with sub-
jectivity. It is to be assessed by the contribution to the military purpose of the attack or
the operation as a whole, as compared with other consequences of the action, such as
the effect upon civilians or civilian objects. It involves weighing the interests arising from
the success of the operation on the one hand, against the possible harmful effect upon
protected persons and objects on the other. There must, therefore, be an acceptable
relation between the legitimate destructive effect and undesirable collateral consequences.
Historically, the principle of proportionality was probably best known in its relation to

a recourse to reprisals, formerly regarded as the last resort of a belligerent subjected to persistent breaches of the law of armed conflict by the adverse party. Any such measures were required to bear a reasonable relationship to the action against which they were directed, for the aim was not to retaliate but to compel the wrongdoer to resume lawful conduct. Today, reprisals against protected persons and objects are increasingly considered to be unlawful.

Attacks which have no direct military purpose are forbidden, even though their indirect purpose may be to terminate the conflict. For this reason, acts of terror against the civilian population of the adverse party are forbidden, despite the fact that the purpose may be to compel the adverse party to terminate its military activities. However, it is forbidden to use the civilian population to ensure immunity for a military object, so that an attack upon civilians brought into the vicinity of a legitimate military objective for this purpose cannot be regarded as illegal.

As has been pointed out, the law of armed conflict rests upon a judicious balance between military necessity and humanitarian principles, which means that, in active combat, commanders must ensure that this balance is preserved, bearing in mind that, in so far as the restrictions imposed by law upon their freedom of action are embodied in treaties, those treaties have been drafted with military considerations in mind. It is equally important for the military commander to appreciate that the law of armed conflict applies to both the state in defence as well as the state in offence. Under customary law, there was no restriction upon the state in defence in so far as the treatment of its own nationals or territory was concerned, even though the competence of the enemy in regard to those persons or that territory was limited. Today, however, both are equally limited by the principles of international law in regard to human rights, while, in so far as the Protocol defines an attack as "any act of violence against the adversary, whether in offence or in defence," any limitations affecting offensive action apply equally to defensive actions. It is, therefore, no longer possible for a state in defence to destroy its own territory or dangerous objects within its jurisdiction without any regard for the long-term effects or for the consequences such action may have upon its own population. However, it must be remembered that even the Charter of the United Nations recognizes that states possess an inherent right of self-defence, so that actions taken against one's own territory for the preservation of the territorial integrity and existence of the state would still be lawful, at least to the extent that such actions would not result in the destruction of one's own population.

Applying these basic principles to aerial conflict in the light of Protocol I, which expressly declares its applicability to aircraft operating against targets on land, or which are being attacked from the land, it becomes possible to supplement the lacunae resulting from the absence of specific treaties directed at controlling air warfare. Intentional bombing of civilians is illegal and objectives aimed at from the air must be military objectives and identifiable as such. To this end, the ground power must itself take such measures as may be necessary to enable the necessary distinction to be drawn. While attacks upon military objectives must be carried out with care to avoid civilian populations in the vicinity being attacked through negligence, incidental injury suffered by that population does not render an otherwise lawful aerial attack unlawful. The decision as to whether an aerial attack should be launched or not, must be made by a commander in the light of all knowledge available to him in the particular circumstances, and if, taking all these considerations into account, it transpires that civilian damage is likely to be excessive, the attack must be suspended or abandoned. All aircraft used in armed conflict should be clearly marked with proper insignia known to the enemy and must indicate clearly that they are military aircraft. In this way, their occupants will be entitled to the protection afforded by international law to lawful combatants, while the occupants of aircraft not so identifiable and taking part in hostile operations are liable to be treated as unprivileged combatants and subjected to trial for breaches of the law of armed conflict. Civilian aircraft, even though manned by military crews or carrying members of the armed forces as passengers, are not permitted to take part in combat. While they may be attacked in certain circumstances, they may only be used for combat purposes if they are incorporated into the air force and are correctly marked.

A problem that presents itself more readily to aircraft than to land forces relates to the risk of infringing the rights of neutrals. The experience of the second World War, and of the period since, despite further developments in navigational aids, illustrates the ease with which belligerent aircraft may accidentally cross a frontier and breach a nation's neutrality by such overflight. If this occurs, the intruder runs the risk of being fired upon, even without warning, although during the second World War warnings were usually issued and fire only resorted to when the warning was disregarded. Belligerent aircraft should endeavour to confine their activities, and this includes flying through air space without taking any offensive action of any kind, to the airspace above their national territory, that of the adverse party or over the high seas and, while doing so, not interfere with the right of neutral aircraft to traverse international airspace even though such aircraft be proceeding towards enemy territory. In the case of sea warfare, such a voyage may be prevented by a blockade, but in the air this type of interdiction is impractical.

If any enemy aircraft seeks to break off combat by entering neutral airspace, the adversary aircraft is not entitled to pursue it unless, in circumstances similar to those relating to the *Altmark* and *H.M.S. Cossack* in Norwegian waters in 1940, there is evidence to indicate that the neutral concerned is unable or unwilling to assert its neutral rights as against the intruder. However, if a neutral state's airspace is penetrated, the neutral state must remember that even the right to protect its air sovereignty is limited by considerations of a humanitarian character and that any force it seeks to apply must be commensurate to the threat to which it is exposed. This may mean that radio signals should be directed at the intruder informing it of the intrusion, or warning shots should be fired and no attack launched until the intruder has been apprised of the intrusion and has disregarded an order to land or depart. In any case, the neutral state involved must make certain that the intruder is not a protected aircraft, for it would be in breach of its own obligations if it immediately launched an attack upon a medical or civil aircraft belonging to one of the belligerents. If a neutral aircraft enters the airspace of a belligerent, or an area which has been declared a combat zone, it does so at its own risk. However, military aircraft or the air defence or anti-aircraft commands of a belligerent are obliged to take similar precautions as a neutral with regard to intruding belligerent aircraft. That is to say, there should be no attack upon such an aircraft before it has been warned to withdraw, and that warning has been disregarded.

As to aerial combat, or ground attack against enemy aircraft, aircraft may be attacked by any weapon the use of which is not contrary to international law. This includes air-to-air and ground-to-air missiles, as well as explosive or incendiary projectiles, even though the employment of such weapons may be restricted or forbidden against individual personnel in land combat. Equally, ramming techniques as between aircraft or suicide attacks against targets on land or at sea, such as those carried out by Japanese *kamikaze* pilots during the second World War, are perfectly legitimate. Just as perfidious use of protected emblems, such as the Red Cross, is forbidden in land or sea warfare, so it constitutes a war crime for a military aircraft to pretend to be a medical aircraft, or for what appears to be a medical aircraft to indulge in combat. While a captured enemy aircraft may be used, this is only so if it is marked with the identification rondels of the force making use of it. In fact, Protocol I now expressly prohibits the use of enemy emblems or insignia during attacks—and this applies both in offence and defence—in order to favour or protect military operations.[26] Similarly, while it is permissible to make use of the call signs of enemy aircraft, it is prohibited falsely to make use of distress signals or the signals reserved for medical aircraft, and, as has been pointed out, although it is perfectly legal to camouflage aircraft or to make use of personal or formation signs, care must be taken that national signs are not obscured and the enemy is not led to believe that his own signs are being used.

Aircraft may be used to enforce a blockade and to effect the seizure of enemy civilian vessels and aircraft, and such craft may be used after their condemnation by a prize court. In the event of enemy military aircraft or warships—which may be attacked so long as they are not in neutral waters—being seized by or with the assistance of aircraft, such use is permitted without any prior recourse to a prize court. Every effort should be made to avoid attacking civil aircraft in flight, for they are *prima facie* assumed to be carrying civilians who may not be made the object of direct attack. If there is any doubt as to the status of an aircraft which appears to be civil, it should be called upon to clarify its status, and only if it fails to do so, or it becomes clear that it is being used for non-civil purposes, such as the ferrying of troops, may it be attacked. It is probably unnecessary to emphasize that civil aircraft should avoid entering areas in which aerial combat is taking place or which have been declared restricted flight areas by the belligerents. If it should appear that an aircraft which is not marked as a military aircraft is intended for absorption into the enemy's air force, it may be attacked while being ferried from the manufacturer to the belligerent for whom it is intended. The crews of such aircraft, together with those of any military aircraft who fall into enemy hands become prisoners of war. The same is true of the civilian crew of any civilian aircraft which has been lawfully attacked, but if the attack is unlawful the crew should be freed or held in accordance with the terms of the 1949 Geneva Convention concerning the treatment of civilians. Civil aircraft on the ground may only be attacked in accordance with the normal rules relating to military objectives. However, since they may be used for transporting troops or military supplies, their status will often depend upon the prevailing military situation. Moreover, airfields are legitimate objects of attack and incidental damage to civil aircraft does not render such an attack unlawful. It must be emphasized that belligerents may agree to confer protection on any aircraft for a specific reason, such as the carriage of negotiators or for a special mercy mission.[27]

Aircraft may not open fire on any personnel who have indicated an intention to surrender, and this restriction applies to ships as well as land forces. Nor may they fire upon shipwrecked persons, including those who may have parachuted into the sea or otherwise come from downed aircraft, at least so long as they have not been picked up. If, however, they have been rescued by a protected vessel, the protected status of the vessel will extend to them. While parachuting airmen are now protected, paratroops may be attacked while in course of descent. This immunity of persons who are seeking to render themselves *hors de combat* applies to all medical transport and personnel, regardless of the theatre in which they are operating. It also extends to enemy merchant ships, so long as they do not actively resist an order to stop when called upon to do so; do not take any

---

[26]Art. 39.
[27]In 1941, arrangements were made for an R.A.F. plane to drop an artificial leg to Wing Commander Bader, then a prisoner of war.

offensive action; await visit and search either by an aircraft landing upon the sea or hovering while awaiting a ship to fulfil this task; are not sailing under convoy of enemy warships or military aircraft; and are not being used for any auxiliary armament, or the like. In so far as neutral vessels are concerned, neutral warships or merchant craft are immune from attack so long as they do nothing to compromise their neutrality or assimilate them to a belligerent. However, a neutral vessel sailing under enemy convoy is a legitimate target, as is one seeking to run a lawful blockade.

In attacks directed from the air against troops or ground targets, all the precautions required in regard to attacks on land must be observed. In other words, such attacks must not be indiscriminate, and care must be taken, to the extent that is feasible, to avoid excessive damage to civilians and civilian objects. Aerial attack or bombardment of an undefended place is prohibited, and before commencing any bombardment effective advance warning should be given if the attack may affect the civilian population, unless circumstances do not permit this.[28] Those involved in any attack must take all reasonable precautions to avoid losses of civilian lives and damage to civilian objects,[29] and to spare hospitals and other places where the wounded and sick are being cared for,[30] as well as buildings dedicated to religion, art, science, historic monuments and the like, provided they are not being used for military purposes,[31] and the burden of proof is, broadly speaking, upon the attacker.

It has long been accepted that aerial attack intended to spread terror among the civilian population is forbidden, and this is now embodied in Article 51 of Protocol I. Moreover, bearing in mind the need to examine all the prevailing circumstances in the light of the information available, any aerial attack which may be anticipated to cause civilian damage excessive in relation to the concrete and direct military advantage anticipated, is illegal. For this reason, aerial attacks which would treat as a single military objective a number of clearly separated and distinct military objectives located in an area containing a concentration of civilians or civilian objects is prohibited. This means that area bombing in such a place is forbidden, although it is still permissible to attack two or more legitimate military objectives within a given area, and these may be attacked during the same aerial assault. However, an aerial attack which cannot be directed against a specific military objective and which is likely, therefore, to affect both military objectives and civilians or civilian objects without distinction, is forbidden.[32] This would imply that saturation bombing or weapons of mass destruction, or fire bombs, the effect of which cannot be controlled, are all illegal. Equally, an air attack with weapons, the effects of which cannot be limited to satisfy the restrictions on behalf of civilians postulated by Protocol I, is also forbidden. This would seem *prima facie* to forbid the use of nuclear weapons. It should be made clear, however, that throughout the negotiations relevant to Protocol I, the International Committee of the Red Cross, as well as the participants in the Conference, were emphatic that the provisions of the Protocol only related to conventional weapons. In fact, at the time of signature, most of the NATO Powers expressed their understanding of the nature of the Protocol as excluding any application to the nuclear arm.

It is, nevertheless, relevant to mention that in *Shimoda* v. *The State*, the Tokyo District

[28]Protocol I, Art. 57, para 2(c).
[29]Art. 57, para 4.
[30]Hague Regs., Art. 27, and Geneva Conventions, 1949, re sick, wounded and shipwrecked.
[31]Hague Regs., Art. 27; see also Protocol I, Arts. 52, 53 and the 1954 Hague Convention for the Protection of Cultural Property in the Event of Armed Conflict (Schindler/Toman, 661) to which Canada is not a party.
[32]Art. 51.

Court had to consider the legality of the dropping of the atomic bombs on Hiroshima and Nagasaki:

> . . . the use of a new weapon is legal, as long as international law does not prohibit it. However, the prohibition in this case is understood to include not only the case where there is an express provision of direct prohibition, but also the case where it is necessarily regarded that the use of a new weapon is prohibited, from the interpretation and analogical application of existing international laws and regulations (international customary laws and treaties). Further, we must understand that the prohibition includes also the case where, in the light of principles of international law which are the basis of the positive international laws and regulations [mentioned by the Court, extending from the Declaration of St. Petersburg of 1868 to the Geneva Gas Protocol of 1925, including the Draft Hague Rules on Air Warfare of 1923], the use of a new weapon is admitted to be contrary to the principles. For there is no reason why the interpretation of international law must be limited to grammatical interpretation. . . .
>
> It is right and proper that any weapon contrary to the custom of civilized countries and to the principles of international law, should be prohibited even if there is no express provision in the laws and regulations. Only where there is no provision in the statutory (international) law, and as long as a new weapon is not contrary to the principles of international law, can the new weapon be used as a legal means of hostility. . . .
>
> We can safely say that the prohibition of indiscriminate aerial bombardment on an undefended city and the principle of military objective . . . are international customary law, also from the point that they are in common with the principle of land and sea warfare. Further, since the distinction of land, sea and air warfare is made by the place and purpose of warfare, we think that there is also sufficient reason for existence of the argument that, regarding the aerial bombardment of a city on land, the laws and regulations respecting land warfare analogically apply since the aerial bombardment is made on land. . . .
>
> It is a long-standing, generally recognized principle in international law respecting air raids, that indiscriminate aerial bombardment is not permitted on an undefended city and that only bombardment of military objectives is permitted. Of course, it is naturally anticipated that the aerial bombardment of a military objective is attended with the destruction of non-military objectives or casualty of non-combatants; and this is not illegal if it is an inevitable result accompanying the aerial bombardment of a military objective. However, it necessarily follows that, in an undefended city, an aerial bombardment directed at a non-military objective, and an aerial bombardment without distinction between military objectives and non-military objectives (the so-called blind aerial bombardment) is not permitted in the light of the above-mentioned principle. . . .
>
> The act of atomic bombing on an undefended city . . . should be regarded in the same light as a blind aerial bombardment; and it must be said to be a hostile act contrary to international law of the day. . . .
>
> It is a well-known fact that Hiroshima and Nagasaki were not cities resisting a possible occupation attempt by land forces at that time. Further, it is clear . . . that both cities did not come within the purview of the defended city, since they were not in the pressing danger of enemy's occupation, even if both cities had antiaircraft guns, etc. against air raids and had military installations. Also, it is clear that some 330,000 civilians in Hiroshima and some 270,000 civilians in Nagasaki maintained homes there, even though there were so-called military objectives such as armed forces, military installations, and munitions factories in both cities. Therefore, since an aerial bombardment with an atomic bomb brings the same result as a blind aerial bombardment from the tremendous power of destruction, even if the aerial bombardment has only a military objective as the target of its attack, it is proper to understand that an aerial bombardment of both cities of Hiroshima and Nagasaki was an illegal act of hostility as the indiscriminate aerial bombardment of undefended cities . . .[33]

[33]1963, 8 Japanese Annual of International Law (1964), 212, 235, 236-237 (reproduced in 32 *I.L.R.*, 626.

Regardless of any argument that the atomic attacks on Hiroshima and Nagasaki might have been legitimate as reprisals in the light of Japanese breaches of the law of armed conflict, and subject to some measure of doubt whether the two cities were, in fact, undefended and not military objectives, if the Tokyo court were correct in its conclusion that the use of the atomic bomb was contrary to the then-existing customary and treaty law of armed conflict as a blind and indiscriminate weapon, it would matter little that signatories to Protocol I had made declarations that the Protocol had no relevance to nuclear weapons, for such weapons would already be illegal and the Protocol would make no difference to this fact. This would mean that any member of an aircrew aware that he was participating in a nuclear attack would be amenable to trial for war crimes.

Assuming that the Protocol has no application to nuclear weapons, and assuming that the Japanese decision is wrong and that there is no law forbidding the use of such weapons, it must, nevertheless, be noted that aerial attacks launched against objects which are indispensable to the survival of the civilian population with the purpose of denying that population its means of sustenance are illegal.[34] It is equally forbidden to launch an aerial attack against dams, dykes and nuclear electrical generating stations, even though they might be legitimate military objectives, if the effect of their destruction would cause the release of dangerous forces and consequently severe losses among the civilian population, but if no such losses would be caused the attack would be legitimate. Similarly, military objectives near such installations may not be attacked if their destruction would result in the escape of dangerous forces from such neighbouring installations. While such works or installations should be indicated by identification marks, the absence of such marks does not mean that they may be attacked.[35] This would seem to imply that the burden is upon the attacking aircraft, which must, therefore, rely upon its intelligence or spotting and identification machinery to indicate the character of the work or installation it is considered desirable to bomb. This means that prior reconnaissance may often be essential, but if this takes place and it is ascertained that a particular objective is in fact a lawful object for attack, the aerial attack launched against that object should be sufficiently close in time to the reconnaissance to ensure that the object in question is still a legitimate objective. However, given modern observation and surveillance techniques, the risk of mistake had been somewhat minimized.

Among other aerial attacks which are forbidden are those which are intended or may be expected to cause long-term, widespread and severe damage to the natural environment. This is a new regulation introduced by Article 55 of the Protocol and the damage envisaged is of a lasting character and not localized. A similar provision is to be found in the Treaty of the Military Use of Environment Modification Techniques of 1977,[36] to which, however, Canada is not a party. Those accepting the Treaty have undertaken not to engage in the military use of such techniques as a means of injuring any other party to the Treaty, if they have widespread, long-lasting or severe effects.

It may well happen that, during an aerial attack, the same military advantage might be gained by bombing one or another of two objectives. Should this be so, the attack should be launched against that objective which is likely to result in less civilian damage,[37] while, if it transpires during an attack that the objective is not or has ceased to be a legitimate military objective, or is subject to some special protection, or the attack is likely

---

[34]Protocol I, Art. 54, para 2.
[35]Art. 56.
[36]16 *I.L.M.* (1977), 88.
[37]Protocol I, Art. 57, Para 3.

to result in civilian damage excessive to the direct military advantage anticipated, given all the circumstances, then this aerial attack should be cancelled or suspended. Since this is a provision newly introduced by Protocol I,[38] it is not binding upon states which, like Canada, have not yet ratified the Protocol.

Perhaps most important from the point of view of those engaged in aerial warfare against the ground, is the rule to be found in the Geneva Conventions and the Protocol forbidding reprisals against civilians and other protected persons and objects. This is now a basic principle of all forms of warfare, regardless of the nature involved. Equally, it must be remembered at all times that, when there are no specific rules relating to air warfare as such, the basic rules of armed conflict referred to earlier, as well as the general rules governing land warfare and the selection of targets, are equally applicable to aerial attacks directed against enemy personnel and ground or sea targets.

[38]Art. 57, para 2(b).

VIII

Lawful and Unlawful Weapons and Activities

There are various activities in armed conflict affecting the use of weapons, such as a decision to launch a gas or nuclear attack, which can only be made at the highest level, political or military. In so far as the ordinary man in the field is concerned, if he considers such an attack to be illegal it is a moral choice for him whether he complies with an order to use such weapons or not. Equally, it is not for him to decide whether a conflict in which his state is involved is just or unjust. Here, too, he is faced with the same moral dilemma, and it is unlikely that in either case those, be they military or civil, who will be called upon to judge him will find in his favour.[1] There are, however, a number of activities and weapons which directly involve the personal responsibility of the man in the field. For the main part, this paper is concerned rather with the latter type of activity than the former, although reference will be made to these, too, where the lawfulness of particular weaponry is directly in question.

Any consideration of the legality of the weapons that may be used or activities indulged in during conflict must, of necessity, look to the purpose for which war is fought. According to Sun Tzu[2] "generally in war the best policy is to take a state intact; to ruin it is inferior to this. To capture the enemy army is better than to destroy it; to take intact a battalion, a company or a five-man squad is better than to destroy them. For to win one hundred victories in one hundred battles is not the acme of skill. To subdue the enemy without fighting is the acme of skill." This view of a Chinese military strategist writing probably in the sixth century B.C. should be compared with those of Clausewitz some 2500 years later. In the first place he pointed out that "to impose our will on the

---

[1]See, e.g., *Levy* v. *Parker* (1973) 1 M.L.R. 2130. See, also, *DaCosta* v. *Laird* (1973) 471 F. 2d 1146, and for consideration of the role of the laws of war in an unlawful war, see Lauterpacht, "Rules of Warfare in an Unlawful War," in Lipsky, *Law and Politics in the World Community*, 1953, 89.
[2]*The Art of War*, tr. Griffith, 1963, III "Offensive Strategy," 77.

enemy is [the] object [of force]. To secure that object we must render the enemy powerless . . . The fighting forces must be *destroyed*: that is they must be *put in such a condition that they can no longer carry on the fight.*"[3] It is clear, therefore, that Clausewitz did not consider it necessary to exterminate the enemy, although since "war is an act of force, there is no logical limit to the application of force."[4] In view of this it is perhaps not surprising that he is cynical about restraints on the use of force. Thus he states that "attached to force are certain self-imposed perceptible limitations hardly worth mentioning, known as international law and custom, but they scarcely weaken it . . . [In fact,] kind-hearted people might . . . think there was some ingenious way to disarm or defeat an enemy without too much bloodshed, and might imagine that is the true goal of the art of war. Pleasant as it sounds, it is a fallacy that must be exposed: war is such a dangerous business that the mistakes which come from kindness are the very worst. . . . [However,] if civilized nations do not put their prisoners to death or devastate cities and countries, it is because intelligence plays a larger part in their methods or warfare [than was the case among savages] and has taught them more effective ways of using force than the crude expression of instinct."[5] Perhaps one can be equally cynical and remark that the 'intelligence' which he regards as playing a larger part in methods of warfare expresses itself in those very rules of international law and custom which he condemns as 'hardly worth mentioning'.

It is clear that the views expressed by Sun Tze and Clausewitz are far removed from those that we find in the Old Testament. During the exodus from Egypt to Canaan we are told of the conflict between the Israelites and King Arad, "and the Lord delivered up the Canaanites; and they utterly destroyed them and their cities"[6] and when Jericho fell "they utterly destroyed all that was in the city, both man and woman, young and old, and ox, and sheep, and ass, with the edge of the sword."[7] There was then no suggestion that any activity was forbidden either by law or by conscience. On the other hand, there were occasions when behaviour was more in accordance with the teaching of Clausewitz and the taking of captives was envisaged rather than utter destruction.[8] Moreover, the Israelites were also enjoined to seek peace rather than war, for "when thou comest nigh unto a city to fight against it, then proclaim peace unto it. And it shall be, if it make thee answer of peace, and open unto thee, then it shall be, that all the people that is found therein shall be tributaries unto thee, and they shall serve thee."[9] It is only if these overtures calling for surrender are rejected that the place in question is to be destroyed, but even then it is only the males that are to be slain, while mercy is shown to the women and children,[10] for the object of the use of force has been achieved. Perhaps the reason for the apparent barbarism of the ancient Israelites may be expressed in the words of Gibbon commenting on the behaviour of the Scythians in the middle of the fifth century:[11]

> In all their invasions of the civilized empires of the South, the Scythian shepherds have been uniformly actuated by a savage and destructive spirit. The laws of war that restrain the exercise of national rapine and murder, are founded on two prin-

[3]*On War*, 1832, Howard and Paret ed., 1976, Bk. I, ch. 1, para. 2, ch. 2, 75, 90 (italics in original).
[4]*Ibid.*, Bk. I, ch. 1, para. 3, 77.
[5]*Ibid.*, Bk. I, ch. 1, paras. 2, 3, 75, 76.
[6]*Numbers*, 21, iii.
[7]*Joshua*, 6, xxi.
[8]*Deuteronomy*, 21, x.
[9]*Deuteronomy*, 20, x, xi.
[10]*Deuteronomy*, 20, xii-xiv.
[11]*The Decline and Fall of the Roman Empire*, 1776-88, ch. 34, Bury ed. 1909, vol. 3, 450 (italics added).

ciples of substantial interest: the knowledge of the permanent benefits which may be obtained by a moderate use of conquest; and a just apprehension lest the desolation which we inflict on the enemy's country may be retaliated on our own. But *these considerations of hope and fear are almost unknown in the pastoral state of nations.*

By the time of the Greek city states and of Rome we find that a different attitude to an enemy is manifest.[12]

The rule and principles of war were considered both in Hellas and Rome to be applicable only to civilized sovereign States, properly organized, and enjoying a regular constitution; and not to conglomerations of individuals living together in an irregular and precarious association. Rome did not regard as being within the comity of nations such fortuitous gatherings of people, but only those who were organized on a civilized basis, and governed with a view to the general good, by a properly constructed system of law. . . . Hence barbarians, savage tribes, bands of robbers and pirates, and the like were debarred from the benefits and relaxations established by international law and custom. . . . [A]s to the general practice of war in Hellas[,] we find remarkable oscillations of warlike policy. Brutal treatment and noble generous conduct are manifested at the same epoch, in the same war, and apparently under similar circumstances. At times we hear of proceedings which testify to the intellectual and artistic temperament of the Greeks; at other times, we read narratives which emphasise the fundamental cruelty and disregard of human claims prevalent amongst the ancient races when at war with each other. In Homer . . . hostilities for the most part assumed the form of indiscriminate brigandage, and were but rarely conducted with a view to achieving regular conquests, and extending the territory of the victorious community. Extermination rather than subjection of the enemy was the usual practice. . . . Sometimes prisoners were sacrificed to the gods, corpses mutilated, and mercy refused to children, and to the old and sickly. On the other hand, acts of mercy and nobility were frequent. . . . The adoption of certain cowardly, inhuman practices, such as, for example, the use of poisoned weapons, was condemned.[13] . . . In reference to the conduct of war in Greece, it is important to remember that it was between small States, whose subjects were to an extraordinary degree animated by patriotism and devotion to their mother-country, that each individual was much more affected by hostilities than are the cities of the large modern States, that every individual was a soldier-politician who saw his home, his life, his family, his gods at stake, and, finally, that he regarded each and every subject of the opposing State as his personal adversary.

In this, he was little different from the guerrillas who opposed Napoleon during the Spanish campaign or some of the nationals in occupied Europe during the Second World War. Also, as was shown during the Spanish Civil War, when the conflict is one of a fundamental ideological character the methods of fighting revert to those of an earlier age.

While both Greeks and Persians seem to have resorted to methods of warfare which would now be condemned, it is of interest to note that among the Greek city States:

Temples, and priests, and embassies were considered inviolable. The right of sanctuary was universally recognized. Mercy was shown to suppliants and helpless captives. Prisoners were ransomed and exchanged. Safe-conducts were granted and respected. Truces and armistices were established and, for the most part, faithfully observed. Solemn oaths were fulfilled. Burial of dead was permitted; and

[12]Phillipson, *The International Law and Custom of Ancient Greece and Rome*, 1911, vol. 2, 195, 207-9, 210; see, also, 212 re the Peloponnesian war.
[13]See, e.g., *The Odyssey*, Lattimore ed., 1965, 34, Bk. I, 11, 260-3.

graves were unmolested. It was considered wrong and impious to cut off or poison the enemy's water supply, or to make use of poisoned weapons. Treacherous stratagems of every description were condemned as being contrary to civilized warfare. And . . . it is essential to emphasize that the non-existence of the law and of universally accepted custom relating to them is not necessarily proved when we point here and there to conduct of a contrary nature.[14]

The conditions here described as prevailing in Greek times are equally valid today, some in the form of treaty law, others in the form of custom.

By the time of the Roman Empire the nature of the state had changed, for Rome constituted a centralized authority and the practices in war[15]

varied according as their wars were commenced to exact vengeance for gross violations of international law, or for deliberate acts of treachery. Their warlike usages varied also according as their adversaries were regular enemies . . . or uncivilized barbarians and bands of pirates and marauders. . . . The Roman conduct [under Germanicus] far transcended in its civilized and humane character that of the German leader, Arminius, who is reported [by Tacitus] to have burnt to death and otherwise barbarously[16] slain the centurions and tribunes of the Varian legions, and nailed their skulls to trees. Undoubtedly, the belligerent operations of Rome, from the point of view of introducing various mitigations in the field, and adopting a milder policy after victory, are distinctly of a progressive character. They were more regular and disciplined than those of any other ancient nation. They did not as a rule degenerate into indiscriminate slaughter, and unrestrained devastation. . . . The *ius belli* imposed restrictions on barbarism, and condemned all acts of treachery. . . . [Livy tells us] there were laws of war as well as peace, and the Romans had learnt to put them into practice not less justly than bravely. . . . The Romans [says Cicero] refuse to countenance a criminal attempt made on the life of even a foreign aggressor. . . .

Apart from these references as to the general conduct *in bello*, in both Greece and Rome other accepted customs prevailed. Thus, the temples as well as ambassadors were respected and prisoners were frequently made captives, though often branded as a sign of possession by the captor, or even freed, while corpses generally were respected and afforded proper burial, "though we read of occasional practices to the contrary, but these infractions were exceptional, and were admittedly opposed to established custom; so that they cannot be said to furnish any index to the conduct and sentiment which obtained universally."[17]

When considering the legality of weapons one must constantly bear in mind the developments in technology over the centuries. Both Greece and Rome, as well as what the western world described as 'primitive' man,[18] relied primarily on hand-to-hand combat or throwing weapons, for by and large conflict was a matter of close combat. In the case of Greece and Rome the striking weapons tended to be the sword, the dagger, the shield and the battering ram, with the spear, javelin, sling or bow and arrow for distance. In the case of less organized societies, their weapons tended to be those that were used for hunting, with their striking weapons

[14]Phillipson, *op. cit.*, 221-3.
[15]*Ibid.*, 227, 228-9.
[16]This is the term used by Tacitus.
[17]Phillipson, *op. cit.*, 275.
[18]For consideration of the meaning of 'primitive', see Green, " 'Civilised' Law and 'Primitive' Peoples," *Law and Society*, 1975, 99.

confined to arm-, foot-, or mouth-propelled instruments. These include war hammers, battle-axes, and swords; thrusting spears; and missile weapons, such as the hurled spear, or javelin, the arrow propelled by arm- or foot-drawn bow, or the blowpipe. The striking edge or point of these weapons is of hard wood, stone, bone, or metal, and occasionally poison is used on the tip of arrow or spear.[19]

This description of weapons is not so very different from the arms used during feudal times, particularly by and against mounted knights in armour. There were, of course, special refinements, such as the mace and the club, the ball and chain, and varied types of lance which were peculiarly useful in unmounting or overthrowing men dressed in iron. Perhaps we may indulge ourselves here and reproduce the description of such a person written by a contemporary:[20]

Do you think Nature would recognize the work of her own hand—the image of God? And if any one were to assure her that it were so, would she not break out in execrations at the flagitious actions of her favourite creature? Would she not say when she saw man thus armed against man, 'What new sight do I behold? Hell itself must have produced this portentous spectacle. . . . I would bid this wretched creature behold himself in a mirror, if his eyes were capable of seeing himself when his mind is no more. Nevertheless, thou depraved animal, look at thyself, if thou canst; reflect on thyself, thou frantic warrior, if by any means thou mayest recover thy lost reason, and be restored to thy pristine nature. Take the looking glass, and inspect it. How came that threatening crest of plumes upon thy head? Did I give thee feathers! Whence that shining helmet? Whence those sharp points, which appear like horns of steel? Whence are thy hands and arms furnished with sharp prickles? Whence those scales, like the scales of fish, upon thy body? Whence those brazen teeth? Whence those plates of brass all over thee? Whence those deadly weapons of offence? Whence that voice, uttering sounds of rage more horrible than the inarticulate noise of the wild beasts? Whence the whole form of thy countenance and person distorted by furious passions, more than brutal? Whence that thunder and lightning which I perceive around thee, at once more frightful than the thunder of heaven, and more destructive to man? I formed thee an animal a little lower than the angels, a partaker of divinity; how camest thou to think of transforming thyself into a beast so savage, that no beast hereafter can be deemed a beast, if it be compared with man, originally the image of God, the Lord of creation?'

As this type of dress for war became outmoded, so did the weapons that were tuned to overcoming it. Thus, although it is not unknown for the modern soldier in extremis to use his rifle as a club, the mace, the broad-axe, the ball and chain, the halberd, the glaive, the paritzan, the military fork, and the like have fallen into desuetude. Not only that, but they have been out of use so long that they would now be considered illegal. When sieges were a common phenomenon in war, the flaming cannon-ball, the battering ram and such defensive weapons as boiling oil were in common use. As modern warfare has ceased to depend on the investment of enemy towns and war has become a long-distance affair with close combat and hand-to-hand engagements the exception rather than the rule, so these weapons have lost their value and by now would be regarded as unlawful, having been replaced by weapons more in line with modern needs and technology. On the other hand, while some things become forbidden by passage of time and desuetude, others which were forbidden become lawful, even though they may again become unlawful by conduct or written law. Thus, during the American War of Independence and the American Civil War it was generally considered illegal to fire on

[19]Wright, *A Study of War*, 1965, 81.
[20]Erasmus, *Bellum*, 1545, Imprint Society ed., 1972, 17.

sentries.[21] Though the Hague Regulations of 1899 and 1907[22] are silent on this, even Davis, the United States delegate to The Hague, still asserted in 1908 that the practice of firing on sentries was strictly forbidden.[23] Today, of course, there is no question that sentries are lawful targets, and what was apparently a customary rule of law is no longer such.

From earliest times there have been attempts to limit the means of warfare by declaring this or that weapon to be unlawful. Thus, as long ago as the Code of Manu,[24] compiled about the second century B.C., it was stated that "when the king fights his foes in battle, let him not strike with weapons concealed, nor with barbed, poisoned, or the points of which are blazed with fire." In 1139 the Second Lateran Council forbade the use of the crossbow and the arc as anathema, a view that coincided with the reaction of the orders of knighthood:

> To the Church these weapons were hateful to God. To the knights they were weapons whereby men not of the knightly order could fell a knight . . . Worse, they were weapons that enabled a man to strike without the risk of being struck.[25]

The Church also forbade Christians from using in their wars "darts or catapults (in order to reduce as far as possible the number of engines of destruction and death), and the prohibition was enforced under pain of anathema."[26] Once again the orders of knighthood agreed with the Church.[27]

> Paolo Vitelli while recognizing and using the cannon 'put out the eyes and cut off the hands of the captured arquebusiers because he held it unworthy that a gallant and . . . noble[28] knight should be laid low by a common, despised foot soldier.'[29]

While the Church and the knights might have condemned the use of particular weapons, so long as the weapons in question proved to be of use such bans had but little influence. Commenting on the Church ban, Belli wrote in 1563:[30]

[21]See, e.g., Lieber Code, 1863, U.S. General Orders No. 100 (Schindler/Toman, 3), Art. 69.
[22]Hague Convention II, 1899, Convention IV, 1907, *ibid.*, 57.
[23]*Elements of International Law*, 1908, 297.
[24]Buhler, *The Laws of Manu*, 1976, 230, Tit. VII, 90.
[25]Draper, "The Interaction of Christianity and Chivalry in the Historical Development of the Law of War," 5 *Int'l Rev. of the Red X*, 1965, 3, 19.
[26]*Corpus juris canonici*, 1500, Decretal V, c. Belli, *De Re Militari et Bello Tractatus*, 1563, Pars VII, cap. III, 29 (Carnegie tr. 186).
[27]Draper, *loc. cit.*, 18.
[28]Draper points out that it was only between knights, and particularly during jousts and tourneys, that the rules of chivalry were observed. He supports this contention by comparing the outrageous and revolting behaviour of the Crusaders at the fall of Jerusalem in 1099 with that of Saladin's capture of the city in 1197, *ibid.*, 11. He also draws attention to the devastation caused by Richard I at the fall of Acre in 1191, and by the Venetians against Christians as well as others at the fall of Constantinople in 1204, during the fourth Crusade, 12, 13 resp. See, however, letter to *The Times* (London) 24 July, 1984, by Major T. J. D. Holmes, pointing out that in 1914 the Emperor Franz Joseph, Colonel in Chief of the 1st King's Dragoon Guards, "sent a letter to the regiment to the effect that the Emperor wished the regiment to know that he was most distressed that his regiment and his country should be in a state of war and went on to explain that he had given orders to all his troops that should any officer or man of the KDG be so unfortunate as to be taken prisoner, he was to be regarded as a personal guest for the duration of hostilities."
[29]This attitude should be compared with that of Kapitänleutnant (Ing) Lenz at the sinking of *The Peleus, In re Eck* (1945) U.N.W.C.C. 1 *War Crimes Reports*, 1, 3, 7; Cameron, *The Peleus Trial*, 1948, 85-6, 116, 131.
[30]Belli, *op. cit.*, 29. See, also, Gardot, "Le Droit de la Guerre dans l'Oeuvre des Capitaines Français du XVIe Siècle," 72 *Hague Recueil* 1948, 397, 416, c. Rabutin, *Memoires*, t. II 229.

But today regard is so far lacking for this rule that firearms of a thousand kinds are the most common and popular implements of war; as if too few avenues of death had been discovered in the course of centuries, had not the generation of our fathers, rivalling God with his lightning, invented this means whereby, even at a single discharge, men are sent to perdition by the hundreds.

It is an historical fact that if a particular state considers certain weapons or methods of warfare are likely to provide it with advantages over an enemy, especially one that is not so well equipped, that state will maintain that use of the particular weapon or means is perfectly lawful. Thus, naval powers have always endeavoured to restrict the limitations on naval warfare or the rights of maritime neutrals as much as possible,[31] while at the same time remaining content with imposing strict limits on the rights of land belligerents. Similarly, we cannot expect that a belligerent possessing sophisticated weapons will abstain from employing them against an enemy which lacks such weapons or is technologically disadvantaged.[32] Perhaps one may emphasise this point with an example from the animal kingdom.[33]

Cobras would advocate the banning of horses, claws and cutting teeth, but would denounce in the strongest terms a proposal to outlaw venom.

There is little point in devoting attention to the regulations which were issued at various times concerning the behaviour of troops during sieges, with their imprecations to respect women, priests, the infirm and others, or not to pillage or destroy private property.[34] The need for these rules has to a large extent become redundant with the disappearance of siege. They are important now only when troops are moving through enemy country or are in occupation thereof. The conduct of the armed forces in such circumstances is now controlled by the ban on looting,[35] respect for private enemy persons[36] or Geneva Convention IV, 1949, as extended[37] concerning the protection of civilians in occupied territory. In addition to these rules relating to the conduct of the individual soldier as regards enemy citizens who are not members of the armed forces—for where they are concerned he is bound to treat the wounded and sick[38] or prisoners of war[39] in accordance with the relevant Conventions—there are certain rules regarding his own conduct which do not touch on the legality of weapons. Thus, it is well established that he must not behave in a treacherous fashion, a prohibition which we now find embodied in the rules against perfidy.[40] This was clearly established as early as the American War of Independence, when, prior to the Battle for Bennington,

---

[31]See, e.g., Report of British Inter-Departmental Committee, 1908: "In the past the interests of Great Britain have led her to take a strict view as to the obligations of a neutral State. This suited her convenience, because she was to a very small extent dependent on the right to use neutral ports, and her strength at sea has enabled her, generally speaking, to insist on her own rules," c. Best, *Humanity in Warfare*, 1980, 246.

[32]Bynkershoek, *Quaestionum Juris Publici*, 1737, Lib. I, cap. I puts it bluntly: "we may destroy an enemy though he be unarmed, and for the purpose we may employ poison, an assassin, or incendiary bombs, *though he is not provided with such things*" (Carnegie tr. 16, italics added).

[33]Bishop, *Justice Under Fire*, 1974, 270.

[34]See, e.g., Gardot, *loc. cit.*, 407-9.

[35]Regulations annexed to Hague Convention IV, n. 22 above, Arts. 28, 47.

[36]Lauterpacht, *Oppenheim's International Law*, Vol. 2, 1951, S. 116.

[37]Schindler/Toman, 427, extended by Protocol I, 1977, *ibid.*, 551, Part IV.

[38]Geneva I, 1949, *ibid.*, 305.

[39]Geneva III, 1949, *ibid.*, 355.

[40]See, e.g., Protocol I, Art. 37.

a proclamation was issued ordering all subjects to swear allegiance to the King and to join His Majesty's forces in suppressing the rebellion. Groups of American militia came into the British camp, and professed their loyalty to the Crown. Many actually took oaths of allegiance, and were then given muskets and ammunition by the Commander, Col. Baum, upon the advice of his credulous Loyalist 'population expert', Col. Skene. The latter also advised the Americans to wear white papers in their hats so that they could be distinguished from the 'rebels'. All these new-found friends were then allowed to leave the camp.
Later, these same groups ranged themselves around Baum's camp without any interference since they were considered to be loyal reinforcements. When Stark led the main body of troops against the British, these 'Loyalists' opened fire, and Baum found himself surrounded by the enemy.
Those Americans who swore an oath of allegiance and took up the King's arms certainly acted in bad faith. . . . It is certain that if Baum had been victorious, he would have been justified in punishing those from among the captured who had violated their oaths.[41]

The individual soldier must also guard against behaving in a manner that was made popular by Spanish guerrillas during the Napoleonic campaigns, and must avoid responding in kind:[42]

The Spanish resistance was popular, passionate and primitive. Goya's 'Disasters of War' etchings do not all represent what he himself witnessed but none of them shows anything that did not happen. Soldiers who have found comrades castrated, maimed, impaled, crucified, are likely to do similar things to the men—and the comrades and womenfolk of the men—whom they believe to be responsible. Peasants who have been tortured by marauding soldiers to tell where their grain and sausage are hidden or who have had their cottages and sheds burned are likely to take it out of the next soldier they meet—who may be the brigade cooks and drummer boys . . . As time went on and the guerrilla bands, besides becoming more familiar to the French, also to some extent, took on regular attributes and recognizable appearance, the French began to deal with them more as equals; in particular, by not killing them when captured, by expecting the guerrilla chieftains to reciprocate, and even by practising that humane courtesy of 'civilized' warfare, the exchange of prisoners. . . . For the law-minded 'regular' soldiers faced with a 'guerrilla' enemy (we will use the word loosely, as regulars use it, to mean anything but an enemy just like themselves), the main question then was, as it has been ever since: whom are we fighting? The definition of belligerent status becomes all-important. Conventional soldiers in the eighteenth century recognized each other easily. Their uniforms showed what they were . . . But who were these nondescript, anomalous, raggedy armed men who began to appear on the battlefield or near it from the early nineties? If no shred of apparent uniform hung upon them, they could only be . . . revolting peasants or bands of brigands. If some kind of uniform or common badge did appear, then it was very important to know what it meant in terms of discipline and command; to whom were they responsible, and were they effectively subordinate to his authority? . . . [I]t was a question not of completely denying legitimacy to 'guerrillas' but of demanding that they be distinguishable from 'brigands', for their own sake, and from civilians, for the sake of civilians.

From the point of view of today's soldier the situation may have changed for the worse. While during the Second World War the allied command demanded that 'resistance' forces should be treated as regular units and entitled to all the rights of ordinary soldiers,

---

[41]Clancy, "Rules of Land Warfare During the War of the American Revolution," 2 *World Polity*, 1960, 203, 245.
[42]Best, *op. cit.*, 116-9.

particularly when they were wearing identification marks,[43] it is now provided[44] that, while normally,

> [i]n order to promote the protection of the civilian population from the effects of hostilities, combatants are obliged to distinguish themselves from the civilian population while they are engaged in an attack or in a military operation preparatory to an attack[, r]ecognizing, however, that there are situations in armed conflicts where, owing to the nature of the hostilities an armed combatant cannot so distinguish himself, he shall retain his status as a combatant, provided that, in such situations, he carries his arms openly:
> (a) during each military engagement, and
> (b) during such time as he is visible to the adversary while he is engaged in a military deployment preceding the launching of an attack in which he is to participate.

This provision is intended to protect members of a national liberation movement and would cover those who are 'farmers by day and soldiers by night'. Such persons are entitled to prisoner of war status, while those who do not satisfy the 'arms' requirements do not become prisoners of war, but are entitled to the same protections. In fact, from the soldier's point of view this development does not make a great deal of difference to his conduct. While he would be entitled to treat a non-combatant carrying arms or indulging in warlike acts as having lost his protective status, the soldier would still be required to treat that person with due regard to the laws of humanity and to hand him over for trial or other treatment by the military authorities. The soldier would have no right to take peremptory action on his own. While a soldier in a regular force is required to wear a uniform or some other distinguishing mark and is not permitted "to make improper use of the national flag or of the military insignia and uniform of the enemy,"[45] he may wear such enemy insignia or uniform as a ruse, but it would be improper for him to continue to wear this when engaging in combat, although use of it outside the zone of combat to gather information would appear legitimate.[46] It is worth mentioning, that in sixteenth century France the wearing of enemy uniform was considered intolerable.[47]

While the modern soldier is, generally speaking, unlikely to behave as did the Spanish guerrillas, or indulge in some of the more unpleasant methods of partisans, he has not always shown the same respect for his enemy dead as did his ancestors, who frequently effected the burial with full military honours. In fact, during the Vietnam War it became common for United States personnel to remove an ear from an enemy corpse as evidence to support a body count. While the Geneva Convention on the Wounded and Sick[48] made provision for the proper interment of the dead and forbade pillage thereof, it was still necessary for the Department of the Army in 1970 to remind United States military personnel that "the mutilation of bodies is a war crime, and an order to cut off ears would therefore be illegal. Equally illegal would be permission to take as souvenirs valuables from dead bodies or from any prisoner."[49]

[43]*Ibid.*, 239-44.
[44]Protocol I, Art. 44(3).
[45]Hague Regulations, Art. 23(f).
[46]H.M.S.O., *Manual of Military Law*, Part III, *The Law of War on Land*, 1958, para. 320, and notes 2 and 3.
[47]Gardot, *loc. cit.*, 464.
[48]Geneva Convention I, Schindler/Toman, 305, Arts. 16, 17.
[49]'The Geneva Conventions of 1949 and Hague Convention IV of 1907', Dept. of the Army, ASubjScd 27-1, 8 Oct. 1970—this document is discussed by Green, "Aftermath of Vietnam: War Law and the Soldier," in Falk, *The Vietnam War and International Law*, Vol. 4, 1976, 147, 168-74.

Equally, the modern soldier should be warned against the temptation to assassinate an enemy leader upon whose head a price has been set and he should also beware of seeking out such a person for this purpose. Among the 'fathers' of international law, both Grotius[50] and Vattel[51] regarded such an act as unlawful if done treacherously. While there is nothing in any of the conventional laws of war condemning assassination, the various military manuals, basing themselves upon the Hague Regulations, which expressly forbid "to kill or wound treacherously individuals belonging to the hostile nation or army,"[52] condemn assassination as a prohibited act.[53] The borderline between an unlawful assassination and a legitimate killing might appear to be somewhat narrow:[54]

> . . . This prohibition applies only to treacherous killing. It is not forbidden to send a detachment or individual members of the armed forces to kill, by sudden attack, members or a member of the enemy armed forces. Thus, for instance, the raid by a British commando party on the headquarters of General Rommel's African Army at Beda Littoria in 1943 was not contrary to the provisions of the Hague Rules. The operation was carried out by military personnel in uniform; it had as part of its objective the seizure of Rommel's operational headquarters, including his own residence, and the capture or killing of enemy personnel therein.

In contrast, for an instance of unlawful assassination we might refer to the American War of Independence:[55]

> In the second year of the Revolution, a British General, Patrick Gordon, was killed by an American scout, Lt. Benjamin Whitcomb, . . . on his own volition [and] not upon the order of his commander.
> In his report to Gates, Whitcomb was very matter-of-fact about the affair: 'Staid at the same place till about twelve o'clock, then fired on an officer.' The shooting was not in self-defense, nor is there any indication that he knew the victim was a general.
> The killing aroused great indignation, General Carleton, in command of the British forces in Canada, and one of the most humane and sensible of the British commanders, issued a very heated General Order to his troops, denouncing the act as an 'assassination', and ordering that no flags, or communications from the Americans were to be received in future.
> Washington also termed it an 'assassination', and said that it was an 'indecent, illiberal, and Scurrilous perrformance . . . highly unbecoming the Character of a Soldier and Gentleman . . .'
> [General] Wilkinson gave this as the American reaction and added a revealing comment as to the difficulty in preventing such acts: 'This abominable outrage upon the customs of war and laws of humanity produced a sensation of strong

[50]*De Jure Belli ac Pacis*, 1625, Lib. III, cap. IV, s. xviii—while Grotius affirms that "to kill an Enemy any where is allowed", he condemns assassination when carried out 'treacherously' as by a spy, or because a price has been set upon the victim's head (Eng. tr., 1738, 569-70; Carnegie tr. 654-5).

[51]*Le Droit des Gens*, 1758, Liv. II, ch. VIII, s. 155, while Vattel recognizes that "when a resolute soldier steals into the enemy's camp and makes his way to the general's tent and stabs him, he does nothing contrary to the natural laws of war . . . [but if it be] committed by means of treachery, . . . [as] by an agent who makes his way as a suppliant or refugee, or as a turncoat, or even as an alien[, then] I assert that the deed is a shameful and revolting one, both on the part of him who executes and of him who commands it" (Carnegie tr., 287-8).

[52]Art. 23(b).

[53]See, e.g., German Gen. Staff, *Usages of War on Land*, 1902, ch. II, tr. Morgan as *The German War Book*, 1915, 65—this also condemns the declaration of outlawry against Napoleon in 1815 as constituting "an indirect invitation to assassination"; Brit. *Manual of Military Law*, op. cit., para. 15; U.S. Dept. of the Army, *The Law of Land Warfare*, FM 27-10, 1956, para. 31.

[54]Brit. *Manual*, para. 115, n. 2.

[55]Clancy, *loc. cit.*, 250-1 (italics in original).

disgust in the army, and men of sensibility did not conceal their abhorence of its perpetrator. *Yet it was impossible in the temper of the times to bring him to punishment without disaffecting the fighting men on that whole frontier'.*

Another officer . . . termed Whitcomb a spy, and admitted that his was an unlawful act, but also offered a sort of apology: 'The act though villanous, was brave, and a peculiar kind of bravery that I believe Whitcomb alone possessed of. He shot Gordon near by their advanced sentinel, [as we have seen had he shot the sentinel there would have been no doubt of his guilt] and notwithstanding a most diligent search was made, he avoided them by mere dint of skulking'.

If Whitcomb was punished, it was no more than reprimand, for he was sent out on another scouting mission after this incident. However, Gates framed his instructions in such a manner as to forbid the spy to fire on anyone, except in self-defence.

We hear a great deal nowadays when an area falls under enemy occupation, or when troops pass through it and are present only temporarily, to the effect that, despite treaty regulations protecting the civilian population and particularly women from sexual assault, rape is a common phenomenon on the part of the occupying troops. It is interesting to note that senior French knights during the sixteenth century were adamant in protecting the modesty of women found in cities which had surrendered,[56] and by an Ordinance promulgated by Coligny violence against women was punishable by death.[57] Gentili, therefore, was only giving expression to actual practice when he wrote in 1612[58] that "to violate the honour of women will always be held to be unjust." It was hardly necessary for him, therefore, to reproduce the views of Alexander who stated: "I am not in the habit of warring with prisoners and women." Now by virtue of the Civilians Convention[59] "women shall be especially protected against any attack on their honour, in particular against rape, enforced prostitution or any form of indecent assault." This means that any soldier who so attacks a woman in an occupied place is not only liable to the processes of his national criminal law, but is also amenable to a charge arising from the treaty law of armed conflict.[60] It should be pointed out that this prohibition refers not only to the period of active operations, but so long as the occupation subsists.

Having commented upon the actions and reactions of some sixteenth and eighteenth century commanders in the field, it is now time to turn our attention to the writings of some of the classical 'fathers' of international law. Their views so far as they were in agreement may be considered as constituting *opinio juris*, and, to the extent that they were consistent with past behaviour or future behaviour conformed to their views, they became the basis of current customary law, so long as it has not been replaced by treaty commitment.

Nearly all the classical writers agree that the purpose of conflict is not the total destruction but merely the defeat of an enemy in order to impose one's will or preserve one's independence. To this end, they all recognize that some restraint upon conduct in war is essential. Typical are the comments of Gentili:[61]

[56]Gardot, *loc cit.*, 452-3.
[57]*Ibid.*, 469, citing Fourquevaux, *La Discipline militaire*, 1592.
[58]*De Jure Belli*, 1612, Lib. II, cap. xxi (Carnegie tr., 257, 251, resp.)
[59]Art. 27.
[60]In sixteenth century France Baron de Taube emphasised the importance of national military codes, pointing out that it was a combination of the law of nations and national military law which formed *"le meilleur frein pratique pour imposer aux armées le respect d'un modus legitimus de mener les guerres"*, Gardot, *loc. cit.*, 467. Such codes were promulgated in England by Richard II, 1383, and Henry V, 1415, and in the Swiss *Sempacherbriff*, 1393, *ibid.*, 468.
[61]*Op. cit.*, Lib. II, cap. III, VI, XXIII, Carnegie tr. 142-4, 159, 272.

In war . . . victory is sought in no prescribed fashion. . . . Our only precaution must be not to allow every kind of craft and every cunning device; for evil is not lawful, but an enemy should be dealt with according to law. . . In dealing with a just and lawful enemy [as distinct from pirates and brigands] we have the whole fetial law and many other laws in common. . . Necessity does not oblige us to violate the rights of our adversaries . . . [but t]he laws of war are not observed towards one who does not himself observe them.

Before passing to any other writer or commenting on the significance of this statement overall, it is necessary to point out that, at least since the 1929 Geneva Convention on Prisoners of War[62] this is no longer true in so far as reprisals against prisoners of war are forbidden, a prohibition that was extended by the 1949 Conventions[63] which extended the ban to protect all 'protected persons and their property'[64] and the 1977 Protocol I made the prohibition even more extensive.[65] The Protocol has not yet received anything like universal acceptance, and has not been ratified by any major power belonging either to NATO or the Warsaw Pact. However, it may well be argued that, since these provisions were adopted by consensus and are in line with earlier stipulations, they are merely spelling out a general rule and amount to customary law so that the individual soldier would be well advised to abstain from any reprisal that he might seek to apply against an enemy on the basis that the latter has disregarded his obligations towards him.

Since Grotius considered that "by the Law of Nations any Thing done against an Enemy is lawful,"[66] it is not surprising to find that he stated that "it is lawful for an Enemy to hurt another both in Person and Goods . . . [and for] both sides [to do so] without Distinction", including within this right the killing of women, infants and even prisoners, "but it is restrained more or less in some Places by the particular Law of each State."[67] Nevertheless, he considered it lawful to use poison, to poison weapons or springs, although not to pollute them otherwise, and he also vehemently condemns rape.[68] At a later stage when discussing Moderation concerning the Right of Killing Men in a Just War,[69] he states, quoting Cicero,[70] "There are certain Duties to be observed even toward those who have wronged us." Therefore, children, women and old men should be spared, as should priests and other religious, and "to these we may justly add those who apply themselves to the Study of Sciences and Arts beneficial to Mankind."[71] To these he adds farmers, prisoners and those who surrender.[72] Finally, he calls for the avoidance of useless fighting, for a show of strength rather than a true warlike action is "wholly repugnant to the Duty of a Christian, and Humanity itself. Therefore all Magistrates ought strictly to forbid these Things, for they must render an account for the unnecessary shedding of Blood to him, whose Viceregents they are."[73] In later chapters[74]

[62]Schindler/Toman, 271, Art. 2.
[63]Convention I, Art. 46; II, Art. 47; III, Art. 13.
[64]Convention IV, Art. 33.
[65]Arts. 20, 51-6. Art. 51(8) specifically states "any violation of these prohibitions [relating to protection of the civilian population] shall not release the Parties to the conflict from their legal obligations with respect to the civilian population and civilians . . ."
[66]*Op. cit.*, Lib. III, cap. IV, s. xviii (1738 tr. 570; Carnegie tr 654).
[67]*Ibid.*, ss. ix, x (564, 565; 648, 649).
[68]*Ibid.*, xv, xvi, xix (567, 568, 572; 651, 657).
[69]*Ibid.*, cap. XI.
[70]*De Officiis*, Lib. I, cap. XI (630; 722).
[71]Lib. III, cap. XI, ss. ix, x (640, 642-3; 734, 736-7).
[72]*Ibid.*, ss. xi, xiii, xiv-xv (643, 644-6; 737-40).
[73]*Ibid.*, s. xix (649; 743).
[74]Cap. XII, XIII, XIV, XIX.

he calls for moderation in laying waste, in regard to captured property and prisoners, and for the exercise of good faith between enemies.

Of particular importance, perhaps, to the individual man in the field is the ban on his acting as if the conflict were a private affair permitting him to commit acts regardless of his being a participant in a public matter. Thus, he may not commit warlike acts after a retreat or an armistice[75] nor keep captured property for himself.[76] Moreover,[77]

> It is not enough that we do nothing against the Rules of rigorous Justice, properly so called; we must also take Care that we offend not against Charity, especially Christian Charity. Now this may happen sometimes; when, for Instance, it appears, that such a plundering doth not so much hurt the State, or the King, or those who are culpable themselves, but rather the Innocent, whom it may render so extremely miserable. . . . But farther, if the taking of this Booty neither contributes to the finishing of the War, nor considerably weakens the Enemy, the Gain arising to himself only from the Unhappiness of the Times, would be highly unbecoming an honest Man, much more a Christian. . .
>
> Yet if a Soldier, or any other Person, even in a just War, shall burn the Enemy's Houses, lay waste their Fields, and commit such other Acts of Hostility, without any Command, and besides when there is no Necessity, or just Cause, in the Opinion of the Divines he stands obliged to make Satisfaction for those Damages. I have with Reason added, what they have omitted, if there be not a just Cause, for if there be, he may perhaps be answerable for it to his own State, whose Orders he hath transgressed, but not to his Enemy, to whom he hath done no Wrong.

The discussion of what is necessary in war and the restraints associated therewith may be terminated by reference to the views of Vattel[78] writing more than a century later and with greater knowledge, therefore, of what states actually do:[79]

> Since the object of a just war is to overcome injustice and violence, and to use force upon one who is deaf to the voice of reason, a sovereign has the right to do to his enemy whatever is necessary to weaken him and disable him from maintaining his unjust position; and the sovereign may choose the most efficacious and appropriate means to accomplish that object, provided those means be not essentially evil and unlawful, and consequently forbidden by the Law of Nature.
>
> *A lawful end confers a right only to those means which are necessary to attain that end. Whatever is done in excess of such measures* is contrary to the natural law, and *must be condemned as evil* before the tribunal of conscience. . . . [A]s it is very difficult always to form a just estimate of what the actual situation demands, and, moreover, as it is for each Nation to determine what its particular circumstances warrant it in doing, it becomes absolutely necessary that Nations should mutually conform to certain general rules on this subject. Thus, when it is clear and well recognized that such a measure, such an act of hostility, is, in general, necessary for overcoming the resistance of the enemy and attaining the object of lawful war, that measure, viewed thus in the abstract, is regarded by the Law of Nations as lawful and proper in war, although *the belligerent who would make use of it without necessity, when less severe measures would have answered his purpose, would not be guiltless* before God and in his own conscience. *This is what constitutes the difference between what is just, proper, and irreprehensible in war, and what is merely permissible and may be done by Nations with impunity.*

[75]*Ibid.*, Cap. XVIII, s. i (684; 788-9). See also, *Grumpelt (Scuttled U-boats) Trial* (1946) 13 *Ann. Dig.* 309.

[76]*Ibid.* (685; 789). See, also, text to n. 35 above re looting.

[77]*Ibid.*, ss. iv, v (686; 790-1).

[78]*Op. cit.*, Vol. II, Liv. III, ch. VIII. See also, Ruddy, *International Law in the Enlightenment*, 1975, 245-56.

[79]*Ibid.*, ss. 138, 137 (Carnegie tr., 280, 279, italics added).

Among the actions which are considered forbidden by Gentili are the killing of those who surrender—it is *only "when we cannot overcome their resistance and bring them to terms by less severe means, [that] we are justified in taking away their lives"*[80]—denial of quarter, reprisals against prisoners, violence against women, children, the aged and the sick, ecclesiastics and men of letters, husbandmen and in general all unarmed persons; equally to be condemned are assassination and the use of poison and poisoned weapons and the poisoning of streams, springs and wells.[81] Many of these activities are condemned by others among the classical writers,[82] but it is Vattel who is most direct in seeking to restrain the horrors of war:[83]

> Necessity alone justifies Nations in going to war; and they should all *refrain from,* and as a matter of duty oppose, *whatever tends to render war more disastrous . . . All acts of hostility which injure the enemy without necessity,* or which do not tend to procure victory, *are unjustifiable, and as such condemned* by the natural law . . . [A]s between Nation and Nation, we must lay down general rules, independent of circumstances and of certain and easy application. Now, we can only arrive at such rules by considering acts of hostility in the abstract and in their essential character. Hence, . . . *the voluntary Law of Nations* limits itself to forbidding acts that are essentially unlawful and obnoxious, such as poisoning, assassination, treason [—this refers to acts committed treacherously against an enemy and not to treason in the sense of national law—], the massacre of an enemy who has surrendered and from whom there is nothing to fear . . . [and] *condemns every act of hostility which,* in its own nature and independently of circumstances, *contributes nothing to the success of our arms* and neither increases our strength nor weakens the enemy. On the other hand, it permits or tolerates every act which in its essential nature is adapted to attaining the end of the war; and it does not stop to consider whether the act was unnecessary, useless, or superfluous in a given case unless there is the clearest evidence that an exception should have been made in that instance; for *where the evidence is clear freedom of judgment can not be exercised.* Thus it is not, generally speaking, contrary to the laws of war to plunder and lay waste to a country. But if an enemy of greatly superior forces should treat in this manner a town or province which he might easily have held possession of, as a means of obtaining just and advantageous terms of peace, he would be universally accused of waging war in a barbarous and uncontrolled manner. The deliberate destruction of public monuments, temples, tombs, statues, pictures, etc., is, therefore, absolutely condemned even by the voluntary Law of Nations, as being under no circumstances conducive to the lawful object of war. The pillage and destruction of towns, the devastation of the open country by fire and sword, are acts no less to be abhorred and condemned when they are committed without evident necessity or urgent reasons.

While, as we have seen, pillage is forbidden under modern law, it was not until 1954 that states entered into a treaty commitment for the protection of cultural property in the event of armed conflict.[84] Similarly, it was not until Protocol I, 1977, that a similar provision was made with respect to the preservation of objects indispensable to the survival of the civilian population, such as foodstuffs, agricultural areas, crops, drinking water installations and the like.[85] The Protocol also extends this prohibition to a method of warfare that might have such long-term effects, but would not be used by the individual soldier.

[80]*Ibid.*, s. 139 (280, italics added).
[81]*Ibid.*, ss. 140, 142, 145-7, 155-7 (280-3, 287, 289).
[82]E.g., Ayala, Belli, Bynkershoek, Gentili, Wolff and Zouche.
[83]Liv. III, ch. VIII, s. 156, ch. IX, ss. 172-3 (289, 294-5, italics added).
[84]Schindler/Toman, 661, as amended by Protocol I, Art. 53.
[85]Art. 54.

By Article 55 it is forbidden to take any warlike action which may damage the natural environment thereby prejudicing the health or survival of the population, while in 1976 there was adopted a Convention on the Prohibition of Military or any other Hostile Use of Environmental Modification Techniques.[86]

The humanitarian considerations expressed in these classical writings find their modern equivalent first expressed in treaty form in the 1868 Declaration of St. Petersburg renouncing the use in time of war of explosive projectiles under 400 grammes weight[87] and which were either explosive or charged with fulminating or inflammable substances. This ban was based on the premise

> That the progress of civilization should have the effect of alleviating as much as possible the calamities of war;
> That the only legitimate object which States should endeavour to accomplish during war is to weaken the military forces of the enemy;
> That for this purpose it is sufficient to disable the greatest possible number of men;
> That this object would be exceeded by the employment of arms which uselessly aggravate the sufferings of disabled men, or render their death inevitable;
> That the employment of such arms would, therefore, be contrary to the laws of humanity.

More general in its application, and of more direct concern to the fighting man, is the Project of an International Declaration concerning the Laws and Customs of War drawn up at Brussels by the European states in 1874[88]

> Art. 12: The laws of war do not recognize in belligerents an unlimited power in the adoption of means of injuring the enemy.
> Art. 13: According to this principle are especially *forbidden*:
> (a) Employment of poison or poisoned weapons;
> (b) Murder by treachery of individuals belonging to the hostile nation or army;
> (c) Murder of an enemy who, having laid down his arms or having no longer means of defense, has surrendered at discretion;
> (d) The declaration that no quarter will be given;
> (e) The employment of arms, projectiles or material calculated to cause unnecessary suffering, . . .
> (f) Making improper use of a flag of truce, of the national flag or of the military insignia and uniform of the enemy, as well as the distinctive badges of the Geneva Convention [—that is to say the Red Cross and its recognized alternatives];
> (g) Any destruction or seizure of the enemy's property that is not imperatively demanded by the necessity of war.
>
> Art. 18: A town taken by assault ought not to be given over to pillage by the victorious troops.

These obligations were given wider application by the Hague Regulations attached to Convention II of 1899 and later to Convention IV of 1907, which the Nuremberg Judgment in 1946[89] regarded as amounting to customary law, and therefore binding on all states,

---

[86]Gen. Ass. Res. 31/72, 16 *I.L.M.* 88.
[87]Schindler/Toman, 95.
[88]*Ibid.*, 25, italics in original.
[89]H.M.S.O., Cmd. 6964 (1946), 65; 41 *Am. J. Int'l Law*, 1947, 172, 248-9.

including those which never became parties to either Convention and regardless of the provision in Article 2 which declared the Convention and Regulations as irrelevant if any belligerent was not a party thereto. In so far as the Hague Conventions are concerned, the parties recognized the difficulty of drawing up a comprehensive code to deal with every circumstance which might arise. They therefore included in the Preamble, in what has come to be known as the Martens Clause, an affirmation that

> Until a more complete code of the laws of war is issued, the High Contracting Parties think it right to declare that in cases not included in the regulations adopted by them, populations and belligerents remain under the protection and empire of the principles of international law, as they result from the usages established between civilized nations, from the laws of humanity, and the requirements of the public conscience.

To some extent the 'usages established by civilized nations' are to be found in the classical writings to which reference has already been made, as well as in the Lieber Code which was based on the laws and customs of war generally accepted at that time, 1863. This, too, recognized

> military necessity, as understood by civilized nations, [as] consist[ing] in the necessity of those measures which are indispensable for securing the ends of the war and which are lawful according to the modern laws and usages of war. . . . Military necessity does not admit of cruelty—that is, the infliction of suffering for the sake of suffering or for revenge, nor of maiming or wounding except in fight, nor of torture to extort confessions. It does not admit of the use of poison in any way . . . [and] disclaims acts of perfidy; and, in general, military necessity does not include any act of hostility which makes the return to peace unnecessarily difficult.[90]

Apart from laying down specific regulations which to a great extent merely reproduce those of the Lieber Code and the Brussels Declaration, the Hague Regulations make it absolutely clear,[91] at the beginning of the section on hostilities in the chapter on the means of injuring the enemy, that "The right of belligerents to adopt means of injuring the enemy is not unlimited. . . . [I]t is especially forbidden . . . to employ arms, projectiles, or material calculated to cause unnecessary suffering," and it should be noted that this prohibition on 'unnecessary suffering' is retained in Article 35 of Protocol I, 1977. From the point of view of the man in the field it is probably true to say that any injury he suffers during war, whether it be caused by rifle, grenade, bayonet or any other means, inflicts 'unnecessary suffering' upon him. However, the test is not subjective, but as with the comments of the classicists on necessity, it is one of proportionality, prohibiting "those measures of military violence, not otherwise prohibited by international law, which are not necessary (relevant and proportionate) to the achievement of a definite military advantage."[92] Thus, it is enough to disable an enemy. It is not necessary to kill him. It is, therefore, forbidden to alter a weapon, such as a bayonet, in order to cause an aggravated wound almost certain to result in death.

Commenting upon the meaning of the ban on weapons causing unnecessary suffering, both British and American *Military Manuals* list lances with barbed heads, irregularly shaped bullets, projectiles filled with broken glass and the use of any substance likely

---

[90]Schindler/Toman, 3, Arts. 14, 16, 17.
[91]*Ibid.*, 57, Arts. 22, 23(e).
[92]Bothe, Partsch and Solf, *New Rules for Victims of Armed Conflicts*, 1982, 195.

to inflame a wound, as well as the use of poison and poisoned weapons.[93] Both Manuals state that explosives in hand grenades are not included, but it is difficult to appreciate how the ban does not exclude claymore and similar grenades which splinter or discharge shards of sharp metal on explosion. The *German War Book*[94] is broadly to the same effect, but this goes on to condemn as "closely connected with the unlawful instruments of war the employment of uncivilized and barbarous peoples in European wars . . . [and] the transference of African and Mohammedan Turcis to a European seat of war [by the French] in the year 1870 was . . . a retrogression from civilized to barbarous warfare, since these troops had and could have no conception of European-Christian culture, of respect for property, and the honour of women, etc."[95] In so far as the modern soldier is concerned, he must bear in mind that he cannot discriminate among the enemy on the basis of sex, race, nationality, religion, political opinions, or any other similar criteria.[96] From this point of view all members of an adverse party are entitled to equal protection.

It is also perhaps of interest to mention, in the light of the German comments on 'barbarous' forces, that one of the first weapons to be specifically banned was the 'Dum-Dum' bullet, in 1907: "The Contracting Parties agree to abstain from the use of bullets which expand or flatten easily in the human body, such as bullets with a hard envelope which does not entirely cover the core or is pierced with incisions."[97] This bullet was apparently invented because of the belief that coloured troops were impervious to ordinary rifle fire. Westlake's explanation of the reason for its invention is slightly less 'imaginative': ". . . it having been found in the British frontier wars [in India] that the impact of an ordinary bullet did not give a shock sufficient to stop the onrush of certain assailants, so that the suffering caused to such assailants by their expansion in the body was not useless, and did not bring them within the condemnation of explosive bullets by the Declaration of St. Petersburg."[98] While it would appear that explosive and incendiary bullets are not illegal when used against aircraft[99] or tanks, there is no doubt that it is illegal for a soldier in the field to alter his normal issue of ammunition so as to expose its core or render it explosive on contact. Nevertheless, he would probably be excused from liability if he could prove that this was the only ammunition issued to him.

One of the easiest weapons that the man in the field can make for himself is the booby trap, but here, too, he should ensure that this means of warfare does not affect innocent persons, such as non-combatants, nor cause unnecessary suffering. Such weapons as the punji stick—a wooden pole with sharpened ends covered with excrement and placed in a hole covered with camouflage, which gives way as soon as stepped on—is clearly illegal.[100] As to booby traps generally, attention must now be paid to Protocol II annexed to the 1981 Convention on Prohibitions or Restrictions on the Use of Certain Conventional Weapons which may be Deemed to be Excessively Injurious or to have Indiscriminate Effects.[101] This defines booby-traps as "any device or material which is designed, con-

---

[93]*Op. cit.*, paras. 110, 111, and 34, 37 resp.
[94]*Op. cit.*, 65.
[95]*Ibid.*, 66-7.
[96]1949, I-Art. 12, II-12, III-16, IV-13, Protocol I-75—the latter also forbids any discrimination on grounds of "language . . . national or social origin, wealth, birth or other status, or any other similar status."
[97]Declaration IV, Schindler/Toman, 103.
[98]Westlake, *International Law*, Part II, *War*, 1913, 78.
[99]Hague Rules on Air Warfare, 1923, Schindler/Toman, 147, Art. 18. These Rules were never officially adopted, but have been considered declaratory of existing law, *ibid.*; see, also, Lauterpacht, *Oppenheim, op. cit.*, Vol. 2, 519, and Spaight, *Air Power and War Rights*, 1947, 42-3, 213.
[100]Bond, *The Rules of Riot*, 1974, 142.
[101]19 *I.L.M.*, 1980, 1523.

structed or adapted to kill or injure and which functions unexpectedly when a person
disturbs or approaches an apparently harmless object or performs an apparently safe
act." The use of such a weapon is only banned, however, if employed as a reprisal against
civilians or is indiscriminately placed so that it "may be expected to cause incidental loss
of civilian life, injury to civilians, damage to civilian objects, or a combination thereof,
which would be excessive in relation to the concrete and direct military advantage anticipated," and there is no indication of how this is to be measured. But, consider

Art. 6:

(1) Without prejudice to the rules of international law applicable in armed conflict
relating to treachery and perfidy, it is prohibited in all circumstances to use:

(a) any booby-trap in the form of an apparently harmless portable object which
is specifically designed and constructed to contain explosive material and to
detonate when it is disturbed or approached, or

(b) booby-traps which are in any way attached to or associated with:
  i)   internationally recognized protective emblems, signs or signals;
  ii) sick, wounded or dead persons;
  iii) burial or cremation sites or graves;
  iv) medical facilities, medical equipment, medical supplies or medical trans-
       portation;
  v)   children's toys or other portable objects or products specially designed
       for the feeding, health, hygiene, clothing or education of children;
  vi) food or drink;
  vii) kitchen utensils or appliances except in military establishments, military
       locations or military supply depots;
  viii) objects clearly of a religious nature;
  ix) historic monuments, works of art or places of worship which constitute
       the cultural or spiritual heritage of peoples;
  x)   animals or their carcasses.

(2) It is prohibited in all circumstances to use any booby-trap which is designed to
cause superfluous injury or unnecessary suffering.

This latter provision would clearly make the use of punji sticks or similar weapons or
traps illegal.[102]

There is probably little to be gained by discussion of further specific 'dos and don'ts'
regulating the military man's behaviour during conflict. Let it suffice that in all he does
he must behave in accordance with certain basic guidelines. As regards his opponents
he must do nothing to cause unnecessary suffering, that is to say once they are rendered
hors de combat by wounds or capture they become protected, and any injury inflicted
should be no more than is required to render them *hors de combat*. Moreover, the fact that
an opponent has disregarded the law in some respect, for example, abusing the protection
offered by a flag of surrender, does not entitle him to take similarly unlawful action. In
so far as non-combatants are concerned, he must control his behaviour so that any injury
suffered by them is incidental to normal conflict and not intentional. At the same time,
he must remember that, like the civilian in peacetime, the military man is presumed to
know the law to which he is subject[103] and any attempt to protect himself by contending

[102]See Fenrick, "New Developments in the Law Concerning the Use of Conventional Weapons in
Armed Conflicts," 19 *Can. Y.B. Int'l Law*, 1981, 229, 245.
[103]See, "The Man in the Field and the Maxim *Ignorantia Juris Non Excusat*," ch. II *supra*.

that he was acting in compliance with orders will, if the orders are manifestly unlawful, serve at most to mitigate any punishment that may be meted out to him.[104]

Broadly speaking, these principles apply equally to members of air and naval as well as land forces. That is to say, for example, airmen should not indulge in indiscriminate bombing,[105] nor should they attack civilian concentrations whether in towns or in flight on the roads. Equally, as with all other forces, air force personnel are forbidden from attacking hospitals or medical personnel and establishments.[106] In so far as aerial combat is concerned, the Hague Rules had already condemned attack upon crew evacuating a damaged aircraft by means of parachute, and this has now been confirmed by Protocol I, which provides, however, that this exemption does not apply to airborne troops.[107]

While the Treaty of Washington, 1922, and that of London, 1930,[108] laid down regulations with regard to submarine warfare, these by and large only have effect for the naval high command and individual submarine commanders. Moreover, it would appear from the Nuremberg Judgment[109] that unrestricted submarine warfare has become so normal in modern warfare that it matters little what the black letter law on the subject is. All that really concerns the normal seaman is that he should not attack hospital ships[110] or open fire upon shipwrecked mariners.[111]

The weapons and activities discussed thus far are of concern primarily to the man in the field, they cannot however be said today as being likely to move unduly the man in the street. He seems to be more concerned with such matters as gas, chemical, bacteriological and nuclear warfare, recourse to which depends on a major policy decision made by governmental authority, with the soldier using such weapons if so ordered. At first blush it might be thought that all these weapons fall under the general ban on the use of poison which, as we have seen, dates from earliest times. It has been suggested that in so far as the European state system is concerned, "for the Church poison was allied to the black arts, to sorcery and to witchcraft. To the knightly order it was but another method of killing an opponent without personal risk."[112]

The 1899 Hague Conference adopted a Declaration[113] agreeing "to abstain from the use of projectiles the sole object of which is the diffusion of asphyxiating or deleterious gases." The only major power refusing to accept this Declaration was the United States, and its reason is of interest:[114]

> That no shell emitting such gases is as yet in practical use, or has undergone adequate experiment, consequently a vote taken now would be taken in ignorance of the facts as to whether the results would be of a decisive character, or whether injuries in excess of that necessary to attain the end of warfare, the immediate disabling of the enemy, would be inflicted.

---

[104]See, "Superior Orders and the Reasonable Man," ch. III *supra*.

[105]Indiscriminate bombing was condemned by the Hague Rules, 1923, n. 99 above, Art. 24, and all indiscriminate attacks, including aerial, are prohibited by Protocol I, Art. 51. It should be noted that, with the exception of the U.S. flyers who bombed Tokyo, no trials for illegal bombing took place in connection with World War II, and this trial is generally condemned as illegal, see Spaight, *op. cit.*, 58-60. Those responsible were subsequently tried and executed, *Re Sawada* (1946) UNWCC, 5 *War Crimes Reports* 1.

[106]See "War Law and the Medical Profession," ch. VI *supra*.

[107]Arts. 20, 42, resp.

[108]Schindler/Toman, 789, 793, resp.

[109]*Loc. cit.*, n. 89 above, 108-9, 112, 303-5, 308, resp.

[110]See, e.g., *Llandovery Castle* (1921), Cameron, *The Peleus Trial*, 1948, App. IX.

[111]See, e.g., *The Peleus Trial, (in re Eck)* (1945) *ibid.*

[112]Draper, *loc. cit.*, n. 25 above, 19.

[113]Schindler/Toman, *op. cit.*, 99.

[114]Hyde, *International Law Chiefly as Interpreted and Applied in the United States*, Vol. 3, 1947, 1819, n. 2.

The reproach of cruelty and perfidy, addressed against these supposed shells, was equally uttered formerly against firearms and torpedoes, both of which are now employed without scruple. Until we know the effects of such asphyxiating shells there was no saying whether they would be more or less merciful than missiles now permitted.

That it was illogical, and not demonstrably humane, to be tender about asphyxiating men with gas, when all were prepared to admit that it was allowable to blow the bottom out of an ironclad at midnight, throwing four or five hundred men into the sea, to be choked by water, with scarcely the remotest chance of escape. If, and when, a shell emitting asphyxiating gases alone has been sufficiently produced, then, and not before, men will be able to vote intelligently on the subject.

Ignoring the evidence during the First World War that such weapons did exist and were capable of use, and Article 171 of the Treaty of Versailles affirming their use to be prohibited, the United States still refused to accede to the 1925 Geneva Protocol[115] which affirmed that "the use in war of asphyxiating, poisonous or other gases, and of all analogous liquids, materials or devices has been justly condemned by the general opinion of the civilized world", and went on to proclaim that its "prohibition shall be universally accepted as part of International Law, binding alike the conscience and the practice of nations . . . [and the Parties] agree to extend this prohibition to the use of bacteriological methods of warfare." Nevertheless, the United States Naval War College concluded that "the use of poisonous gases and those that cause unnecessary suffering is in general prohibited; the use of smoke screens and of tear gas has not been included in the category of prohibited acts, but the use of bacteriological warfare has been prohibited."[116] Despite this statement, the United States Field Manual on the Law of Land Warfare[117] published in 1956 still stated: "The United States is not a party to any treaty, now in force, that prohibits or restricts the use in warfare of toxic or nontoxic gases, of smoke or incendiary materials,[118] or of bacteriological warfare. . . . The Geneva Protocol . . . signed on behalf of the United States and many other powers, has been ratified or adhered to by and is now effective between a considerable number of States. However, the United States Senate has refrained from giving its advice and consent to the ratification of the Protocol by the United States, and it is accordingly not binding on this country." This statement is, however, no longer correct, since the United States adhered to the Protocol in 1975 though with reservations attached[119]—in fact, many of the parties to the Protocol reserved the right to make use of such weapons in the event of their prior use against them. The only other major belligerent in the Second World War which had not become a party to the Protocol was Japan, which adhered in 1970. Since we are concerned with the law as it is, the fact that the General Assembly of the United Nations has passed Resolutions[120] condemning the use of bacteriological or chemical weapons is of little relevance, for the Resolutions of the General Assembly lack binding authority. They are, however, at least when adopted unanimously or by consensus, evidence of a general understanding and to that extent they may be considered as confirming that the use of such weapons is contrary to the current view of the existing law. On the other hand,

---

[115]Schindler/Toman, *op. cit.*, 109.

[116]*International Law Situations*, 1935, 106.

[117]*Op. cit.*, para. 38.

[118]See Protocol on Prohibitions or Restrictions on the Use of Incendiary Weapons, annex to 1981 Convention *loc. cit.*, n. 101 above.

[119]The reservation printed in Schindler/Toman, 119, does not fully reflect the United States' attitude, see Presidential Statement, 22 Jan. 1975, and Executive Order 11850, 8 Apr. 1975, 14 *I.L.M.*, 299, 794, resp.

[120]See, e.g., Res. 2603 A (XXIV) 1969, 3318 (XXIX) 1974, Schindler/Toman, 125, 205, resp.

although evidence can be marshalled as to the existence of a customary rule from the practice of abstention from resort to such weapons or from the statements of policy-makers banning certain chemical and biological agents, still the evidence is far from overwhelming, and it is quite possible to reach, with complete intellectual honesty, a differing determination. The split of authority among reputable international jurists makes evidence of the existence of a customary rule doubtful, and, if it is in existence, evidence of its extent equivocal[121]

In the absence of any other international agreement on the subject of chemical and bacteriological weapons—the Convention on the Prohibition of the Development and Stockpiling of Bacteriological (Biological) and Toxin Weapons and on Their Destruction, 1972,[122] does not materially alter the situation and appears to have been completely disregarded by the major powers—nothing further need be said on the subject, save to point out that there have been allegations that the Soviet Union has made use of such weapons in Afghanistan and a United Nations Commission has confirmed that gas and other chemical agents have been used against Iran in the Gulf War in 1983 and 1984.[123] Further, most major powers have trained their forces in the use of anti-gas and chemical tactics and are reported to be manufacturing or stockpiling such weapons for the future.

As regards nuclear weapons, the situation is confused. Some are convinced that such weapons clearly fall within the prohibition on poison or their indiscriminate character,[124] while others are prepared to concede their use by way of reprisals.[125] It has been suggested that the use of such weapons is contrary to the laws of humanity, but that they may be used against a belligerent which, by its conduct, has placed itself outside the ambit of civilized states.[126] In addition to these doctrinal views there is some judicial comment implying that the use of atomic weapons is so outrageous as to prevent any finding of guilt in respect of more traditional war crimes.[127] Perhaps not surprisingly, the Tokyo District Court has held that the atomic bombing of both Hiroshima and Nagasaki was "an illegal act." The Court recognized that this was a new weapon and that there was no legal prohibition directly in point:[128]

Of course, it is right that the use of a new weapon is legal, as long as international law does not prohibit it. However, the prohibition in this case is understood to include not only the case where there is an express provision of direct prohibition but also the case where it is necessarily regarded that the use of a new weapon is prohibited, from the interpretation and analogical application of existing laws and regulations (international customary laws and treaties). Further, we must understand that the prohibition includes also the case where, in the light of principles of international law which are the basis of the above-mentioned positive international laws and regulations [—the court cited various international instruments beginning with the Declaration of St. Petersburg and concluding with the Geneva Gas Protocol—], the use of a new weapon is admittedly to be contrary to the principles. For there is no reason why the interpretation of international law must

[121]Thomas and Thomas, *Legal Limits to the Use of Chemical and Biological Weapons*, 1970, 246.
[122]G. A. Res. 2826 (XXVI), adopted by 110 in favour, none against and France abstaining, 11 *I.L.M.*, 309. It is not included in the Schindler/Toman collection.
[123]*The Times* (London), 28 Mar. 1984.
[124]E.g., Singh, *Nuclear Weapons and International Law*, 1959.
[125]Schwarzenberger, *The Legality of Nuclear Weapons*, 1958, 48.
[126]See Lauterpacht, *Oppenheim, op. cit.*, Vol. 2, 351.
[127]See dissent by Mr. Justice Pal at the Tokyo Trial 1946, Pal, *International Military Tribunal for the Far East, Dissentient Judgment*, 1953, 620-1.
[128]*Shimoda et al* v. *Japan* (1963) 8 *Jap. Ann. Int'l Law* 1964, 212, 235.

be limited to grammatical interpretation, any more than in the interpretation of municipal law.

. . . It is right and proper that any weapon contrary to the custom of civilized countries and to the principles of international law, should be prohibited even if there is no express provision in the laws and regulations. Only where there is no provision in the statutory (international) law, and as long as a new weapon is not contrary to the principles of international law, can the new weapon be used as a legal means of hostility.

Both the British and United States Manuals agree that there is no 'statutory' ban on the use of nuclear weapons, the former stating that "their use is governed, therefore, by the general principles" relating to the means of carrying on war,[129] while the latter is more specific:[130] "The use of explosive 'atomic weapons', whether by air, sea or land forces, cannot as such be regarded as violative of any customary rule of international law or international convention restricting their employment." While it is true that there have been numerous technological advances since these documents were published, and while it may be considered that the provisions of Protocol I, 1977, against indiscriminate attack to protect the civilian population and the ban on "methods or means of warfare which are intended, or may be expected, to cause widespread, long-term and severe damage to the natural environment"[131] imply the illegality of nuclear weapons, this was far from being the intention of some of the major powers responsible for drafting the Protocol. The International Committee of the Red Cross stated in introducing its draft that "problems relating to atomic, bacteriological and chemical weapons are subjects of international agreements or negotiations by governments, and in submitting these draft Protocols the ICRC does not intend to broach these problems," and the United Kingdom, the United States and the Soviet Union expressed concurrence in this view.[132] When signing the Protocol both the United Kingdom and the United States made declarations that the new rules in the Protocol were "not intended to have any effect on and do not regulate or prohibit the use of nuclear weapons."[133]

It was pointed out earlier when discussing feudal weapons that as weapons ceased to have relevance and fell into desuetude, they came to be regarded as unlawful, a point that is actually made in the German War Book.[134] Nowadays, rather than falling into desuetude it is simpler to make an agreement declaring such weapons illegal. Thus, with the virtual disappearance of static and trench warfare, flame has become of less value as a weapon in land warfare, but such weapons remain of value in tank, air and naval warfare. In a Protocol attached to the 1981 Convention[135] a ban is placed on the use of weapons which are

primarily designed to set fire to objects or to cause burn injury to persons through the action of flame, heat or a combination thereof, produced by a chemical reaction of a substance delivered on the target. Incendiary weapons can take the form of, for example, flame throwers, fougasses, shells, rockets, grenades, mines, bombs and other containers of incendiary substances.

But they do not include

[129]Para. 113.
[130]Para. 35.
[131]Arts. 51, 52, 57, 35.
[132]Bothe, Partsch and Solf, *op. cit.*, 188-9.
[133]Schindler/Toman, 635, 636.
[134]*Op. cit.*, 66.
[135]See n. 118 above.

Munitions which have incidental incendiary effects, such as illuminants, tracers, smoke or signalling systems; [or]
Munitions designed to combine penetration, blast or fragmentation effects with an additional incendiary effect, such as armour-piercing projectiles, fragmentation shells, explosive bombs and similar combined-effects munitions, in which the incendiary effect is not specifically designed to cause burn injury to persons, but to be used against military objectives, such as armoured vehicles, aircraft and installations or facilities

when, of course, they are almost certainly specifically designed to cause burn injury to the crews of such vehicles or aircraft. The Protocol does not forbid the use of such weapons against the man in the field, although the reservation with regard to armoured vehicles and aircraft would seem to imply this. It does, however, expressly forbid their use against civilians or civilian objects. The remaining prohibitions are somewhat contradictory:

It is prohibited in all circumstances to make any military objective located within a concentration of civilians the object of attack by air-delivered incendiary weapons. It is further prohibited to make any military objective located within a concentration of civilians the object of attack by means of incendiary weapons other than air-delivered incendiary weapons, except when such military objective is clearly separated from the concentration of civilians and all feasible precautions [defined as 'those . . . which are practicable or practically possible taking into account all circumstances ruling at the time, including humanitarian and military considerations'] are taken with a view to limiting the incendiary effects to the military objective and to avoiding, and in any event to minimizing, incidental loss of civilian life, injury to civilians and damage to civilian objects.
It is prohibited to make forests or other kind of plant cover the object of attack by incendiary weapons except when such natural elements are used to cover, conceal or camouflage combatants or other military objectives, or are themselves military objectives.

A further Protocol was agreed upon at the same time. It will be recalled that Captain Mahan explained the unwillingness of the United States to accept the 1899 ban on gas projectiles on the basis that they had not yet been invented.[136] In 1980, however, no representative found it difficult to agree to the Protocol prohibiting the use of "any weapon the primary effect of which is to injure by fragments which in the human body escape detection by X-rays." One can only presume that it is more difficult to agree to weapons the invention of which is clearly within the horizons of invention, than to agree upon a ban on one that has not been invented and which is considered as being beyond the realm of invention!

---

[136]See text to n. 114 above.

IX

The Status of Mercenaries in International Law

The activities of white mercenaries during the Congolese and Angolan civil wars; the trial of a number of them at Luanda after the establishment of an independent Angolan government; and the inclusion of a special Article (47) denying them combatant status in the 1977 Protocol I Additional to the Geneva Conventions of 1949 relating to the Protection of Victims of International Armed Conflicts[1] have focused attention on what has long been a reality in so far as the armed forces of a number of countries are concerned. The uproar that these events caused might well lead one to assume that the problem is new. To adopt such an attitude, however, not only indicates a lack of historical knowledge, but also an ignorance of classical international law.

While modern writers on the law of war have not drawn any distinction between the status of mercenaries and others and have not seen any need to make any specific reference to their existence, many of the classical writers were concerned since princes often made use of foreign troops to fight their wars,[2] even it would seem against their own sovereign. Thus, Bynkershoek records[3] that

> at the beginning of the second English war when the States-General gave permission to some Scotch mercenaries to depart if they did not wish to serve in the Netherlands, some remained in the service of the States-General, ready to serve against any and every enemy, even the English. Charles II, however, issued an edict proscribing these men as traitors. But when peace was made with England the men requested the States-General to use their influence with the English King to have the edict replaced so that they might again acquire property in England by right of inheritance and by the other customary practices in vogue in England. The States-General did as requested on October 24, 1688. . . .

[1]For the text *see* Schindler/Toman, 551.
[2]See, e.g., Mockler, *The Mercenaries*, Chs. 2-5 (1969); Bayley, *Mercenaries for the Crimea* (1977).
[3]Bynkershoek, *Quaestionum Juris Publici* Book II, Ch. XXV, § 6, (Carnegie tr. 279-80).

It is true that Ayala[4] was of opinion that "sovereigns should be urged to employ as soldiers in war natives rather than foreigners, for the latter serve for pay rather than glory." His reason for arguing thus did not depend on any doubt as to the right of a foreigner to be a soldier, but he feared that such foreigners might not be easy to disband at the end of hostilities, and he cites the instance of

> the Emperor of Constantinople [who having] no forces of his own, summoned Turkish auxiliaries to protect him from his neighbours; but he could not get rid of them at the end of the war; and that is how the whole of Greece fell under the rule of Turkey. I, therefore, do not approve of the policy of Cyrus, who declared that soldiers should not be selected out of citizens, but be brought from afar like the best horses, nor of that ancient custom of the Alexandrians, who would not allow of any but foreign soldiers.

Ayala, thus, pays no attention to the justness of the cause or the motive of the alien soldier, he is merely concerned with the ultimate safety of the prince in whose service he is.

Others among the classicists were more concerned with the justness of the cause than in the safety of the country of enlistment or the status or nationality of any of the soldiers enlisted, although they tended to be more condemnatory of the alien than the liege national who might be involved in an injust cause. Thus Vitoria[5] was prepared to argue that

> if it is evident that the war is unjust, or if this is known to be the case, or if the subjects are conscious that the war is unjust, they may not fight, even when the prince exercises compulsion upon them. The reason for this is that such a prince is committing a mortal sin, and one must obey God rather than him. . . . I also maintain that those who are prepared to go forth to every war, who have no care as to whether or not a war is just, but follow him who provides the more pay, and who are, moreover, not subjects, commit a mortal sin, not only when they actually go to battle, but whenever they are thus willing. I further contend that, when the case is doubtful, allies . . . may not, when they themselves are subjects, furnish aid to the other side. However, it should be observed in this connection that there may exist a doubt as to the right of the matter—as to whether a particular city belongs to France. But *let us suppose the city is in the possession of our king; it is then indubitable that the war in which the city is defended by the Spanish king, is a just war; and accordingly, any person whosoever may offer aid to the Spanish king.*

Grotius,[6] too, condemned any ally who fought without regard to the justice of the cause and since

> those Alliances which are entered into, with the Design and Promise of Assistance in any War, without regarding the Merit of the Cause, are altogether unlawful; so there is no Course of Life more abominable and to be detested, than that of mercenary Soldiers, who without ever considering the Justice of what they are un-

[4]Ayala, *De Jure et Officiis Bellicis et Disciplina Militari*, Book III, Ch. II, § 16 (Carnegie tr. 188-189); see also, Mockler, *op. cit.*, at 181 *et seq.*, re mercenary revolt in Congo.
[5]Vitoria, *De Bello* Art. I, para. 8, in Scott, *Francisco de Vitoria and His Law of Nations*, App. F, CXVIII, CXIX-CXX (1934).
[6]Grotius, *De Jure Belli ac Pacis*, Book II, Ch. XXV, § IX, § X, (1738 tr., 505-7; Carnegie tr. 585-586)—in his notes, Barbeyrac disagrees with the interpretation Grotius gives to the classical authorities he cites.

dertaking, fight for the Pay; who *By their Wages the Goodness of the Cause compute.* . . . The Case of a Soldier . . . is really a miserable one, *Who to support his Life to Death resorts.* . . . Did they sell only their own Lives it were no great Matter: but they sell also the Lives of many an harmless inoffensive Creature: . . . by how much it is worse to kill without a Reason, than with one. . . . Philip of Macedon said of that sort of Men, *who got their Livelihood by fighting, that War was Peace to them, and Peace War.* . . . *To bear Arms is* . . . *no Crime, but to bear Arms on the account of Booty is Wickedness with a Witness.* Nay, it is so to fight for Pay, if that be the sole and principal View; tho' it is otherwise very justifiable to receive Pay, for *who ever goes to War at his own Cost?*[7]

It has been said that Suarez developed the law of nations as elaborated at Salamanca by Vitoria out of the teachings of Aquinas.[8] While he believes that the cause should be just, he is somewhat more charitable than either Vitoria, his predecessor, or Grotius, his Protestant successor, towards the individual soldier. Thus, he asserts[9] that

common soldiers, as subjects of princes, are in no wise bound to make diligent investigation, but rather may go to war when summoned to do so, provided it is not clear to them that the war is unjust. This conclusion may be derived from the following arguments: first, when the injustice of the war is not evident to these soldiers, the united opinion of the prince and of the realm is sufficient to move them to this action; secondly, subjects when in doubt are bound to obey their superiors. . . . A greater difficulty arises with soldiers who are not subjects and who are called mercenaries. The opinion commonly held seems to be that these soldiers are bound to inquire into the justice of a war, before they enlist. . . . However, such an opinion comes into conflict with the following difficulties. First, it would be necessary for each individual mercenary soldier to inquire into the cause of the war. But such an investigation is contrary to all custom, and humanly speaking, is impossible; for . . . the reason of the war cannot be explained to all, nor are all capable of appreciating that explanation. Secondly, (if the opinion in question were valid,) even soldiers who were subjects could not take part in a doubtful war without examining the cause, save when they were under strict orders of such sort that they would be disobedient in not doing; for in that case their disobedience would alone excuse them. But as long as they were not under orders, it would be (morally) safer not to fight. However, this consequence is contrary to all custom, and that obligation (to investigate the cause of war) would be harmful to the state. Thirdly, if permanent mercenaries could, previously to a war, bind themselves to fight even in doubtful cases by giving their consciences into the keeping of the prince's conscience, why would not those mercenaries do the same who enlist at the outbreak of a war? For, from a moral standpoint, the same principle is involved in the performance of an action and in binding oneself to perform it. The confirmation of this argument lies in the fact that just as one is not allowed to proceed to an unjust war, neither is he allowed to undertake the obligation of serving in such a war, nor even in any war indiscriminately, whether just or unjust; and the reason for these restrictions is that to fight in an unjust war is to act unjustly. Therefore, conversely, if one is permitted to bind himself to service in a doubtful war, the obligation involved in such a case is not wicked; and therefore, it would be permissible so to bind oneself for pay, here and now, although no previous obligation exists. Nor does it seem to be of much importance that a given (mercenary) was already regarded as a subject before the war, by reason of his pay. For one might say the same thing of a contract made on the eve of the outbreak of the war, since, at such a time also, soldiers bind themselves to obedience in all matters in which obedience is legitimate; so that it makes no difference from the

---

[7]1 *Epistle to the Corinthians*, 9:7.
[8]Scott, *The Catholic Conception of International Law*, 128-130 (1934).
[9]*De Triplici Virtate Theologica*, Disp. XII, De Bello, § VI, paras. 8, 10, 11, 12 in Suarez, *Selections from Three Works* (Carnegie tr. 832, 833-836).

standpoint of justice, whether this contract was made before the war, or whether it is made now, (at the moment when the conflict begins). Fourthly, in a similar doubtful situation, any person is permitted to sell arms to these princes and to the soldiers; nevertheless, if they do so, the same danger is present, namely, that the act may contribute to the injury of innocent persons, if by any chance, the war is in fact unjust. The antecedent is commonly accepted as true. The proof of the consequent is, that both kinds of cooperation are very pertinent to actual wars; and although soldiers seem . . . to cooperate more immediately, nevertheless the persons who furnish arms are ordinarily able to do more harm. . . . Lastly, . . . the first and essential element is that one who is not a subject, submits himself to another for the sake of payment, and in so doing, inflicts no injury upon any person; neither, generally speaking, does he expose himself to the danger of any wrongdoing. And for the rest, he is exercising his right, when he sells his own property or his own labour, a right of which he is not bound to deprive himself to his own detriment. With regard to these (mercenary) soldiers, there is, in addition, a special argument; for each of them has the authority of the prince and that of the whole state to support him, a fact which involves a great probability (that their conduct is just). Hence, all the circumstances being weighed, it would by no means seem that mercenaries who serve in that condition (when there is great probability that the war is just), are choosing the course that is (morally) less safe. These arguments are clearly convincing; nor do I find any difference in actual fact between subjects and non-subjects. So it is that Vitoria, too, speaks simply of "soldiers," without distinction. . . . [I]f the doubt (as to the justice of a war) is purely negative, it is probable that the soldiers in question may take part in that war without having made any examination of the question, all responsibility being thrown upon the prince to whom they are subject. . . . If, however, the doubt is positive . . . , then . . . (those who are about to enlist) should make an inquiry into the truth of the matter. If they are unable to ascertain the truth, they will be bound to follow the course of action which is more probably just, and to aid him who is more probably in the right. . . . Finally, if the arguments on both sides contain an equal probability, the soldiers may under such circumstances conduct themselves as if the doubt were purely negative; for the balance is equal, and the authority of the prince turns the scale.

Another early writer who was concerned with the justness of a war, and particularly with the safety of the soul of the soldier participating in an unjust war whether as a mercenary or otherwise, was Belli, who, although among the classicists of international law, is not normally regarded as one of the great writers thereon. Writing earlier than any of those already mentioned, Belli[10] proclaimed that

[v]olunteers . . . should beware of putting themselves in jeopardy . . . because of peril to their souls; for . . . it is not lawful to serve in an unjust war. . . . Furthermore, the mercenary soldiers, too, should have a care—who, . . . the instant they hear the mention and tumult of war, rush to the clinking coin, with never a thought of justice or injustice. For such . . . are manifestly doomed to endless perdition, if they do not reform. . . . [S]uch soldiers should not be absolved, unless they renounce their calling, or at any rate return to the service of justice.

Having expressed his concern for the soul of a serviceman engaged in an unjust war, Belli reaffirms that distinctions cannot be drawn between the volunteer and the hired man, for both are soldiers.[11] He is, unlike Ayala, not concerned that they may be difficult to disband when hostilities cease, but rather with the fear that they may desert and so cause the defeat of their employer. He cites in this connection the defeat of Scipio the

[10]Belli, *De re Militari et Bello Tractatus*, Pars. Sec., Cap. II, S. 5 (Carnegie tr. 64).
[11]*Ibid.*, Pars. Ter., Cap. I, s. 12, at 106.

Elder by Hasdrubal and "almost in our times, [the case of] Ludovico Sforza, [who] through the defection of the Swiss lost Milan, and [in 1500] fell into the hands of Louis XII, King of France."[12]

It is often pointed out that the Peace of Westphalia, 1648,[13] marks a watershed in the European law of nations. It is interesting to note therefore that Pufendorf,[14] writing some 25 years later in 1672, had nothing detrimental to say about the use of mercenaries. He comments that it is frequently said, in respect of the use in war of the help of any persons whose support may be secured, that "a distinction should be drawn between traitors to and deserters from their masters, who voluntarily offer their services, and those who are led by promises or rewards to break their faith," and confesses that he does not understand the reason why the former is considered legitimate, but not the latter, for "when I am permitted to kill a man with an iron lance, why may I not attack him as well with one of silver?" He reminds us, however, that he who has once shown perfidy towards his liege lord cannot be expected to remain completely faithful to his new master. It is perhaps of interest that he does not deal with the problem of the mercenary from a third State, although it would appear that he is fully aware of their existence, for when discussing who may take booty under a declaration to this effect, he states this relates only to citizens, for "mercenary troops are owed nothing beyond their pay, unless it be the desire to use them generously, or to reward them for some distinguished service, or to incite them to great fortitude."

A somewhat different approach—perhaps more practical and less philosophical—is to be found in the writings of the eighteenth century. Wolff[15]—almost foretelling German views on expansionism—pointed out that

> the greater its power for resisting foreign attack, the more powerful the nation is. And since for resisting foreign attack, . . . or even for obtaining by force its own right from another nation which refuses to concede it, both a number of soldiers . . . and enormous expenditures are required . . . the power of a nation depends upon the number of men who can perform military service, and upon its wealth. And since it is just the same whether the soldiers are natives or foreigners hired for a price, a nation is still rated as powerful, if it is rich enough to hire for a price as many foreign soldiers as it needs.

Perhaps the country which is best known as a source of mercenaries is Switzerland. It is interesting, therefore, to note the views of Vattel[16] on the subject, and one cannot but be impressed by the chauvinism which underlies much of his comments.

> Mercenary soldiers are foreigners who voluntarily enter into the service of the State for a stipulated pay. As they are not subjects of the sovereign they owe him no service in that capacity, and consequently the pay he offers them is the motive of their service. By their contract they bind themselves to serve him, and the Prince on his part agrees to certain conditions set down in the terms of enlistment. These terms are the rule and measure of the respective rights and obligations of the contracting parties, and they should be scrupulously obeyed. . . . [Vattel then takes

---

[12]*Ibid.*, Pars. Oct., Cap. I, ss. 28-29, at 228; *see also*, Mockler, *supra* note 2, at 96-98, who points out that both parties were aided by Swiss mercenaries.

[13]See, e.g., Gross, "The Peace of Westphalia, 1648-1948," 42 *Am. J. Int'l L.* 20 (1948); *Essays on International Law and Organization*, 1984, vol. 1, 3.

[14]Pufendorf, *De Jure Naturae et Gentium*, Book VIII, Ch. VI, ss. 18, 20, (Carnegie tr. 1308, 1311).

[15]Wolff, *Jus Gentium Methodo Scientifica Pertractatum*, Ch. 1, s. 69, at 41 (Carnegie tr., 41).

[16]Vattel, *Le Droit des Gens, ou Principes de la Loi Naturelle*, Book III, Ch. II, ss. 13-14, (Carnegie tr., 239-40).

issue with French commentators who have criticised Swiss mercenaries for having left their employment on the employing prince's failure to pay.] But . . . the Swiss . . . have never quit service at the first payment overdue; and when they have found a sovereign sincerely desirous to pay them, but actually unable to do so, their patience and their zeal have always kept them faithful to him. Henry IV owed them immense sums, but they never forsook him in his greatest necessity, and that brave man found the Swiss Nation as generous as it was courageous. I mention the Swiss in this connection because, in fact, they were often mere mercenaries. But troops of that sort are not to be confused with the Swiss who at the present day serve various powers with the permission of their sovereign and in virtue of alliances existing between those powers and the Swiss Confederation or some individual canton. These latter troops are real auxiliaries, although paid by the sovereign whom they serve. The question has been much discussed whether the profession of a mercenary soldier be legitimate or not, whether individuals may, for money or other rewards, engage as soldiers in the service of a foreign prince? The question does not seem to me very difficult of solution. Those who enter into such contracts without the express or implied consent of their sovereign are wanting in their duty as citizens. But when the sovereign leaves them at liberty to follow their inclinations for the profession of arms, they become free in that respect. Now, every free man may join whatever society pleases him best and seems most to his advantage, and may make common cause with it and take up its quarrels. He becomes in some measure, at least for a time, a citizen of the State into whose service he enters; and as ordinarily an officer is free to leave the service when he thinks fit, and a private soldier at the expiration of his term, if that State should enter upon a war that is manifestly unjust, the foreigner may leave its service. *Such mercenary soldiers, by learning the art of war, will render themselves more capable of serving their country,* if ever it has need of them. This last consideration furnishes us with the answer to a question proposed at this point: Can the sovereign properly allow his subjects to serve foreign powers indiscriminately as mercenaries? He can, and for this simple reason—that in this way his subjects learn an art the knowledge of which is both useful and necessary. *The tranquillity, the profound peace which Switzerland has so long enjoyed in the midst of wars which have agitated Europe, would soon become disastrous to her if her citizens did not enter into the service of foreign princes and thereby train themselves in the art of war and keep alive their martial spirit.* Mercenary soldiers enlist freely. A sovereign . . . should not even resort to deceit or stratagem to lead [foreigners] to enter into a contract which, like every other, should be founded upon good faith.

Vattel's reference to Swiss whom he describes as "auxiliaries," since they serve with permission of their sovereign by virtue of alliances, typifies the situation prevailing in Europe right up until the Crimean War. It has already been pointed out that Swiss mercenaries served on both sides during the conflict between Louis XII and Sforza and during the years immediately following enabled the Confederacy almost to create a powerful central European State, "but as always with the Swiss, their mercenary spirit ruined their political enterprises."[17] By virtue of the Perpetual Peace of 1516[18] Switzerland became virtually a mercenary recruiting ground for France, with the Swiss agreeing never to supply mercenaries to the enemies of France, although Swiss regiments did serve in the armies of Savoy, Holland, Spain, Austria and England. However, the French connection remained supreme until the massacre of the Swiss Guard during the French Revolution and Napoleon's intervention in Swiss affairs at the time of the Helvetic Republic. Now, in accordance with the Swiss Constitution,[19] military capitulations, that is to say agreements for the supply of mercenary troops to foreign countries, may not be

[17]Mockler, *op. cit.*, 102.
[18]Dumont, 4 *Corps Universel Diplomatique*, 248.
[19]Art. 11.

concluded. While, if Vattel's views are accepted, only alien volunteers should be used as mercenary troops, by the time of the American War of Independence England at least was arranging with the various German princes for the wholesale employment of entire regiments, for "many of the small princes depended for almost their entire revenue upon hiring out their subjects at exorbitant prices." Despite the fact that George II complained that "this giving commissions to German officers to get men in plain English amounts to making me a kidnapper which I cannot think a very honourable occupation,"[20] German troops were in fact employed against the American rebels, when the United Provinces refused to make its Scots Brigade available.[21]

The English traditionally were opposed to a standing army on British soil and it was always difficult to secure sufficient local recruits. It therefore became necessary to recruit abroad and "in 1695 approximately ¼ of the grand total was made up of Dutch, Danish and Hanoverians and by the end of the century this proportion had risen to one half. . . , while by the middle of the Seven Years' War the national army of 97,000 was supplemented by some 60,000 foreign troops."[22] The English attitude is well expressed by Lord Egremont in 1756:[23]

> I shall never be for carrying a war upon the continent of Europe by a large body of national troops, because we can always get foreign troops to hire, This should be our adopted method in any war on the continent of Europe.

Typical of the period is the Treaty of 1776 between George III and the Langrave of Hesse-Cassel,[24] whereby

> [h]is Britannic Majesty, being desirous of employing in his service a body of 12,000 men, of the troops of his most serene highness the reigning landgrave of Hesse Cassel; and that prince, full of attachment for his Majesty, desiring nothing more than to give him proofs of it,

it was agreed that fully equipped troops of fit men should be made available immediately for "there is no time to be lost," and

> this body of troops shall not be separated, unless reasons of war require it, but shall remain under the orders of the general, to whom his most serene highness has entrusted the command. . . .

While George III undertook to pay to the landgrave a fixed sum in respect of every man supplied, together with certain additional items, as well as an annual subsidy,

> with regard to the pay and treatment, as well ordinary as extraordinary, of the said troops, they shall be put on the same footing in all respects with the national British troops, and his Majesty's department of war shall deliver, without delay, to that of his most serene highness, an exact and faithful state of the pay and treatment enjoyed by those troops.

---

[20]Mockler, *op. cit.* 115—*see* his Ch. 5 for a full discussion.
[21]Bayley, *op. cit.* 5.
[22]*Ibid.,* 4-5.
[23]Cobbett, *Parliamentary History*, XIV, col. 1283.
[24]Parry, 46 *Consolidated Treaty Series*, 127; *see also*, Treaty with Brunswick for 3964 men, and with Hesse-Hanau for 668 men, *ibid.,* 119, 163.

The Treaty was not popular with Parliament, both on account of its expense and in view of the unpopularity of the American war. Perhaps it is enough to cite the comments of the Duke of Richmond,[25] comments which have a familiar ring today:

> Let us consider the means we have to prosecute this war. The British troops, we find, fail not, my Lords, in point of courage, but they show an honest backwardness to engage their fellow citizens. To Germany we have recourse for assistance: 17,000 German mercenaries [he clearly made no distinction, as did Vattel, between individual hirelings and "auxiliaries" obtained under treaty] are at least obtained; with these and a small British army, many of whose regiments consist entirely of recruits some of whom are of the worst description—for I have been told that even the prisons have been ransacked to augment their numbers—in this country to engage a nation who are enthusiastic in their case, have no hopes but in success, are united in every tie, have every stimulative to courage that shame or ambition can give an army of brothers? The mercenaries we employ, for they are justly called so since that man must be deemed a mercenary soldier who fights for pay in the cause in which he has no concern, are a motley barrel of various nations who are yet in Germany, are yet to be conveyed across the Atlantic; some will perish on the way, some desert, but I will suppose the remnant landed on the American shore. Will conquest immediately follow? Impossible to expect it.

It hardly needs mentioning that the presence of the German mercenaries ultimately made no difference to the result of the war.

During the Crimean War, in view of the difficulty in securing allies, Britain considered the advisability of raising a foreign legion, as had been done under the authority of statute during the Napoleonic wars, although then it could be argued that the Germanic Legion was fighting for the liberation of its own soil, while George III was a Germanic king *vis-à-vis* Hanover. The Foreign Enlistment Act of 1854[26] authorized the enlistment of foreign volunteers in separate regiments, not to be employed in the United Kingdom other than during the period of training, that the number in the United Kingdom was not to exceed 10,000, that they were not to be billeted in private households, and were to be amenable to the British articles of war. Problems arose since some European countries, for example, Switzerland and the German *Bund*, fearing their neutrality, had made recruitment by foreign powers within their territory criminal. Nevertheless, British-German, British-Swiss and British-Italian Legions of 9682, 3294 and 3581 officers and men were ultimately raised and saw service under the British flag.[27] While the British Army continued to employ foreign units, for example the Gurkha Regiments, as part of its regular armed forces, this was the last occasion on which governmental efforts were directed at securing the services of mercenary units. In so far as France was concerned the need to make use of mercenaries was not the same, since general conscription provided a much larger solid core of trained personnel, while for foreign service, particularly in the colonial territories, the Foreign Legion comprising foreign personnel serving under French authority and on personal contract was available from 1831. While by an extended application of the definition both the Gurkhas and the Foreign Legion might be considered as mercenaries—and this term has even been applied by one writer to the International Brigade in Spain as well as British officers seconded to the Arab Legion[28]—they would hardly fall within the term as currently used, or perhaps even as used by the classicists,

[25]Mockler, *op. cit.* 122-123.
[26]18 & 19 Vict. c. 2.
[27]House of Commons, *Sessional Papers*, XXVII, 151.
[28]Mockler, *op. cit.*, 14.

for all of these were serving as embodied personnel within the regular forces of those under whose flag they served. However, at times it would appear that even today the Foreign Legion is being used almost as a traditional mercenary unit although not for the purpose of a foreign war as for suppressing a rebellion. Thus, in April 1978 some 300 Foreign Legion troops were sent by France to assist Chad in combatting Chad National Liberation Front rebels.[29] This may perhaps be compared with the actions of Louis-Philippe who, in 1835, during the Carlist war hired the Legion to Queen Cristina.[30] However, there is no evidence of any hire arrangement with Chad, merely provision of aid by an ally.

The Crimean War seems to have proved a watershed in both the doctrinal writing and state practice with regard to the service of non-nationals in conflict situations. In his *Institutes of the Law of Nations*,[31] Lorimer proposed some rules concerning the enlistment of neutrals based on the distinction "between the position of the neutral State in its corporate capacity, and when viewed as an aggregate of private persons," a distinction which is now becoming more and more disregarded, not only as regards the problem of State trading, but also more generally,[32] and particularly in the attitude of third world countries when assessing the activities of nationals of the first world. He saw nothing wrong in a neutral national's enlisting in belligerent forces and was of opinion that by so doing he abandoned all claim to protection by his own nation, being regarded from the moment of enlistment as a citizen of the belligerent State concerned.[33] In his view there was to be no distinction between volunteering and enlisting, so that presumably both were to be treated alike. Moreover, enlistment was to be permitted even within the neutral State, and it was not to be considered a breach of neutrality that the State in question permitted him to retain his domicile and enjoy any private rights resulting therefrom. Calvo, too, seemed to see nothing wrong in the employment of foreign mercenaries, whom he regarded as being entitled of full rights under international law.[34] The general view of nineteenth century writers seems to have been that the use and enlistment of foreign volunteers was legitimate, and there was a tendency to accept that the provision of such personnel under an agreement made between a non-belligerent sovereign and a country at war, or about to enter into war, was not incompatible with neutrality. It was, of course, open to the belligerent against whom such "treaty" mercenaries were operating to regard the arrangement as an unneutral act amounting to a *casus belli* authorizing warlike acts against the *soi-disant* neutral.

Whether nationals would be allowed to serve in a foreign army depended, in the absence of specific treaty[35] between two States seeking to protect themselves, not on the requirements of international law but on the provisions of municipal law. A good many countries, concerned about the danger of the presence of foreign troops upon their own territory, had passed legislation forbidding the stationing within the territory of such

---

[29]*The Times* (London), 21 April, 1978. In May the Legion went to Zaire to rescue Europeans and suppress a rebellion.
[30]Mockler, *op. cit.*, 135.
[31]Lorimer, 2 *Institutes of the Law of Nations*, 179-180 (1884).
[32]See, e.g., Garcia-Mora, *International Responsibility for Hostile Acts by Private Persons against Foreign States*, 68 (1962).
[33]See, e.g., Schwarzenberger, 1 *International Law* 593 (1957).
[34]Calvo, *Derecho Internacional*, 483 (1868).
[35]See, e.g., Jay Treaty, 1794, 52 Parry, *supra* note 24, at 243, Art. 21; see also, Central American Treaty of Peace and Amity, 1923, Hudson, 2 *International Legislation*, 901, Art. 14; Habana Convention on Civil Strife, 1928, 4 *ibid.*, 2416, Art. 1; see *however*, Habana Convention on Maritime Neutrality, 1928, *ibid.*, 2402, Art. 23—"Neutral States shall not oppose the voluntary departure of nationals of belligerent States *even though they leave simultaneously in great numbers*; but they *may* oppose the voluntary departure of their own nationals going to enlist in the armed forces." (Italics added.)

personnel, if enlisted.[36] Some countries went further and forbade their nationals from enlisting in alien armies and alien causes. Thus, as early as 1794, the United States Congress enacted[37]—and it is still law today:[38]

> Every citizen of the United States who, within the territory or jurisdiction thereof, accepts and exercises a commission to serve a foreign prince, state, colony, district, or people, in war, by land or by sea, against any prince, state, colony, district, or people, with whom the United States are at peace, shall be guilty of a high misdemeanor. . . .

In practice, it would seem that this Act was primarily concerned with the fitting out of raiding naval vessels,[39] a matter which was eventually dealt with by the Declaration of Paris, 1856,[40] having over centuries been regarded as an act of extreme infamy and akin to piracy.[41]

The present law of the U.S. is wider than that originally enacted, for it now forbids anyone in the U.S., regardless of nationality, from recruiting or enlisting or leaving the U.S. to serve "any foreign prince, state, colony, district or people," whether as a soldier, marine or seaman, but there is no reference to the service being in a campaign against a state with which the U.S. is at peace.[42] There are certain exceptions. The ban does not apply to nationals of a belligerent allied to the U.S., unless he "shall hire or solicit a citizen of the U.S. to enlist or go beyond the jurisdiction of the U.S. with intent to enlist or enter the service of a foreign country."[43] Equally no offence is committed by

> any subject or citizen of any foreign prince, State, colony, district, or people who is transiently within the United States and enlists or enters himself on board any vessel of war, letter of marque, or privateer, which at the time of its arrival within the United States was fitted and equipped as such, or hires or retains another subject or citizen of the same foreign prince, state, colony, district, or people who is transiently within the United States to enlist or enter himself to serve such foreign prince, state, colony, district, or people on board such vessel of war, letter of marque, or privateer, if the United States shall then be at peace with such foreign prince, state, colony, district, or people.[44]

This would suggest that it might be possible for the subjects of a belligerent with which the U.S. is at peace to time their arrival in the U.S. to coincide with that of a vessel visiting the U.S. with the sole purpose of enlisting such nationals, and it would appear not to matter that the U.S. might be at peace with the State against which the enlistment is directed.

Finally, an offence is committed by

> [w]hoever within the United States, knowingly begins or sets on foot or provides or prepares a means for or furnishes the money for, or takes part in, any military

[36]See note 26 *supra*.
[37]2nd Cong. Sess. I, c. 50, s. 3.
[38]18 *U.S.C.* § 958.
[39]See, e.g., *The Charming Betsey* (1804), 2 *Cranch* 62. *See also, The Alabama Arbitration* (1872), Moore, 1 *International Arbitration* 653, in which Great Britain was held liable for having allowed such fitting out.
[40]Schindler/Toman, 699.
[41]Butler and Maccoby, *The Development of International Law*, 165 (1928).
[42]18 *U.S.C.* § 959 (a).
[43]*Ibid.*, § 959 (b).
[44]*Ibid.*, § 959 (c).

or naval expedition or enterprise to be carried on from thence against the territory
or dominion of any foreign prince or state, or of any colony, district, or people
with whom the United States is at peace. . . .[45]

This would seem to cover the advertising for and recruiting of mercenaries to serve in
such places as the Congo or Angola[46] subject to the question of whether the liberation
movement against which they were operating could be considered as a district or people
with whom the U.S. was at peace.

Perhaps more important than the fine or imprisonment envisaged by these provisions,
at least in the case of U.S. citizens, is the provision in the 1952 Immigration andNationality
Act,[47] providing for the loss of nationality by any U.S. national, whether by birth or
naturalization, who enters or serves in the armed forces of a foreign State without the
prior written authorization of the Secretary of State and Secretary of Defense.

In practice, the U.S. has appeared hesitant to apply the penal clauses here referred to.
During the First World War, and before the U.S. became a belligerent, U.S. citizens
formed the Escadrille Américaine, which became the Escadrille Lafayette after German
protests at the presence of an American squadron with the French air force. No action
was taken against these *"citoyens Américains volontaires pour la durée de la guerre,"* and after
the U.S. joined the Allies, the Lafayette Squadron became 103 Pursuit Squadron U.S. Air
Service.[48] There was a similar group of American airmen with the R.A.F.—the Eagle
Squadron—prior to Pearl Harbour, while Chennault's Flying Tigers only became part of
the U.S.A.A.F. in the summer of 1942.[49] During the Middle East crisis of 1956, when it
was known that American Jews were joining the Israeli forces, the Department of State
pointed out that no authorization had been issued "in any individual case and there is
no intention of departing from this policy."[50] There is, however, no record of any prosecution. A somewhat different attitude has been adopted towards service in revolutionary
forces. After the victory of the Castro forces in Cuba the U.S. Embassy stated that while
citizens who fought with the Revolutionary forces would not necessarily be expatriated,
"such persons who continue voluntarily to serve with these forces, if and when they
become an integral part of the armed forces of the Republic of Cuba" are so liable, and
this was reiterated by the State Department shortly thereafter. "Thus, a distinction was
made between serving in the revolutionary forces of Castro and serving in the armed
forces of a foreign State."[51] The significance of this became clear in *U.S. ex rel. Marks* v.
Esperdy[52] in which an equally divided Supreme Court[53] upheld a decision expatriating
Marks by reason of his service in the Cuban armed forces after the conclusion of the
revolution and the establishment of the Castro Government. It would seem, however,
that since *Afroyim* v. *Rusk*[54] this would no longer be the case, for the Supreme Court held
that non-voluntary expatriation was unconstitutional. While this decision arose out of
the exercise of the franchise by a citizen during a foreign election, it seemingly is of
general application[55] and would indicate that *Marks* v. *Esperdy* would not be followed.

[45]*Ibid.*, § 960.
[46]See, e.g., Burchett and Roebuck, *The Whores of War*, ch. 6, 10 (1977); see also, *The Times* (London)
9 May 1978, citing Stockwell, *In Search of Enemies; A CIA Story* (1978).
[47]8 *U.S.C.* § 1481 (a) (3).
[48]Spaight, *Air Power and War Rights*, 462-463 (1947).
[49]*Ibid.*, 463-465.
[50]Whiteman, 8 *Digest of International Law*, 171 (1967).
[51]*Ibid.*, 173-174.
[52](1963), 315 F2d 673; (1964), 377 *U.S.* 214.
[53]4 votes to 4, Justice Brennan did not participate.
[54](1967), 387 *U.S.* 253.
[55][1975] *U.S. Digest*, 817.

Twenty-five years after the American precedent, and as a result of activities on behalf of the revolting Spanish American colonies,[56] England passed its first Act[57] "to prevent the enlisting or engagement of His Majesty's subjects to serve in Foreign Service, and the fitting out or equipping, in His Majesty's Dominions, vessels for warlike purposes, without His Majesty's licence." The Preamble declared that such action

> in or against the Dominions or Territories of any foreign prince, state, potentate, or persons exercising or assuming to exercise the powers of government in or over any foreign country, colony, province or part of any province, or against the ships, goods or merchandise of any foreign prince, state, potentate or persons as aforesaid, or their subjects, may be prejudicial to and endanger the peace and welfare of this Kingdom.

This being so, the Act repealed previous legislation, such as the Act of 1754 forbidding service as officers in the French forces and that of 1769 requiring British subjects accepting commission in the "Scotch Brigade in the Service of the States General of the United Provinces" to take the oath of allegiance. To take such service as was proscribed by the Act without royal licence was made a misdemeanor, punishable by fine and/or imprisonment at the discretion of the Court. The Act was not made retroactive so that persons already serving were able to continue. The Act further provided that any vessel at a British port with such persons aboard might be detained, while any vessel fitted out in British territory for this purpose was made liable to forfeiture, and any person who added to or changed the military equipment of any warship was equally guilty of a misdemeanor. The Act made no reference to any requirement that the foreign ruler be at peace with England, and clearly forbade enlistment in foreign service whether the ruler concerned was at peace or war. *Prima facie*, the wording of the Act was such that it would apply to any government *de facto* or *de jure* and to any band of rebels describing itself as a government provided it controlled some territory, and it would appear that recognition by England was irrelevant.

Problems affecting the Act arose during the American Civil War, particularly with regard to the fitting out of ships for the Confederacy, culminating in the *Alabama Arbitration*.[58] To some extent the award could not have been completely unexpected, for in a Report by the Law Officers[59] it states that

> in the event of war breaking out, an act prohibited by the Foreign Enlistment Act would be illegal, and would be punishable by the law of this country, even though it might be done in fulfilment of some contract entered into before the breaking out of war: and it might probably be the duty of Her Majesty's Government, either of its own accord or on the requisition of either belligerent, to exercise the powers given to them by that statute, in order to prevent and to punish any such act. And we must add, that we think it hardly probable that a contract with a foreign Government, for building in this country an armour-plated ship could be completed, after the breaking out of war between that Government and another foreign State, without some acts amounting to an "equipping, furnishing, fitting-out, or arming," within the meaning of the 7th section of the Foreign Enlistment Act, and therefore punishable by the laws of this country.

---

[56]McNair, 2 *International Law Opinions*, 328 et seq. (1956).
[57]*(1819)*, 59 Geo. III c. 69.
[58]See note 39 *supra*, and 3 McNair, *op. cit.*, 171 et seq.
[59]11 August 1862, *ibid.*, 225.

It was partly as a result of the experience of the American Civil War that a new Foreign Enlistment Act was passed in 1870[60] and it is still the law of Great Britain on this matter. It should be pointed out, however, that

the Foreign Enlistment Act is no measure of the international obligations of Great Britain. It goes far beyond them, and its extreme stringency is presumably designed to arm Her Majesty's Government with power to interpose in possible contingencies which it would be difficult to anticipate. . . .[61]

By virtue of the new Act, it is a misdemeanor punishable at the discretion of the court by fine and/or imprisonment, to a maximum of two years, for

any person [who], without the license of Her Majesty, being a British subject, within or without Her Majesty's dominions, accepts or agrees to accept any commission or engagement in the military or naval service of any foreign state at war with any foreign state at peace with Her Majesty, and in this Act referred to as a friendly state, or whether a British subject or not within Her Majesty's dominions, induces any other person to accept or agree to accept any commission or engagement in the military or naval service of any such foreign state as aforesaid. . . .

The Act then contains a number of detailed provisions with regard to the use of ships for this purpose, including the obligation to remove immediately any illegally enlisted persons who shall not be allowed to return to the ship. If a ship is built to the order of a belligerent State at war with a friendly State or is delivered to the order of such State or its agent and is employed in the military or naval service of such State, it shall, until the contrary is proved, be deemed to have been built for that purpose and the burden of proof is upon the builder. Perhaps more important at the present time is the provision that forbids in British territory the preparation or fitting out of "any naval or military expedition against the dominions of any friendly State . . . [and] every person engaged in such preparation or fitting out, or assisting therein, or employed in any capacity in such expedition" equally commits an offence. This wording is probably wide enough to cover any British subject volunteering in any capacity as a member of a force engaged in hostilities against a foreign friendly State, while any ship, arms or munitions used in or forming part of such an expedition is forfeit to the Crown. Reflecting the embarrassment of the British government over the *Alabama*, if the Secretary of State is satisfied that a ship is being built, commissioned or equipped contrary to the Act, and is to be taken out of the jurisdiction he may order the ship to be seized, detained and searched, and if the suspicions are justified then it may be detained until its release is ordered. The Act does not apply to any commissioned ship of any foreign State, which is in accord with the view expressed by the Law Officers in 1866[62] that

the Peruvian warship *Independencia*, supposing that she had violated the Foreign Enlistment Act of 1819 in recruiting British subjects within British jurisdiction and taking on board arms and ammunition within British jurisdiction, with a view to warlike operations against Spain, would, if she returned within British jurisdiction under a regular commission from the Peruvian Government, be entitled to the immunity of a foreign public armed ship.

---

[60]33 & 34 Vict. c. 90.
[61]*Law Officers' Report*, 12 February 1895, 3 McNair, *op. cit.,* 170.
[62]I *ibid.,* 103.

It might be possible to argue, however, that if such a ship had in fact recruited British nationals while lying in British waters she had abused her status by exercising a sovereign act in Britain without the consent of the Crown, and had therefore subjected herself to the same sort of treatment as had been threatened against the Chinese Embassy in 1896 when Sun Yat Sen was wrongly detained.[63] It is also possible that such a ship would not be granted permission to return to British waters, at least for some time.

The most important Section of the Act is Section 30, the interpretation Section:

> "foreign State" includes any foreign prince, colony, province, or part of any province or people, or any person or persons exercising or assuming to exercise the powers of government in or over any foreign country, colony, province, or part of any province or people.

In the view of the Law Officers, this definition would include rebels as a foreign State at peace with Her Majesty, so as to make it an offence for a British ship to be employed in the military or naval service of the Peruvian Government for the purpose of suppressing a rebellion. In the instant case, the Commander of the British Pacific Station had cautioned the ship which he had found in Peruvian waters, so that the master and crew "were engaged in the commission of a breach of neutrality, [and] Admiral de Horsey would, on the high seas, have been justified in stopping the vessel and preventing her proceeding on her voyage whilst the Peruvian troops remained on board."[64] It would also seem to be the case that rebels would be regarded as a foreign friendly state even though there had been no recognition of insurgency or belligerency, and the Law Officers have doubted whether a British ship, "fitted out as a privateer and to be used in the service of an unrecognized nationality, could be dealt with as a piratical vessel."[65] The Law Officers have also pointed out[66] that for the purposes of the Foreign Enlistment Act, a protectorate, in this case Madagascar then engaged in hostilities against France as the protecting State, is a friendly foreign State, so that "when a state of hostilities exists between two such States, and they are recognized by Her Majesty's Government as belligerents, the Foreign Enlistment Act would apply to either." They considered, however, that since British interests had not yet been affected by the instant hostilities there was no obligation upon Britain to apply the Act. They did not say that recognition of belligerency was a prerequisite, but they did interpret the 1877 Report concerning the Peruvian rebellion:[67]

> It would seem that the term "rebels" was probably meant only to cover such "rebels" as by establishing a more or less stable Government, and, by obtaining general recognition as belligerents, might fairly be said to have constituted themselves into a separate "State" within the meaning of that expression as generally employed.

The other definition which is of importance in Section 30 is that of "military service," for this includes "any employment whatever, in or in connection with any military operation." This definition is not wide enough to include service in an air force, for the Act only refers to military and naval forces and expeditions and as a penal statute falls to be construed with strict regard to the statutory language used. It is not permissible

---

[63]Satow, *Guide to Diplomatic Practice*, 218 (Bland ed., 1957; Gore-Booth ed., 1979, 110); see also, *ibid.*, for incident affecting Soviet Embassy in Paris in 1929.
[64]Report, 7 December 1877, cited in Lauterpacht, *Recognition in International Law*, 266 (1947).
[65]Report, 10 October 1876, 2 McNair, *op. cit.*, 368.
[66]Report, 27 February 1895, I *ibid.*, 58.
[67]See note 64 *supra*.

for courts of law to extend the definitions of statutory offences by analogy in order to deal with new situations which they regard as equally reprehensible.[68]

While the Reports of the Law Officers of the Crown are important and may affect government policy in a particular case, their significance must not be exaggerated. True, a Report may serve as a precedent or guideline or give an indication of what the government considers the law to be, and may well be followed in the future. It is not, however, an authoritative and binding interpretation of the law, while its contents are, generally speaking, not even known to the general public. For such a statement reference must be made to the courts and the judgments in both the United Kingdom and the United States are somewhat sparse, at least in so far as individual volunteers or the preparation and equipping of a military expedition are concerned. What decisions there have been have for the most part related to ships.[69] The unwillingness to prosecute is brought home quite clearly by the experience of the Spanish Civil War. While British volunteers served on both sides, and while Britain pursued a policy of non-intervention and the Foreign Office issued a public warning that the Act applied,[70] no volunteer was ever prosecuted. The English case which does deal with an armed expedition is *R. v. Jameson*[71] arising out of the Jameson Raid against the South African Republic, although the judgment was concerned with technical details affecting the validity of the indictment rather than the substance of the charge. Jameson was subsequently sentenced to fifteen months in jail, although he only served six.

It is, of course, not only the United Kingdom and the United States which have legislation directed against foreign enlistment. In so far as Commonwealth countries are concerned, the British Act was extended to most of them and still prevails. Some, however, have enacted their own legislation. Thus Ghana[72] has made it a felony punishable with life imprisonment "to accept or induce any engagement in the military service of any other country." The Canadian Act[73] is very similar to its English forebear, the definition of "foreign State" in whose service enlistment may be forbidden being identical. Unlike the Act of 1870 the Canadian Act makes no reference to a State at peace with Canada, but uses instead "a friendly foreign State" which is clearly a synonym, and the Act provides that it is an offence for any Canadian, wherever he may happen to be, to accept an engagement in the armed forces of "any foreign State at war with any friendly foreign State," while any person in Canada, regardless of nationality, who induces another to leave with such intent equally commits an offence. The Act likewise forbids any Canadian from leaving Canada for this purpose and also forbids any person within Canada from fitting out any army, naval or air expedition to proceed against the dominions of any friendly State. The Act thus reflects the development since 1870 of war in the third dimension. As regards recruiting, this is forbidden within Canada in so far as it relates to the "armed forces of any foreign State or other armed forces operating in such a State." It is clear, therefore, that there can be no doubt as to the application of the Act as regards rebels, whether recognized or not, and whether a state of belligerency is recognized. Moreover, since the Act relates to operations by "other armed forces operating in a State," it would appear that it would operate in an area where the governing power, for example, a foreign ruler, had withdrawn and fighting was being conducted

---

[68](Diplock) Report of the Committee of Privy Councillors appointed to inquire into the Recruitment of Mercenaries, *Cmnd.* 6569, para. 25 (1976).
[69]For a list of cases, see Burchett and Roebuck, *op. cit.*, at 184, n. 10.
[70]10 January 1937, that is before any recognition of the Nationalists, see Lauterpacht, *op. cit.*, 273.
[71][1896] 2 *Q.B.* 425.
[72]Foreign Enlistment Act, 1961.
[73]*R.S.C.* 1970, c.F.-29.

between a variety of forces each describing itself as a national liberation movement. This interpretation finds support in the provision that the Governor General in Council may by order or regulation provide for the application of the Act "to any case in which there is a state of armed conflict, civil or otherwise, either within a foreign country or between foreign countries." It should be noticed that the Act again recognizes modernity, in that it uses the generic term "armed conflict" rather than the technical term "war." The Governor General is also authorized to provide for the requirement of consent before any prosecution is launched, and may, in addition to the normal punishment of fine and/or two years imprisonment, provide for the restriction, cancellation or impounding of passports, whether within Canada or elsewhere, should he consider that necessary. Such a provision, of course, is rather more formal than real. Strictly there is nothing to stop a Canadian from leaving Canada without a passport, and it depends on foreign not Canadian law whether any country will admit him if he has no passport. It is hardly likely that the authorities in whose service he is seeking to enlist himself will be unduly worried whether he does or does not carry a passport.

The Penal Codes of Belgium, France and Sweden, for example, all forbid recruiting for foreign service, while Sweden and Belgium both enacted special legislation during the Spanish Civil War. Perhaps not surprisingly in view of her special relationship to the area Belgium passed no such legislation during the Congo Civil War[74] when a number of Belgian nationals, both *colons*[75] and others, played a significant role, sometimes as specially enlisted mercenaries.[76] However, all these national enactments are of local significance only and do not as such have any importance in international law unless there is some rule of the latter which would be infringed if the states in question failed to enforce their criminal law in this regard.

In assessing whether international law has any bearing in this regard it is necessary to avoid political assessments or subjective analysis. International law applies universally and not on an eclectic basis. Moreover, in examining the activities of mercenaries nothing is to be gained by the use of such language as would imply that those on the "wrong" side were fighting for loot and reward, while those who were on the "right" side were motivated by some higher ideal. Thus, we read in one violent attack on mercenaries that as *Whores of War* they were "hijacking a country,"[77] with "economic power abused to hire human bodies with the specific intentions of avoiding public association with them and responsibility for their welfare, and using money to exploit moral weakness."[78] What does one say of the validity of a work which attempts to discriminate between the whites who were fighting for the various nationalist movements in Angola in 1976?

> There were plenty of white Angolans fighting with the MPLA, which led the mercenaries to assume that they were often confronted by Cubans when they were not. . . . [These] fought for what they believed in: true independence, an end to colonialist oppression and exploitation. . . . If [the blacks with the FNLA] . . . went back to their villages or rallied to the MPLA, it was because their sympathies were with those who really fought to end oppression and exploitation.[79]

[74]Burchett and Roebuck, *op. cit.*, 220-226.
[75]Mockler (*op. cit.*) condemns as mercenary, Schramme who, in 1964 and 1966, "was pacifying the area where he owned plantations" (at 177) and who regarded himself as "a planter and administrator, in uniform only through force of circumstances" (at 206).
[76]*Ibid.*, ch. 8.
[77]Burchett and Roebuck, *op. cit.*, 37.
[78]*Ibid.*, 6.
[79]*Ibid.*, 117.

It is equally difficult to accept as objective comment anything written by those who can say of two mercenaries charged at the Luanda trial,[80] one of whom on whose own testimony had probably killed FAPLA personnel, while the other had not, that the former "succeeded in convincing the Tribunal that he sincerely regretted what he had done and recognized the enormity of the use of mercenaries," and was sentenced to thirty years, while the latter's demeanour, if not his actual words, betrayed regret that his effort had not succeeded. He never displayed any regret for his own activities and was executed. The former was "a money-motivated mercenary," the other "a political mercenary,"[81] but he believed in the wrong politics.

What does international law say of those who enlist in foreign service? Does it regard such persons as committing any illegality and does their country of origin carry any liability? As we have seen, the "fathers of international law" were somewhat divided in their views. So, also, were some countries affected by mercenary activities. Thus, in 1818 before the passage of the first British Foreign Enlistment Act the Law Officers were called upon to advise on the status of British nationals serving the Spanish American colonial insurgents. Spain intimated that it intended treating any such aliens they might capture as insurgents. According to the Report[82]

> [t]he Spanish Government has undoubtedly the Right of War against such Persons, and the letter of the Spanish Minister describes "the Foreigners as *waging War against His Majesty*," but the ordinary laws of War would not justify severity in the nature of punishment, which appears to be the measure in the contemplation of the Spanish Government. It is certain also, that Foreigners may be guilty of Treason, against the Sovereign of a State in which they have only an occasional residence. But cases of that kind have usually been very distinguishable in principle from the present case, which is merely that of Individuals joining the Forces of Persons exercising the powers of Government, in Provinces, that have been in a state of Revolt, asserting their Independence for some years. . . .

A somewhat similar problem arose, after the enactment of the modern Act, when it was learned in 1895 that the French military authorities engaged in fighting a civil war in Madagascar considered themselves "justified in treating as 'condottieri' the British subjects who have taken service with the Hovas, and, if captured, in at once shooting them," while apparently not intending to treat captured Hovas in the same way. In their Report,[83] the Law Officers stated that

> the French authorities are *not* entitled to discriminate between British subjects serving in the armed forces of the Malgasy Government and Hovas in the like service to the prejudice of the former.
> The French authorities are *not* entitled to shoot British subjects serving in the Hova forces whom they may take prisoners in open fight during the pendency of the present hostilities in Madagascar. We assume that the British subjects are regularly incorporated in the regular forces of the Hovas. It is open to, and . . . desirable, for Her Majesty's Government to communicate with the French Government upon the subject . . . with a view to preventing what . . . would be a violation of international law.
> If the fighting now in progress between the French and the Hovas were merely a civil brawl, or a local popular tumult, the French might legitimately treat persons

[80]See below, text to no. 116, 131.
[81]Burchett and Roebuck, *op. cit.*, 46, 74-75.
[82]21 July 1818, 2 McNair, *op. cit.*, 335.
[83]16 April 1895, *ibid.*, 370.

who take part in it as rioters and murderers. Or, if British subjects took part in
hostilities against the French without being incorporated in any regular forces, they
might be treated as private individuals unwarrantably engaged in lawless warfare. . . .
But a state of war does exist between France and Madagascar. Her Majesty's Government, as a neutral Power, have not thought fit to recognize belligerency. . . .
But the duties imposed upon belligerents by international law are in no sense
dependent upon, and have no relation to the action of, neutral Powers which is
dictated by their policy and interests. If a state of war exists as distinguishable from
a civil brawl, the authorized soldiers of one belligerent when captured by the other
belligerent must be treated as prisoners of war to whatever nationality they belong,
subject always to the risk of such reprisals as are recognized by international law,
in case the Government they serve has violated the law.

While the activities and attitudes of neutral powers are "dictated by their policy and
interests," by the end of the nineteenth century the European powers were involved in
codifying the international law regarding neutrality. As to the practice almost immediately
prior to this, perhaps one might refer to the Swiss decision in 1870 at the time of the
Franco-German War to allow French and German nationals to traverse Switzerland in
order to join their units so long as they were in civilian clothing and unarmed. She would
not, however, permit France to open an office for the purpose of sending Alsacian
volunteers through Switzerland to the south of France.[84] By the end of the century

the majority of writers maintain[ed] that the duty of impartiality must prevent a
neutral from allowing the levy of troops. . . . If the levy and passage of troops
must be prevented by a neutral, he is all the more required to prevent the organization of a hostile expedition from his territory against either belligerent. Such
organization takes place when a band of men combine under a commander for the
purpose of starting from the neutral territory and joining the belligerent forces.
Different, however, is the case in which a number of individuals, not organized
into a body under a commander, start in company from a neutral State for the
purpose of enlisting with one of the belligerents. Thus in 1870, during the Franco-
German War, 1200 Frenchmen started from New York in two French steamers [the
Lafayette and the *Ville de Paris*] for the purpose of joining the French Army. Although
the vessels carried also 96,000 rifles and 11,000,000 cartridges, the United States
did not interfere, since the men were not organized in a body, and since, on the
other hand, the arms and ammunition were carried in the way of ordinary com-
merce.[85]

That Oppenheim's view was, broadly speaking, an expression of the by then generally
accepted view of international law is shown by the terms of the 1907 Hague Convention
No. V respecting the Rights and Duties of Neutral Powers and Persons in War on Land:[86]

Corps of combatants cannot be formed nor recruiting agencies opened on the
territory of a neutral Power to assist the belligerents. A neutral Power must not
allow any [such] acts to occur on its territory. . . . The responsibility of a neutral
Power is not engaged by the fact of persons crossing the frontier separately to offer
their services to one of the belligerents.

[84]Oppenheim, 2 *International Law*, 703-704 (7th ed., by Lauterpacht, 1952, reproducing 1st ed. 352-
353 (1906).
[85]*Ibid.*, 1st ed., 353; *see however, Wiborg v. U.S.* (1896), 163 *U.S.* 632, in which it was held that "the
elements or the expedition . . . were combined or in process of combination; there was a concert
of action" (654).
[86]See Schindler/Toman, 847, Arts. 4-6.

There is no clarification in the Convention as to the meaning of the word "separately" or how many individuals may be allowed to cross at any one time. Presumably so long as they do not constitute an organized corps of combatants no liability on the part of the neutral State concerned could arise. As to any individual who does cross and enlist, Article 17 confirms the views of the British Law Officers that while

> a neutral cannot avail himself of his neutrality . . . if he voluntarily enlists in the armed force of the parties [,] in such a case, the neutral shall not be more severely treated by the belligerent as against whom he has abandoned his neutrality than a national of the other belligerent State could be for the same act.

Thus, such a "neutral" national enjoys all the rights of a normal combatant, including those of a prisoner of war. In so far as the fitting out of ships to assist belligerents is concerned, the 1907 Hague Convention XIII concerning the Right and Duties of Neutral Powers in Naval War[87] reflects the limitations and restrictions of the foreign enlistment enactments of the United States and the United Kingdom, but it makes no reference to criminal liability. The neutral State is required "to employ the means at its disposal to prevent the fitting out . . . [and] to display the same vigilance to prevent" departure. Apparently, since failure to take such steps would constitute a breach of neutrality, a belligerent whose rights had been adversely affected would be entitled to regard such failure as a *casus belli*.

As has already been pointed out, no action was taken against those who volunteered during the Spanish Civil War, regardless of whether they joined the International Brigade supporting the government or served with the rebels. This was probably due to the fact that the Republic and the Nationalist authorities represented a political cleavage that crossed frontiers and found some support in most of the countries from which the foreign fighters—be they called volunteers, mercenaries or conscripts—originated. Again, as has been seen, in the case of the Eagle Squadron between 1939 and 1941, or the volunteers serving with Israel in the Middle East, no authority, private individual or organ of the media seemed unduly worried by such activists or their doings.

It was only when white settlers struggling against the activities of local rebels, described as National Liberation Movements, became involved, by assisting one of the local rebel movements, usually the least radical, that the problem took on a new aspect. The term "mercenary" suddenly acquired an obscene flavour, and the profession of arms as conducted by professionals prepared to serve an alien master came to be regarded with such obloquium that it seemed almost to have sunk to the level of the supreme crime against mankind. The first intimation of this change in attitude came during the struggle for independence in the Belgian Congo, the United Nations having decided in 1960 to take steps to provide the Republic with such military assistance as it might require and calling upon third States to do nothing to impede the government's efforts to restore order, while urging Belgium to withdraw its forces as speedily as possible. While the United Nations Force was operating, an attempt was made by the Province of Katanga to secede, which automatically raised the possibility of U.N. military involvement in an internal armed conflict. The Katangese secessionists were assisted by foreign mercenaries, some of whom were in fact Belgian local landowners,[88] but a number of African States strongly objected to their presence, contending that they were interfering with the activities of

---

[87]*Ibid.*, 855, Art. 8.
[88]See note 75, *supra*.

the U.N. force, were unlawfully interfering in the internal affairs of an African country, were using the activities of the Kantangese as a cover for a possible return of European imperialism, and, probably more importantly, because many of them feared possible secessionist activities by tribal minorities within their own countries. In its resolution of 21 February 1961,[89] the Security Council, with France and the Soviet Union abstaining, reiterated its concern at the situation in the Congo, and urged

> that measures be taken for the immediate withdrawal and evacuation from the Congo of all Belgian and other paramilitary personnel and political advisers not under the United Nations command, and mercenaries.

By November, not much having been done to this end, and with the General Assembly having resolved[90] that the "central factor" was the continued presence of Belgian and other foreign military and paramilitary personnel, political advisers and mercenaries, the Security Council, with France and the United Kingdom abstaining, resolved[91] "to secure the immediate withdrawal and evacuation from the Congo of all foreign military, paramilitary and advisory personnel not under the United Nations Command, and all mercenaries," deprecated "the secessionist activities illegally carried out by the provincial administration of Katanga, with the aid of external resources and manned by foreign mercenaries," and authorized the Secretary-General "to take vigorous action, including the use of requisite measures of force, if necessary, for the immediate apprehension, detention pending legal action and/or deportation of all foreign military and paramilitary personnel and political advisers not under the United Nations command, and mercenaries . . . [and] prevent the entry or return of such elements under whatever guise. . . ." It is essential to note that in these Resolutions the Security Council was not concerned with the status of mercenaries and in fact was treating them in exactly the same way as any other foreign military personnel in the Congo other than as part of the U.N. command. The main thrust of the Resolutions was the prevention of Katangese secession and the termination of the civil war, with the concomitant consolidation of the power and authority of the Republic. The Council's condemnation of the mercenaries, as of other foreign military personnel, was solely on the basis that they formed one of the resources being employed to secure Katanga's secession and thus to thwart the Resolutions of the Council and the purpose for which its Force had been sent to the Congo. Any attempts to use these Resolutions as a ground for condemning mercenaries or their employment *per se* is fraudulent misrepresentation of the activities and objectives of the Security Council. It was not until the beginning of 1963, after military confrontation between the mercenaries and the United Nations forces,[92] that the U.N. was able to declare that the Katanga revolt was over. In 1964, however, a further revolt took place against the authority of the Republican Government and the mercenaries were back again, which culminated in 1966 in a further attempt by the Katangese to secede, although on this occasion it appeared that the mercenaries were prepared to serve on either side,[93] and in 1967 there was a revolt by the mercenaries themselves which appeared likely to overthrow President Mobutu. The Security Council's Resolution was again noncommittal in so far as the mercenaries as such were concerned.[94] Having condemned

---

[89]Doc. S/4741.
[90]Res. 1599 (XV), adopted by 61-5-33.
[91]S/5002.
[92]Mockler, *op. cit.*, 168-170.
[93]*Ibid.*, 171-193.
[94]Res. 239 (1967).

any State which persists in permitting or tolerating the recruitment of mercenaries and the provision of facilities for them, with the objective of overthrowing the Governments of States Members of the United Nations, [called] upon Governments to ensure that their territory and other territories under their control, as well as their nationals, are not used for the planning of subversion, and the recruitment, training and transit of mercenaries designed to overthrow the Government of the Democratic Republic of the Congo [,]

the Council decided to remain seized of the question and requested the Secretary-General to "follow closely the implementation of this Resolution," which was hardly one that could be implemented in any way that the U.N. could inspire or control. What the Security Council meant by implementation became a little clearer by the end of the year. It had been known for some time that the mercenaries were using the Portuguese colony of Angola as their marshalling area and the base from which attacks against the Congo were being launched. In November 1967, without a vote, the Security Council con-demned[95] the failure of Portugal to prevent the mercenaries from using Angola in this way, and called

upon all countries receiving mercenaries who have participated in the armed attacks against the Democratic Republic of the Congo to take appropriate measures to prevent them from renewing their activities against any State.

It is clear that the Security Council was not prepared to state that mercenarism was a crime or that mercenaries were not entitled to treatment as prisoners of war or the protection of the international law of armed conflict. All it was willing to do was call upon member States to take the measures they might consider necessary to prevent mercenaries from taking action against any State. In other words, the most that can be said of the action of the Security Council at this time is that it called upon members to enforce their foreign enlistment legislation.

The General Assembly too had passed resolutions concerning the Congo, but these are of less significance than those of the Security Council. There is no need at this juncture to consider how far such resolutions, even if constantly reiterated, are binding in law. What is more important is that, with the presence of the United Nations force in the Congo, and the constant consideration of the problem by the Security Council, the role of the Assembly was somewhat reduced. Moreover, attempts to condemn the mercenaries as such failed to secure the requisite two-thirds majority in the Assembly. Further, to some extent the African members of the U.N. were able to express their views through the Organization of African Unity where they were free of western pressures and could give vent to their ideological concerns for national liberation. It soon became clear that from the point of view of this Organization, whatever be the actual issue that led the members to pass a condemnatory resolution, they were really only concerned with those mercenaries who were engaged in hostilities against forces that the Organization regarded as struggling for their self-determination and national liberation. From 1964 until 1971 the Organization passed a series of resolutions condemning the recruitment and use of mercenaries, and by 1971 had resolved that it was time to draft a convention condemning mercenarism as a crime, especially when directed against African liberation movements.[96] While these resolutions and proposals may have had some moral effect upon the members

[95]Res. 241 (1967).
[96]Burchett and Roebuck, *op. cit.*, 233.

of the Organization, they were of course completely irrelevant as regards any State not such a member, even though that State might itself promote the recruitment of mercenaries for service in Africa.

Both the Organization of African Unity and the United Nations became concerned with the problem again during the civil war in Angola. As early as 1966 problems had arisen between Portugal and Congo, with the latter accusing Portugal of allowing mercenaries to operate from its colonial territories against the Congo. Portugal stated that there were no mercenaries in Angola and no camps for operations against the Congo. The Security Council, having called upon all States not to interfere in the domestic affairs of the Congo simply urged Portugal "not to allow foreign mercenaries" to use Angola as a base.[97] A further Resolution pretty well to the same effect was passed in 1967[98] when the Council called upon

> all countries receiving mercenaries who have participated in the armed attacks against the Democratic Republic of the Congo to take appropriate measures to prevent them from renewing their activities against any State.

More substantively, it condemned Portugal for having failed in violation of earlier resolutions,

> to prevent the mercenaries from using the territory of Angola under its administration as a base for operations

against the Congo. Within a year the scene of activity had shifted. The military operations were now being carried on in Portugal's colonial territories and the scene of international concern was the General Assembly. Thus, in 1968, having condemned the Portuguese failure to grant independence to "territories under Portuguese domination," and "the collaboration between Portugal, the minority racist regime of South Africa and the illegal racist minority regime in Southern Rhodesia, which is designed to perpetuate colonialism and oppression in Southern Africa," the General Assembly[99] called upon all States as a matter of urgency

> to take all measures to prevent the recruitment or training in their territories of any persons as mercenaries for the colonial war being waged in the Territories under Portuguese domination and for violations of the territorial integrity and sovereignty of the independent African States.

The Resolution, continuing with its anti-colonial bias, deplored the Portuguese policy of settling "foreign immigrants" in the colonial territories. In addition, there was one new feature in the Resolution. Traditionally, colonial powers having been allowed to treat their dependent territories as "private property" and what they have done therein has been regarded as falling within the reserved domain of domestic jurisdiction. This has, of course, been affected on the political level by the series of General Assembly resolutions, and in some cases conventions, on human rights and independence for non-self-governing territories, but these did not introduce any rules of international law regulating the conduct of internal conflicts. The Geneva Conventions of 1949 relating to humanitarian

[97]Res. 226 (1966).
[98]Res. 241 (1967).
[99]Res. 2395 (XXIII).

principles in armed conflict made only the slightest inroads into this position by including in each of the four, what is known as common Article 3. This is to apply in the case of armed conflict not of an international character occurring in the territory of one of the High Contracting Parties, and which is binding on all parties to the conflict. By its Resolution, the General Assembly called upon Portugal to observe the provisions of the 1949 Prisoners of War Convention.[100] It should be pointed out that this merely imposes observance of the minimal conditions of humanity and requires reciprocal application. There is, however, nothing to indicate that the rebels applied its provisions to their prisoners. Moreover, the Assembly completely ignored the fact that when Portugal ratified the Conventions she made a reservation concerning Article 3,[101] to which no opposition appears to have been expressed:

> As there is no actual definition of what is meant by a conflict not of an international character, and as, in case this term is intended to refer solely to civil war, it is not clearly laid down at what moment an armed rebellion within a country should be considered as having become a civil war, Portugal reserves the right to not to apply the provisions of Article 3, in so far as they may be contrary to the provisions of Portuguese law, in all territories subject to her sovereignty in any part of the world.

Again it should be noted that the Resolution is not general in character and does not condemn mercenarism as such nor the use of mercenaries. It is only concerned with their use by Portugal in its African territories and against African States. The same is true of the 1973 Resolution concerning Guinea.[102]

> The use of mercenaries by colonial and racist regimes against the national liberation movements struggling for their freedom and independence from the yoke of colonialism and alien domination is considered to be a criminal act and the mercenaries should accordingly be punished as criminals.

It must not be thought that the General Assembly always looked at the problem of mercenaries in the context of a particular struggle. In 1965, when considering the need for a condemnation of intervention in the affairs of third States, the Assembly[103] may be considered to have dealt with the problem in a somewhat indirect fashion, when it stated that

> no State shall organize, assist, foment, finance, incite or tolerate subversive, terrorist or armed activities directed towards the overthrow of the regime of another State, or interfere in civil strife in another State.

The ideological background for this is to be seen in the Preamble which reaffirms

> the principle of non-intervention proclaimed in the charters of the Organization of American States, the League of Arab states and the Organization of African Unity and reaffirmed at the conferences held at Montevideo, Buenos Aires, Chalpultepec and Bogota, as well as in the decision of the Asian-African Conference at Bandung, the First Conference of Heads of State or Government of the Non Aligned Countries at Belgrade, in the Programme for Peace and International Co-operation adopted

---

[100]Schindler/Toman, 355—for Art. 3, *see* 362 (This Article is common to all 4 1949 Conventions).
[101]*Ibid.*, 512.
[102]Res. 3103 (XXVIII).
[103]Res. 2131 (XX).

at the end of the Second Conference of Heads of State or Government of Non-Aligned Countries at Cairo, and in the declaration on subversion adopted at Accra by the Heads of State and Government of the African States.

That this Resolution was not regarded with excessive seriousness by some members of the U.N., even though it had been adopted by 109 to 1, with only the United Kingdom abstaining, became clear when it was reaffirmed a year later by 114 to 9, with 2 abstentions.[104] Then, in 1969, by 78 to 5 with 16 abstentions, the Assembly reaffirmed[105] its Declaration on Independence for Colonial Countries and Peoples,[106] which by its very title indicates that its provisions are not of general application, but solely concerned with colonial independence. Within this context the Assembly found it possible to state in general terms, that is to say not in relation to any particular conflict, that

> the practice of using mercenaries against movements for national liberation and independence is punishable as a criminal act and that the mercenaries themselves are outlaws, and calls upon the Governments of all countries to enact legislation declaring the recruitment, financing and training of mercenaries in their territory to be a punishable offence and prohibiting their nationals from serving as mercenaries.

While the Resolution condemns mercenaries as outlaws, this is only true if they are opposing national liberation and independence. In addition, the Assembly, aware that its resolutions are only *voeux* did no more than call upon States to make recruitment and enlistment of mercenaries for such campaigns criminal offences. It did not even go to the extent of calling upon the International Law Commission to codify the law on mercenaries, nor on the members of the U.N. to enter into negotiations for a treaty to this end. Without the will to act, a mere affirmation is as empty as the original resolution, and in 1970 to mark the tenth anniversary of the adoption of the aforesaid Declaration, the Assembly,[107] after deploring the fact that the colonial powers, particularly Portugal, South Africa and Southern Rhodesia were still "colonial" or racist rulers, and noting with grave concern that many territories were still under "colonial domination and racist regimes," reiterated its declaration that

> the practice of using mercenaries against national liberation movements in the colonial Territories constitutes a criminal act and calls upon all States to take the necessary measures to prevent the recruitment, financing and training of mercenaries in their territory and to prohibit their nationals from serving as mercenaries.

Could anything be clearer that the General Assembly is not concerned with mercenarism or mercenaries as such, but only when they are employed against national liberation movements in colonial territories? On this basis, presumably, the General Assembly is not concerned with mercenaries who may be serving on behalf of a national liberation movement—seemingly it agrees with the view that such persons have the right ideological approach[108]—nor if they are serving on one or both sides in a traditional type of armed conflict. Here it should be remembered, however, that the General Assembly definition of colonialism, imperialism, foreign rule, racism, and the like, is highly subjective, so

[104]Res. 2225 (XXI).
[105]Res. 1514 (XV).
[106]Res. 2548 (XXIV).
[107]Res. 2707 (XXV).
[108]See note 79 *supra*.

that since 1975 when it was decided[109] by the barest majority (72 to 35, and 32 abstaining) that Zionism is racist it would seem that Jewish and other non-Israelis going to fight for Israel would be "criminal" mercenaries, while non-Palestinians fighting in the Palestinian cause would be looked upon as fighters in the twentieth century version of a just war.

The somewhat jaundiced attitude of the U.N. towards issues when it might be possible to argue that national liberation is in question is to be seen also in the definition of aggression.[110] Among the acts in article 3 described as constituting aggression is

the sending by or on behalf of a State of armed bands, groups, irregular or mercenaries, which carry out acts of armed force against another State. . . .

However,

[n]othing in this definition, and in particular Article 3, could in any way prejudice the right to self-determination, freedom and independence . . . of peoples forcibly deprived of that right . . . , particularly peoples under colonial and racist regimes or other forms of alien domination; nor the right of these peoples to struggle to that end and to seek and receive support. . . .

It is clear, therefore, that a people allegedly engaged in or supporting a struggle for national liberation would be able to argue that, far from acting as an aggressor by employing mercenaries, it was in fact acting in a perfectly lawful fashion, while the mercenaries and the countries from which they were coming were carrying out obligations imposed upon them by the U.N.

While the members of the U.N. were not prepared to carry any of these resolutions into effect so as to make mercenarism a crime, the same end was reached in some countries in so far as Rhodesia was concerned by reason of legislation consequent upon resolutions condemning the white régime in that country—Zimbabwe—whereby nationals were forbidden from having relations with that régime, but such measures do not refer to mercenaries specifically and have to be read in the context of the Zimbabwe issue.[111]

Matters took a new turn in 1976 because of the events connected with the Angolan civil war. In November, the General Assembly, reflecting the emotions occasioned by Angola, carried its prejudicial discrimination to its logical conclusion, for it now bluntly declared[112] not only

that the practice of using mercenaries against movements for national liberation and independence constitutes a crime [but also] that the mercenaries are criminals.

If one recalls the number of members of the Organization of African Unity which are in the U.N. it is only surprising that such a declaration had not been made much earlier. In 1972 the Organization had prepared a draft Convention for the Elimination of Mer-

[109]Res. 3379 (XXX).
[110]Res. 3314 (XXIX).
[111]See, e.g., statement by Prime Minister Callaghan in British House of Commons, 10 March 1976 (*The Times*, 11 March 1976); proceedings under the Southern Rhodesia Act 1956 and the 1968 Order in Council (U.N. Sanctions Order No. 2) against Roy Dovaston for advertising for "emigrants" (*ibid.*, 14, 16 April 1977); and report of Rhodesian Commission of Justice and Peace (summarized by Louis Heren, *ibid.*, 23 April 1977).
[112]Res. 31/34 (GAOR, *Supp.* 39 (A/31/39), 93).

cenaries in Africa.[113] In so far as the draft condemns the employment of aliens to overthrow the government of any member State or undermine its independence there is perhaps nothing to quarrel with. But the definition goes on to include any such person who

> is employed, enrols or links himself willingly to a person, group or organization whose aim is . . . to block by any means the activities of any liberation movement recognized by the Organization of African Unity . . . [and] the actions of [such] a mercenary . . . constitute offences considered as crimes against the peace and security of Africa and punishable as such.

The clear meaning of this is that such persons will not be regarded as legitimate combatants or, in so far as they are, would be liable to trial for crimes against peace. Such a policy is clearly discriminatory[114] and runs counter to the whole trend of international humanitarian law which regards all combatants, regardless of nationality, as entitled to equal treatment when captured. That this was also the effect of the General Assembly's 1976 Resolution becomes clear from the statement made by the U.S. representative in Committee III:[115]

> [The] paragraph . . . is contrary to the 1949 Geneva Conventions and general international law in suggesting that individual combatants can be treated as "criminals" solely on the basis of the political acceptability of the cause for which they are fighting or the fact that they may be regarded as "mercenaries" by other parties to the issue in question.

Others must have had similar views, for the Resolution, while carried by 109 to 4, had 24 abstaining.

It is time now to refer to the events in Angola.

By the time the Portuguese announced their intention to withdraw from Angola, there were three distinct liberation movements and fighting soon broke out among them for the reins of power. The MPLA (Popular Movement for the Liberation of Angola) proclaimed a government and this received recognition from the majority of the members of the Organization of African Unity, but the FNLA (National Front for the Liberation of Angola) and UNITA (National Unity for the Total Independence of Angola) continued the struggle—it is perhaps worth pointing out here that both the FNLA and MPLA had been admitted to the first two sessions of the Geneva Conference on Humanitarian Law, 1974 and 1975, as fully recognized national liberation movements. The movements opposed to the MPLA recruited a number of non-African "white" mercenaries who were promised high wages and were organized in a separate unit under their own command, and apparently with their own disciplinary code. It was reported that these mercenaries had committed a number of atrocities against Angolan citizens from both sides, and also that their commander had killed or ordered the killing of a number of his men who had refused to fight. Some of these mercenaries were captured and the Government of Angola brought ten British and three United States nationals to trial for the crime of mercenarism, crimes against peace, murder, brutality, looting and the like. The trial was held in accordance with Angolan law, namely, the 1966 Code of Discipline of the MPLA which had become Angolan law by the Constitution of November 1975. It is hard to see how the accused were subject to this law, although it is possible that in so far as murder and

---

[113]OAU, Doc. CM/433/ Rev. L, Annex 1 (reprinted in Burchett and Roebuck, *op. cit.*, 234).
[114]See note 82 *supra*.
[115][1976] *U.S. Digest* 13.

the like were involved, even the Angolan government might have been able to try them for war crimes. From our point of view what is important is the charge concerning mercenarism. According to the indictment this was based on declarations by the heads of State and government of the Organization of African Unity and General Assembly resolutions, most of which, as we have seen, referred to the employment of mercenaries in specific conflicts. None of these resolutions or declarations created law, while the introductory paragraphs of the Organization of African Unity's draft Convention itself stated that "existing laws do not really cover the specific problem of mercenarism." The judgment states:[116]

> Mercenarism was not unknown in traditional penal law, where it was always dealt with in relation to homicide. . . . Yet it is important that in modern penal law, and in the field of comparative law, the mercenary crime lost all autonomous existence and was seen as a common crime, generally speaking aggravated by the profit motive which prompts it. And this mercenary crime, which is known today as "paid crime to order," comes within the law of criminal complicity, it being through them that the responsibility of he who orders and he who is ordered is evaluated. . . . [The judgment then states that mercenarism is therefore provided for in Article 20(4) of the Penal Code.] . . . This annuls the objection of the defence that the crime of mercenarism has not been defined and that there is no penalty for it. It is in fact provided for with penalty in most evolved penal systems. As a material crime, of course!

This would seem to imply that if mercenarism is a crime it can only be so if another common crime has also been committed to which it can be associated as an inherent part. This does not seem to have been possible in the case of Gearhart, the American executed for mercenarism, and this led American spokesmen to comment on this execution in the light of the legal status of mercenarism. Thus Secretary of State Kissinger stated[117]

> there is absolutely no basis in national or international law for the action now taken by the Angolan authorities. The "law" under which Mr. Gearhart was executed was nothing more than an internal ordinance of the MPLA issued in 1966, when the MPLA was only one of many guerrilla groups operating in Angola. Furthermore, no evidence whatsoever was produced during the trial of Mr. Gearhart in Luanda that he had even fired a shot during the few days he was in Angola before his capture.

Somewhat similar arguments were put forward by Assistant Secretary of State Schaufele in testimony before the House International Relations Committee Special Subcommittee on Investigations:[118]

> The recruitment of mercenaries within the territory of the United States to serve in the armed forces of a foreign country is an offense under our Neutrality Laws.[119] . . . A legally accepted definition of what constitutes a mercenary does not exist in international law. Nor is the act of serving as a mercenary a crime in international law, not to mention Angolan law where the Angolan authorities were forced to use a set of guidelines for their combatants the MPLA issued in 1966. The general international practice appears to consider mercenaries in the same status

[116]See "Report on the Trial of Mercenaries," by Lockwood, a Canadian observer at the trial, 7 *Manitoba L.J.* 183, 198-199 (1977).
[117][1976] *U.S. Digest* 714.
[118]*Ibid.*, 714-715.
[119]See text to note 37 *et seq., supra.*

as other combatants and therefore to be treated as such under the terms of the
Geneva Convention of 1949 [on Prisoners of War]. This has certainly been American
practice back to the Revolutionary War and was reflected in our treatment of captured Hessian troops. This was also the case in the Civil War when there had been
combatants on both sides who fought for hire, adventure, or beliefs and who could
be considered by some as mercenaries. . . . The act of being a mercenary is not a
crime in international law and mercenaries were entitled to the same status and
protection as other combatants under the 1949 Geneva Conventions and the rules
of warfare. Mr. Gearhart was not charged with any other specific crime. No evidence
was presented that he had harmed anyone during the few days he was in Angola
before his capture.

Even authors who have condemned the use of mercenaries especially in Angola, treating
them as below contempt, and condemning Gearhart as a monetary mercenary, have
tended to agree that his sole crime was that of mercenarism, aggravated by a refusal to
express humility at this fact.[120]

It was not only in the U.S. that the reports of mercenary activities in Angola and the
trial in Luanda had repercussions, generally of a character condemning mercenaries and
those who acted as recruiting agents. Almost simultaneously with the opening of the
trial, a Labour Member of the British Parliament was given leave by 184 votes to 89 to
introduce the Advertisement for the Recruitment of Mercenaries (Prohibition) Bill,[121] with
the aim of ending mercenary recruitment in Britain, although it did not forbid Britons
from going as mercenaries, even though Mr. Hughes had described the trade of mercenary as "obscene." "It reduces man below the level of beasts, for animals do not kill
without purpose or reason, as a mercenary does. We owe a duty to end this despicable
trade." The House of Commons was saved the need of further consideration of this Bill
by reason of the fact that the Diplock Committee established in February delivered its
Report in August.[122] The Commission defined "mercenaries" in the "broad sense" as
"persons who serve voluntarily for pay in armed forces other than the regular forces of
their own country," and recognized that this was wide enough to include the Gurkha
Regiments in the British Army, the International Brigade, the Eagle Squadron, British
Jews in the Israeli Army, as well as the *condottiere* of Renascence Italy. The Committee
pointed out that mercenaries were motivated by a variety of reasons, not always monetary, for they might include

a conscientious conviction that the merits of [the] cause are so great as to justify
his sacrificing his own life if need be in order to ensure that it will triumph. The
soldier of conscience may be found fighting side by side with the soldier of fortune
in the same ranks and for the same rate of pay. . . . [A]ny definition of mercenary
which required positive proof of motivation would . . . either be unworkable or so
haphazard in its application as between comparable individuals as to be unacceptable. . . .

To serve as a mercenary is not an offence under international law. Under the
Geneva Conventions . . . a mercenary serving as a member of an organised armed
force of one party to a conflict which would be recognised in international law as
involving a "state of war" between the parties to it, is entitled to the same treatment
as a combatant and as a prisoner of war as any other member of that force. . . .

. . . [W]e do not think there are any means by which it would be practicable to
prevent a United Kingdom citizen from volunteering while he is abroad to serve
as a mercenary and from leaving the United Kingdom to do so, we should regard
any attempt to impose such a prohibition upon him by law as involving a depri-

[120]See text to note 81 *supra*.
[121]*The Times*, 16 June 1976.
[122]See note 68 *supra*.

vation of his freedom to do as he will which would require to be justified by a much more compelling reason of public policy than the prohibition of active recruiting of mercenaries within the United Kingdom. . . . No administrative action can stop a United Kingdom citizen from volunteering for service as a mercenary once he is abroad, but his journey from this country to a foreign destination, though it cannot be prevented, can be hindered and made more difficult for him by his not possessing a valid passport. At common law, . . . a citizen of the United Kingdom has the right to leave this country and to return to it unhindered and at his own free will. A similar right in every human being is recognised by article 13(2) of the Universal Declaration of Human Rights. . . . A passport . . . merely makes it easier for him to exercise that right . . . [and] if he establishes his identity by other means, an immigration officer has no legal power to prevent his embarkation. . . .

Since there is no legal right in a person to receive a passport and, since when granted it remains the property of the Crown, it may be refused or withdrawn. In fact, passports were withdrawn from 8 persons who had served as mercenaries in the Congo in 1961, from 3 who served there in 1967/8, 4 who served in Nigeria in 1968, and 54 who served in Angola, but in each case "the stable door was shut after the horse had gone," and there was, anyway, nothing to stop the person involved from leaving again, especially as "an applicant for a passport is not required to state why he wants it."

As has already been pointed out, the Diplock Report emphasized that as the Foreign Enlistment Act was a penal statute it had to be interpreted narrowly,[123] and

[t]he stautory language used in the Act . . . is adapted to conditions as they existed in 1870 as respects relations between sovereign states, the kinds of armed conflict that had taken place in foreign territory during the previous decades and means of transport and of waging war that were then available. The immense changes in those conditions which have taken place in the last hundred years and particularly since World War II have resulted in there being important omissions from the Act and a number of obscurities in the statutory language affecting most of the ingredients of the offences. These make the application of the Act to United Kingdom citizens who participate in a particular internal conflict in a foreign State a matter of grave legal doubt and the commission of an offence almost incapable of satisfactory proof.

The Committee pointed out that the Act referred to foreign enlistment, and therefore could have no application to enlistment in the forces of a Commonwealth country, even though that country might be at war. Equally, since by the Ireland Act[124] the Republic of Ireland is not a "foreign State," the Act would not apply in that case either. It then stated[125] that

A fortiori the Act would have no application to service in the army or air force of the régime in Southern Rhodesia, since this still remains, *de jure* a Crown colony.

One cannot refrain from enquiring why the Report fails to mention that enlistment in these forces would therefore amount to treason?[126]

One of the problems that arose in connection with Angola, as it has and will in similar cases, related to the status of the parties to the conflict, a question which concerned the

[123]*Ibid.*

[124]12, 13 & 14 Geo. 6 c. 41, s. 2.

[125]Para. 32.

[126]See, e.g., Green, "Southern Rhodesian Independence," 14 *Archiv des Völkerrechts* 155 *et seq.* (1969).

Legal Officers of the Crown on earlier occasions.[127] On this matter the Report was rather full,[128] and tended to illustrate a continuity in the official interpretation:

> The expanded definition of "foreign State" prevents its being confined to a government that is recognised by HM Government as the *de jure* government over a particular area. It is . . . broad enough to make it an offence to enlist in armed forces raised by rival governments . . . or forces . . . raised by insurgents . . . in their . . . struggles for independence. But the questions whether and, if so, when the Act becomes applicable to particular cases of internal struggles for power between rival forces within a State in the varied circumstances in which such struggles may arise today, are capable of raising so many doubts as to make this part of the Act unsuitable . . . to continue to be used as a penal statute.
> The expanded definition . . . is capable of including within its ambit armed forces raised by groups of persons who are *de facto* exercising governmental powers over a particular identifiable area even though their right to do so *de jure* is recognized neither by HMG nor by any other sovereign State. But the description of the offences requires that the persons on whose behalf the force is raised should also constitute an entity possessed of characteristics which in international law entitle it to recognition as being "at war" with another State and so enable it to exercise belligerent rights vis-à-vis neutral States.
> . . . [T]his requires not only that the persons controlling the force should be claiming to be entitled to act as an independent sovereign government but that they should also have been actually exercising effectively and with some degree of permanence exclusive governmental powers over an identifiable part of the territory to which they lay claim; and their opponents must either be a government which is recognized *de jure* by HMG or must also satisfy the same criteria as a *de facto* government.

And it is extremely doubtful whether these conditions were in fact satisfied at the time of the Angola situation. In fact, the Committee commented that

> [u]ntil the status in international law of each of the parties to the struggle in Angola was clear, the United Kingdom Government had no power in law to stop the enlistment or recruitment of mercenaries for service on behalf of any of those parties.
> [Further,] it would be necessary to prove that HMG had recognised the persons on whose behalf the armed force was raised and the persons against whom they were fighting as being *de facto* or *de jure* at the time that the accused enlisted. So in practice no offence can be committed until HMG . . . is prepared to accord that recognition formally [—a view that does not appear to tally with earlier interpretations]; and it would be a breach of the United Kingdom's own obligations under international law to grant this recognition to a *de facto* government before the criteria were satisfied.

Since, in its practice, the United Kingdom tends to base its recognition policy on political rather than legal criteria, and since there is no record of any country ever having been held liable for premature recognition, it is perhaps unfortunate that the Committee did not give any indication of the basis for this last assertion.

Many of the recent conflicts, particularly in Africa, have been fought between, or have involved the use of guerrilla forces, and in the light of its above comments the Diplock Committee considered it

doubtful whether the Act could ever apply to enlistment in guerrilla forces or in

---

[127]See notes 64-66, *supra.*
[128]Paras. 34-36.

security forces engaged in their suppression if the guerrillas were not purporting to act as the regular government of a particular part of the State's territory but were seeking to bring down the existing régime throughout the territory by force of arms.

In the light of this statement it would appear that the Foreign Enlistment Act could probably not be invoked against any mercenaries participating in the activities of SWAPO (South West African People's Organization) or the ANC or PAC (African National and Panafricanist Congress) against South Africa.

[Moreover,] since the offence consists of enlistment and not a continuing offence of service as a mercenary the applicability of the Act to a particular mercenary might depend upon the stage that had been reached in an internal struggle between rival factions at the time he enlisted. A mercenary who had enlisted before the group on whose behalf the force was raised had won and exercised control over an identifiable area of the disputed territory and had been formally recognised . . . as a *de facto* government would have committed no offence, while his comrade-in-arms who had enlisted in the same force after that event would be liable to conviction.

It is highly probable that however carefully legislation was worded, the same practical difficulties would exist and the same loopholes present themselves. This led the Committee to the conclusion[129] that it would not be

practicable or just to try to define an offence of enlisting as a mercenary in such a way that guilt would depend upon proof . . . of a particular motive as activating the accused to do so. . . . [A] penal prohibition sought to be imposed by the State upon what an individual does abroad involves a restriction on the liberty of the individual which can only be justified on compelling grounds of public interest. . . . Accordingly we would recommend *the abolition of any statutory offence by a United Kingdom citizen of enlisting as a mercenary while abroad or of leaving the United Kingdom in order to do so.* . . . [W]e see *no advantage in retaining a statutory offence of enlisting in the United Kingdom for service as a mercenary abroad.* . . . We do not think that it can be justified . . . to impose a general prohibition on United Kingdom citizens from serving . . . in the armed forces of a foreign State at a time when there are no hostilities in which that force is engaged. To make it a criminal offence . . . for him not to desert that force as soon as it became involved in external or internal conflict, to which the United Kingdom was not itself a party, would . . . be an impermissible affront to the sovereignty of the foreign State concerned

and the Committee was, therefore, opposed to the idea of making mercenarism criminal. On the other hand, it was opposed to recruitment and advertising therefor, so that

any fresh legislation creating . . . new offences in relation to recruitment . . . should take the form of an enabling Act empowering HMG . . . by Order in Council . . . requiring affirmative resolutions by both Houses of Parliament to apply the provisions of the Act to the armed forces specified in the Order. . . . The description of proscribed forces need not necessarily be by reference to the name that they bore; it could be by reference to the area in which they were operating. . . .

If such an Act were passed, the concept that service would need to be on behalf of a "foreign" State would end, for the proscribed forces could be operating equally in a

---

[129]Paras. 42-50 (italics added).

Commonwealth country or a colony. As yet, there is no indication that the British Government has accepted the recommendations in the Diplock Report. Equally, there has been no official indication of any intent to pass legislation making enlistment as a mercenary illegal or taking any steps to forbid recruitment or advertising. In Australia, on the other hand, the government has itself introduced legislation[130] forbidding recruitment and advertisement for service with the armed forces of a foreign country, as well as the preparing for or engaging in incursions into foreign countries. But it does not prohibit enlistment of mercenaries outside Australia.

While third States were considering the problems arising from the employment of their nationals in Angola, other developments on an international level were taking place.

In an effort to give credibility to their show trial, the Government of Angola invited 51 "Commissioners" from 37 countries to attend the proceedings and draft an international convention on the suppression of mercenarism, prepare a general declaration on the subject and report on the fairness of the trial. Some of the members of the Commission were appointed by governments friendly to the MPLA, some were nominated by political parties, while some were personal invitees known for their sympathy for left-wing political movements. What is important is that this so-called "International Commission of Enquiry on Mercenaries" had no official international status, cannot be regarded as a normal international body representing any countries or learned bodies, and has about as much credibility as the so-called Russell Trial of Lyndon Johnson.[131] In the normal way, one would be able to ignore it as a pure propaganda effort, despite the fact that some of its members may truly have been imposed-upon "innocents abroad." However, some politicians from the third world have given its findings almost an official status. The only thing that need be said of the relation between the Commission and the trial is that the former produced its general declaration and the draft convention before the judgment was delivered. Despite the comment that the trial was fair[132] one cannot but feel that its condemnation of mercenarism as such must have contributed to the attitude of a tribunal which did not consist solely of trained judges or lawyers. In its Declaration[133] the Commission accepted as truth the allegations made against the mercenaries at their trial, accepting the Angolan government's propaganda statement that the recruitment, despatch and equipment of the mercenaries could not have been effected without the tacit approval of the countries where they had been recruited or equipped, and Great Britain and the United States were specifically mentioned—allegations which both governments vehemently denied. It then proceeded to allege that mercenaries were being recruited all over the world, in defiance of international public opinion, and to confront liberation movements as part of an imperialistic counter-offensive against the progress of freedom and world peace. Since it was considered that Namibia and Zimbabwe were in imminent danger of mercenary activities the Commission called upon the world, its organizations, its governments and its people to adopt without delay the proposed Convention making mercenarism criminal. The draft,[134] taking as its basis the variety of resolutions and declarations concerning Africa already referred to, which were regarded

[130]Crimes (Foreign Incursions and Recruitment) Bill, 1977.
[131]*Against the Crime of Silence* (ed. by Duffett, 1968).
[132]Lockwood, *loc. cit.*, 193—Mr. Lockwood here states that he is commenting from a "purely procedural point of view;" it could hardly have been otherwise, since his Committee on "fairness" started 3 days after the trial opened and he left before it concluded.
[133]Original French text supplied by Dr. Al-Faluji, Head, Iraqi Delegation, Geneva Conference on Humanitarian Law in Armed Conflict.
[134]Original French text supplied by Dr. Al-Faluji; Eng. tr., in Burchett and Roebuck, *op. cit.*, 237–240.

as "indicative of the development of new rules on international law making mercenarism an international crime," declares that

> [t]he crime of mercenarism is committed by the individual, group or association, representatives of States and the State itself which, with the aim of opposing by armed violence a process of self-determination, practises any of the following acts:
> (a) organises, finances, supplies, equips, trains, promotes, supports or employs in any way military forces consisting of or including persons who are not nationals of the country where they are going to act, for personal gain, through the payment of a salary or any other kind of material recompense;
> (b) enlists, enrols or tries to enrol in the said forces;
> (c) allows the activities mentioned in paragraph (a) to be carried out in any territory under its jurisdiction or in any place under its control or affords facilities for transit, transport or other operation of the above mentioned forces.

This makes no reference to increased pay as an inducement to enlistment, so that an alien serving in a regular armed force only becomes a mercenary if that armed force is engaged in activities against the "process of self-determination," and no attempt is made to indicate how one decides that the operations against which such forces are sent are in fact in aid of this process. Since no State recognized the existence of Rhodesia, it was probably true to say that there was no Rhodesian nationality, so that its military forces consisted of people who did not possess the nationality of the country where they were acting, namely Zimbabwe, and since it would appear that the African countries at least recognized the "Popular Front" as engaged in the "process of self-determination" logically every member of the Rhodesian forces was guilty of the crime of mercenarism. Since a number of countries in the Third World have equated the Palestine Liberation Organization with a popular liberation movement and have secured the passing of a General Assembly resolution equating Zionism with imperialism,[135] one is compelled to assume that the same would be considered true of all members of the Israel armed forces, at least those of them fighting against the PLO, for it might have been possible to argue that Israeli forces engaged against Egyptian forces in, for example, Sinai, were engaged in a regular armed conflict, even though there was little doubt that in such circumstances Egypt and its Arab and African friends would have maintained that it was fulfilling its obligations as a member of the U.N. on behalf of self-determination.

Perhaps the most striking feature of the definition is that it includes States and declares that they, too, if their governments allow the recruitment of mercenaries, are guilty of crime—a somewhat new development in international law, and probably one that could only have been invented by a body not terribly concerned with, or competent in, the realities of international law and politics. When a State representative becomes a criminal under this definition, he is to be punished for his acts or omissions. As to the State, "any other State may invoke such responsibility: (a) in its relations with the State responsible, and (b) before competent international organizations." At present, it is somewhat doubtful whether the International Court of Justice would be willing to take on this jurisdictional responsibility, and whether there would be mutual declarations under the "Optional Clause" to grant jurisdiction. The draft makes no provision for a competent tribunal to be established, merely providing that in the event of a dispute as to interpretation or application the issue shall be settled by negotiation or a competent international tribunal or arbitrator acceptable to all parties—does this include the national liberation movement involved?

[135]See note 109 *supra*.

Assuming one is prepared to accept the view that mercenarism is a crime in itself, there could be little quarrel with the provision that the individual concerned is personally responsible for all other criminal acts he may have committed, nor perhaps with the principle that the maxim *aut punire aut dedere* is to operate. While one might agree that war crimes and other common crimes are not to be regarded as political offences,[136] this becomes more difficult to accept when mercenarism within this wide definition is equally regarded as a common crime. The position is made even more unacceptable by article 4 of the draft which postulates that "mercenaries are not lawful combatants. If captured they are not entitled to prisoner of war status." Not only does this discriminate among those engaged in armed conflict, but it means that until such time as the conflict becomes one opposed to self-determination the individual soldier is a protected combatant. After the conflict changes its character, any legitimate act of war committed by him becomes illegal and he may find himself on trial, not merely for mercenarism but for murder in respect of any member of the national liberation movement concerned that he may have killed in the course of battle.

The only thing that may be said in favour of this draft is that, since it is tied in with the concept of self-determination, it may be shortlived, for, hopefully, it will not be long before all peoples have achieved this, and this twentieth century version of a political Sermon on the Mount will have dropped from the vocabulary of international law. Unfortunately, however, the concept is subjective and every revolutionary movement and its supporters claim to be engaged in a struggle for self-determination and national liberation, as has been made clear by the Soviet reaction in June 1978 to the possible creation of a Pan-African Peace-keeping Force supported by the western powers and directed to preserving some at least of the African governments against foreign subversion and incursions.

At one time it appeared as if this draft might be peddled at the Geneva Conference on Humanitarian Law in Armed Conflict. However, general support was given to a more modified version put forward by Nigeria which omitted the objectionable ideological features of the Luanda draft. It is true that Article 47 of Protocol I relating to the Protection of Victims of International Armed Conflicts, 1977,[137] retains the undesirable discriminatory provision denying a mercenary his status as a combatant or a prisoner of war. However, the definition of a mercenary is less objectionable. The most important change from Luanda lies in the fact that the definition is now general in scope and no longer has any reference to struggles for national liberation, even though these by Article 1 have been elevated to the level of international armed conflicts.[138] What is perhaps of great significance is that there is no provision on mercenaries in Protocol II[139] concerning non-international conflicts. While this may clarify some of the issues with regard to internal conflict and guerrilla activities mentioned in the Diplock Report,[140] the matter remains confused in that the borderline between a Protocol I and a Protocol II situation is not clear, and all one dare say is that if the movement concerned is not in control of part of the national territory, but is operating from outside, Protocol I cannot apply—a fact which was seemingly not sufficiently appreciated by some of the third world countries at Geneva, and would probably have excluded many of the incidents in which mercenaries were engaged in Africa between 1960 and 1977. According to Article 47

[136]See, e.g., Green, "Political Offences, War Crimes and Extradition," 11 *I.C.L.Q.* 329 (1962).
[137]Schindler/Toman, 551.
[138]See, e.g., "The New Law of Armed Conflict," ch. I *supra*.
[139]Schindler/Toman, 619.
[140]See text to note 128 *supra*.

[a] mercenary is a person who:
(a) is specially recruited locally or abroad in order to fight in an armed conflict;
(b) does, in fact, take a direct part in the hostilities;
(c) is motivated to take part in the hostilities essentially by the desire for private gain and, in fact, is promised by or on behalf of a Party to the conflict, material compensation substantially in excess of that promised or paid to combatants of similar ranks and functions in the armed forces of that Party;
(d) is neither a national of a Party to the conflict nor a resident of territory controlled by a Party to the conflict;
(e) is not a member of the armed forces to the conflict, and
(f) has not been sent by a State which is not a Party to the conflict on official duty as a member of the armed forces.

Perhaps the most notable aspect of the Article is that it no longer describes the mercenary as a criminal, although it does lay him open to proceedings as an unprivileged person taking part in hostilities when he is not granted the status of combatant. Then there is no suggestion that the State involved in any way in his recruitment is itself criminally liable. Nor does it require the parties to the Protocol to make mercenarism a crime or forbid enlistment within their territory. In addition, the segments of the definition are cumulative, so that embodiment of the mercenaries within the armed forces of a party to the conflict would remove from those persons the slur of mercenarism, subject to the contention of course that they only enlisted for reasons of reward and were paid on a higher scale than nationals holding the same rank and performing the same task. It is probable, however, that mercenaries enlisted into technical units may well hold the same rank and be described as performing the same tasks, but since they hold abilities not possessed by the locals their pay might in fact be higher. Since the mercenary is one who takes a direct part in the hostilities and has been specially recruited for this purpose, "advisers" would not fall within the condemning rubric. However, Polisario—the national liberation movement in the Sahara—has announced its intention to treat French technicians captured in Mauretania as mercenaries, an announcement that was bitterly condemned by France.[141] Equally exempt are members of the armed forces sent by their government, even if they are described—as were the German and Italian supporters of Franco's Nationalists in Spain—as volunteers. Thus, Cubans in Angola or Ethiopia would not be mercenaries, nor for that matter would be the "traditional mercenary" of the critics, namely the French Foreign Legion operating on behalf of the Government of Zaire in 1978. Nor would it include the Gurkha units of the British Army, or officers seconded to, or on contract as members of, foreign units. Since residents are not regarded as mercenaries even though they are specially recruited and receive a higher pay than the regular servicemen, it would seem that, for example, non-Israelis wishing to serve in the Israeli forces would merely be required to take up residence for such period of time as is prescribed by Israeli law in order to become lawful combatants. The same was not true for the Rhodesians, for the Protocol definition still involves nationality considerations. Their situation was not helped by the decision of the World Council of Churches,[142] seeking apparently to plug the loophole in the Protocol concerning punishment, at least in so far as Rhodesia was concerned, calling on member-churches

to urge their government to treat enlistment in the armed forces of the illegal

[141]*Le Monde*, 25 May 1977.
[142]*The Times*, 6 August 1977.

Rhodesian regime as a criminal offence, to punish offencers accordingly, and to outlaw any recruitment for this purpose.

While the Protocol definition may have omitted some of the most unpleasant parts of the Luanda formula, it retains the motive test. A mercenary "is motivated essentially by the desire for private gain," so that any non-national captured would have to be examined as to the motive which led him to enlist. His comrade paid the same, but motivated—at least, so he says—by ideological sympathy, though this of course could not protect him in a campaign against national liberation, would not be considered a mercenary and would be a lawful combatant entitled to prisoner of war status. One should not overlook the warning of Brian C.J. in 1477:[143]

It is common knowledge that the thought of man shall not be tried, for the Devil himself knoweth not the thought of man

or as it has been expressed more recently[144]

I do not see how intent can make infringement of what otherwise is not. The less legal rights depend on someone's state of mind, the better.

The Protocol has come into force only for some, but since the various resolutions of the U.N. and other international organizations in this area are not law-making, and since it is of the essence of humanitarian law and of the law of war that it should be even-handed, so that even those engaged in an unlawful war remain protected by the law,[145] for most countries mercenaries are still legally combatants, entitled to treatment as prisoners of war and only liable to trial for such crimes against the law of war or the criminal law that they may commit. International law, as yet, does not regard mercenarism as an offence. Moreover, since the drafting of Protocol I it has become noticeable that the African countries, the very countries that led the campaign against mercenaries, are no longer so concerned when alien troops, even so mercenary a unit as the French Foreign Legion, are engaged in keeping a recognised African government in power. True, it would seem that ideology is here important. If the proposed Pan-African Peacekeeping Force comes into existence, it may no longer be necessary for the Foreign Legion to play a part on the African stage. But will the role of such a force be any different from that of, for example, the Cubans operating on behalf of left-wing governments in Africa, ostensibly at the invitation of such governments? If the British Foreign Secretary can say at the 1978 Lord Mayor's Banquet[146] that "they are like the private armies of the Middle Ages," which moved around "tilting the military balance indiscriminately at the whim of the feudal baron," then the Soviet Union is equally entitled to describe the western-sponsored and supported Pan-African Peacekeeping Force as a tool of the imperialists directed at destroying the national liberation movements of Africa—it is of course unfortunate, as the Soviet and Cuban role in Ethiopia and Somalia illustrate, that today's idealists are yesterday's neocolonialists, and *vice-versa*. So long as the present political

---

[143]Cited with approval in *Brogden v. Metropolitan Rly. Co.*, [1876-7] 2 *A.C.* 692 (Lord Blackburn).
[144]*Mercoid Corp. v. Mid-Continent Investment Co.* (1944), 320 *U.S.* 661, 678 (Jackson J.).
[145]See, e.g., Lauterpacht, "Rules of Warfare in an Unlawful War," in *Law and Politics in the World Community*, 89, 112 (ed. by Lipsky, 1953) and in Oppenheim, 2 *International Law*, 231 (7th ed., by Lauterpacht, 1952); *see also*, Schwarzenberger, *The Law of Armed Conflict*, 98-99, 105-106 (1968) and *International Law and Order*, 235 (1971).
[146]*The Times*, 6 April 1978.

temper prevails, with its rival power interests, it will matter little how the treaty text defines mercenaries. In any case if the Diplock Report and events in Africa since the signature of Protocol I are any indication, it may well be that Article 47 will be subject to reservation. Since there were hints at Geneva that if such a politically motivated provision were in fact reserved, the majority of third world states would not ratify the Protocol as such, it may well be the law will remain as it has always been. The new threats to independence in Africa may herald a period in which the African States themselves strengthen their Pan-African Peacekeeping Force, with a leavening of white mercenaries, leading us back to a period when the profession of arms is again like any other, open to those who wish to follow it, and made use of by those employers who require the services of such professionals. Morality, particularly when fed by propaganda and pseudo-idealism, may condemn the profession. While law should reflect the morality of those it governs, it should not be affected by the vagaries of the season, nor should it hesitate when morality runs away from justice to be the medium through which level-handed justice and humanity remain supreme.

Since the adoption of the Protocol, the question of the status of mercenaries has come up for discussion in the General Assembly of the United Nations at the initiative of Nigeria. In its Working Paper,[147] which comprised a draft international convention, Nigeria accepted the definition of Article 47 of Protocol I. However, it goes beyond the Protocol in that it proclaims mercenarism to be a crime. Moreover, it widened its scope to include not only those who serve as mercenaries, but also those recruiting or making use of them. By its proposed Article 2

"1. The crime of mercenarism is committed when an individual, group or association, or body corporate registered in that State or representative of a State or the State itself with the aim of opposing by threat or armed violence the territorial integrity of another State or the legitimate aspirations of national liberation movements jeopardizes the process of self-determination or manifests by overt acts any of the following:
(a) Organizes, finances, supplies, equips, trains, promotes, supports, or employs in any way individuals, bands or military forces consisting of or including persons who are not nationals of a Party to the conflict and who act for personal gain through payment of salary or any other kind of material recompense;
(b) Participates as an individual, group or association or body corporate or enlists in any force;
(c) Advertises, prints or causes to be advertised any information regarding paragraphs (a) and (b) of this article;
(d) Allows or tolerates the activities mentioned in paragraphs (a), (b) and (c) of this article to be carried out in any territory or place under its jurisdiction or control or affords facilities for transit, transport, or other operation of the above-mentioned forces;
(e) Actually participates in any way in any of the acts mentioned in paragraphs (a), (b), (c) and (d) of this article which results in destruction of life and property.
2. Any person, group or association representative of a State or the State who:
(a) Attempts to commit any act of mercenarism (hereinafter referred to as 'the offence') mentioned in article 2;
(b) Participates as an accomplice of any one who commits or attempts to commit the offence also commits the offence for the purposes of this Convention.
3. The offence if committed shall be deemed *an offence against the peace and security of a State*" (italics added) [—and thus an act of aggression].

---

[147]U.N. Doc. A/AC.207/L.3, 23 Jun. 1981.

This definition of the 'crime' of mercenarism abandons any concept of reciprocity or equality upon which the law of armed conflict has always been considered to depend. Its wording makes it clear that it is only a person enlisting against a national liberation movement who is envisaged as committing a criminal act, and not any person who enlists on behalf of such a movement. In addition, it appears to retreat from the Protocol definition with which it opened, in that it seems to abandon the need for the 'mercenary' to receive payment higher than that given to a member of the force in which he has enlisted, since it condemns the payment of *any* salary. One wonders whether this would mean that an alien ideologue serving without pay in a national force against a national liberation movement would now be considered a mercenary. It also implies that the State employing alien personnel to cope with an 'ethnic' rebellion against its rule might be guilty of mercenarism.

The Nigerian draft was considered by an ad hoc committee established by the General Assembly with the objective of drafting a Convention[148] and during its work it became clear that a number of states accepted these implications adopting the view that

> international law prohibited the use of force by a colonial power in order to prevent a people under its illegal domination from exercising its inherent right of self-determination and independence, it recognized that peoples under colonial and foreign domination could resort to force in order to exercise that right, so that the refusal by a colonial, racist and foreign Government to allow a people under its domination to exercise its right to self-determination and independence authorized other States to intervene and actively support the oppressed people in the exercise of that right. . . . Since the practice of resorting to mercenaries resulted in a direct form of interventionism, it should be viewed as a threat to international peace and security, a crime against the peace and security of mankind [—and thus an act of aggression—] and a dangerous manifestation of international terrorism. The use of mercenaries against national liberation movements similarly constituted a criminal act and mercenaries themselves were criminals.[149]

Perhaps all that need be said about this part of the Report is that its conception of what constitutes current international law is controversial to say the least, and the sentiment expressed is more indicative of political ideology than of a desire to codify the law, especially as the only national liberation movements recognized at present are the African National Congress, the Palestine Liberation Organization and the South-West Africa People's Organization, and even then the recognition is by no means universal. Fortunately, the Report made no concrete proposals, but indicated that there was a dichotomy of view between what might be described as the traditional approach adopted by the older western states and that, expounded above, put forward by those from the Third World which now form a majority in the General Assembly.

To date, no new draft Convention has come up for consideration. If earlier instances, such as the processes for adopting the 1977 Protocols, are followed it would seem likely that, given the pressure from Third World countries, and the unwillingness of older states, particularly the western democracies to give any offence to those countries, it is probable that any new Convention, however undesirable some of its features may be, will be adopted by consensus.[150] However, the mercenary in the field may take some

---

[148]G.A. Res. 35/48 (1980).
[149]Report of the Ad Hoc Committee on the Drafting of an International Convention against the recruitment, Use, Financing and Training of Mercenaries, G.A. *Official Records*, 36th Sess. Supp. No. 43 (A/36/43), para. 17. This para. is typical of the larger part of the Report.
[150]For comments on the implications of consensus, see, e.g., Kaufman, *United Nations Decision Making*, 1980, pp. 128, 209-12; Moskowitz, *The Roots and Reaches of United Nations Actions and Decisions*, 1980, pp. 195-7.

consolation from the fact that the western democracies are unlikely to discriminate against him in any conflicts *inter se*, and that any Convention will almost certainly take a number of years to come into effect. However, he must recognize that this will in no way inhibit those countries which have maintained that mercenarism is a crime, and he must realise that if he participates in any campaign against a national liberation movement and is captured he will be denied any rights as a prisoner of war, and will almost certainly stand trial for his crime with the virtual certainty of a death sentence at the end thereof.

X

War Crimes, Extradition and Command Responsibility

Traditionally war crimes have been defined as "violations of the laws or usages of war committed during war."[1] Broadly speaking the 'laws' in question have been defined in the Hague Regulations attached to Hague Convention IV, 1907, respecting the Laws and Customs of War on Land,[2] as well as in some of the other Conventions adopted that year, together with such Declarations as that of 1868 Renouncing the Use, in Time of War, of Explosive Projectiles under 400 Grammes Weight.[3] In addition to this Hague Law, there has been adopted a series of Geneva Conventions in 1949,[4] as supplemented by the Protocols of 1977.[5] This Geneva Law is primarily concerned with modifying the horrors of war as they affect those who are *hors de combat*, although Protocol I of 1977 does in fact to some extent have an impact on the Hague Law as well as that of Geneva. This it does, for example, by changing the concept of international war so as to apply to armed conflicts conducted in the name of self-determination.[6] Concomitantly, this has affected the description of combatants.[7] Moreover, the Protocol has made a major deviation from established law by removing the reciprocity that formerly applied as between belligerents on behalf of those engaged in such a national liberation effort,[8] while at the

[1]See, e.g., War Crimes Act (Canada), 10 Geo. VI, c. 73, 1946, s. 1(f).
[2]Schindler/Toman, 57.
[3]Declaration of St. Petersburg, *ibid.*, 95.
[4]I—Wounded and Sick; II—Wounded, Sick and Shipwrecked; III—Prisoners of War; IV—Civilian—*ibid.*, 305, 333, 355, 427, resp.
[5]Protocol I—international armed conflicts; Protocol II—non-international armed conflicts, *ibid.*, 551, 619, resp.
[6]Pr. I, Art. 1(4).
[7]See, e.g., Art. 44(3).
[8]*Ibid.*, and Art. 44(4). It would appear that members of the armed forces of a recognised state are still required to wear uniforms, while this is not necessarily true for others, e.g., members of a national liberation movement, engaged in conflict.

same time removing mercenaries from the protection of the law of armed conflict.[9] In addition, the Conventions and Protocol I have added to the concept of war crimes a new category of offences, known as 'grave breaches' which are particularised in the documents in question.[10]

In addition to the rules laid down in treaties and conventions, there are certain usages that have grown up over the centuries that have to be complied with and the breach whereof would amount to a war crime.[11] In any codification of law there is always the risk that the final document will not be adequate to cover all the potential issues that might arise. This is perhaps more true in the case of armed conflict, where advances in technology must of necessity have an effect that is perhaps not quite so marked in other cases. Thus, the Preamble to Hague Convention IV embodies what is known as the Martens Clause:

> It has not been found possible at present to concert regulations covering all the circumstances which arise in practice;
> On the other hand, the High Contracting Parties clearly do not intend that unforeseen cases should, in the absence of a written undertaking, be left to the arbitrary judgment of military commanders.
> Until a more complete code of the laws of war has been issued, the High Contracting Parties deem it expedient to declare that, in cases not included in the Regulations adopted by them, the inhabitants and the belligerents remain *under the protection and the rule of the principles of the law of nations, as they result from the usages established among civilized peoples, from the laws of humanity, and the dictates of the public conscience.*[12]

This Martens Clause has stood the test of time and is reproduced in almost identical terms in Article 1 of Protocol I of 1977:

> In cases not covered by this Protocol or by other international agreements, civilians and combatants remain under the protection and authority of the principles of international law derived from established custom, from the principles of humanity and from the dictates of public conscience.

It is of course a simple matter to specify obligations in this way, but this does not help the man in the field who may be placed in the position of having to determine whether the act he has been ordered to perform is in fact according to the laws and usages of conflict. Equally, the easiest line of defence for an accused to adopt is that, since the law is difficult to ascertain or may be controversial, and since he has received no special instruction therein, he cannot be expected to differentiate between orders which are in compliance with the law of war and those which are not. However, the maxim *ignorantia juris non excusat* applies as much to members of the armed forces as it does to civilians charged with an offence under the criminal law.[13] This fact was already recognized as early as 1880 when the Institute of International Law drew up its Oxford Manual:[14]

[9]*Ibid.*, Art. 47. See, e.g., "The Status of Mercenaries in International Law," Ch. IX *supra.*
[10]1949, Conv. I, Art. 50; II, Art. 51; III, Art. 130; IV, Art. 147; Pr. I, Arts. 11, 85.
[11]See, e.g., Keen, *The Laws of War in the Middle Ages*, 1965, ch. 3—"The Trial of Military Cases." See, also, Schwarzenberger, *International Law*, vol. 2, *The Law of Armed Conflict*, 1968, ch. 34—"The Breisach Trial of 1474."
[12]Italics added.
[13]See, e.g., Green, "Scientia Juris and the Soldier," 9 *Id Dritt* (Univ. of Malta L.R.) 1978, 37; "The Man in the Field and the Maxim *Ignorantia Juris Non Excusat*," ch. II *supra.*
[14]Schindler/Toman, 35, 37 (italics added).

By [drawing up its Manual, the Institute] believes it is rendering a service to military men themselves. In fact, so long as the demands of opinion remain indeterminate, belligerents are exposed to painful uncertainty and to endless accusations. A positive set of rules, . . . if they are judicious, serves the interests of belligerents and . . . strengthens the discipline which is the strength of armies; it also ennobles their patriotic mission in the eyes of the soldiers by keeping them within the limits of respect due to the rights of humanity. But in order to attain this end it is not sufficient for sovereigns to promulgate new laws. *It is essential, too, that they make these laws known among all people, so that when a war is declared, the men called upon to take up arms to defend the causes of the belligerent States, may be thoroughly impregnated with the special rights and duties attached to the execution of such a command.*

In keeping with this injunction, the 1949 Conventions impose an obligation upon the High Contracting Parties[15]

to disseminate the text of the present Convention as widely as possible in their respective countries, and, in particular, to include the study thereof in their programmes of military and, if possible, civil instruction, so that the principles thereof may become known to the entire population, in particular to the armed fighting forces, the medical personnel and the chaplains.

Protocol I of 1977 is even more specific, for in addition to repeating this obligation "to include the study [of the Conventions and Protocol] in their programmes of military instruction and to encourage the study thereof by the civilian population," the High Contracting Parties are obliged to ensure that[16]

any military or civilian authorities who, in time of armed conflict, assume responsibilities in respect of the application of the Conventions and this Protocol shall be fully acquainted with the text thereof.

Moreover, recognizing that instruction in the law of armed conflict is somewhat specialised in character, the Protocol provides for the attachment of legal advisers to military commanders.[17] These advisers have a dual function. They shall be available for advising "on the appropriate instruction to be given to the armed forces," and, perhaps even more importantly, they shall "advise military commanders at the appropriate level on the application of the Conventions and this Protocol," thus it is hoped making the issue of unlawful orders less likely than would otherwise be the case.[18]

In addition to pleading ignorance of the law, those accused of offences against the law of armed conflict invariably contend that as members of the forces they are obliged to obey all orders they receive, since non-compliance will result in a court martial for disobedience. However, it is clearly laid down in both statute and military manuals that it is only lawful orders that are entitled to compliance.[19] Moreover, with the increase in education and the realisation that, particularly in time of war, armies are now largely citizen armies it is being more and more accepted that soldiers cannot be regarded as

[15]I, Art. 47; II, Art. 48; III, Art. 127; IV, Art. 144.
[16]Art. 83(2).
[17]Art. 82.
[18]See, e.g., "The Role of Legal Advisers in the Armed Forces," ch. IV *supra.*
[19]See, e.g., Canadian National Defence Act, R.S.C., c. N-4; U.K., *Manual of Military Law,* Part I, 1972, 296; *U.S. v. Carr* (1872) 25 Fed. Cas. 306, 308; *U.S. Uniform Code of Military Justice,* Art. 90, 10 U.S.C., s. 890; U.S. *Manual for Courts Martial* 1969, ss. 169, 216.

automata, but that they are required to exercise some moral judgment,[20] so that they will not obey every order they receive without question.[21]

Closely related to the defence of superior orders is the argument that military orders are acts of state and as such should be considered as being political in character. As a result, the plea is frequently put forward to secure exemption from extradition when the offender involved is alleged to be a war criminal. For some years this enabled fugitive war criminals to feel secure from arrest on an international warrant, since it was the contention of the International Criminal Police Organization (Interpol) that, since it was precluded by its Constitution[22] from participating in the arrest of political offenders, it was incompetent to cooperate in seeking out war criminals.[23] Not long after the Eichmann incident,[24] however, Interpol seems to have changed its policy, for in 1964 Gerhard Bohne, accused of participating in the mass killing of 15,000 mental patients, was arrested in Buenos Aires at the request of Interpol.[25] On that occasion the Argentine Supreme Court ruled that his acts did not fall within the traditional Argentine understanding of a political crime, which it defined as one attacking the state as a political personality and possessed of "an aggressive purpose and end" in the pursuit of the offender's interests.[26] In addition, the Court held that "International law has progressively denied favourable treatment in the case of acts which, though directed against governmental authority, are regarded as serious crimes in the eyes of moral and common law." In view of this it rejected the contention that euthanasia, which, "in view of its cruelty and immorality, was clearly against the common feelings of civilized people," could ever have any relation to a political or military offence.

The Argentine court in its judgment referred to Belgian decisions as well as earlier judgments of its own, but made no reference to *Re Castioni*[27] which may be considered to have established the definition of a political offence as understood in Anglo-American law:[28]

> . . . it must at least be shown that the act is done in furtherance of, done with the intention of assistance, as a sort of overt act in the course of acting in a political manner, a political rising, or a dispute between two parties in the State as to which is to have the government in its hands. . . .

If we accept this as the current definition, which it in fact appears to be,[29] it is manifestly

[20]See, e.g., *Keighley* v. *Bell* (1866) 4 F. & F. 763; *U.S.* v. *Hutto* (1970/71) 39 C.M.R. 108: "[A] member of the United States Army is not and may not be considered, short of insanity, an automaton, but may be inferred to be a reasoning agent who is under a duty to exercise moral judgment in obeying the order of a superior officer" [this quotation is taken from a copy of the Instructions of the Judge Advocate, supplied by courtesy of the Librarian of the U.S. Judge Advocate General's School of Law; see, also, Norene, *Obedience to Orders as a Defence to a Criminal Act*, 1971—unpublished JAG School thesis, 68-77].
[21]See Green, *Superior Orders in National and International Law*, 1976; Dinstein, *The Defence of 'Obedience to Superior Orders' in International Law*, 1965; Keijzer, *Military Obedience*, 1978.
[22]1956, as amended, Art. 3: "It is strictly forbidden in the Organization to undertake any intervention or activities of a political, military, religious or racial character."
[23]See, e.g., Green, "Political Offences, War Crimes and Extradition," 11 *I.C.L.Q.* 1962, 329.
[24]See Green, "The Eichmann Case," 23 Modern L.R. 1960, 507.
[25]*The Times* (London), 16 Dec. 1965.
[26]This is the definition put forward by Roque Sáenz Peña, as Argentine delegate at the South American Convention, Montevideo, in 1889, and cited by the Court at para. 11 of the judgment—I am grateful to Mme. Judge Arguas for having supplied me with the text of the judgment, dated 24 Aug. 1966.
[27][1891] 1 Q.B. 149, 157, *per* Denman J.
[28]See, e.g., Green, *Law and Society*, 1975, Ch. IX, "Hijacking, Extradition and Asylum," 365-392.
[29]See, e.g., Green, *ibid.*, Ch. VIII, "The Right of Asylum in International Law," 324-330; Bassiouni, *International Extradition and World Public Order*, 1974, 370-429; Shearer, *Extradition in International Law*, 1971, Ch. 7; Papadatos, *Le Délit Politique*, 1954.

clear that a war crime, in so far as it has been committed by order of a government or in accordance with government policy, cannot constitute a political offence to provide the offender with immunity from extradition. In fact the Argentine decision in *Bohne* is fully in line with that of the Ghana Court of Appeal in *The State* v. *Director of Prisons, ex parte Schumann*.[30] Here, too, the accused was alleged to have participated in the Nazi euthanasia programme and the application submitted by the German Federal Government was based on murder. However, all the judges made it clear that they regarded the offences for which Schumann's extradition was requested as war crimes. The defendant contended that the acts with which he was charged were legal in Germany when committed, that they were committed in accordance with superior orders received from governmental authorities, and that as acts of State they were political in character. In delivering judgment, the Chief Justice referred to both the Nuremberg[31] and Eichmann[32] judgments, and continued:[33]

> . . . we have it on record from the evidence of . . . an official of the Ministry of Justice in West Germany, and formerly a Public Prosecutor, that murder has always been a crime in Germany and it was a crime during the entire period of the Nazi era. The fact that for political reasons murder of the type with which the appellant is charged was not punishable during the Nazi régime does not by any reason render its prosecution now unlawful. I am unable to accept as tenable any of the grounds advanced by the appellant's counsel in support of his submission that the offence involved in these proceedings is of a political character.
> The offence of murder with which the appellant is charged is, having regard to all the circumstances in which the offence was committed, no more of a political character than the offence of, say, robbery with violence or burglary committed by a political party activist in a desperate bid to seek means of replenishing the dwindling coffers of his political party. . . .

Justice of Appeal Crabbe in delivering a concurring judgment pointed out that this was the first extradition case to come before the Ghanaian court, and therefore he referred to a number of foreign decisions relating to the definition of 'political offence'[34] and in the light thereof held[35]

> . . . It is clear . . . that the dominant motive of the appellant in killing those thousands of lunatics and Jews was anything but political. There was no political rivalry in Nazi Germany, and the appellant has not conceded that fear of prosecution for a political offence or political persecution led him to commit the offences with which he is charged. Finally, the appellant admitted before us that he is not at odds with the present Government of the Federal Republic of Germany on 'some issue connected with the political control or government of the country'. In my judgment the appellant is a 'fugitive from justice' and must be surrendered for trial.

Even Justice of Appeal Lassey expressed[36]

---

[30][1969] G.L.R. 703; 39 I.L.R. 433.
[31]13 *Ann. Dig.* 203.
[32]36 *I.L.R.* 5.
[33]At 439.
[34]*Re Castioni, loc. cit.,* n. 27 above; *Re Meunier* [1894] 2 Q.B. 415; *Ex p. Kolczynski* [1955] 2 W.L.R. 116; *Ex p. Schtraks* [1962] 3 W.L.R. 1013; *Re Ezeta* (1894) 62 F. 972; *Karadzole* v. *Artukovic* (1958) 247 F. 2d 198; *Re Noblot* (1928-Switzerland) 4 Ann. Dig. 350.
[35]At 450.
[36]At 450-452.

some sympathy with the appellant, not because in actual fact the killings complained of . . . are not inhuman, atrocious and heinous in themselves, but because different views may be taken by different people with different political thinking or systems as regards the political events which led up to the commission of the offences in Germany at the time . . . [particularly as] there is no doubt that the killings were done in circumstances which were not entirely without some political significance . . . [since they] were committed on the orders of the ruling political party in Germany at the time and they were so committed in fulfilment of the political programme or ambitions of the ruling political party, namely, the Nazi Party in Germany, prior to and during the Second World War [, went on to state that t]he crucial question here is this: In those circumstances is it necessary to widen the scope or meaning of those magic words, 'of a political character', if only for reasons of humanity? . . . [I]n order to determine the political character of the particular offence so as to make it not extraditable there must necessarily be present at the time of the commission of the particular crime some element of organized or violent opposition or resistance to the execution of the planned policy of the ruling political party and the offence must be committed in the conflict which might result between the opposing parties. In this context any such offence committed either by the agents of the ruling political party seeking to carry out their principal's orders or by the agents of those who dislike or resist the carrying into effect of the particular political policy may be brought under the category of an offence 'of a political nature or character' and therefore excusable in extradition proceedings. This . . . should be one of the tests in determining whether in any particular circumstances an offence committed against the municipal laws of a State by a national who has sought asylum or refuge in another State is of a political nature or not. Merely carrying out wicked or inhuman orders or plans of a governing political party by State agents against the persons or properties of individuals or groups of individuals who manifestly do not demonstrate any organized violent resistance to the execution of those plans would not stamp the offences committed in such a situation with political character so as to afford the perpetrators an excuse from due prosecution. It is absolutely absurd to me to hold that what is clearly murder committed in one territory in response to the superior orders of a ruling political party against helpless victims in a lunatic asylum should not lie[37] and the offender [should not be] extradited because it was done in obedience to the superior order of a governing political party.

. . . [N]either the helpless lunatics in the mental institution at Munsungen nor the Jews in Auschwitz appeared to have offered any organized resistance to the Nazi Party in Germany, notwithstanding the possibility that as individuals they may not have liked the policy of the Nazi régime which was out to exterminate them from the face of the earth. The offences . . . were not committed against the numerous victims in the course of any open conflict or rebellion between the agents of the Nazi Party and the lunatics in Munsungen Institute or the Jews in Auschwitz. These offences are clearly extraditable. . . .

Despite the implication that might be read into the latter part of this statement that had the lunatics and Jews in question been 'enemies' of the Nazi Party or of Germany then the political defence might have been valid, it is suggested that in the light of Lassey J.A.'s general condemnation of these offences that would probably be a misreading of his intention.

It might be of interest to point out that, unlike some of the United Nations,[38] Ghana was under no general obligation to seek out or extradite war criminals, other than in circumstances where their offences might be extraditable under a normal extradition

[37]It should not be overlooked, however, that in *Re Brandt* (The Doctors' Trial) (1947) 14 Ann. Dig. 296, the U.S. Military Tribunal implied that had the victims been German nationals it would have lacked jurisdiction (298).
[38]The name of the wartime alliance against the Axis.

treaty. Others, however, had assumed specific obligations to this end,[39] while there had been a variety of General Assembly Resolutions to the same effect.[40] Nevertheless, it became clear almost as soon as the War ended that the major Allied powers entered into active competition to secure the services of leading Nazi scientists and intelligence personnel who might prove useful to them should any conflict arise between themselves. In fact, it has now been made public that in some cases they were even prepared to shelter wanted offenders against extradition requests received from allied nations.[41] Furthermore, on occasion they became excessively legalistic in construing what offences might be regarded as war crimes either *eo nomine* or when described as common crimes. This, despite the fact that, for example, both the United States and the United Kingdom had originally indicated that they would even be prepared to hand over those who were guilty of treason in that they had assisted the enemy—a political offence if ever there was one. Thus in *Chandler* v. *United States*[42] the United States Court of Appeals for the 1st Circuit went so far as to state that "a State might choose to turn over to a wartime ally a traitor who had given aid and comfort to their common enemy." Similarly, the British Government at first adopted the view that since they could always deport an undesirable alien there was no need for any special agreement for the treatment of traitors, they were prepared to deport any "aliens against whom there was a prima facie case that they were . . . guilty of treachery involving active assistance to the enemy. . . . [T]hey would be satisfied with only two conditions before turning them over to the requesting State: that the wanted persons were nationals of the requesting State, and that there was prima facie evidence "that they had actively assisted a State at war with their own country'."[43] Nevertheless, as early as May 1949 the British Government announced that no further war criminals, let alone traitors, would be handed over to a demanding State in the absence of a satisfactory explanation for the delay that had elapsed prior to the request being made.[44] As recently as February 1983 it was disclosed by the Dutch Government that the Canadian Government had refused to surrender a convicted member of a Dutch Nazi group who had escaped from a detention camp shortly after the War. The man had been convicted in 1948 and sentenced to twenty years, but Canada pointed out that the conviction was not for murder but only for helping the Germans. However, the Dutch contended that his conviction for this criminal offence had in fact included two murders. This did not alter the opinion of the Canadian authorities that extradition could not be acceded to.[45]

The United States has recently adopted a new policy whereby those accused of war crimes have been returned to stand trial in Germany. This has not been done by way of extradition for war crimes, although the media, at least outside the United States, have tended to suggest that this was the case. Under United States law[46] immigration and nationality depend upon good moral character, and wilful misrepresentation or concealment of a material fact constitutes a violation for which revocation and setting aside of the entrance or naturalization is prescribed. This has enabled the United States authorities to contend successfully that a person who had, when applying for entry or naturalization, wilfully suppressed that he was a member of the Nazi Party or Gestapo

---

[39]See H.M.S.O., *History of the United Nations War Crimes Commission*, 1948, Ch. 13.
[40]E.g., 13 Feb. 1946, 15 Dec. 1946, 31 Oct. 1947, see also, Green, *loc. cit.*, n. 23 above, 344-348.
[41]See, e.g., U.S. protection of Klaus Barbie, *Globe and Mail* (Toronto), 29 Mar. 1983.
[42](1948) 171 F. 2d 921, 935.
[43]Foreign Office Letter of 29 Mar. 1945, *op. cit.*, n. 39 above, 398-399.
[44]Parliamentary Debates (Lords), Vol. 162, col. 388, *per* Lord Henderson.
[45]*Globe and Mail* (Toronto), 26 Feb. 1983.
[46]Immigration and Nationality Act, 8 U.S.C.

or had in fact committed war crimes had failed to satisfy the good moral requirement of the legislation and was therefore illegally within the country and as such liable to deportation[47] to Germany where he might in fact stand trial for war crimes. In other cases, as, for example, that of Archbishop Valerian Trifka, the individual concerned has been permitted to leave the United States after being denaturalized rather than submitting to deportation proceedings.

While judicial proceedings may be the concomitant of deportation in so far as the United States is concerned, this is by no means the case everywhere. In 1983, for example, Klaus Barbie, "The Butcher of Lyon," was deported from Bolivia to France. Barbie had been twice sentenced to death in France *in absentia* for a variety of war crimes but had escaped, apparently with the assistance of United States military authorities,[48] to South America, and France had made a number of unsuccessful attempts to recover him. With the election of a new more liberal President in Bolivia, the Bolivian attitude changed. Both France and the Federal German Republic were seeking his extradition to try him for offences committed during the War, and the President of Bolivia announced he was being expelled from Bolivia by presidential order. It was indicated that, though no extradition treaty existed, Barbie was being sent to France as the only country prepared to accept him. However, there is no evidence to indicate that Barbie was given a chance to seek asylum elsewhere. Even had France been able to proceed by way of extradition to secure his return from Bolivia there would have been certain difficulties. For reasons connected with the French legal processes it was decided to indict Barbie for crimes against humanity,[49] hardly an offence which would have been listed as extraditable in any treaty, although there is today a tendency to include in such treaties offences against international law, which are now being increasingly excluded from characterization as political offences.

A somewhat parallel case has arisen in Canada, although there on a judicial level. Moreover, the issue has been complicated somewhat by the implications of the Canadian War Crimes Act[50] and the recently enacted Charter of Rights.[51] By section 4 of the Regulations embodied in the Schedule to the former:

(1) Any Canadian flag, general or air officer commanding any Canadian forces, wherever such forces may be serving, whether in the field or in occupation of enemy territory or otherwise, . . . shall have power to convene military courts for the trial of persons charged with having committed war crimes and to confirm the findings and sentences of such courts: Provided that no military court shall be convened for the trial of any person for a war crime unless the case has been certified by the Judge Advocate General . . . as approved for trial.

In the light of this a number of survivor organizations and their sympathisers, both in and outside of Canada, have contended that the Canadian authorities are failing in their statutory responsibilities by not instituting war crimes proceedings against those persons in Canada, some of whom have acquired Canadian nationality, regarding whom there

[47]See, e.g., *U.S.* v. *Walus* (1978) 453 F. Supp. 699; *U.S.* v. *Federenko* (1979) 597 F. 2d 246.
[48]*Globe and Mail*, 29 Mar. 1983.
[49]*The Times*, 25 Feb. 1983. A defence contention that his transfer to France was illegal in the absence of treaty was dismissed on the ground that 'the conditions of his arrest were in full conformity of the law. Moreover, the Court held that in accordance with the Nuremberg Principles those accused of war crimes and crimes against peace or humanity should be sent back to the countries of commission for trial there. The defence intimated that an appeal would be lodged with the European Commission on Human Rights, *ibid.*, 8 Oct. 1983.
[50]1946, 10 Geo. VI, c. 73.
[51]Constitution Act, 1982, Part I.

is evidence of their involvement in the commission of war crimes. Since it has been suggested that the purpose of the War Crimes Act was to provide for the establishment of Canadian military tribunals to operate against alleged war criminals in those areas of occupied Europe or the Far East in which Canadian forces might find themselves after the end of the Second World War, and since further it is hardly likely that the Canadian public would tolerate the arrest of a civilian on the warrant of a military officer to stand trial by a military court for an offence against non-Canadians committed some forty years ago outside of Canada,[52] these pressure groups have argued that such persons should be tried for grave breaches against the Geneva Conventions of 1949, enacted into Canadian law by the Geneva Conventions Act.[53] This, of course, ignores the fact the crimes with which war criminals are charged were all committed by 1945 at the latest, and to try them for offences created by treaties in 1949 and ratified by Canada in 1965 would run counter to the Anglo-American common law principle against retroactive legislation and would be contrary to Article 15 of the International Covenant on Civil and Political Rights,[54] ratified by Canada in 1976, and Section 11(g) of the Canadian Charter of Rights, unless it can be argued that grave breaches qualify, under both instruments, as crimes under international law already clearly established, or "according to the general principles of law recognized by the community of nations." However, if this be so, it would be preferable to proceed by way of extradition for the common crimes which most grave breaches in fact are.

This, in fact, seems to be the procedure being pursued in Canada, since it is not possible to proceed by way of denaturalization or cancellation of the right of immigration as in the United States, for at the time that Axis personnel came to Canada after the Second World War they were not asked the type of question that United States immigration officers asked, nor was it possible to cancel naturalization after it had been granted. Extradition proceedings are, therefore, the only route available for dealing with such people. Helmut Rauca entered Canada in 1950 and became a naturalized Canadian citizen in 1956. He had been a member of the Gestapo and was the officer in charge of selecting Jews for extermination in camps in German occupied Lithuania. The Federal Republic of Germany sought his extradition under its extradition treaty with Canada[55] and in accordance with the terms of Canada's Extradition Act,[56] alleging Rauca's responsibility for the murder of approximately 11,500 persons between August 1941 and December 1943. The defence based its arguments on s. 6(1) of the Canadian Charter of Rights and Freedoms which guarantees to every citizen the right to 'remain' in Canada. Although this was intended as a guarantee against arbitrary expulsion, it was claimed that it provided a complete guarantee against expulsion for whatever reason. However, s. 1 of the Charter provides that all the rights guaranteed therein are subject to "such reasonable limits prescribed by law as can be demonstrably justified in a free and democratic society." In his judgment in *Federal Republic of Germany* v. *Rauca*[57] Chief Justice Evans of the Ontario High Court pointed out that in construing the Extradition Treaty and the Act he was adopting "the well-recognized rule that courts apply a fair and liberal interpretation with a view to fulfilling Canada's international obligations in the community of nations."[58] The learned Chief Justice indicated that the real issue turned on the interpretation of the s. 1 limitation. He stated:[59]

[52]See "Canadian Law and the Punishment of War Criminals," Ch. XII *infra*.
[53]1964-65, c. 44, R.S.C. 1970, c. G-3.
[54]1966, G.A. Res. 2200 (XXI)A.
[55]Signed 11 Jul. 1977, in force 30 Sept. 1979.
[56]R.S.C. 1970, c. E-21.
[57](1982) 38 O.R. 2d 705, confirmed on appeal (1983) 41 O.R. (2d) 225.
[58]At 708.
[59]At 715-717.

The overriding provision in s. 1 places a statutory restriction upon those rights and freedoms set out in the Charter and provides that those guaranteed rights and freedoms are subject 'to such reasonable limits prescribed by law as can be demonstrably justified in a free and democratic society.' In my view, the 'limits' to be applied require the court to adopt an objective standard in assessing the restrictions 'prescribed by law' and that the demonstrable justification which modifies the reasonable limits be interpreted in a manner that leans slightly in favour of the individual when the competing rights of the individual and of society are being balanced in the courts. The addition of the words 'in a free and democratic society' sets out the parameters within which these competing rights must be resolved. . . . [Since] the alleged infringement or violation is either evident or readily established and results from governmental policy or legislative action [, t]he government is charged with the onus of demonstrating that the restriction is reasonable within the meaning of s. 1.

The phrase 'reasonable limits' in s. 1 imports an objective test of validity. It is the judge who must determine whether a 'limit' as found in legislation is reasonable or unreasonable. The question is not whether the judge agrees with the limitation but whether he considers there is a rational basis for it—a basis that would be regarded as being within the bounds of reason by fair-minded people accustomed to the norms of a free and democratic society. That is the crucible in which the concept of reasonableness must be tested. The phrase 'prescribed by law' requires the limitation to be laid down by some rule of law in a positive fashion and not by mere implication. The rule of law containing the limitation will normally be statutory although it is possible that it may be found in delegated legislation or in the form of a common law rule.

In the phrase 'as can be demonstrably justified', the key word is the word 'justified' which forms the cornerstone of the phrase. It means to show, or maintain the justice or reasonableness of an action; to adduce adequate grounds for; or to defend as right or proper. The legal use of the word is to show or maintain sufficient reason in court for doing that which one is called upon to answer for. The notion of justification is qualified by the word 'demonstrably' which means in a way which admits of demonstration which in turn means capable of being shown or made evident or capable of being proved clearly and conclusively. . . .

. . . [T]he onus is upon the Federal Republic of Germany to establish that the 'limits', *i.e.* extradition laws, are reasonable, are prescribed by law and are demonstrably justified in a free and democratic society . . .

The court must decide what is a reasonable limit demonstrably justified in a free and democratic society by reference to Canadian society and by the application of principles of political science. Criteria by which these values are to be assessed are to be found within the Charter itself, which means that the courts are entitled to look at those societies in which as a matter of common law freedoms and democratic rights similar to those referred to in the Charter are enjoyed. Parliament operating in 'a free and democratic society' has enacted the Extradition Act and approved the treaty. Following the usual presumptive canon of construction of legislation validity the courts should be extremely . . . reluctant to characterize the limitation as *not* justifiable in a free and democratic society unless it is obviously unreasonable.

. . . Although I accept that extradition is *prima facie* an infringement of the s. 6 mobility rights of a citizen, I am satisfied that the Requesting State has established that extradition is a procedure prescribed by law and is a reasonable limitation on one's guaranteed rights and freedoms which can be demonstrably justified in our society.

I am satisfied that such statutory restriction which has as its objective, the protection and preservation of society from serious criminal activity, is one which members of a free and democratic society such as Canada would accept and embrace. To hold otherwise would be to declare that a procedure which has been accepted in our country for over a century and in most other democratic societies is no longer a reasonable and proper method of protecting our society from serious criminal activities . . .

At this point it is perhaps of interest to mention the decision of the English court in *R. v. Governor of Pentonville Prison, ex p. Budlong and Kember*.[60] The defendant, a British national, claimed that the attempt to extradite him to the United States was in contravention of Article 48 of the Treaty of Rome[61] guaranteeing freedom of movement, "subject to limitations justified on grounds of public policy, public security or public health." Judge Griffiths rejected the contention, holding that extradition is "far more analogous to the implications of domestic criminal law than to deportation."

Although Chief Justice Evans held that Rauca was amenable to extradition under the Treaty and the Act, and that to extradite him would in no way infringe the Charter of Rights, this did not mean that he would in fact be extradited. As the Chief Justice pointed out,[62] "the fact that a court may decide there is sufficient evidence to warrant extradition does not preclude the right of the fugitive to be exempted from surrender at the political level. The executive is not required to surrender a fugitive, whether a Canadian citizen or not, even though a court may decide that a *prima facie* case has been established against the fugitive." It is always open to the executive to decide to afford any person present in the territory asylum, regardless of the offences that he may have committed or the claims of another state to have him surrendered to it.[63]

While Rauca did not attempt to plead the defence of superior orders and while the Ghanaian Supreme Court held in the *Schumann* case[64] that this was a matter for the Court before which the substantive issue was to be heard, it is important to note that rejection of the plea and conviction of the perpetrator of the act does not exempt the superior issuing the order from liability.[65] This is, in fact, already implicit in Hague Convention IV, 1907,[66] Article 3 of which provides that "a belligerent party which violates the provisions of the Regulations [attached to the Convention] shall, if the case demands, be liable to pay compensation. It shall be responsible for all acts committed by persons forming part of its armed forces." The liability of Supreme Commanders and of their political masters was spelled out in the London Agreement for the Prosecution and Punishment of the Major War Criminals of the European Axis (the Nuremberg Charter), 1945:[67]

> Art. 6. . . . Leaders, organizers, instigators and accomplices participating in the formulation or execution of a common plan or conspiracy to commit any of the foregoing crimes [Art. 6(b) deals specifically with war crimes] are responsible for all acts performed by any persons in execution of such plan.
>
> Art. 7. The official position of defendants, whether as Heads of State or responsible officials in Government Departments, shall not be considered as freeing them from responsibility or mitigating punishment.

That senior personnel were aware of the potential risks they ran is made clear by the answer given by Himmler during the one short interrogation he received before committing suicide:[68]

---

[60][1980] 1 All E.R. 701, 717.

[61]298 *U.N.T.S.* 11.

[62]At 708.

[63]See, e.g., LaForest, *Extradition To and From Canada*, 1977, 134-137. Rauca was extradited and charged in the Federal Republic, but died before trial.

[64]*Loc. cit.*, n. 35 above, 452, *per* Lassey, J.A.

[65]See, e.g., Parks, "Command Responsibility for War Crimes," 62 *Mil.L.R.* 1973, 1.

[66]*Op. cit.*, n. 2. above.

[67]Schindler/Toman, 823, 826.

[68]Letter to *The Times*, 7 Jan. 1983, from Niall MacDermott, formerly i.c. counter-intelligence H.Q. 21 Army Group.

Himmler was asked what comment he had to make on the horrors of Belsen and other such camps. His reply was to say rhetorically: 'Am I responsible for the excesses of my subordinates?' all of whom had pleaded that they were acting under superior orders.

Equally interesting is the statement made by Barbie to the investigating magistrate. Having stated that his memory was somewhat 'vague' as to events that had occurred, he conceded that some of his subordinates "were capable of torture," and that "it is possible that I wrote a report for my superiors that orders had been carried out."[69]

Perhaps even more significant are the decisions of war crimes tribunals. From this point of view the Judgment of the Nuremberg Tribunal may be discounted, for it dealt with the highest levels of command and not with direct responsibility for specific actions. For our purpose we may refer to both a Canadian and a United States decision. By the Canadian War Crimes Regulations:[70]

> Where there is evidence that more than one war crime has been committed by members of a formation, unit, body, or group while under the command of a single commander, the court may receive that evidence as *prima facie* evidence of the *responsibility of the commander for those crimes*.
> Where there is evidence that a war crime has been committed by members of a formation, unit, body, or group and that an officer was present at or immediately before the time when such offence was committed, the court may receive that evidence as *prima facie* evidence of the responsibility of such officer or non-commissioned officer, *and of the commander* of such formation, unit, body, or group, for that crime.

Kurt Meyer, Commanding Officer of the 25th Panzer Grenadier Regiment, was tried by a Canadian tribunal for having ordered his troops to deny quarter to prisoners, for having ordered the killing of Canadian prisoners, and for having been responsible for such killings carried out by men under his command. As to the liability of Meyer as a commander, the Judge Advocate stated:[71]

> [A]n officer may be convicted of a war crime if he incites and counsels troops under his command to deny quarter, whether or not prisoners were killed as a result thereof. It seems to be common sense to say that not only those members of the enemy who unlawfully kill prisoners may be charged as war criminals, but also any superior military commander who incites and counsels his troops to commit such offences . . .
> [The] broad question 'When may a military commander be held responsible for a war crime committed by men under his command in the sense that he may be punished as a war criminal?' is not easily answered. . . .
> . . . [T]he facts proved by the prosecution must be such as to establish the responsibility of the accused for the crime in question or to justify the Court in inferring such responsibility. The secondary onus, the burden of adducing evidence that he was not in fact responsible for any particular war crime then shifts to the accused . . .
> [T]he Regulations do not mean that a military commander is in every case liable

---

[69]*The Edmonton Journal,* 13 Mar. 1983, *Globe and Mail,* 14 Mar. 1983, both citing *Le Progrès de Lyon.*
[70]Re-enacted as Schedule to War Crimes Act, n. 50 above, s. 10(4), (5), italics added.
[71]Reported as *Abbaye Ardenne Case* (1945) 4 Law Reports of Trials of War Criminals 97; the extract printed here is taken from the unpublished transcript, 840-845 (reproduced in "Canada's Role in the Development of the Law of Armed Conflict," see ch. XIII *infra*).

to be punished as a war criminal for every war crime committed by his subordinates but once certain facts have been proved by the Prosecution, there is an onus cast upon the accused to adduce evidence to negative or rebut the inference of responsibility which the Court is entitled to make. All the facts and circumstances must then be considered to determine whether the accused was in fact responsible. . . . The rank of the accused, the duties and responsibilities of the accused by virtue of the command he held, and the training of the men under his command,[72] their age and experience, anything relating to the question whether the accused either ordered, encouraged or verbally or tacitly acquiesced in the killing of prisoners, or wilfully failed in his duty as a military commander to prevent or to take such action as the circumstances required to endeavour to prevent, [the acts in question] are matters affecting the question of the accused's responsibility. In the last analysis, it is for the Court, using its wide knowledge and experience of military matters, to determine, in the light of the relevant factors and the provisions of the Regulations, the responsibility of an accused in any particular case. . . . The giving of the order may be proved circumstantially, that is to say, you may consider the facts you find to be proved bearing upon the question whether the alleged order was given, and if you find that the only reasonable inference is that an order that the prisoners be killed was given by the accused . . . , and that the prisoners were killed as a result of that order, you may properly find the accused guilty. . . . [I]t is not necessary for you to be convinced that a particular or formal order was given, but you must be satisfied before you convict, that some words were uttered or some clear indication was given by the accused that prisoners were to be put to death . . .

Perhaps far better known than the *Meyer* case is *Re Yamashita*[73] decided by a United States tribunal. In this instance the accused was not charged with having issued particular orders, so much as with having failed to control the troops under his command and prevent them from committing the war crimes in question. Although the defence argued that successful American operations had virtually severed Yamashita's lines of communication and made contact with his forces impossible, the President of the Court declared:

The Prosecution presented evidence to show that the crimes were so extensive and widespread, both as to time and area, that they must either have been wilfully permitted by the accused, or secretly ordered by the accused. Captured orders issued by subordinate officers of the accused were presented as proof that they, at least, ordered certain acts leading directly to exterminations of civilians under the guise of eliminating the activities of guerrillas hostile to Japan . . .
. . . As to the crimes themselves, complete ignorance that they had occurred was stoutly maintained by the accused, his principal staff officers and subordinate commanders, further, that all such acts, if committed, were directly contrary to the announced policies, wishes and orders of the accused. The Japanese Commanders testified that they did not make personal inspections or independent checks . . . to determine for themselves the established procedures by which their subordinates accomplish their missions. . . .
This accused is an officer of long years of experience, broad in its scope, who has had extensive command and staff duty in the Imperial Japanese Army in peace as well as in war . . . Clearly, assignment to command military troops is accompanied by broad authority and heavy responsibility. This has been true of all armies throughout recorded history. It is absurd, however, to consider a commander a murderer or rapist because one of his soldiers commits a murder or a rape. Never-

---

[72] In *U.S.* v. *Keenan* (1969) 39 C.M.R. 108, 117, it was held that the fact that the actions ordered were in keeping with the training received would not excuse obedience to an order palpably illegal on its face.
[73] (1946) 4 Reports of Trials of War Criminals 1, 34-35. See also, Parks, *loc. cit.*, 103.

theless, where murder and rape and vicious, revengeful actions are widespread offences, and there is no effective attempt by a commander to discover and control the criminal acts, such a commander may be held responsible, even criminally liable, for the lawless acts of his troops, depending upon their nature and the circumstances surrounding them. Should a commander issue orders which lead directly to lawless acts, the criminal responsibility is definite and has always been so understood. . .

The principle of command responsibility, especially as enunciated in *Yamashita*, has now been embodied in treaty, although it must be recognized that while the treaty in question is in force it has not been ratified by any leading member of NATO or the Warsaw Pact. However, it should be noted that a number of national military codes, in addition to the Canadian War Crimes Regulations, already recognize this as an established principle,[74] so that it may now be considered a rule of the international customary law of armed conflict. Protocol I, 1977,[75] provides

The fact that a breach of the Conventions or of this Protocol was committed by a subordinate does not absolve his superiors from penal or disciplinary responsibility, as the case may be, if they knew, or had information which should have enabled them to conclude in the circumstances at the time, that he was committing or was going to commit such a breach and if they did not take all feasible measures within their power to prevent or repress the breach.

In addition to imposing this liability upon a commander who fails to prevent his forces from committing breaches of the law of armed conflict, the Protocol also imposes a positive obligation upon the High Contracting Parties to ensure that commanders behave properly in this regard:[76]

The High Contracting Parties and the Parties to the conflict[77] shall require military commanders, with respect to members of the armed forces under their command and other persons under their control, to prevent and, where necessary, to suppress and report to competent authorities breaches of the Conventions and of this Protocol.
In order to prevent and suppress breaches, High Contracting Parties and Parties to the conflict shall require that, commensurate with their level of responsibility, commanders ensure that members of the armed forces under their command are aware of their obligations under the Conventions and this Protocol.
The High Contracting Parties and Parties to the conflict shall require any commander who is aware that subordinates or other persons under his control are going to commit or have committed a breach of the Conventions or of this Protocol, to initiate such steps as are necessary to prevent such violations of the Conventions or this Protocol, and, where appropriate, to initiate disciplinary or penal action against violators thereof.

While there has been no opportunity to test the authority of these provisions, the events in the refugee camps at Shatila and Sabra, Lebanon, in September 1982, which

[74]See, e.g., *British Manual of Military Law*, Part III, The Law of War on Land, 1958, para. 631—fn. 1(b) cites Dutch and French legislation to the same effect; see, also, U.S. Dept. of the Army, The Law of Land Warfare, FM27-10, 1956, para. 501; U.S. Dept. of the Air Force, International Law—The Conduct of Armed Conflict and Air Operations, AFP 110-31, 1976, para. 15-2d.
[75]*Loc. cit.*, n. 5 above, Art. 86(2).
[76]Art. 87.
[77]Art. 96(3) makes it possible for a national liberation movement engaged in a conflict seeking self-determination, in accordance with Art. 1(4), to undertake to apply the Conventions and Protocol in that conflict.

led to the establishment of a Commission of Inquiry by the Government of Israel and recommendations critical of a number of senior officers as well as the Minister of Defence,[78] are of significance in any modern discussion of this issue. The problem in this case is complicated somewhat by the fact that the Minister of Defence was a member of the Reserve and by his actions indicated that he considered himself competent to take decisions as if he were a commander in the field.[79] A further problem lies in the fact that the Government of Lebanon did not regard the Israeli incursion into Lebanon as a *casus belli* so there was no war or other form of armed conflict between Israel and Lebanon. The Israeli incursion was directed against the Palestine Liberation Organization which Israel considered as a conglomeration of terrorists lacking any form of international status. Further, Israel refused to sign the Protocol or the Final Act of the drafting Conference because the representative of the Palestine Liberation Organization was permitted to sign, and that Organization has not since made any declaration in accordance with the Protocol. It would appear, therefore, that Israel does not regard itself as being involved in any war or other type of armed conflict with the Palestine Liberation Organization. However, in its Report the Kahan Commission called the Israeli incursion into Lebanon, as did the Government of Israel, "The 'Peace for the Galilee' war,"[80] but, nevertheless, referred to those against whom it was directed as 'terrorists'. This leads one to consider what is a 'war'—or, as it now tends to be described, an international armed conflict—and what is the function of the law of war.

It is true that the Hague Conventions consider a declaration of war to be necessary and, although it is generally accepted that an *animus belligerendi* should exist on the part of those engaged, practice indicates that in fact a functional approach tends to be adopted,[81] at least for the purposes of the law of contract[82] or of insurance.[83] Moreover, there is no doubt that both the members of the Palestine Liberation Organization who had established themselves in Lebanon and the Israeli forces operating against them clearly possessed an *animus belligerendi*, and it was the intention of the Israeli forces to destroy their military potential. In addition, arrangements were made for the withdrawal of the P.L.O. forces as organized military units and they were permitted to leave with their weapons. Even though the Israeli authorities contended that Organization members in their hands were terrorists and not entitled, as prisoners of war, to be released at the end of active hostilities,[84] they nevertheless demanded that their own personnel be treated as prisoners of war and arrangements were subsequently made for the exchange of such prisoners with those held by the Israelis. It is submitted that if the captives of one are to be regarded as prisoners of war and treated as such, the same is true for the captives of the other party. Perhaps even more important is the purpose for which the laws regarding warfare and armed conflict have developed. As we have seen,[85] the purpose of such laws and customs is to preserve the "usages established among civilized peoples, the laws of humanity and the dictates of the public conscience." In other words, the

[78]The Authorized English Translation of the Final Report of the Kahan Commission, 1983, is reproduced in 22 I.L.M., 1983, 473-520.
[79]Report, 68; *I.L.M.* 502.
[80]Report, 9; *I.L.M.* 477.
[81]See, e.g., Green, "Armed Conflict, War and Self-Defence," 6 Archiv des Völkerrechts 1957, 387.
[82]See, e.g., *Kawasaki Kisen Kabushiki Kaisha of Kobe* v. *Bantham S.S. Co.* [1939] 2 K.B. 544.
[83]See, e.g., *Shneiderman* v. *Metropolitan Casualty Co. of New York* (1961) 220 N.Y.S. 2d 947; *Pan American World Airways Inc.* v. *Aetna Casualty & Surety Co.* (1974) 505 F. 2d 989; *Mitchell* v. *Laird* (1973) 476 F. 2d 533, re the war in Vietnam.
[84]Prisoners of War Convention, 1949, n. 4 above, Art. 118; see also Levie, *Prisoners of War in International Armed Conflict*, 1978, 417-429.
[85]See Martens Clause, n. 12 above.

purpose is to mitigate the horrors of conflict and to the greatest extent possible apply humanitarian principles to both combatants and non-combatants alike. Since Israel is a civilized state—and the appointment and findings of the Kahan Commission emphasise this—its armed forces behave in accordance with these principles. In fact, Israeli military authorities do not hesitate to prosecute and punish their own personnel accused of breaches of the law of armed conflict, particularly in so far as civilians and other non-combatants are concerned.[86] In view of this, there is little doubt that the operations in Lebanon may be measured in accordance with the law of war.

In assessing the liability of any Israeli in respect of the massacres, it must be remembered that the atrocities were committed by Lebanese, either by Phalangists or members of Major Haddad's forces which depend for their existence and their *matèriel* on the Israelis. Neither of these groups is part of the Israeli forces, nor is it under direct Israeli command. However, Israeli forces were in control of the area in which the camps were situated and Phalangist forces were sufficiently under their control for the Chief of Staff at the beginning of the war to have "told the Phalangists that they should refrain from all fighting [and a]fter Israel Defence Forces reached the area under Christian control, the Phalangists commanders suggested that a company of theirs . . . set up a training base . . . [T]he [Israeli] Chief of Staff agreed to this, but made his agreement conditional on the Phalangist forces' exercising restraint and discipline, as the area was Druze. At first, this condition was honored; afterwards there were outbursts of hostilities between the Phalangists and the Druze. . . . The Druze committed some murders, and the Phalangists took revenge; a small I.D.F. force was stationed in the area in order to prevent such actions."[87] Here we have clear evidence that the Israeli military authorities were aware of the possibility of Phalangist misconduct if they were given freedom to act as they wished, together with evidence that the Israelis were able to control such misconduct. Moreover, any one with any appreciation of the situation in Lebanon, of the strains between the P.L.O. and the Phalangists, and with knowledge of previous atrocities and massacres, must have anticipated that a massacre was likely to ensue if the Phalangists were allowed into the P.L.O. areas, especially after the assassination of President Bashir Jemayel. That this was recognized by elements in Israel is indicated in the Kahan Report:[88]

> . . . The Phalangist leaders proposed removing a large portion of the Palestinian refugees from Lebanese soil, whether by methods of persuasion or other means of pressure. They did not conceal their opinion that it would be necessary to resort to acts of violence in order to cause the exodus of many Palestinian refugees from Lebanon. . . . [T]he Mossad[89] . . . maintained close contacts with the Phalangist leadership. In addition, the Intelligence branch of the I.D.F. participated, albeit in a more limited capacity, in the contacts with the Phalangists . . . [B]oth the Mossad and Military Intelligence specifically dealt with drawing up evaluations on the Phalangists, and each one of them was obligated to bring these evaluations to the attention of all interested parties. . . . [T]he battle ethics of the Phalangists, from the standpoint of their attitude to non-combatants, differ greatly from those of the I.D.F. When the war began in June 1982, the prevailing opinion among the Mossad agents who had maintained contacts with the Phalangist leadership was that the atrocities and massacres were a thing of the past, and that the Phalangist forces had reached a stage of political and organizational maturity that would ensure that such actions would not repeat themselves. . . . [However,] there were various facts

[86]*The Times*, 2 Aug. 1982, 18 Feb. 1983; see, for the acquittal of two senior officers charged with having ordered such acts, *ibid.*, 20 Sept. 1983.
[87]Kahan Report, 10; *I.L.M.*, 7.
[88]*Ibid.*, 8, 11-12; *I.L.M.*, 476-7, 478.
[89]Institute for Intelligence and Special Assignments (Israel's "C.I.A.").

that were not compatible with this outlook. During the meetings that the heads of the Mossad held with Bashir Jemayel, they heard things from him that left no room for doubt that the intention of this Phalangist leader was to eliminate the Palestinian problem in Lebanon when he came to power—even if that meant resorting to aberrant methods against the Palestinians in Lebanon. . . . Furthermore, certain actions of the Phalangists during the war indicated that there had been no fundamental change in their attitude toward different segments of the Lebanese population, such as Druze and Palestinians, whom the Phalangists considered enemies. There were reports of Phalangist massacres. . . , as well as the liquidation of Palestinians carried out by the intelligence unit of Elie Hobeika. . . , also, a document which mentions the Phalangist attitude toward terrorists they had taken prisoner. . . . These reports reinforced the feeling among certain people—and especially among experienced intelligence officers—that in the event that the Phalangists had an opportunity to massacre Palestinians, they would take advantage of it.

Despite this knowledge, it was decided that "searching and mopping up the camps will be done by the Phalangist/Lebanese Army." The Chief of Staff testified before the Commission "that the entry of the Phalangists into the refugee camps [at Sabra and Shatila] was agreed upon between the Minister of Defence and himself."[90] It was reported that the Minister had spoken with the Prime Minister, and it was agreed "following the murder of President-elect Bashir Jemayel I.D.F. forces entered West Beirut to prevent possible grave occurrences and to ensure quiet."[91] In fact, the Prime Minister informed the representative of the United States embassy[92]

> that I.D.F. forces had entered West Beirut beginning in the morning hours, that there were no real clashes, that the I.D.F. action was undertaken in order to prevent certain possible events, and that we were concerned that there might be bloodshed even during the night. The Prime Minister also said that the Phalangists were behaving properly [—at this time the Minister of Defence was acutally in Beirut—]; their commander had not been injured in the assassination and was in control of his forces; he is a good man and we trust him not to cause any clashes, but there is no assurance regarding other forces. He added that the primary immediate task was to preserve quiet, for as long as quiet is maintained it will be possible to talk; otherwise there might have been pogroms. . .

At a military briefing held the same day, it was stated[93]

> that the I.D.F.'s entry into West Beirut was perceived as vital not only by the Christians [Phalangists] but also by the Muslims [—the majority of the P.L.O. were Muslims as were the inhabitants of the camps—], who regarded the I.D.F. as the only factor that could prevent bloodshed in the area and protect the Sunni Muslims from the Phalangists. . . . [Nevertheless,] the Deputy Chief of Staff reported his impression of the meeting of Phalangist headquarters in Beirut that day and said that the intention was to send the Phalangists into the refugee camps and afterwards perhaps into the city as well. He added that 'this might create an uproar', because the armed forces in West Beirut that were then quiet might stir up a commotion upon learning that the Phalangists are coming in behind the I.D.F.

In view of statements of this kind it cannot be suggested that the Israeli authorities in Beirut, including the Minister of Defence, did not know of the dangers involved if the

[90]Kahan Report, 13, 14; *I.L.M.* 478, 479.
[91]*Ibid.*, 15; 479.
[92]*Ibid.*, 16; 480.
[93]*Ibid.*, 17; 480.

Phalangists entered the camps. However, the Minister stated "he would send the Phalangists into the refugee camps,"[94] although it would appear that in reporting to the Prime Minister he did not mention this fact:[95]

> the fighting has ended. The refugee camps are surrounded. The firing has stopped. We have not suffered any more casualties. Everything is calm and quiet. . . . All the key points are in our hands. Everything's over.

The Chief of Staff's view is summed up in the words that "there's such a dual kind of situation that they're confused. They're seething with a feeling of revenge, and there might have been rivers of blood there. We won't go into the refugee camps."[96] Following the Minister's decision that the Phalangists could be allowed into the camps, Brigadier Yaron, chief infantry and paratroop officer and in charge of the forward command post, "spoke with the Phalangists about the places where the terrorists were located in the camps and also warned them not to harm the civilian population. He has mentioned that, he stated, because he knew that the Phalangists' norms of conduct are not those of the I.D.F. and he had arguments with the Phalangists over this issue in the past."[97]

It would appear from the above quotations in the Kahan Report that the Minister of Defence and at least some of the officers most directly involved clearly had foreknowledge of the dangers involved in allowing the Phalangists to enter the camps, and regarded themselves as being in supreme command with the Phalangists as much under their orders as their own troops. Thus, in the Defence Minister's Summary of 15 September 1982 it expressly states:[98]

> F. Only one element, and that is The I.D.F. shall command the forces in the area. For the operations in the camps the Phalangists should be sent in.

In view of this, the Israeli commanders and the Minister of Defence who had, with this foreknowledge, authorised the use of the Phalangists—in fact, since the decision to use the Phalangists was of a highly political character, he was the only person, whether with or without the agreement of his fellow ministers, who could give this order—must accept responsibility for the actions of these troops, even if they did not constitute allies in the ordinary sense of this word. If ever there was evidence to satisfy the terms of Protocol I, this is it. Clearly, "they knew, or had information which should have enabled them to conclude in the circumstances at the time, that [their subordinates were] . . . going to commit a breach" if they had the opportunity.

Apart from the issue of foreknowledge, there is also the question of whether the Israeli personnel involved took sufficient preventive or repressive measures once they ascertained what was happening. Although the Israelis set up an observation post to supervise the actions of the Phalangists, it appears that they were unable to see effectively from the post thus established,[99] a failure which in some respects might be compared to Yamashita's failure to ensure that he was able to observe the activities of those under his command. In addition, there was some measure of active cooperation in at least the

[94]*Ibid.*, 18; 480.
[95]*Ibid.*, 18; 481.
[96]*Ibid.*
[97]*Ibid.*, 19; 481.
[98]*Ibid.*
[99]*Ibid.*, 14, 19, 21; 479, 481, 482.

initial activities of the Phalangists in the camps. The latter required illumination and this was provided by the Israelis,[100] originally "by a mortar company, and subsequently also by aircraft; but because the illumination from the planes interfered with the evacuation of casualties of an I.D.F. unit, this source of illumination was halted; mortar illumination continued intermittently throughout the night." At a very early moment in the course of events it became clear to Israeli military personnel, as a result of radio communication that had been overheard, that the massacre had already begun or was about to begin. Despite some reports to the effect that as many as 300 inhabitants of the camps, believed to be women and children as distinct from terrorists, had been killed, there was still an unwillingness on the part of some senior officers to believe the reports that they were receiving, though they were conveyed up the chain of command. Seemingly, some of the senior officers were satisfied with the warnings that they had issued to the Phalangists "not to harm civilians" and with the assurance that "appropriate orders to that effect" would be given. It would seem, however, that no steps were taken to see whether this had in fact been done and whether such orders, if given, were being obeyed. Moreover, despite this hesitancy, there is some evidence to suggest that not only were some senior officers aware of what was happening, but that they had anticipated these occurrences and decided to 'allow' them to occur. Thus, on the night of September 16, that is to say the night the massacre commenced, at a meeting of the Cabinet, the Chief of Staff[101]

> provided details about the I.D.F.'s operation in West Beirut and about his meetings with Phalangist personalities. He said, inter alia, that he had informed the Phalangist commanders that their men would have to take part in the operation and *go in where they were told*, that early that evening they would begin to fight and would enter the extremity of Sabra, that the I.D.F. would ensure that they did not fail in their operation . . . [and that] the Phalangists *would go in there 'with their own methods'*, . . . The Chief of Staff explained that the camps were surrounded 'by us', that the Phalangists would begin to operate that night in the camps, that *we could give them orders* whereas it was impossible to give orders to the Lebanese army, and that I.D.F. would be assisted by the Phalangists and perhaps also the Lebanese Army in collecting weapons. With respect to the consequences of Bashir's assassination, the Chief of Staff said . . . two things could happen. One was that the entire power structure of the Phalangists would collapse. . . . 'A second thing that *will happen*—and it will make no difference whether we are there or not—*is an eruption of revenge*. . . . It will be between all of them, and neither the Americans nor anyone else will be of any help. *We can cut it down*, but today they already killed Druze there . . . and one dead Druze is enough so that tomorrow four Christian children will be killed; . . . and that is how it will begin, if we are not there—it will be an eruption the likes of which has never been seen; I can already see in their eyes what they are waiting for. . . . [T]hey have just one thing left to do, and that is revenge; and it will be terrible . . . [t]he whole establishment is already sharpening knives . . .'

Despite this conviction in the high command that a massacre was inevitable, it was nevertheless stated by the Chief of Staff that the Israel Defence Force would not enter the camps, but that the Phalangists would. Apparently only the Deputy Prime Minister was aware of the possibility that Israel would be blamed for complicity, but his warnings went unheeded.[102]

Even after it became known that the killings had started, the Israeli officers on the spot

---

[100]*Ibid.*, 21; 482.
[101]*Ibid.*, 25-6; 484 (italics added).
[102]*Ibid.*, 27; 484.

did nothing to bring matters to an end, although they suggested that an attempt would be made to ensure that "they will organize in a more orderly manner—we will see to it that they are moved into the area", but all that seems to have happened, at least in the early stages, was that one of the Operations Branch officers at the forward command post replied to the Phalangist request for more illumination that "the Phalangists had killed 300 people and he was not willing to provide them with illumination," although he subsequently "ordered that limited illumination be provided."[103] The Kahan Commission's report makes it clear that reports of large-scale killings were being reiterated and reported back, but at no time does it appear that any effort was made by the officers on the spot or the Minister of Defence or any other person with authority to order Israeli troops to take any steps to bring the situation to an end other than telling the Phalangist commanders to stop where they were and advance no further. Whatever the confusion as between the various military branches involved—and there were many—it is difficult not to conclude that there was at least negligence on the part of the Israeli officers present, in so far as they failed to take such action as was open to them to attempt to control the activities of troops within their area of command or to confirm that their orders were being obeyed. Rather than this, the attitude seems to have been that the Phalangists should "continue action, mopping up the empty camps south of Fakhami until tomorrow at 5:00 A.M., at which time they must stop their action due to American pressure . . ."[104] Moreover, it would appear that no attempt was made to ascertain from the Phalangists whether the rumours of large-scale killings were in fact true or not. While it would appear that officers on the spot had failed in their duty as commanders to ensure that all troops under their command behaved properly and had equally failed to react when told of happenings to the contrary, it is equally clear that the Minister of Defence, who from the beginning had made it clear that he regarded himself as being in overall authority, equally failed to take any positive action when made aware of the situation.[105]

That the Israeli command was aware of its responsibility over the Phalangists is clear from the fact that when it was realised the Phalangists had not vacated the camps a further order to this effect was issued and complied with, but no attempt was made to seek out any of those responsible for what had occurred nor to arrest or otherwise discipline any Phalangist officer who had permitted such action or refused to obey the orders received from the Israelis. Perhaps the relationship of the Israeli command to the situation is best expressed in the comment of Brigadier Yaron, senior infantry and para-troop officer:[106]

> The mistake, as I see it, the mistake is everyone's. The entire system showed insensitivity, I am speaking now of the military system. I am not speaking about the political system. The whole system manifested insensitivity. . . . On this point everyone showed insensitivity, pure and simple. Nothing else. So you start asking me, what exactly did you feel in your gut on Friday . . . I did badly, I cannot, how is it possible that a divisional commander—and I think this applies to the Division Commander and up—how is it possible that a Division Commander is in the field and does not know that 300, 400, 500 or a thousand, I don't know how many, are being murdered there? If he's like that, let him go. How can such a thing be? But why didn't he know? Why was he oblivious? That's why he didn't know and that's why he didn't stop it . . . but I take myself to task . . . I admit here from this rostrum we were all insensitive, that's all.

[103]*Ibid.*, 28; 485.
[104]*Ibid.*, 35; 488.
[105]*Ibid.*, 35-8; 488-9.
[106]*Ibid.*, 47; 493.

Insensitivity and failure to know what was happening within his command as explained by Brigadier Yaron cannot possibly be accepted as excuses by a commander—a fact which the Commission itself recognized when it recommended that he be barred from field command for three years.[107]

While the Commission accepted that there was no direct responsibility on Israel for the atrocities, it went on to say, in words which clearly indicate its awareness of the principle of command responsibility:[108]

> If it indeed becomes clear that those who decided on the entry of the Phalangists into the camps should have foreseen from the information at their disposal and from things which were common knowledge—that there was danger of a massacre, and no steps were taken which might have prevented this danger or at least greatly reduced the possibility that deeds of this type might be done, then *those who made the decisions and those who implemented them are indirectly responsible for what ultimately occurred, even if they did not intend this to happen and merely disregarded the anticipated danger.* A similar indirect responsibility also falls on those who knew of the decision; it was their duty, by virtue of their position and their office, to warn of the danger, and they did not fulfill this duty. *It is also not possible to absolve of such indirect responsibility those persons who, when they received the first reports of what was happening in the camps, did not rush to prevent the continuation* of the Phalangists' actions *and did not do everything within their power to stop them.* . . . It may be that from a legal perspective, the issue of responsibility is not unequivocal, in view of the lack of clarity regarding the status of the State of Israel and its forces in Lebanese territory.[109] If the territory of West Beirut may be viewed at the time of the events as occupied territory—and we do not determine that such indeed is the case from a legal perspective—then it is the duty of the occupier, according to the rules of usual and customary international law,[110] to do all it can to ensure the public's well-being and security. Even if these legal norms are invalid regarding the situation in which the Israeli government and the forces operating at its instructions found themselves at the time of the events, still, as far as the obligations applying to every civilized nation and the ethical rules accepted by civilized peoples go, the problem of indirect responsibility cannot be disregarded . . . [T]he development of ethical norms in the world public requires that *the responsibility be placed not just on the perpetrators, but also on those who could and should have prevented the commission of those deeds* which must be condemned. . . .

Having dealt with the problem of the indirect responsibility of the commanders in this way, it only remains to mention the Commission's view of the liability of the Minister of Defence himself:[111]

> It is true that no clear warning was provided by military intelligence or the Mossad about what might happen if the Phalangist forces entered the camps. . . . But . . . even without such warning it is *impossible to justify the Minister of Defence's disregard of the danger of a massacre.* . . . [There was] the widespread knowledge regarding the Phalangists' combat ethics, their feelings of hatred toward the Palestinians and their leaders' plans for the future of the Palestinians when said leaders

[107]*Ibid.*, 93-6, 106; 512-4, 519.
[108]*Ibid.*, 54-5; 496 (italics added).
[109]See p. 229 above.
[110]Here, the Commission, like the Nuremberg Tribunal, appears to have adopted the view that the Hague Regulations, Section III of which relates to Military Authority over the Territory of the Hostile State, have become part of customary law. See also the IVth (Civilians) Geneva Convention, 1949.
[111]Report, 67-71; 502-3 (italics added).

would assume power. Besides this general knowledge, the Defence Minister also had special reports from his not inconsiderable meetings with the Phalangist heads before Bashir's assassination. . . . In the circumstances that prevailed after Bashir's assassination, *no prophetic powers were required to know that concrete danger of acts of slaughter* existed when the Phalangists were moved to the camps without the I.D.F.'s going with them in that operation and without the I.D.F. being able to maintain effective and ongoing supervision of their actions there. *The sense of such a danger should have been in the consciousness of every knowledgeable person who was close to the subject, and certainly in the consciousness of the Defence Minister, who took an active part in everything relating to the war. His involvement in the war was deep, and the connection with the Phalangists was under his constant care.* If in fact the Defence Minister, when he decided that the Phalangists would enter the camps without the I.D.F. taking part in the operation, did not think that that decision could bring about the very disaster that in fact occurred, the only possible explanation for this is that *he disregarded any apprehensions about what was to be expected* because the advantages to be gained from the Phalangists' entry into the camps distracted him from the proper consideration in this instance.

As a politician responsible for Israel's security affairs, and as a Minister who took an active part in directing the political and military moves in the war in Lebanon, it was the duty of the Defence Minister to take into account all the reasonable considerations for and against having the Phalangists enter the camps, and not to disregard entirely the serious conditions mitigating against such an action, namely that the Phalangists were liable to commit atrocities and that *it was necessary to forestall this possibility as a humanitarian obligation* and also to prevent the political damage it would entail. . . .

[T]he Minister of Defence *made a grave mistake when he ignored the danger of acts of revenge and bloodshed by the Phalangists* against the population in the refugee camps. . . . Regarding [his] responsibility, it is sufficient to assert that he issued no order to the I.D.F. to adopt suitable measures. Similarly, in his meetings with the Phalangist commanders, [he] made no attempt to point out to them the gravity of the danger that their men would commit acts of slaughter . . .

Had it become clear to the Defence Minister that no real supervision could be exercised over the Phalangist force that entered the camps with the I.D.F.'s assent, *his duty would have been to prevent their entry.* The usefulness of the Phalangists' entry into the camps was wholly disproportionate to the damage their entry could cause if it were uncontrolled. . .

. . . It might perhaps be inferred from [the Phalangists'] military organization that their soldiers would heed the orders of their commanders and not break discipline; but at the very least, *care should have been taken that the commanders were imbued with the awareness that no excesses were to be committed and that they give their men unequivocal orders to this effect.* The routine warnings that I.D.F. commanders issued to the Phalangists, which were the same kind as were routinely issued to I.D.F. troops, could not have had any concrete effect. . . . [R]*esponsibility is to be imputed to the Minister of Defence for having disregarded the danger of acts of vengeance and bloodshed* by the Phalangists against the population of the refugee camps, and *having failed to take this danger into account when he decided to have the Phalangists enter the camps.* In addition, *responsibility is to be imputed* to the Minister of Defence *for not ordering appropriate measures for preventing or reducing the danger of massacre as a condition for the Phalangists' entry into the camps.* These blunders constitute *the non-fulfilment of a duty with which the Defence Minister was charged. . .*

The Commission, however, did not consider that the Minister was in any way responsible for not ordering the removal of the Phalangists when he first heard of the killings. They based this decision on the fact that he was told at the same time that the operation had ceased and that the Phalangists had been ordered to withdraw. It might be suggested, though, that since the Minister was clearly in supreme command he might have been expected to make further enquiries for himself and that he showed a similar amount of indifference or negligence as to the realities of the situation as he had shown when deciding to order the Phalangists in.

It is not necessary to consider the findings of the Commission with regard to other individuals, either military or civilian. Nor is it necessary to comment upon the recommendations of the Commission or the manner in which Israeli authorities have carried them out. Any disciplinary or punitive acts against individual members of the Israeli forces as a result of the Report will depend upon Israeli law, and may well follow the internal I.D.F. inquiry which the Commission recommended.[112]

Enough has been said about the camps massacre and sufficient citation made of the Kahan Report to indicate the major contribution it may have made in assessing the nature of command responsibility. Combined with the Yamashita principle and the wording of Articles 86 and 87 of Protocol I, we now have a clear and dogmatic expression of what is understood by command responsibility in so far as it affects not only the military commanders most directly concerned but also any governmental minister who by his office or his actions is assimilated to a military commander.

[112]*Ibid.*, 4; 475. However, the retention of the Minister in the Cabinet, albeit in a different portfolio, and the rehabilitation of some of the censured commanders, raise doubts as to the intentions of the Government of Israel.

XI

The Law of Armed Conflict and the Enforcement of International Criminal Law

It is a well-known fact that, despite the variety of definitions of international criminal law,[1] there is no international means of enforcing that law. The attempt made in the days of the League of Nations to establish an international criminal court was an abysmal failure,[2] and the efforts that have been made since[3] have been equally unsuccessful. However, it cannot be denied that states do exercise a measure of international criminal jurisdiction over offences that may be described as *contra jus gentium* whether by customary law[4] or by convention.[5] In most cases the Convention creating an international crime requires the parties thereto to amend their criminal legal codes to give effect to the

[1]See, e.g., Schwarzenberger, 'The Problem of an International Criminal Law', in Mueller and Wise, *International Criminal Law*, 1965, 3; Ryu and Silving, 'International Criminal Law—A Search for Meaning', in I Bassiouni and Nanda, *A Treatise on International Criminal Law*, 1972, 22; Bassiouni, *International Criminal Law*, 1980, 22; Green, 'Is There an International Criminal Law?' 21 *Alberta Law Rev.*, 1983, 251.

[2]See, e.g., Convention for the Prevention and Punishment of Terrorism, 1937, 7 Hudson, *International Legislation* 863; Statute for an International Criminal Court, 1937, *Ibid.*, 879.

[3]See, e.g., Green, "New Trends in International Criminal Law," 11 *Israel Yearbook on Human Rights*, 1981, 9. For a general history of efforts to establish an international criminal law, see Ferencz, *An International Criminal Court*, 1980.

[4]See, e.g., opinion of Judicial Committee of Privy Council in *Re Piracy Jure Gentium* [1934] A.C. 586, which should be compared with the decision of Sir Wm. Scott in *The Le Louis* (1817) 2 Dods. 210, 165 Eng. Rep. 1464. See also Canadian Criminal Code, s. 75(1): "every one commits piracy who does an act which by the law of nations is piracy."See also Geneva Convention on the High Seas, 1958, 450 UNTS 82, Art. 15, and U.N. Convention on the Law of the Sea, 1982, 21 *I.L.M.* 1261, Art. 101.

[5]See, e.g., Genocide Convention, 1948, 78 *UNTS* 277, (Schindler/Toman, 171) Art. I: "The Contracting Parties confirm that genocide . . . is a crime under international law which they undertake to prevent and punish."

provisions of the Convention[6] and then leaves the process of enforcement to the local judicial process.[7] It rests, therefore, with the national authorities whether they are willing to bring their criminal legal regulations into line with their international obligations. Further, the decision whether to prosecute in any case will depend upon a political decision made by the minister in charge of criminal prosecutions. Taking the Genocide Convention as an example, it must be conceded that this offence is not one likely to be perpetrated as a matter of private enterprise. It requires the instigation, connivance, collusion or acquiescence of state authority and, so long as the prosecution is to be instituted in accordance with the criminal law of the territory in which it has occurred, there is little chance of, for example, the President instructing the Chief Justice to institute proceedings against the Commander in Chief or the Chief of Police. Recent events in Latin America and elsewhere would seem to confirm this.[8] It is only in the event of genocide being committed in occupied territory that the accused is likely to be amenable to a foreign jurisdiction, and in such circumstances it is likely that the law of armed conflict will apply.

It is probably true to assume that in the eyes of the general public the most grievous international crime is war. And this view has received support in judicial practice in so far as aggressive war is concerned. Thus, the International Military Tribunal at Nuremberg was instructed by its constitutent instrument[9] to condemn as crimes against peace the "planning, preparation, initiation or waging of a war of aggression, or a war in violation of international treaties, agreements or assurances, or participation in a common plan or conspiracy for the accomplishment of any of the foregoing." On the authority of this instruction, the Tribunal stated[10] that "war is essentially an evil thing. Its consequences are not confined to the belligerent State alone, but affect the whole world. To initiate a war of aggression, therefore, is not only an international crime; *it is the supreme international crime* differing only from other war crimes in that it contains within itself the accumulated evil of the whole." This view of the criminality of an act of aggression was adopted by the General Assembly of the United Nations by consensus[11] in its Resolution defining aggression:[12] "A war of aggression is a crime against international peace. Aggression gives rise to international responsibility. [Moreover, n]o consideration of whatever nature, whether political, economic, military or otherwise, may serve as a justification for aggression." Despite this latter protestation, the Resolution affirms[13] that nothing in the definition of aggression can "in any way prejudice the right to self-determination, freedom

---

[6]Art. V: "The Contracting Parties undertake to enact, in accordance with their respective Constitutions, the necessary legislation to give effect to the provisions of the present Convention and, in particular, to provide effective penalties for persons guilty of genocide . . ."

[7]Art. VI: "Persons charged with genocide . . . shall be tried by a competent tribunal of the State in the territory of which the act was committed, or by such international penal tribunal as may have jurisdiction with respect to those Contracting Parties which shall have accepted its jurisdiction."

[8]See, e.g., Kuper, *International Action Against Genocide*, 1982, published by the Minority Rights Group, London.

[9]Charter of the International Military Tribunal, Art. 6(a), annexed to Agreement for the Prosecution and Punishment of the Major War Criminals of the European Axis, 1945, 82 *UNTS* 280, Schindler/Toman, 823.

[10]*Judgment*, U.K., Cmd. 6964 (1946), 13; 41 *Am. J. Intl. Law*, 1947, 172, 186 (italics added).

[11]To proceed by consensus has become common practice in the General Assembly and other international bodies, especially when it is believed that unanimity is unlikely to be achieved. The procedure enables states to avoid committing themselves. See, e.g., Kaufmann, *United Nations Decision Making*, 1980, 129-31; Moskowitz, *The Roots and Reaches of United Nations Actions and Decisions*, 1980, 195-7.

[12]Res. 3314 (XXIX); the text of the draft definition which was adopted by the Assembly without amendment is reprinted in 13 *I.L.M.* 1974, 712.

[13]Art. 5.

and independence, as derived from the Charter, of peoples forcibly deprived of that right and referred to in the Declaration on Principles of International Law concerning Friendly Relations and Cooperation among States in accordance with the Charter of the United Nations,[14] particularly peoples under colonial and racist regimes or other forms of alien domination; nor the right of these peoples to struggle to that end and to seek and receive support,[15] in accordance with the principles of the Charter[16] and in conformity with the above-mentioned Declaration."

While international bodies might have reserved their condemnation as criminal for wars of aggression, the general public, particularly in view of the risk that any major international conflict is likely to be waged with nuclear weapons, tend to condemn any war as criminal. Even if this be so, one cannot overlook the fact that if a conflict arises there is a whole panoply of law, both customary and conventional,[17] which regulates its conduct and specifies what may or what may not be done when war occurs. Moreover, it has even been suggested that it is in time of conflict that the law with regard to human rights becomes most real and effective.[18] What is more, from feudal times on states, including those not involved in a particular conflict, have taken upon themselves the right to try and to punish those individuals involved in the conflict who have conducted themselves in a manner considered to be in breach of accepted methods of behaviour.[19] By the time of Elizabeth I the existence of a law of war and the criminality of breaches thereof were so well established that Shakespeare has the Welsh captain Fluellen say in *Henry V* "Kill the poys and the luggage! 'tis expressly against the law of arms: 'tis as arrant a piece of knavery . . . as can be offer'd."[20] In fact, Henry regarded this act as such an atrocity that he ordered the slaughter of all his prisoners.

In so far as the written law of war is concerned, nothing appeared concerning the trial of individual offenders save in national military codes. Thus, by the time of the establishment of the Commonwealth England had promulgated its Lawes and Ordinances of Warre[21] regulating the behaviour of the armed forces, forbidding, among other things, marauding of the countryside, individual acts against the enemy without authorization from a superior, private taking of booty, or private detention of an enemy prisoner. On the other hand, as early as [?] 1360 Legnano had enquired in his *De Bello de Represaliis et de Duello*[22] "whether a soldier should be punished with death, who bravely charges the enemy with his company and utterly routs them, contrary to the commands of the general?" In a fifteenth century manuscript we read "a dialogue between a pursuivant and his instructor, an old herald. 'How shall I learn about the law of arms?' asks the pursuivant. 'I tell you,' says his master, 'that you will find it in a book called the *Tree of Battles*, and for this reason, you must get a clerk's learning; and you should also follow the wars, for there you will hear of the judgements that are delivered from time to time, which are not all mentioned in the *Tree of Battles*.' "[23] Through the sixteenth to eighteenth

---

[14]Res. 2625 (XXV) Annex, 9 *I.L.M.* 1970, 1292.

[15]By Art. 3(g) aggression includes "the sending by or on behalf of a State of armed bands, groups, irregulars or mercenaries, which carry out acts of armed force against another State of such gravity as to amount to the acts" defined as aggression in the text.

[16]In fact, there is nothing in Art. 2 of the Charter, which sets out the principles, that directly relates to self-determination or to condemnation of "colonial and racist regimes."

[17]For a collection of most of these conventions see Schindler/Toman.

[18]See, e.g., "Human Rights and the Law of Armed Conflict," ch. V *supra*.

[19]See Keen, *The Laws of War in the Late Middle Ages*, 1965, 34, 192-7.

[20]Act IV, Scene 7, I. 1 (this statement is based on Holinshed's *Chronicles*).

[21]Clode, 1 *Military Forces of the Crown*, 1869, App. VI.

[22]Carnegie tr. by Brierly, 253 (ch. xxx).

[23]Keen, *op. cit.*, n. 19 above, 21, who states that the *Tree of Battles* was written by Honoré Bonet, and is to be found in numerous heraldic MSS. of the fifteenth century (n. 1).

centuries we have a series of 'classical' writings on the law of war[24] which enunciate what is lawful and what is not in times of conflict. This law is expressive of the common practice of the armies of Europe and became so generally accepted that by the time of the outbreak of the American Civil War Professor Lieber of Columbia College, New York, was able to prepare a code based on accepted practices, and this was promulgated by President Lincoln as Instructions for the Government of Armies of the United States in the Field.[25] Here we find clear reference to personal liability on the part of those who breach at least some portions of the law of armed conflict. Thus,[26] "The law of war does not only disclaim all cruelty and bad faith concerning engagements concluded with the enemy during the war, but also the breaking of stipulations solemnly contracted by the belligerents in time of peace, and avowedly intended to remain in force in case of war between the contracting powers. It disclaims all extortions and other transactions for individual gain; all acts of private revenge, or connivance at such acts. Offenses to the contrary shall be severely punished, and especially so if committed by officers. . . . All wanton violence committed against persons in the invaded country, all destruction of property not commanded by the authorized officer, all robbery, all pillage or sacking, even after taking a place by main force, all rape, wounding, maiming, or killing of such inhabitants, are prohibited under the penalty of death, or such other severe punishment as may seem adequate for the gravity of the offence. A soldier, officer or private, in the act of committing such violence, and disobeying a superior ordering him to abstain from it, may be lawfully killed on the spot by such superior. . . . Crimes punishable by all penal codes, such as arson, murder, maiming, assaults, highway robbery, theft, burglary, fraud, forgery, and rape, if committed by an American soldier in an hostile country against its inhabitants, are not only punishable as at home, but in all cases in which death is not inflicted, the severer punishment shall be preferred. . . . Whoever intentionally inflicts additional wounds on an enemy already wholly disabled, or kills such an enemy, or who orders or encourages soldiers to do so, shall suffer death, if duly convicted, whether he belongs to the Army of the United States, *or is an enemy captured after having committed his misdeed.*" In so far as the violators of these Instructions were members of the United States forces no problem of jurisdiction could arise, since such persons remain at all times subject to their national law as may be seen from the trial of *Wirz*[27] or more recently of *Calley*.[28] In the case of a captured enemy, however, jurisdiction must be based on authority derived from international law and this source is clearly referred to in the Lieber Code:[29] "There exists no law or body of authoritative rules of action between hostile armies, except that branch of the law of nature and of nations which is called the law and usages of war on land. All municipal law of the ground on which the armies stand, or of the countries to which they belong, is silent and of no effect between armies in the field."

While the Lieber Code formed the basis of the Brussels Project of an International Declaration concerning the Laws and Customs of War,[30] the Oxford Manual of the Laws of War on Land adopted by the Institute of International Law,[31] and Hague Convention II with respect to the Laws and Customs of War on Land as amended as Convention IV

---

[24]E.g., Belli, 1563; Ayala, 1582; Gentili, 1612; Grotius, 1625; *etc.*
[25]General Orders No. 100, 1863, Schindler/Toman, 3.
[26]E.g., Arts. 11, 44, 47, 71 (italics added).
[27]*U.S.* v. *Wirz* (1865) H. R. Exec. Doc. No. 23, 40th Cong., 2nd Sess., 1867-8, vol. 8.
[28]*U.S.* v. *Calley* (1971: 1973) CM 426402, 46 *C.M.R.* 1131; 48 C.M.R. 19; 1 *M.L.R.* 2488.
[29]Arts. 40, 41.
[30]1874, Schindler/Toman, 25.
[31]1880, *Ibid.*, 35.

of 1907,[32] none of them specifies individual liability for breaches of the laws and regulations that they enunciate. The only punitive provision that we have is to be found in Article 3 of Hague Convention IV of 1907:[33] "A belligerent party which violates the provisions of the said Regulations [respecting the Laws and Customs of War on Land appended to the Convention] shall, if the case demands, be liable to pay compensation. It shall be responsible for all acts committed by persons forming part of its armed forces."

Despite this failure to provide for the prosecution of individuals who may have broken particular rules of the law of armed conflict, belligerents have not hesitated to try members of the enemy forces or their auxiliaries for alleged breaches of that law. This is not the place to discuss whether a particular trial has been justified or not, but merely to indicate that belligerents have claimed the right to try alleged lawbreakers not possessing their own nationality for such offences. Thus, in July 1916 the German authorities executed a British merchant navy officer, Captain Fryatt, for having, while in command of an unarmed merchant vessel, refused to obey the summons of a German U-boat to surrender and having, instead, unsuccessfully tried to ram it. Acting on the principle that persons not entitled to combatant status have no legal right to participate in hostilities,[34] the Germans executed Fryatt for "a franc-tireur crime against the sea forces of Germany."[35] Similarly, medical personnel who are entitled to immunity because of their medical status lose that status and protection if they indulge in activities related to the war which are outside the scope of their function as medical personnel. In 1915 the Germans executed Edith Cavell, a British nurse, who had pleaded guilty to harbouring, in the hospital of which she was matron, British, French and Belgian soldiers, supplying them with money and clothes and helping them to escape, contending that it was her duty to enable her countrymen to escape from Belgium, where they were liable to be shot. However lofty or patriotic such actions might have been, they could hardly be considered as falling within the scope of proper medical activities.[36] While she was not charged with a war crime under the international law of war, she was tried for an offence against Article 58

---

[32]1899, 1907, *Ibid.*, 57.

[33]*Ibid.*, 65.

[34]See, e.g., 1st ed. of Oppenheim, *International Law*, vol. 2, 'War and Neutrality', 1906, s. 254: "Since International Law is a law between States only and exclusively, no rules of International Law can exist which prohibit private individuals [—and this means all persons not in the armed forces—] from taking up arms and committing hostilities against the enemy. But private individuals committing such acts do not enjoy the privileged treatment of members of armed forces, and the enemy has according to a customary rule of International Law the right to consider and punish such individuals as war criminals. Hostilities in arms [—and this would include such acts as ramming a submarine—] committed by private individuals are . . . [acts which] the enemy has the right to consider and punish as acts of illegitimate warfare. . . ." This comment is repeated verbatim in all later editions of Oppenheim up to and including the 5th, the first edited by Lauterpacht. In the 6th and 7th, also edited by Lauterpacht, this is abbreviated to "Private individuals who take up arms and commit hostilities against the enemy do not enjoy the privileges of armed forces, and the enemy has, according to a customary rule of International Law, the right to treat such individuals as war criminals."

[35]For allied criticism of the action against Captain Fryatt, see I Garner, *International Law and the World War*, 1920, 407-14, and 3rd (Roxburgh) ed. of Oppenheim, which describes the execution as "nothing less than judicial murder," vol. 2, 258, a description which has been maintained in every edition of Oppenheim, see 7th (Lauterpacht) ed., 1952, 574.

[36]Her execution was condemned in highly emotional language by Garner, vol. 2, 104-5, and she is regarded as a great Allied patriot who suffered judicial murder. It is interesting to note that none of the commentators mentions her abuses of her medical status. Roxburgh, *op. cit.*, 347, n. 2, says that "even if . . . the charge was proved, so that the sentence might perhaps have been justified according to the letter of the law, the execution was an outrage, especially as the victim was a woman who had with equal devotion nursed German as well as French and English wounded"—but this is a duty of medical personnel in time of war. All Lauterpacht says in the 7th ed., is "see Garner, ii, ss, 382-386." See, also, 'War Law and the Medical Profession', ch. VI *supra*.

of the German Military Penal Code with war treason[37] in that "with the object of helping a hostile power, or prejudicing the German or allied troops" she guided soldiers to the enemy.

In the Treaty of Versailles[38] we find the first attempt to establish an international tribunal to try offences against the law of armed conflict. By Article 227 of the Treaty provision was made for the trial of the former Emperor of Germany by a special tribunal to be established by the Allied and Associated Powers, "for a supreme offence against international morality and the sanctity of treaties, . . . In its decision the tribunal will be guided by the highest motives of international policy, with a view to vindicating the solemn obligations of international undertakings and the validity of international morality. It will be its duty to fix the punishment which it considers should be imposed." It is interesting to note that no attempt was made to allege that William II had broken any of the laws of armed conflict, nor was it intimated that the tribunal would operate within the framework of international law. Although the Article provided for a request for the ex-Kaiser's surrender by The Netherlands, to which he had fled, that country refused to surrender him.

Article 228 provides for trial of German personnel by either Allied or German tribunals, with the former taking precedence and without regard for the principle *non bis in idem*: "The German Government recognizes the right of the Allied and Associated Powers to bring before military tribunals persons accused of having committed acts in violation of the laws and customs of war. Such persons shall, if found guilty, be sentenced to punishments laid down by law. This provision will apply notwithstanding any proceedings or prosecution before a tribunal in Germany or in the territory of her allies. The German Government shall hand over to the Allied and Associated Powers, or to such one of them as shall so request, all persons accused of having committed an act in violation of the laws and customs of war, who are specified by name or by the rank, office or employment which they held under the German authorities," and Article 229 provided that "persons guilty of criminal acts against the nationals of one of the Allied and Associated Powers will be brought before the military tribunals of that power." In fact, the German authorities refused to hand any such person over, but they did institute a series of trials before the German Supreme Court,[39] of which the most famous is probably that relating to the *Llandovery Castle*[40] which has largely formed the basis for the modern doctrine of superior orders. It is true that the accused were charged in all instances with offences against the German Military Penal Code. But it is clear from, for example, the *Llandovery Castle* decision that the German Supreme Court was aware that it was dealing with acts which constituted offences against the law of war:[41] "The firing on the boats was an offence against the law of nations. . . . [I]n war at sea the killing of shipwrecked people, who have taken refuge in lifeboats, is forbidden. . . . Any violation of the law of nations in warfare is . . . a punishable offence, so far as, in general, a penalty is attached to the

---

[37]In his 2nd ed., 1912, Oppenheim states that a belligerent has the right to try enemy personnel, 'whether soldiers or not', who commit acts of war treason, and among the examples of such 'treason' he includes "(6) Liberation of enemy prisoners of war," S. 255, and in refering to this Lauterpacht makes his Cavell/Garner reference, n. 36 above.

[38]1919, 112 B.F.S.P. 1, 13 *Am. J. Intl. Law*, 1919, Supp.

[39]Summaries of these trials are reproduced in 2 *Ann. Dig.*, but the full texts of the judgments in the *Dover Castle* and the *Llandovery Castle* are reproduced in Cameron, *The Peleus Trial*, 1948, App. X, IX, resp., and of the *Müller* case in Schwarzenberger, *International Law and Totalitarian Lawlessness*, 1943, 113. See also Mullins, *The Leipzig Trials*, 1921.

[40]2 *Ann. Dig.* 437.

[41]*Ibid.*, 437-8; Schwarzenberger, *op. cit.*, 144.

deed. The killing of enemies in war is in accordance with the will of the State that makes war . . . , only in so far as such killing is in accordance with the conditions and limitations imposed by the Law of Nations. The fact that his deed is a violation of international law must be well-known to the doer. . . . The rule of international law, which is here involved, is simple and is universally known.''

There is no guarantee that in any war it is only one belligerent or alliance of belligerents—the defeated—that will be responsible for the commission of war crimes.[42] There is however no provision in the Treaty of Versailles imposing an obligation upon any Allied or Associated Power to bring members of its own forces to trial for committing breaches of the law of war. While it is clear that almost every breach of the law of war would also constitute a breach of national military or criminal law, this lacuna meant that it was completely within the discretion of such Power to decide the extent to which it would proceed against its own personnel for war crimes.

Even though the Leipzig Trials had made it clear that the written international law of armed conflict was inadequate in so far as the wounded and sick and medical transports and personnel[43] or prisoners of war[44] were concerned, there is little effort in the Geneva Conventions of 1929 to deal with this problem. The Convention for the Amelioration of the Condition of the Wounded and Sick in Armies in the Field[45] provides that "the Governments of the High Contracting Parties shall propose to their legislatures should their penal laws be inadequate, the necessary measures for the repression in war of any act contrary to the provisions of the present Convention. They shall communicate to one another . . . the provisions relative to such repression. . . . On the request of a belligerent, an enquiry shall be instituted, in a manner to be decided between the interested parties, concerning any alleged violation of the Convention: when such violation has been established the belligerents shall put an end to and repress it as promptly as possible." There is no indication of what action is to be taken against a High Contracting Party which fails to enact such legislation, nor does the Convention indicate the sort of punitive measures, if any, which are envisaged as part of the process of 'repressing' violations. In so far as the Convention relative to the Treatment of Prisoners of War[46] is concerned, there is no mention of the possibility of breaches or the requirement for their repression. All that is provided[47] is that "the provisions of the present Convention shall be respected by the High Contracting Parties in all circumstances . . . [and they] shall communicate to each other . . . such laws and regulations as they may adopt to ensure the application of the present Convention."

---

[42]It is interesting in this connection to note the statements in the text *International Law*, published by the Academy of Sciences of the U.S.S.R. Institute of State and Law in 196? as 'A textbook for Use in Law Schools' and edited by Kozhevnikov. In the chapter on the Laws and Customs of War, which he wrote, it states: "Imperialist States . . . frequently violate the laws and customs of war and ignore the undertakings which they have given under the terms of international treaties. The history of modern war demonstrates that imperialist aggression is customarily accompanied by the gross violation of all the universally recognized laws and customs of war and of the most elementary principles of humanity. . . . The founders of Marxism-Leninism vigorously opposed the infringement of the elementary principles of humanity by aggressors. . . . It should be emphasised that even before the emergence of the socialist State, the behaviour of [imperial] Russian troops in all the wars that the Russian people had to wage in defence of their independence and honour was marked by the strict observance of the laws and customs of war and the principles of humanity. . . . The Soviet Union's unswerving observance of the laws and customs of war during the Great Patriotic War was a vivid demonstration of socialist humanism. . ." 415-8.
[43]Both the *Dover Castle* and the *Llandovery Castle*, n. 39 above, dealt with the sinking of hospital ships.
[44]The *Müller* case, n. 39 above, concerned the ill-treatment of prisoners of war.
[45]118 *LNTS* 303, Schindler/Toman, 257, Arts. 29, 30.
[46]118 *LNTS* 343, *Ibid.*, 271.
[47]Arts. 83, 85.

When it became known during the Second World War[48] that mass atrocities of a variety
of kinds were being perpetrated in German–occupied Europe, the United Nations[49] issued
the Moscow Declaration[50]: . . . The three Allied Powers [United Kingdom, Soviet Union
and United States], speaking in the interest of the 32 United Nations, hereby solemnly
declare and give full warning of their declaration as follows—At the time of the granting
of any armistice to any Government which may be set up in Germany, those German
officers and men and members of the Nazi Party who have been responsible for or have
taken a consenting part in . . . atrocities, massacres and executions will be sent back to
the countries in which their abominable deeds were done in order that they may be
judged and punished according to the laws of these liberated countries and of the Free
Governments which will be erected therein. Lists will be compiled in all possible detail
from all these countries. . . . These Germans who take part [in such acts] . . . know that
they will be brought back to the scene of their crimes and judged on the spot by the
peoples they have outraged. Let those who have hitherto not imbrued their hands with
innocent blood beware lest they join the ranks of the guilty, for most assuredly the three
Allied Powers will pursue them to the ends of the earth[51] and will deliver them to the
accusers in order that justice may be done.[52] The above declaration is without prejudice
to the case of the major criminals whose offences have no particular geographical location
and who will be punished by a joint decision of the Governments of the Allies." Although
the Declaration indicated that trials would take place in accordance with "the laws of the
liberated countries and of the Free Governments which will be erected therein", many
of the trials that did take place referred not only, and in some cases not even, to such
law, but also clearly indicated that charges were being brought in respect of breaches of
the law of war.[53]

In regards to the warning issued to "the major criminals whose offences have no
particular geographical location", the leading members of the Alliance gave substance
to their threat by the London Charter establishing the International Military Tribunal at
Nuremberg.[54] This not only provided for the trial of named individuals, but set out the
charges on which they could be tried and for the first time in modern history[55] set up an
international tribunal possessing criminal jurisdiction over persons who did not possess

[48]See, e.g., Statement by Foreign Secretary Eden, 17 Dec. 1942, Hansard, *Commons*, vol. 385, cols.
2082-4; see, also the Collective Notes (Punishment for War Crimes, No. 2) presented to the Governments of the U.K., U.S.S.R., and U.S.A., 21 Jul. 1942, published by H.M.S.O.
[49]This was the name of the wartime alliance against the Axis Powers.
[50]1 Nov. 1943, U.K., H.M.S.O., *The History of the United Nations War Crimes Commission and the
Development of the Laws of War*, 1948, 107-8. See, also, the Inter-Allied Declaration on Punishment
for War Crimes, of 13 Jan. 1942, published by H.M.S.O.
[51]In fact, it did not take very long before the western Powers stopped their search for and return
of alleged war criminals.
[52]Recently, the United States has removed the naturalization or immigrant status of some former
Nazis who had entered the United States without disclosing their membership of the Party, and has
returned such persons to stand trial in the German Federal Republic, see, e.g., *U.S.* v. *Walus* (1978)
453 F. Supp. 699, *U.S.* v. *Federenko* (1979) 597 F. 2d 246. See also Canadian case of *Federal Republic
of Germany* v. *Rauca* (1982) 38 O.R. (2d) 705 (1983) 41 O.R. 2d 225; but see, "Canadian Law and the
Punishment of War Criminals," ch. XII, *infra*.
[53]For a collection of war crimes trials in a variety of jurisdictions, see the 15 volumes of *Law Reports
of Trials of War Criminals* published by H.M.S.O. for the United Nations War Crimes Commission,
1947-9. Later cases may be found in various volumes of the *Annual Digest* and the *International Law
Reports*. See, also, *Eichmann* v. *Attorney-General of the Government of Israel* (1962) 36 I.L.R., 5-342; see
also Green, "Legal Issues of the Eichmann Trial," 37 *Tulane Law Rev.*, 1963, 98.
[54]See n. 9 above. Similar provisions were made with regard to the Major War Criminals in the Far
East Theatre.
[55]See, however, Schwarzenberger, *International Law*, vol. 2, "The law of Armed Conflict," 1968,
ch. 39, for an account of the trial at Breisach of Peter von Hagenbach by a tribunal of 28 judges
drawn from the towns of the Hanseatic League.

the nationality of their judges, whose crimes were for the main part not committed in the territories of which those judges were nationals, and whose victims possessed a variety of nationalities covering the entire gamut of the United Nations. Apart from the specially created offences like waging aggressive war, or conspiring so to do, in breach of existing treaties, the jurisdiction of the Tribunal was directed against war crimes, "namely, violations of the laws and customs of war" and "crimes against humanity." At first sight, the latter appears to be a newly created field of international criminal law. However, the Charter provided[56] that such crimes had to be "in execution of or in connection with any crime within the jurisdiction of the Tribunal," thus making them dependent upon the crime against peace or war crimes as that term is normally understood. This has led some commentators to suggest that in fact the concept of crimes against humanity as outlined by the Charter and applied by the Tribunal[57] has in fact added nothing to the development of international criminal law or the law of armed conflict.[58]

Perhaps from the point of view of non-Conventional international criminal law in the field of armed conflict the statement of the Nuremberg Tribunal regarding Hague Convention IV is of most significance. One of the difficulties with regard to this Convention in both World Wars was that it possessed a 'general participation' clause. By Article 2: "The provisions contained in the regulations (Rules of Land Warfare) . . . as well as in the present Convention do not apply except between contracting powers, and then only if all the belligerents are parties to the Convention." This 'general participation' clause was common to the 1907 Conventions and had been considered by the Judicial Committee of the Privy Council in *The Blonde*[59] in relation to Hague Convention VI governing the Conversion of Merchant Ships into War-Ships.[60] Without actually deciding the point, the Board used language which raised extreme doubt whether non-ratification by states which possessed no ships or harbours and which, therefore, did not make or suffer captures could render the mutuality upon which the Convention rested ineffective, so as to destroy its application.[61] The Nuremberg Tribunal was far more direct and specific:[62] "The rules of land warfare expressed in the Convention undoubtedly represented an advance over existing international law at the time of their adoption. But the Convention expressly stated that it was an attempt 'to revise the general laws and customs of war', which it thus recognized to be then existing, but by 1939 these rules laid down in the Convention were recognized by all civilized nations, and were regarded as being declaratory of the laws and customs of war which are referred to in Article 6(b) of the Charter" defining war crimes.

This interpretation of what may now be regarded as customary rules of armed conflict is of significance in estimating the long-term contribution of the Nuremberg Judgment to the development of the potential enforceability of international criminal law in relation to the law of armed conflict. In December 1946 the General Assembly of the United Nations adopted a Resolution[63] affirming the Principles of International Law recognized by the Charter of the Nuremberg Tribunal. The Resolution did not, however, indicate

---

[56]Art. 6(c).
[57]*Op. cit.*, n. 10 above, 65 249, resp.
[58]See Schwelb, "Crimes Against Humanity," 23 *Brit. Y.B. Intl. Law*, 1946, 178, 205-12.
[59][1922] 1 A.C. 313.
[60]1907, Schindler/Toman, 703.
[61]At 324-6.
[62]*Op. cit.*, n. 10 above, 65, 248-9, resp. See also *Tokyo Judgment* (Intl. Mil. Trib. for Far East) (1948) 13 *Ann. Dig.* 356, 365-6.
[63]Res. 95 (I), Schindler/Toman, 833.

what these Principles were, but directed the International Law Commission to formulate them "in the context of a general codification of offences against the peace and security of mankind." While it has not since been possible to draft this general code, the Commission was able to formulate the Principles of International Law recognized in the Charter of the Nuremberg Tribunal and in the Judgment of the Tribunal.[64] Accepting that crimes against peace, war crimes and crimes against humanity are "punishable as crimes under international law [and that] complicity in the commission of [any such] crime . . . is a crime under international law,"[65] the Commission set out five basic Principles: "Any person who commits . . . a crime under international law is responsible therefor and liable to punishment. The fact that internal law does not impose a penalty for an act which constitutes a crime under international law does not relieve the person who committed the act from responsibility under international law. The fact that a person who committed an act which constitutes a crime under international law acted as Head of State or responsible Government official does not relieve him from responsibility under international law. The fact that a person acted pursuant to order of his Government[66] or of a superior[67] does not relieve him from responsibility under international law, provided a moral choice was in fact possible to him.[68] Any person charged with a crime under international law has the right to a fair trial on the facts and law."

In regard to the problem of criminality under international law, the relevant Principle has little substance in the absence of an international criminal court, or recognition of the existence of universal jurisdiction over such offences enabling any country in which the accused might find himself to try and punish him for his international crime. As to the Head of State, enunciation of his personal liability is essential in view of the traditional immunity which international law confers upon him exempting him from both the civil and criminal jurisdiction of any foreign state.

While the Nuremberg Tribunal was established to try specifically named individuals and having done so became *functus officio*, other tribunals exercising jurisdiction over war criminals have applied the findings of that Tribunal as if they constituted a precedent,[69] without making any reference to the Principles of the Charter or the Judgment as declared by the General Assembly or the International Law Commission. Thus the Tokyo Tribunal[70] and a variety of war crimes tribunals in Europe[71] did not hesitate to apply the law as laid down by the Nuremberg Tribunal, while Control Council Law No. 10[72] made the Judgment *res judicata* and of binding authority for the Occupation courts in Germany.[73] More-

[64]Y.B.I.L.C., 1950, Vol. II, 374, Schindler/Toman, 835.
[65]Principles VI, VII.
[66]See *The State* v. *Director of Prisons, ex p. Schumann* (1966) 39 I.L.R. 433, extradition case decided by Ghana Court of Appeal.
[67]See, e.g., Dinstein, *The Defence of 'Obedience to Superior Orders' in International Law*, 1965; Green, *Superior Orders in National and International Law*, 1976; Keijzer, *Military Obedience*, 1978.
[68]Neither the Nuremberg Charter (Art. 8) nor the Tribunal (Judgment, *op. cit.*, n. 10 above, 83, 92, 118, and 271-2, 283, 316, resp.) refers to the question of choice; both accept that obedience to orders may be taken into consideration by way of mitigation.
[69]See, e.g., Kelsen, "Will the Judgment in the Nuremberg Trial Constitute a Precedent in International Law?" 1 I.L.Q., 1947, 153.
[70](1948) Intl. Mil. Trib. for the Far East, 15 *Ann. Dig.* 356, 362-3.
[71]*Re Roechling* (1948) General Trib. of Mil. Govt. for French Zone, *Ibid.*, 398, 405; *Re Garbe* (1947) Oberlandsgericht, Kiel, *Ibid.*, 419, 420; *Re Ahlbrecht* (No. 2) (1948) Netherlands, Special Crim. Ct., Arnhem, 16 *ibid.*, 396, etc.
[72]20 Dec. 1945, XV Dept. of State, *Bulletin* No. 384, 10 Nov.1946, 862; the text is summarised in 11 Whiteman, *Digest of International Law* 895, and reproduced in full in Taylor, *Nuremberg Trials: War Crimes and International Law*, International Conciliation pamphlet No. 450, Apr. 1949, 358.
[73]See, e.g., *Re Von Leeb* (German High Command Trial) (1948) U.S. Mil. Trib., Nuremberg, 13 *Ann. Dig.* 376, 377.

over, the Nuremberg Judgment and the Nuremberg Principles were quoted and consciously applied by both the District Court and the Supreme Court of Israel in the *Eichmann* case.[74]

After the series of war crimes trials consequent upon the conclusion of the Second World War, the first opportunity to test whether states would in fact enforce the principles of international criminal law relevant to armed conflict came in relation to the Korean War. While we have no published report of either side in that conflict trying any member of its enemy's forces for war crimes, we do have reports of courts martial held by the United States authorities charging American personnel with offences which, had they been committed by enemy personnel, would have been classified as war crimes.[75] Similar trials of United States personnel by United States courts martial took place in connection with activities by such personnel in Vietnam, of which the most notorious is that of *Calley*.[76] In these cases it is unnecessary to charge war crimes since jurisdiction already exists under the individual's national law, a fact which was demonstrated by an English court martial at the end of World War II when a member of the Royal Army Medical Corps was tried for ill-treating German prisoners.[77] Similarly, Israeli personnel have been tried for offences against Arab individuals which could as easily be described as war crimes.[78]

An attempt to carry offences against the law of armed conflict into the realm of international criminal law by way of convention may be seen in the Geneva Conventions of 1949.[79] The parties to each of these "undertake to enact any legislation necessary to provide effective penal sanctions for persons committing, or ordering to be committed, any of the grave breaches [defined in the Convention, and places itself] under the obligation to search for persons alleged to have committed, or to have ordered to be committed, such grave breaches, and shall bring such persons, regardless of their nationality, before its own courts. It may also, if it prefers, and in accordance with the provisions of its own legislation, hand such persons over for trial to another High Contracting Party concerned, provided such High Contracting Party has made out a *prima facie* case. [Moreover, e]ach High Contracting Party shall take measures necessary for the suppression of all acts contrary to the provisions of the present Convention other than grave breaches. . . ."[80] The Conventions then proceed to specify the 'grave breaches' to which these undertakings refer, and these may be considered as being paraphrases of the war crimes and crimes against humanity detailed in the Nuremberg Charter, but amended and extended to recognize activities committed during World War II or having special reference to the persons to whose protection the particular Convention is directed.[81] The definition of 'grave breaches' was extended even further by Protocol I additional to the Geneva Conventions of 1949, and relating to the Protection of Victims of International Armed Conflicts.[82] In this instrument, however, certain acts are named as grave breaches which are

---

[74]*Loc. cit.*, n. 53 above, 39-42, 45-8, *etc.*, 288, 295, *etc.*, resp.

[75]See, e.g., *U.S. v. Kinder* (1954) 14 C.M.R. 742. In fact, the court accepted the view of the U.S. Mil. Trib. at Nuremberg in *Re Ohlendorf* (Einsatzgruppen Case) (1948) 4 Nuremberg Mil. Tribs. 470; see also *U.S. v. Schreiber* (1955) 18 C.M.R. 226.

[76]See n. 28 above. See also *U.S. v. Griffen* (1969) 39 C.M.R. 108; *U.S. v. Hutto* (1969) *ibid*, 586.

[77]*Re Captain Smith, The Times* (London), 8, 10, 12, 14 Apr., 1, 28, 29 May, 1, 17 Jun. 1948.

[78]*Military Prosecutor v. Melinki* (Kafr Kassem incident) *Jerusalem Post*, 16-18 Oct. 1958, 22, 24 Nov. 1959.

[79](I) Wounded and Sick; (II) Wounded, Sick and Shipwrecked; (III) Prisoners of War; (IV) Civilians, Schindler/Toman, 305, 333, 355, 427, resp.

[80]Arts. 49, 50, 129, 146, resp.

[81]Arts. 50, 51, 130, 147, resp.

[82]1977, Schindler/Toman, 551, Arts. 11, 85.

completely innovative, giving expression to the political ideologies of the majority of members of international society. This is the case with "practices of *apartheid* and other inhuman and degrading practices involving outrages upon personal dignity, based on racial discrimination,"[83] which reflects the fact that there exists a United Nations Convention on the Suppression and Punishment of the Crime of *Apartheid*[84] which, by 31 December 1983, had received only 77 ratifications and accessions, primarily from members of the Soviet *bloc* and the Third World, and not including a single member of NATO or any western-oriented state.

The Protocol makes one major departure in so far as criminal liability for breaches of the law of armed conflict are concerned. The decision in *Re Yamashita*[85] made it clear that a commander is liable for the offences of his subordinates if he knows of their acts or should have known of them or has failed to prevent their commission. There has, however, never been a clear statement in black letter law to this effect, other than the broad statement in the Nuremberg Charter[86] making "leaders, organizers, instigators and accomplices in the formulation or execution of a common plan or conspiracy to commit any of the [crimes against peace, war crimes or crimes against humanity specified in the Article] responsible for all acts performed by *any* persons in execution of such plan." Protocol I now provides[87] that "the High Contracting Parties and the Parties to the conflict shall repress grave breaches, and take measures necessary to suppress all other breaches, of the Conventions or this Protocol which result from a failure to act when there is a duty to do so. The fact that a breach of the Conventions or of this Protocol was committed by a subordinate does not absolve his superiors from penal or disciplinary responsibility, as the case may be, if they knew, or had information which should have enabled them to conclude in the circumstances at the time, that he was committing or was going to commit such a breach and if they did not take all feasible measures within their power to prevent or repress the breach. The High Contracting Parties and the Parties to the conflict shall require military commanders, with respect to members of the armed forces under their command and other persons under their control, to prevent and, where necessary, to suppress and to report to competent authorities breaches of the Conventions and of this Protocol. In order to prevent and suppress breaches, High Contracting Parties and Parties to the conflict shall require that, commensurate with their level of responsibility, commanders ensure that members of the armed forces under their command are aware of their obligations[88] under the Conventions and this Protocol. The High Contracting Parties to the conflict shall require any commander who is aware that subordinates or other persons under his control are going to commit or have committed a breach of the Conventions or of this Protocol, to initiate such steps as are necessary to prevent such violations of the Conventions or this Protocol, and, where appropriate, to initiate disciplinary or penal action against violations thereof." Further, the parties have undertaken[89] to offer each other every assistance in connection with criminal proceedings in respect of grave breaches, including cooperation in the matter of extradition.

---

[83]Art. 85(4)(c).

[84]1973, Gen. Ass. Res. 3068 (XXVIII) Annex, 13 *I.L.M.* 1974, 50.

[85](1946) 4 War Crimes Reports 1, 34-5. See also *Abbaye Ardenne Case (in Re Meyer)* (1945) *ibid.* 97—a fuller extract taken from the unpublished transcript is reproduced in "Canada's Role in the Development of the Law of Armed Conflict," ch. XIII *infra*. See also Parks, "Command Responsibility for War Crimes," 62 *Mil. L.R.* 1973, 1.

[86]Art. 6 *in fine* (italics added).

[87]Arts. 86, 87.

[88]To assist commanders in this task, Art. 82 provides for the attachment of legal advisers, see "The Role of Legal Advisers in the Armed Forces," ch. IV *supra*, while Art. 83 calls for the inclusion of the study of the Conventions and the Protocol in programmes of military instruction.

[89]Art. 88.

While it is true that the Protocol only creates law for those who have ratified it, except in those matters which may be considered as declaratory of customary law, and to date a mere handful of states have in fact ratified, not including any leading member of NATO or the Warsaw Pact, nevertheless there is some evidence to suggest that some states already regard these provisions with respect to the liability of commanders if not as declaratory of the law, then as providing guidelines which might be followed. This becomes clear from the Report of the Kahan Commission set up by Israel to inquire into the events at the Refugee Camps in Beirut.[90] Even though Israel has not even signed the Protocol it would appear that the members of the Commission were aware of the relevant articles, for their comments regarding direct and indirect, as well as personal responsibility of the various commanders involved, not only reflect these provisions, but may be considered to go beyond them.[91]

Apart from the measures taken by the individual parties to a conflict to ascertain, repress and punish offences against the Conventions or the Protocol, it is open to the Protecting Power or the representatives of the International Committee of the Red Cross to make representations with regard to any breach that may come to their notice. Moreover Protocol I provides for the establishment of an International Fact-Finding Commission.[92] The Conventions had already provided,[93] "at the request of a Party to the conflict, [for] an enquiry [to] be instituted, in a manner to be decided between the interested Parties, concerning any alleged violation. . . . If agreement has not been reached concerning the procedure for the enquiry, the Parties should agree on the choice of an umpire who will decide upon the procedure to be followed. Once the violation has been established, the Parties to the conflict shall put an end to it and shall repress it with the least possible delay." The Conventions do not provide any procedure should one of the parties to the conflict refuse to cooperate. By the Protocol, however, it is envisaged that the Commission shall be a standing body "consisting of fifteen members of high moral standing and acknowledged impartiality . . . [who] shall serve in their personal capacity . . . [with] equitable geographical representation assured. . . . The Commission shall be competent to enquire into any facts alleged to be a grave breach as defined in the Conventions and this Protocol or other serious violation of the Conventions or of this Protocol; [and to] facilitate through its good offices, the restoration of an attitude of respect for the Conventions and this Protocol. In other situations, the Commission shall institute an enquiry at the request of a Party to the conflict only with the consent of the other Party or Parties concerned." It would seem, therefore, that in so far as grave breaches are concerned the Commission can be called on to operate even in the absence of consent of the party against whom the accusation has been made. In so far as other breaches of the law of armed conflict may be alleged, the possibility of action by the Commission is somewhat reduced. On the other hand, it must be pointed out that in March 1984 the United Nations agreed to a request by Iran in conflict with Iraq to investigate allegations that the latter had been using chemical and gas weapons contrary to the Geneva Protocol of 1925[94] to which both states were parties. Although Iraq denied the allegation and refused to cooperate, the commission visited hospitals in Europe to which casualties had been sent, as well as hospitals in Iran, and considered the accusation justified.[95]

---

[90]1973, 22 *I.L.M.* 473.
[91]At 493-6, 496-9, 502-3, 505-14. See also "War Crimes, Extradition and Command Responsibility," ch. X *supra.*
[92]Art. 90.
[93]I-Art. 52, II-53, III-132, IV-149.
[94]Protocol for the Prohibition of the Use of Asphyxiating, Poisonous or Other Gases, and of Bacteriological Methods of Warfare, Schindler/Toman, *op. cit.*, 109.
[95]*The Times*, March 28, 1984.

Since no permanent international criminal tribunal has been established to hear charges brought against individuals alleged to have committed breaches of the law of armed conflict, it might be argued that the position regarding the enforcement of international criminal law in its relation to the law of armed conflict is no different from the position with regard to any other alleged international crime. In all cases, action depends upon the parties concerned following through their obligations under the relevant treaties or acting upon the rights conferred upon them by customary law. However, in the law of armed conflict we find there is a wider concept of jurisdiction, while the alleged offender is in many cases already in the hands of the country against whose personnel the offence is alleged to have been committed, thus giving a greater likelihood of prosecution. In so far as nationals are concerned, countries tend to be conscious of the need to maintain their own image in the eyes of the world as well as to preserve some sense of discipline based on humanitarianism among their troops. In view of this, we cannot dismiss as idle idealism the words in the Preface to the *Oxford Manual*.[96] "The Institute [of International Law] has contented itself with stating clearly and codifying the accepted ideas of our age so far as this has appeared allowable and practicable. By so doing, it believes it is rendering a service to military men themselves. In fact so long as the demands of opinion remain indeterminate, belligerents are exposed to painful uncertainty and endless accusations. A positive set of rules, on the contrary, if they are judicious, serves the interests of belligerents and is far from hindering them, since by preventing the unchaining of passion and savage instincts—which battle always awakens, as much as it awakens courage and manly virtues,—it strengthens the discipline which is the strength of armies; it also ennobles their patriotic mission in the eyes of the soldiers by keeping them within the limits of respect due to the rights of humanity. But in order to attain this end it is not sufficient for sovereigns to promulgate new laws. It is essential, too, that they make these laws known among all people, so that when a war is declared, the men called upon to take up arms to defend the causes of the belligerent States, may be thoroughly impregnated with the special rights and duties attached to the execution of such a command." Such laws must carry their own sanctions if they are to be of any significance. Since most of the war crimes, crimes against humanity and grave breaches mentioned in this paper are likely to stir the public in the countries of which the victims are nationals or allies, or are of such a grave character as to stimulate horror or disgust among the nationals of the countries of which the offenders are members of the armed forces, as was the case in the United States at the time of the My Lai massacre or in Israel in relation to the massacres in the camps, we may rest reasonably assured that in this field, at least, international criminal law has meaning and is likely to be enforced.

[96]*Op. cit.*, n. 31 above.

XII

Canadian Law and the Punishment of War Crimes

War crimes may be defined as offences resulting from breaches of the laws and usages of war. For the main part these laws are to be found in such treaties as the Hague Conventions of 1899 and 1907,[1] the Geneva Conventions of 1949[2] and the 1977[3] Protocols additional thereto, although when considering particular conflicts it may be necessary to seek the law in earlier treaties, such as the Geneva Conventions of 1929[4] which were in force at the time of the Second World War. In addition to this treaty law, some of the rules, particularly those relating to the means and methods of warfare which have not been consolidated in the Hague Conventions, must be looked for in customary law which to a great extent stems from ancient usages of chivalry as they prevailed among medieval knights.[5] It is generally considered that those against whom *prima facie* cases of war crimes exist may be tried by any state into whose power they fall, even though the state in question might have been neutral during the conflict in which the alleged offence was committed. This is because the law of war, like other aspects of international law, is regarded as part of the legal heritage of mankind and not the sole possession of any one state, so that there is a concern on the part of all to see that the law is observed and that breaches are punished.

Insofar as members of the forces of a prosecuting power are concerned, no jurisdictional problems arise. Such persons are automatically subject to their own military law, and probably also to their own system of national criminal law. In the case of Canada the

---

[1] See Schindler/Toman, at various pages, the most significant—II, 1899 and IV, 1907—appear at 57 et seq.
[2] I, Wounded and Sick; II, Wounded, Sick and Shipwrecked; III, Prisoners of War; IV, Civilians, *ibid.*, 305, 333, 355, 427 resp.
[3] Protocol I, *ibid.*, 551; Protocol II, *ibid.*, 619.
[4] Wounded and Sick, *ibid.*, 257; Prisoners of War, *ibid.*, 271.
[5] See Keen, *The Laws of War in the Middle Ages*, 1965, 2-3, 19-22, 242-7.

253

National Defence Act[6] specifically provides in section 120 for the trial of offences by persons subject to the Code of Service Discipline whether committed in or out of Canada which would, when committed in Canada, constitute offences under the Criminal Code[7] or any other Act of the Parliament of Canada. For the main part, particularly when directed against individuals or private property, acts which would be in breach of the laws and customs of war would in fact constitute offences against the Criminal Code, although there are certain offences which are so closely connected with the conduct of war, such as the disregard of the white flag or the sinking of a warship after surrender,[8] that they would not infringe any Canadian domestic law. Most systems of penal law restrict the operation of their own legislation to their own nationals, to those aliens who commit offences while present in national territory, and sometimes those who commit offences against nationals while abroad. From a Canadian point of view, probably the majority of war crimes, other than those committed against the inhabitants of occupied territory or members of the armed forces, are directed against aliens in alien territory by foreign personnel. While international law may permit the trial of such offenders by any country securing custody over them, legal systems which stem from England normally consider it necessary to enact specific legislation permitting the trial of foreign offenders who have committed their offences outside the national territory. Perhaps the best known decision to this effect is *R* v. *Keyn* concerning the sinking of *The Franconia*[9] which led to the enactment of the Territorial Waters Jurisdiction Act, 1878.[10] For our purposes it is sufficient to draw attention to the War Crimes Regulations of 1945 and the War Crimes Act of 1946[11] which govern the problem of war crimes trials under Canadian law, although it should be pointed out that many of the formerly occupied countries of Europe passed somewhat similar legislation.[12] In their cases, however, the legislation was often intended to ensure that nationals who had collaborated with the Germans either individually or as members of local administrations would be triable.

Until the Second World War drew attention to the fact that many of the breaches of the laws and customs of war committed by Axis personnel were directed against civilians, prosecutions had arisen from abuse of the means and methods of war, such as the sinking of protected hospital ships,[13] or in connection with the ill-treatment of military personnel who had been rendered *hors de combat* by reason of capture.[14] In fact, the few war criminal trials conducted by the Canadian armed forces arising from events occurring during the Second World War, such as that of Kurt Meyer, were all concerned with outrages against Canadian prisoners of war.[15]

While Canadian trials were so restricted, it does not mean that the potential did not exist for trying those alleged to have committed offences against civilians, whether Canadian nationals or not, and whether the offenders were military or civilian personnel. Before considering the contents of the War Crimes Regulations it is perhaps useful to consider the provisions contained in the 1929 Geneva Convention on Prisoners of War,

[6]R.S.C. 1970, c.N-4 (as amended).
[7]R.S.C. 1970, c.C-34 (as amended).
[8]See Protocol I, Arts. 40, 41.
[9](1876) L.R. 2 Ex.D. 53.
[10]41 & 42 Vict. c.73 (U.K.).
[11]10 Geo. VI, c.73, to which the Regulations are annexed. It should be noted that though not included in the 1970 Revised Statutes of Canada, the Act is still in force.
[12]See references in H.M.S.O., *History of the U.N. War Crimes Commission and the Development of the Laws of War*, 1948.
[13]See, e.g., *The Llandovery Castle* (1921) Cameron, *The Peleus Trial*, 1948, App. IX.
[14]See, e.g., Cuddon, *The Dulag Luft Trial*, 1952; Whiting, *Massacre at Malmedy*, 1971.
[15]See *Trial of Kurt Meyer* (Abbaye Ardenne Case) (1945) 4 *War Crimes Reports* 97.

with regard to judicial proceedings against such personnel. By Article 45 prisoners of war are subject to the laws, regulations and orders in force in the armed forces of the detaining power and by Article 46 they may not be sentenced to any penalties other than those prescribed for similar acts by members of the detaining power's forces. This means that if the latter are not punishable by their own law for any particular act it would not be possible for a prisoner of war to be tried for that act, even though it might amount *prima facie* to a war crime. Moreover, sentence may only be pronounced upon a prisoner of war by the same tribunals and in accordance with the same procedure as in the case of persons belonging to the armed forces of the detaining power and the prisoner is entitled to the same appellate rights as such personnel.[16] This would imply that the establishment of *ad hoc* tribunals to try war criminals would be contrary to the obligations of the detaining power unless such tribunals were similar in every respect to the courts martial which would possess jurisdiction over local military personnel charged with similar offences, and this by and large was true of the tribunals set up under the Regulations. Insofar as the Nuremberg International Military Tribunal and similar judicial bodies are concerned, their legal basis rests on the unconditional surrender of Germany or Japan and the international agreements signed by the states responsible[17] which to a limited extent made amendments to the procedural clauses of the Geneva Convention. In this connection it should be mentioned that although the Geneva Convention is humanitarian in character and appears to confer rights upon the individual prisoner, it is nevertheless a treaty like any other treaty. This means that the rights and obligations it creates are the rights and obligations of the states parties thereto, and individual prisoners are protected only to the extent that some party to the treaty is prepared to take up the case on their behalf. As to German or Japanese war criminals tried by United Nations (this was the official title of the alliance against the Axis) tribunals, by virtue of the surrender of the governments concerned and the assumption of supreme power by the victors it may be argued, certainly in the case of Germany, that that state ceased to exist[18] and that the tribunals established for the trial of such offenders were in fact municipal tribunals operating under the law of the sovereign power.[19] A somewhat similar case may be made for Japan by virtue of the powers conferred upon MacArthur and acquiesced in by the Emperor.[20] This is of major significance, even if it is contended that the commitment to treat captives as prisoners of war remains though their home state has ceased to exist.

The War Crimes Act of 1946 is a simple piece of legislation. It re-enacts the War Crimes Regulations which were originally promulgated by Order in Council on August 30, 1945, with effect from that promulgation, and states that anything done under the Regulations shall be deemed to have been done under authority of the Act. The Act also provides that it shall remain in force until its repeal by proclamation of the Governor in Council. Although no such proclamation has been issued, the Act is not included in the current edition of the Revised Statutes of Canada. To a great extent the Regulations, which now constitute the Schedule to the Act, are procedural and descriptive. It may be of interest

---

[16]Articles 63, 64.
[17]London Charter—Agreement for the Prosecution and Punishment of Major War Criminals of the European Axis, 1945, Schindler/Toman, 823.
[18]See, e.g., Schwarzenberger, *International Law*, vol. 1, 1957, 297-8.
[19]*Ibid.*, vol. 2, *The Law of Armed Conflict*, 1968, 468, discussing the Nuremberg Judgment, 1946, Cmd. 6964, 38.
[20]See U.S. Dept. of State, *Occupation of Japan, Policy and Progress*, 1946—the Charter of the Tribunal appears at 146 *et seq*. See also Green, "Law and Administration in Present-Day Japan," 1 *C.L.P.* 1948, 188.

to note that the sole definition of a war crime embodied in the Regulations is "a violation of the laws or usages of war committed during any war in which Canada has been or may be engaged at any time after the ninth day of September, 1939." This means that Canada has not by these Regulations provided for the trial by Canadian tribunals of any war crime committed during a conflict in which Canada remains neutral, nor does it authorize a Canadian trial of any prisoner accused of war crimes committed between the initial assault on Poland and the Canadian entry into the war, nor would it extend jurisdiction to war crimes connected with, for example, the holocaust or German acts against German nationals prior to September 9th, even though such acts might be connected with what the Nuremberg Tribunal was authorized by its constituent Charter to punish as part of the planning, initiation or preparation of a war of aggression or conspiracy in relation thereto.[21] At the same time it must be remembered that while the Act is still in force, so that any charge brought in connection with a war in which Canada might be a party subsequent to the Second World War would be subject to the law as it now exists, charges relating to the Second World War would have to be confined to the law as it existed during that War. This means that persons accused in relation thereto could not be charged with grave breaches as these are defined under the 1949 Geneva Conventions, for these did not become operative for Canada until the enactment of the Geneva Conventions Act 1964-65.[22]

Even less relevant would be the grave breaches listed in Protocol I of 1977 which has not yet been ratified by Canada. Equally, even though many of the crimes committed in occupied Europe during the Second World War amounted to genocide, no person charged under Canadian law in connection with war crimes committed during the Second World War could be tried for genocide, for this only became a clearly established crime under international law by virtue of the Genocide Convention which came into force in 1951,[23] and for Canada in December 1952, becoming a criminal act by virtue of an amendment to the Criminal Code.[24] Any attempt to charge a person with genocide in relation to acts committed during the Second World War, or grave breaches as defined in the 1949 Conventions would be met by the plea that in accordance with Article 15 of the International Covenant on Civil and Political Rights,[25] to which Canada acceded in May 1976, "no one shall be held guilty of any criminal offence on account of any act or omission which did not constitute a criminal offence, under national or international law, at the time when it was committed." When Israel tried Adolf Eichmann it did not charge him expressly with genocide for, as the Court pointed out, while the Convention reaffirmed that such acts had always been contrary to international law, its terms with regard to the trial and punishment of genocide as a conventional crime were intended to operate *in futuro*, so that the Israeli Law for the Prevention and Punishment of Genocide, 1950, "does not apply with retroactive effect and does not therefore pertain to the offences dealt with in the present case."[26] Moreover, such legislation being retroactive would be contrary to the Canadian Charter of Rights and Freedoms.[27]

It was the intention of the Parliament of Canada, as of every country concerned with the pursuit and trial of war criminals, to exercise their jurisdiction either with regard to

---

[21]See Nuremberg Judgment, *loc. cit.* n. 19 above, 65, 41 *Am. J. Int'l Law* 1947, 249. See also Schwelb, "Crimes against Humanity," 23 *Brit. Y.B. Int'l Law* 1946, 178, 205-12.

[22]R.S.C. 1970, c.G-3.

[23]1948, 78 *U.N.T.S.* 277.

[24]S.281.1, enacted R.S.C. 1970, c.11 (1st Supp.), s.1.

[25]Gen. Ass. Res. 2200 (XXI)A, 1966, 6 *I.L.M.* 360.

[26]*Att. Gen., Israel v. Eichmann* (1961) 36 *I.L.R.* 5 and 35.

[27]Constitution Act 1982 [Canada Act 1982 (U.K.) c.11], s. 11(g).

alleged war criminals found within their territory or in such parts of Europe as were subject to their *post bellum* occupation. Moreover, it was intended that war criminals should not evade justice because of procedural or jurisdictional deficiencies and that such justice should not be long delayed. In fact, a practice has grown up whereby western powers to whom demands for the extradition of alleged war criminals have been made have in recent years refused such demands. The refusal has been based on the ground that after so long a period it would be inequitable to return the accused—a policy which is frequently adopted with regard to long-delayed requests under normal extradition processes—coupled with the realization that such delay imposes difficulties upon the defence as well as upon the prosecution, as Yugoslavia, for example, found out when trying a Canadian-naturalized Yugoslav visitor to his native land in 1979.[28] Moreover, when such demands have been made by countries in eastern Europe the western powers have feared that these demands are more connected with political ideology and victimization than justice against war criminals and have refused to comply. That this is not an unjustifiable fear is perhaps evident from the fact that when such countries do try war criminals nowadays the charges are for the main part brought against their own nationals who have collaborated with the Germans, and in respect of offences against their own nationals.

Although it has been suggested that the United States has during the last two or three years been willing to extradite persons against whom *prima facie* evidence of war crimes exists, this is not in fact the case and is largely a result of misdescription by the media. Under United States law a naturalized person may have his nationality revoked if there is evidence that he committed perjury on entering the United States or in connection with the application for naturalization. Those affected by the new policy either denied their membership in the Nazi Party or that they had in any way been connected with criminal activities.[29] With regard to persons resident in Canada or who may have acquired Canadian citizenship, there is nothing to suggest that they were questioned on such matters so there would be no basis in law for similar action to be taken. In any case, it would appear that any documents that might be relevant would have been destroyed by now.

The fact that the German Federal Republic is continuing to try Germans accused of war crimes against civilians is completely irrelevant as a precedent, for there are special reasons of an emotional, moral and political character underlying this policy. Again it is irrelevant that the General Assembly of the United Nations adopted in 1968 by 58 votes in favor to seven against, with 36 abstentions, and 25 members absent, a Convention on the Non-Applicability of Statutory Limitations to War Crimes and Crimes against Humanity.[30] This Convention entered into force in November 1970 and has been ratified by only 26 states, not including Canada, the Federal Republic, or any western power. Presumably, with the possible exception of the special situation concerning Germany, the entire western world—and much of the third world—tends to consider that time should operate as a barrier.

To return to the War Crimes Regulations, the first point to note is that they provide for the United Kingdom Army Act "as made applicable from time to time to members of the Canadian military forces" to apply so far as practicable to the courts established in accordance with the Regulations. The Army Act, of course, no longer has any relevance

[28]*Re Bakich* (1977), *Edmonton Journal*, 29 Mar. 1979, *Calgary Herald*, 30 Mar. 1979.
[29]See, e.g., *U.S.* v. *Walus* (1978) 453 F.Supp. 699; *U.S.* v. *Federenko* (1979) 597 *F.2d* 246.
[30]754 *U.N.T.S.* 73.

to the Canadian forces and there is no provision for statutory succession in the National Defence Act or that part of it which constitutes the Code of Service Discipline, nor are there provisions for war crimes trials in that Act. It may be impossible, therefore, even were the Regulations applicable, for them to be carried into effect at the present time, although by § 36(h) of the Interpretation Act,[31] it might be possible to argue that since the relevant provisions of the Army Act have not been repealed they still apply, even though the United Kingdom Army Act and provisions regarding war criminals have themselves been radically amended.[32] Be that as it may, the Regulations provide that

> any Canadian flag, general or air officer commanding any Canadian forces, wherever such forces may be serving, whether in the field or in occupation of enemy territory or otherwise . . . shall have power to convene military courts for the trial of persons charged with having committed war crimes and to confirm the findings and sentences of such courts: provided that no military court shall be convened for the trial of any person for a war crime unless the case has been certified by the Judge Advocate General . . . as approved for trial.[32]

The use of the phrases "wherever such forces may be serving" and "or otherwise" might suggest that this Regulation applies to Canada itself. However,

> if it appears to a convening officer that a person then within the limits of his command or otherwise under his control has at any place committed a war crime he may direct that such person if not already in custody shall be taken into and kept in custody pending trial in such manner and on such charge as he may direct.[33]

The reference to "already in custody" implies that the Regulations were intended to apply to prisoners of war. However, recognizing that with the surrender many persons, including civilians not in custody, were likely to be charged as war criminals, the Regulations made provision for the local commander to have such persons taken into custody. At the present time it is difficult to envisage a situation, unless there has been a proclamation invoking the War Measures Act,[34] whereby a commanding officer of forces stationed in Canada would have any authority to arrest civilians regardless of the offences in which they were alleged to be implicated. This difficulty is compounded when it is realized that the Regulations go on to provide that

> the commanding officer of any body of naval, military or air forces having charge of an accused shall be deemed to be the commanding officer of the accused for the purposes of all matters preliminary and relating to trial and punishment.[35]

Once again it is difficult to see where a local commander would acquire the authority to place under his command a Canadian civilian, or one present in Canada, and to hold such person for trial by a military court.

Assuming such peremptory action to have been taken, it may be presumed that every civil and human rights organization in the country would leap to the defence of the person involved. Moreover, it is difficult to see how such a procedure could be considered to comply with Section 7 of the Canadian Charter of Rights and Freedoms guaranteeing

---

[31]R.S.C. 1970, c.I-23.
[32]This has been replaced by the Armed Forces Act 1981, c.55 (U.K.).
[33]Regulation 4(1).
[34]Regulation 6(1).
[35]R.S.C. 1970, c.W-2.

everyone "the right to life, liberty and security of the person and the right not to be deprived thereof except in accordance with the principles of fundamental justice," and Section 15 guaranteeing equality before and under the law, with equal protection and equal benefit of the law without discrmination. Here would be an instance of a Canadian civilian or an alien lawfully present in Canada being subjected to military arrest and trial not by the ordinary courts nor in accordance with the processes of law to which such persons are normally subject, a procedure hardly compatible with equality before the law and the protection of the law. As recently as July 1980 the Supreme Court had occasion to deliver a majority opinion supporting trials by court martial within Canada of persons within the armed forces and charged with acts constituting offences against the Criminal Code.[36] On that occasion, the Chief Justice delivered a very strong dissent, while there was a further opinion by some of the majority judges suggesting that in a future case on somewhat different facts the decision might well be otherwise. One hesitates to assess how the Supreme Court would react when faced with a case concerning a civilian resident in Canada, not otherwise liable to military discipline, arrested on the fiat of a military officer and subjected to a trial for offences committed at least 39 years ago outside of Canada and not affecting Canadian nationals as victims, and particularly in view of the very relaxed rules concerning evidence provided for by Regulation 10 which cannot be considered consistent with the Charter. Moreover these rules are completely incompatible with the rules of evidence applicable to Courts Martial at the present time.

While it might be considered distasteful or even unjust that persons present in Canada against whom there is evidence of complicity in the commission of war crimes during the Second World War should go unpunished, it seems clear that there is no basis in Canadian law as it now exists, and that includes the War Crimes Act, whereby such persons could be brought to trial. Any attempt to amend the law would run counter to the common law dislike of retroactive criminal legislation, while at the same time controverting Canada's international treaty obligations, as well as the Charter.

As to the trial of any person charged with war crimes arising from any conflict in which Canada might be a party in the future, the War Crimes Act is today probably irrelevant. It is inconsistent with the 1949 Geneva Convention on Prisoners of War, since by Article 102 "a prisoner of war can be validly sentenced only by the same courts according to the same procedure as in the case of members of the armed forces of the Detaining Power," which would preclude the establishment of the type of special tribunal envisaged by the Act, as well as the type of evidence which may be received by such a tribunal. However, by virtue of the Geneva Conventions Act certain grave breaches have been recognized as crimes, so long as the act in question "would, if committed in Canada, be an offence under any provision of the Criminal Code or other Act of the Parliament of Canada,"[37] even if committed outside of Canada. It is debatable whether "any Act of the Parliament of Canada "includes the Geneva Conventions Act itself, for if it does not the Act does not render all grave breaches criminal. As to the tribunal before which a charge is to be laid, "the offence is within the competence and may be tried and punished by the court having jurisdiction in respect of similar offences in the place in Canada where that person is found in the same manner as if the offence has been committed in that place, or by any other court to which jurisdiction has been lawfully transferred." This would seem to do away with the need of any special tribunal of the kind envisaged by the War Crimes Act, especially as section 7 of the Geneva Conventions Act provides that

---

[36]*MacKay* v. *The Queen* [1980] 2 *S.C.R.* 370.
[37]S.3(1).

every prisoner of war is subject to the Code of Service Discipline as defined in the National Defence Act and every prisoner of war who is alleged to have done or omitted to do anything that is, by virtue of section 3, an offence under the Criminal Code or any other Act of the Parliament of Canada shall be deemed to have been subject to the Code of Service Discipline at the time the offence was alleged to have been committed.

Insofar as non-military personnel, described in the Act as "protected internees," are alleged to have committed war crimes they would not be covered by this provision, and it would appear from the 1949 Geneva Convention relative to the protection of civilians that they may only be tried by non-political military courts sitting in occupied territory.[38] Even for military personnel, it would now appear that there may be no tribunal which under Canadian law could try an accused charged with traditional war crimes not amounting to grave breaches of the Geneva Conventions.

In 1982 the problem became real for Canada. The Federal Republic of Germany made a request for the extradition of one Rauca, charged with responsibility for massacres during the Second World War. For the main part, the issue turned on the claim that a person possessing Canadian citizenship, whether by birth or naturalization, was exempt from extradition on the basis of sections 1[39] and 6[40] of the Charter of Rights and Freedoms. However, in the course of the proceedings reference was made to the War Crimes Act, it being suggested that trial in Canada in accordance with the Act was an alternative to extradition and more compatible with the spirit of the Charter. However, both the High Court and the Court of Appeal in Ontario upheld the validity of the Extradition Act[41] as fully compatible with the Charter being within such "reasonable limits prescribed by law as can be demonstrably justified in a free and democratic society" as required by s.1. In the High Court Chief Justice Evans bluntly rejected the possibility of the War Crimes Act as having any application,[42] while the Court of Appeal held that "the War Crimes Act is not a statute of general application and by its very terms does not cover the present factual situation where the crimes were not committed against Canadian citizens. Further, a proceeding against the appellant under the Act would run afoul of s.11 (f) of the Charter which guarantees, except in the case of an offence under military law tried before a military tribunal, the right to trial by jury where the maximum punishment for the offence is imprisonment for five years or more. We . . . are not persuaded that at present there is an alternative to extradition or to make extradition an unreasonable limit not demonstrably justifiable in a free and democratic society."[43]

It would appear, therefore, that the Courts have confirmed that under Canadian law as it stands at present there is no competence under the War Crimes Act to try a Canadian citizen in Canada for offences against non-Canadians when committed abroad. They have further confirmed that there is nothing in the Canadian Charter of Rights and Freedoms to prevent such an accused being extradited to stand trial in a country having jurisdiction over those offences.

[38]Convention IV, Art. 66.
[39]"The Canadian Charter of Rights and Freedoms guarantees the rights and freedoms set out in it subject only to such reasonable limits prescribed by law as can be demonstrably justified in a free and democratic society."
[40]"(1) Every citizen of Canada has the right to enter, remain in and leave Canada."
[41]R.S.C. 1970, c.E-21.
[42]*Re German Federal Republic and Rauca* (1982) 38 O.R. (2d) 705, 708.
[43](1983) 41 O.R. (2d) 225, 245-6.

XIII

Canada's Role in the Development of the Law of Armed Conflict

Perhaps the most important contribution made by Canada to the development of armed conflict law, and one that is possibly equal in significance to that made by any other country, was not in fact made by Canada as such, but rather in response to Canadian actions. During the 1837 rebellion, Canadian forces had seized an American vessel, *The Caroline*, which had been used to support the rebels, and tipped it over Niagara Falls. In response to United States protests, the Canadian authorities justified their action on the ground of self-defence. In negotiations with the British, who then governed Canada, Daniel Webster, United States Secretary of State, propounded a formulation of the plea of self-defence which has stood the test of time. In his words,[1] preventive action in foreign territory is only justified in the case of "an instant and overwhelming necessity for self-defence, leaving no choice of means, and no moment of deliberation." This concept of the right is so universally accepted today that it was adopted in its Judgment[2] by the International Military Tribunal at Nuremberg when rejecting Germany's explanations of the invasions of Denmark and Norway. Other than having occasioned the definitive formulation of the concept of self-defence, Canada made no positive and original contribution to the development of the law of armed conflict until it participated in the discussions leading to the adoption in 1977 of the two Protocols additional to the Geneva Conventions of 1949,[3] which have served to extend the scope of humanitarian law in both international and non-international armed conflicts.

In the meantime, through the medium of its judicial decisions, Canada, in applying generally accepted rules of the law of war, made a positive contribution to the *corpus* of evidence as to what makes up this law. This being so, it is useful to draw attention to

[1]Note of August 6, 1842, 2 Moore, *Digest of International Law*, 412.
[2]U.K., Cmd. 6964 (1946), at 28.
[3]Schindler/Toman, Pr. I (international) 551, Pr. II (non-int'l), 619.

at least some of these decisions, bearing in mind that during the period in question many of the decisions were reflective of the views of the United Kingdom and its courts.

Since World War II, largely because of the difficulty of being certain that the legal conditions for the existence of a "war" are real,[4] it has become popular in the doctrine as well as in treaties to talk of armed conflict, even though the man in the street may regard the two as synonymous. Much has been made of the fact that an *animus belligerendi* may exist without a declaration or even a breach of diplomatic relations,[5] but as long ago as 1812 Dr. Croke, sitting in the Halifax Court of Vice-Admiralty, was aware that the situation *de facto* might not always accord with the requirements *de jure*. In the case of *The Brig Dart*,[6] the question in issue was whether the seized ship was enemy property, and Dr. Croke said:

> What shall constitute a state of war between two countries has been often debated, and the doctrines which have been laid down in our English law books may seem at first sight to be at variance with each other. If we look at the older authorities, we find it to be an established maxim, that no war can subsist without the concurrence of the king, that if all the subjects of England should make war with a king in league with the King of England, without the royal assent, such war is no breach of the league. "That is a time of hostility," said Lord Chief Justice Hale, "when war is proclaimed by the king against a foreign prince or state. *This and this only renders them enemies.*" It is not however to be understood to be necessary that war should be *solemnly declared* by the King of England. If a war *de facto* subsists between Great Britain and any other country, without a regular declaration, the subjects of that country would be alien enemies. But I apprehend that where there is no express declaration of war, the hostilities exercised on the part of Great Britain must be sanctioned by the sovereign, or there must be some acts, or other proceedings, which show his intention of placing the country in a state of hostility in respect to any given country. If not an express declaration, there must be something equivalent to it. Whatever declaration of war there may be made by foreign powers, whatever hostile acts may be committed by them, or whatever means may be adopted to repel them by the sole authority of the subjects in virtue of the right of self-defence, the state of mutual and reciprocal hostilities between any country and the British dominions cannot legally commence till the king, in whom solely the power of peace and war is vested, either by express declaration, or by some other manifestation of his hostile intentions, such as having recourse to arms, has placed his dominions in a state of warfare. When such manifestation is made, and not before, the complete legal state of hostilities exists, with all its consequences. . . .

This was not the only occasion on which Dr. Croke showed a concern with realities rather than formalities. In the same year, when deciding the validity of the seizure of the *Zodiack*,[7] to which a passport or safe-conduct had been given, he demonstrated an awareness that international law depended upon usage, and a realism that is not always expressed even today. It is interesting to note that even in 1812 he took the line that the rules relating to such documents were such that "no officer in His Majesty's service can be ignorant of them," a rule that applies today where service personnel are concerned, even though not all of them, and even less the members of the public, are aware of the fact.[8] He pointed out that there need be no treaty between the countries concerned, nor

---

[4]See, e.g., Hague Convention III, 1907, on the opening of hostilities in Scott, *The Hague Conventions and Declarations of 1899 and 1907*, 1918, 96.

[5]See, e.g., *Kawasaki Kisen Kabushiki Kaisha of Kobe* v. *Bantham S.S. Co.*, [1939] 2 K.B. 544. For a discussion of the differentiation in terminology, see Green, "Armed Conflict, War and Self-Defence," 6 *Archiv des Völkerrechts* 387 (1957).

[6](1812) Stewart, 301 (italics in original).

[7](1812) Stewart, 333.

[8]See, e.g., *Llandovery Castle* (1921), arising from the unlawful sinking of a British hospital ship carrying Canadian medical personnel (reported in Cameron, *The Peleus Trial*, 1948, App. IX). See also, "The Man in the Field and the Maxim *Ignorantia Juris Non Excusat*," ch. II *supra*.

even a special agreement between the parties directly involved, for when dealing with such matters it must be accepted that "they are founded upon a compact of which the terms are partly expressed, and partly understood from general usage, and they depend upon the established conventional law of nations."

There is little point in considering at length the role that the Canadian courts may have played in regard to questions of enemy status, whether of individuals, vessels, or corporations, or problems concerning trading with the enemy or treasonable activities on, or apparently on behalf of the enemy. These are either applications of the common law, English statutes or, later on, Canadian legislation. In other words, even though problems of enemy status and the like are regularly dealt with in works and manuals of armed conflict law, they remain matters of municipal law and are really only affected by international law to the extent that they operate within the general framework of what that law permits. If authority be needed to emphasize this point, it may be found in the decision of Dr. Croke in the Halifax Vice-Admiralty Court in *The Schooner Nancy*[9] or, more than a century later, in Maclean, J.'s judgment *In the Matter of the War Measures Act, 1914.* The latter pointed out that "subject to any legislation to the contrary, and subject to . . . The Treaty of Peace (Germany), Order 1920 (Canada), it may be said that the law of this country does not confiscate the property of an enemy,"[10] a principle which was not embodied in this form in any generally accepted treaty, although both Professor Lieber's Instructions for the Government of the Armies of the United States in the Field,[11] and the Regulations annexed to Hague Convention IV of 1907 regarding the laws and customs of war on land[12] acknowledged a similar protection insofar as enemy private property in occupied territory was concerned. Equally interesting from the point of view of Canadian recognition of the limits of the law of armed conflict long before such limits found their way into treaty form is the judgment of Dr. Croke relative to the American ship *The Marquis de Somerueles.*[13] In the Hague Regulations of 1907 it was recognized that cultural establishments should be immune from attack, but it was not until 1954 with the adoption of the Convention for the Protection of Cultural Property in the Event of Armed Conflict[14] that proper treaty arrangements were made to this effect. Yet in 1813, Dr. Croke recognized that "the same law of nations, which prescribes that all property belonging to the enemy shall be liable to confiscation, has likewise its modifications and relaxations of that rule. The arts and sciences are admitted amongst all civilized nations, as forming an exception to the severe rights of warfare, and are entitled to favour and protection. They are considered not as the premium of this or of that nation, but as *the property of mankind at large*, and as *belonging to the common interests of the whole species.* . . . We are at war in the just defense of our national rights, not to violate the charities of human nature."

International lawyers have become accustomed to attributing much of the development of international maritime law, particularly in time of armed conflict, to the judgments of Sir William Scott, Lord Stowell. It is perhaps only because the Canadian practice in the same sphere is not sufficiently well known that the name of Dr. Croke does not parallel

---

[9](1805) Stewart, 49; see also *Topay v. Crow's Nest Pass Coal Co.* (1914), 18 D.L.R. 784, and *Re Beranik* (1915), 25 D.L.R. 564.

[10][1925] Ex. C.R. 196, 199; see also his decision in *Sec. of State for Canada v. Alien Property Custodian for the United States* [1930] Ex. C.R. 75.

[11]General Orders No. 100, 1863 (Schindler/Toman, 3), Art. 37.

[12]Reg. 53 (*ibid.*, 57).

[13](1813) Stewart 482.

[14]Schindler/Toman, 661 (italics added; cf. Convention Preamble, which speaks of "the cultural heritage of all mankind").

that of Stowell. Reference has already been made to some of his decisions concerning issues relating to the War of 1812, but in the case of *The Curlew*,[15] in fact the only British decision before World War I concerning requisition, he propounded a statement that may be regarded as the definitive proposition of the law of prize:

> By the law of nations, as universally received and practised in all civilized countries, before captures can be considered as prize, they must undergo a sentence of condemnation, after a regular judicial proceeding, in which all parties claiming an interest may be heard. Till a capture becomes thus invested with the character of prize, the right of property is in abeyance, and the possession of it by the country which has made the seizure, is a sacred trust, a mere custody for the benefit of those who may be ultimately entitled to it. The suits which are prosecuted in those courts are proceedings *in rem*, and the party who obtains a decision in his favor is entitled to the ship or goods themselves, agreeable to the rule of the civil law, *si in rem actum sit coram judice, si contra possessorum judicaverit, jubere ei debet, ut Rem Ipsam restituat.*[16]
> Till adjudication, therefore, the capture being in a mere state of legal sequestration, cannot be alienated or disposed of, in whatever hands the laws of the country may place it, or whosoever may be ultimately entitled to the perquisite of prize. Neither the government of the country nor the captors can apply it to their own use, or employ it in their own services; nor can it be discharged from that custody either by sale, or upon security, without the consent of all parties interested (upon the maxim of *volenti nulla fit injuria*), or for the ultimate benefit of all parties (which afford a presumption of such consent) as in the case of perishable and perishing commodities, or of the probability of a great length of time intervening before the ultimate decision. It does then seem that a Court of Admiralty upon the *general principles* of the law of nations, to which it is bound to adhere can, generally speaking, decree the delivery of property so situated, unless upon very particular and special grounds. . . .

Not only did Dr. Croke explain the law of prize in these simple terms, but at a later point in his judgment he virtually foretold the decision in *The Zamora*[17] when he drew attention to the limitations of a government order with regard to the seizure and detention of vessels. During the same war Dr. Croke made it clear that a principle which had developed by the end of the Thirty Years' War that a captive did not belong to the captor[18] applied equally to the law of maritime prize:

> To prevent the inconveniences and abuses which might take place if they were left entirely under the disposal of those who took them, and to restrain the irregular and piratical practices which might be apprehended; prizes are generally considered as the property of the nation at large, and governments have given the captors only a limited and conditional interest in them, subject to all the rules imposed by the law of nations, and their own municipal regulations.[19]

A later Canadian case in prize is interesting, for, though it expounds views similar to Dr. Croke's on the nature of prize Jurisdiction, it may be regarded as a governmental statement of a later vintage. During the hearing on *The Bellas*,[20] the Deputy Minister of Justice, Mr. Newcombe, appearing as counsel, pointed out:

[15](1812) Stewart, 312 (italics in original); see also *La Reine des Agnès*, (1803) Stewart 9.
[16]Justinian, *Institutes*, Lib. IV, tit. 17, s. 2.
[17][1916] 2 A.C. 77.
[18]Thus, Art. 63 of the Treaty of Westphalia, 1648, provided for the release of all prisoners of war by both sides without payment of any ransom; see Levie, *Prisoners of War in Int'l Armed Conflict*, 5 (1978).
[19]*The Cossack*, (1813) Stewart, 313.
[20](1914) Ex. Ct. of Canada (Official Stenographer's Notes, c. MacKenzie and Laing, *Canada and the Law of Nations*, 515 (1938).

[A prize] court proceeds according to the course of the Admiralty, as evidenced by the instructions of its own Sovereign; and subject to these instructions, according to the law of Nations, or perhaps, with great deference, I may more accurately say, the practice of Nations, as embodied in the municipal system of the country, and so far as the international practice is consistent with the Statutes, rules and regulations for the time being in force.

Nineteenth-century Canadian judges not only made their contribution to the development of the law of prize, they were also concerned in expounding upon the rights and duties of neutrals. Insofar as neutral duties are concerned, perhaps the most significant Canadian judgment is that in *The Chesapeake*.[21] As a result of a plot concocted in Canada, certain British subjects claiming to be agents of the Confederate States seized a northern vessel, killed the second engineer, and made other crew members prisoners. Eventually, the extradition of those involved was requested in respect of piracy, murder, and robbery on the high seas. Privateering had just been made illegal by the 1856 Declaration of Paris and the accused argued that they were not privateering since, though neutral, they were properly commissioned by the Confederacy. In the Vice-Admiralty Court of New Brunswick, Ritchie, J., said:

neutrals taking commissions as privateers and acting on them are likewise [as are nationals of belligerents] free from the imputation of piracy.

They may make themselves amenable for the violation of the laws of their own country,[22] and may denude themselves of the right to claim her protection to shield them from the consequences of their acts, but they cannot be dealt with by the belligerents against whom they are acting as pirates. But as neutrals they stand in a very different position from belligerents. Belligerents . . . may make captures without commissions. Neutrals can only protect themselves by commissions from, or by acting under authority of the belligerent government, or on board commissioned vessels, or under duly authorized officers. They cannot, without any commission or authority, fit out in a neutral country a hostile expedition against a power at peace with such country, and under pretense of acting in the name of, or on behalf of, a belligerent power, commit acts on the high seas that would, unless protected by belligerent rights, be acts of piracy, and not be held responsible criminally for such acts. And therefore it behooves persons not belligerents, but subjects of a neutral power, engaging in acts of hostility, if they wish to escape the imputation of criminality, to be well assured when they depredate upon the shipping of a nation at peace with the one to whom they owe allegiance and in opposition to the municipal law and natural policy of their own government . . . that they are acting under the authority of a commission which will bear the test of a strict legal scrutiny.

The late H. A. Smith, in his *Crisis in the Law of Nations*,[23] drew attention to one of the consequences of the modern development towards total war, and questioned whether the old distinction between combatants and civilians had not disappeared, especially in those instances where a country had more or less subjected the entire population to conscription in aid of the war effort. At the time of the Napoleonic Wars this was already a matter that caused concern to Dr. Croke. *The Tamaahmah*[24] was seized while carrying fifty French passengers, including women and children, from the United States to Bordeaux, then under blockade. The learned judge commented:

[21](1864) Stockton, 208, 284.
[22]See Foreign Enlistment Act, R.S.C. 1970, c. F-29.
[23](1947), ch. 3.
[24](1811) Stewart, 254.

It has been decided in several cases[25] that carrying soldiers and sailors to France, though not regular corps, and not intended for any particular service, is engaging in a trade of a contraband nature. There is no proof that many of these passengers were not of that description. Under the present government of France, where the whole body of subjects is under conscription, every man is a soldier or a sailor. Every man capable of bearing arms on board this vessel, might, and probably would be seized immediately upon his arrival in France, and sent to fight against Great Britain and her allies. Though a few straggling or accidental persons might innocently be permitted on board a general passage vessel, yet where a vessel is employed for that purpose only, and carries a whole cargo of the enemy's subjects, such a cargo can scarcely be considered as of an innocent character. . . . [If the vessel were going to an open port,] it might be a question of some nicety to determine how far persons, not professedly of the military state might come under the principles of [immunity]. Very different is the case here. . . . In this case, the port being under a rigorous blockade, the only question is how far the employment in which the vessel is engaged, is of a favourable nature, and such as to form an exception to the strict rules of blockade. Whatever doubt there might be in the other case, in this there can be none . . .

It was not until World War II that Canadian courts again made a contribution to the evidence of what constitutes the international law of armed conflict. During that war a number of enemy prisoners of war were transshipped from Europe to Canada and established in camps in that country. It was obvious, therefore, that the chances of the judiciary being faced with problems relative to the status and rights of prisoners were very real. In German prisoner-of-war camps it was not uncommon to find that Nazi prisoners tried to assert party discipline and exercise control over their compatriots, even to the extent of subjecting them to trial and ultimate execution.

Insofar as Canada is concerned, perhaps the best-known instance of this occurred not in Canada itself, but in relation to German troops which had surrendered to the 1st Canadian Army in Europe in 1945. Even though it was maintained that these had surrendered and were not in fact prisoners of war, from the legal point of view this was in fact their status. The Germans were left in control of their own discipline and, although the Allied Command had abolished all German courts martial, a trial by German officers was instituted of two German deserters. The Canadian authorities were informed of what was about to happen and knew that the death penalty might be imposed. This in fact occurred and the Canadians supplied the rifles for the firing squad. When this matter was raised in the House of Commons in 1966,[26] the Minister of National Defence described the whole affair as "most regrettable," but suggested that "in view of the fact that it is now over twenty years since the war ended, nothing is to be gained by our carrying this matter further." While there was nothing in the 1929 Prisoners of War Convention which would make such a proceeding illegal, it can hardly be considered that it was the intention of the parties that prisoner of war "kangaroo" courts would be tolerated, and since 1949[27] such a situation could not repeat itself.

More in keeping with maintenance of the rule of law and the purpose for which the law concerning prisoners of war has evolved is the decision of the Appellate Division of the Supreme Court of Alberta in *R. v. Perzenowski and Others*,[28] in which the Court held

---

[25]E.g., *The Friendship* (1803), 4 C. Rob. 420.

[26]H.C. Deb., October 11, 1966, at 8510; December 21, 1966, at 11445-46.

[27]Prisoners of War Convention (Schindler/Toman, 355), Arts. 84, 96, 99; moreover, no sentence of death may now be carried out on a prisoner of war until six months after notification to the Protecting Power, Arts. 100, 107.

[28][1946] 3 W.W.R. 678; see also *R. v. Werner*, [1947] S.A.L.R. 828.

that an "execution" of a prisoner of war carried out by fellow prisoners, in the belief that he was a traitor and that they were acting in accordance with German military law and the orders of a superior, was murder and could not be justified either on the basis of German law or of superior orders.

Of more significance from the point of view of Canada's contribution to the development of the law of armed conflict, or of evidence as to accepted practice relating to this law, is a group of decisions concerning the rights of escaping prisoners of war. The Hague Regulations provided that captured escapees could be subjected to disciplinary punishment,[29] and the 1929 Convention[30] was only more specific with regard to the punishment of an unsuccessful escape, providing that "attempted escape, even if it is not a first offence, shall not be considered as an aggravation of the offence in the event of the prisoner of war being brought before the court for crimes or offences against persons or property committed in the course of such attempt." The difficulty with this provision is that it gives no indication of what offences are to be considered as being part and parcel of the attempted escape, and which are those merely "committed in the course of such attempts." In *R. v. Krebs*[31] the Magistrate's Court of the County of Renfrew, Ontario, held that an escaping prisoner of war who breaks and enters a dwelling house and steals articles for the purpose of facilitating his escape or assisting him to preserve his liberty is not criminally liable. This is the first reported case in this field, although Lord Campbell had suggested in *R. v. Sattler*[32] that a prisoner of war who killed a guard in the course of escaping would probably not be guilty of murder, for it could easily be argued that this constituted part of his escape and, as such, an act of war which, despite his capture, he was still entitled to undertake. The learned magistrate pointed out:

> The accused is not punishable at common law for an attempt to escape [nor is he punishable in the eyes of international law for so doing]. He is not punishable at common law for doing anything reasonably calculated to assist in that escape, and in my opinion the same holds for anything done in an endeavour to preserve his liberty once gained.
> The accused owes no allegiance to the Crown. He is an open and avowed enemy of the Crown, a man taken in war and a man who, if it is not his duty, may quite reasonably feel that it is his duty to escape from the domains of his captor state, and, if he can, return to the state to which he owes allegiance and perform his duty to that state.[33]
> . . . [M]y opinion is that a prisoner of war is not punishable for anything he may reasonably do to escape, or having escaped, to preserve his liberty. . . . [W]hat the accused did was done with a view to facilitating his escape. . . .

The importance of the *Krebs* case lies in its being the first to deal with the alleged criminal responsibility of an escaping prisoner of war. Unfortunately, it was only decided at the magistrate's level and Galligan, P.M., made no reference to the Prisoners of War Convention, 1929, or any other rule, customary or conventional, of the international law of armed conflict. An Alberta Police Court Magistrate had to deal with a similar problem in *R. v. Schindler*,[34] and he expressly disagreed with *Krebs*, which he regarded as expressive of the law as it existed before the adoption of the 1929 Convention. He pointed out that

---

[29]Regulation 8.
[30]Arts. 47-51.
[31](1943), 80 C.C.C. 279.
[32](1858), 169 E.R. 1105.
[33]By the National Defence Act, R.S.C. 1970, c. N-4, s. 66(b), it is the duty of every Canadian taken prisoner of war to attempt to escape if the opportunity offers.
[34][1944] 3 W.W.R. 125.

as a result of the Convention[35] a "prisoner of war in Canada is in the same position as a member of His Majesty's Canadian Forces . . . [and] subject to the civil laws of this country for crimes committed while escaping or attempting to escape or after he has escaped from lawful custody."

The Ontario Court of Appeal tended to agree with the *Schindler* decision in *R. v. Brosig*.[36] Not only did the court support the view that under the Convention it was proper to treat prisoners of war as one's own troops insofar as compliance with the criminal law is concerned, but Robertson, C.J.D., expressly rejected the view that there was any rule of the common law or any other system which exempted prisoners of war from local criminal jurisdiction. Nevertheless, both the judges who delivered judgments left open the possibility that an offence committed as essentially part of the escape might be exempt, and upheld the view of the lower court that theft of perfume to disguise the smell of perspiration might fall into this category. Finally, in *R. v. Kaehler and Stolski*,[37] the Appellate Division of the Alberta Supreme Court, while agreeing that there was no exemption granted by the common law, went on to point out that since a prisoner of war is entitled to the protection of the laws of Canada, he equally has to show obedience to that law, even though he was brought to Canada against his will. This case has an added interest from the international law point of view, for defence counsel was instructed by the Swiss government as Protecting Power under the Convention. Harvey, C.J.A., pointed out that, despite the number of prisoners of war held in England, Canada, and the United States, there appeared to be no decisions on their criminal liability while escaping other than those here referred to. He accepted the *Brosig* view that the 1929 Convention was part of the law of Canada,[38] but was of opinion that none of the provisions of the Convention "would justify the conclusion that offences committed in aid of escape occupy a preferred position." He pointed out that since Article 51[39] forbade the construing of attempted escapes as aggravating criminal liability, while Article 52 called for leniency when "appraising facts in connexion with escape or attempted escape," it would appear that the Convention drew no distinction and "clearly envisages offences punishable by the Courts when committed in the course of an attempt to escape." Moreover, these provisions were embodied into the Regulations concerning Prisoners of War passed under the War Measures Act,[40] whereby prisoners of war were clearly made subject to Canadian law as if they were members of the Canadian Forces. While it may be true that a prisoner of war is under a duty to seek to escape, "any such duty . . . is to his own country and armed forces, not to Canada, and even if he had the right there is no rule applicable to our armed forces, and therefore to prisoners of war, that a legitimate end justifies illegitimate means."

The Chief Justice denied that there was a right to escape, since the Convention recognized that recaptured escapees were liable to disciplinary punishment. However, it is suggested that this goes too far. The fact that the Convention recognizes the right of a Detaining Power to punish a recaptured escapee does not deny that the prisoner has a right to attempt to escape, especially as the Convention provides that if he is recaptured after rejoining his own forces he cannot be punished for the escape. This is nothing but an example of two rights existing in parallel, the one becoming a real right only after it

---

[35]Arts. 45, 51, 56, 60-75.
[36](1945) 83 C.C.C. 199.
[37](1945) 83 C.C.C. 353.
[38]At 358, citing Order in Council P.C. 4121, December 13, 1939 (Proclamations and Orders in Council passed under the authority of the War Measures Act, vol. 1, at 218).
[39]See text *supra* note 30.
[40]R.S.C. 1927, c. 206 (the Regulations were appended to the O. in C.).

has been successfully exercised. There can, however, be no quarrel with the view of the Chief Justice that the Convention distinguishes between the offence of attempting to escape and offences which may be committed in that endeavour, nor possibly with his contention that since the prisoner of war is under protection he is equally under the obligation to obey the law, even to the extent of being liable for an offence which might be directly related to his escape, although by virtue of the Convention such offences should not be punished with any severity.

To some extent the law as enunciated by the Canadian judgments herein referred to has been altered by the 1949 Prisoners of War Convention. While the Convention in Article 93 repeats the provision concerning non-aggravation to be found in Article 51 of the 1929 Convention, it goes on to provide that "offences committed by prisoners of war with the sole intention of facilitating their escape and which do not entail any violence against life or limb, such as offences against public property, theft without intention of self-enrichment, the drawing up or use of false papers, the wearing of civilian clothing, shall occasion disciplinary punishment only" as distinct from penal sanctions. This would mean that, although prisoners of war are subject to the same law as Canadian Forces personnel, any charge similar to those brought in *Krebs, Schindler, Brosig,* or *Kaehler* could not be treated as criminal *simpliciter*, but each would have to be carefully investigated to ascertain whether the items stolen could in fact be regarded as "facilitating escape" and committed "without intention of self-enrichment."

It has not only been in regard to the treatment of prisoners of war that Canadian tribunals have made their contribution to the development of the law of armed conflict. Canadian courts have also been involved in trying war criminals. In *Re Jung and Schumacher* and *Re Holzer*, both heard by Canadian military tribunals in 1946 and both relating to the murder of Canadian prisoners, the Judge Advocate advised the Court on the validity of the defence of superior orders in accordance with the terms of the British Royal Warrant on war crimes trials and the British Manual of Military Law, while recognizing the possibility that the Court, especially in view of the exercise of duress against one of the accused in *Holzer*, might mitigate its sentence.[41] Neither court, however, really made any positive contribution to the law, other than to show that Canadian military tribunals took the same view of the law as did the British and most Allied tribunals.

In one area of the law on war crimes a Canadian tribunal did make a positive contribution, although this has been overshadowed by the contemporaneous *Yamashita* case, which was heard by a United States war crimes tribunal and ultimately confirmed by the Supreme Court,[42] and which is generally regarded as having given expression to the law with regard to command responsibility. Kurt Meyer, Commanding Officer of the 25th S.S. Panzer Grenadier Regiment, was charged with having ordered his troops to deny quarter to prisoners, with having ordered the killing of Canadian prisoners, and with having been responsible for such killings carried out by men under his command. The charges were laid in accordance with the following provisions of the War Crimes Regulations of 1945:[43]

Where there is evidence that a war crime has been committed by members of a formation, unit, body or group and that an officer or non-commissioned officer was

[41]These comments are based on the unpublished transcripts. The relevant extracts concerning the defence of superior orders are reproduced in Green, *Superior Orders in National and International Law*, 288-92 (1976).
[42](1945) 4 *War Crimes Reports*, 1; (1946) 327 U.S. 1.
[43]Re-enacted as a Schedule to the War Crimes Act, 1946, c. 73, s. 10 (4) and (5) (italics added).

present at or immediately before the time when such offence was committed, the court may receive that evidence as *prima facie* evidence of the responsibility of such officer or non-commissioned officer, *and of the commander* of such formation, unit, body, or group, for that crime.

There was evidence[44] to show that Meyer's troops had been responsible for other murders of prisoners, that he knew of the deaths of at least some of the forty-one Canadian prisoners in respect of whom the charges were brought, that at least one sergeant had been present at some of the killings, and that some of the killings had taken place in the vicinity of his headquarters. Moreover, he stated that he knew of the killings and had seen some of the bodies.

In his summing up, the Judge Advocate[45] commented upon the obligations and the discretionary powers of the members of the war crimes tribunal as follows:

They may draw upon their knowledge of human nature and the common experiences of men in battle, and they may take judicial notice of matters within their general military knowledge and also of the laws and usages of war,[46] but insofar as the particular allegations of fact set forth in the charges are concerned, they must disregard . . . any consideration which might affect [their] judgment which is not relevant to this trial. The accused is not to be prejudiced because he is a member of an enemy force and the Court is not concerned with public opinion expressed in the press or elsewhere or with questions of policy or expediency. . . .

The Judge Advocate then proceeded to deal with the individual charges, and, as regards the accusation of ordering the denial of quarter, he stated:

[A]n officer may be convicted of a war crime if he incites and counsels troops under his command to deny quarter, whether or not prisoners were killed as a result thereof. It seems to be common sense to say that not only those members of the enemy who unlawfully kill prisoners may be charged as war criminals, but also any superior military commander who incites and counsels his troops to commit such offences. . . . If you find that those prisoners [of war], or some of them, were killed by members of the 25 SS Panzer Grenadier Regiment, you will have to decide whether the accused was responsible for those acts. . . .

[The] broad question "When may a military commander be held responsible for a war crime committed by men under his command in the sense that he may be punished as a war criminal?" is not easily answered. . . .

. . . [T]he facts proved by the prosecution must be such as to establish the responsibility of the accused for the crime in question or to justify the Court in inferring such responsibility. The secondary onus, the burden of adducing evidence to show that he was not in fact responsible for any particular war crime then shifts to the accused. . . .

[T]he Regulations do not mean that a military commander is in every case liable to be punished as a war criminal for every war crime committed by his subordinates but once certain facts have been proved by the Prosecution, there is an onus cast upon the accused to adduce evidence to negative or rebut the inference of respon-

[44]The account given here is based on the unpublished transcript, pages 839, 840-45.

[45]The Judge Advocate was the legal adviser to the Court. He took no part in reaching the actual judgment, but he summed up the evidence and expounded the law for the Court. Military tribunals did not render a reasoned judgment, and the summing up of the Judge Advocate, when the judgment was in line with his advice, must be regarded as expounding the Court's view of the law.

[46]In the *Neitz* case (1946), the Judge Advocate made the same point: "It is for you to say what the customs and usages of war are, and . . . in the final analysis, whether there has been a breach of those laws and customs . . . and to do so you may draw upon military knowledge which has been acquired from your years of experience in your profession" (unpublished transcript, page 197).

sibility which the Court is entitled to make. All the facts and circumstances must then be considered to determine whether the accused was in fact responsible for the killing of prisoners referred to in the various charges. The rank of the accused, the duties and responsibilities of the accused by virtue of the command he held, the training of the men under his command, their age and experience, anything relating to the question whether the accused either ordered, encouraged or verbally or tacitly acquiesced in the killing of prisoners, or wilfully failed in his duty as a military commander to prevent, or to take such action as the circumstances required to endeavour to prevent, the killing of prisoners are matters affecting the question of the accused's responsibility. In the last analysis, it is for the Court, using its wide knowledge and experience of military matters, to determine, in the light of the relevant factors and the provisions of the Regulations, the responsibility of an accused in any particular case. . . .

The giving of the order may be proved circumstantially, that is to say, you may consider the facts you find to be proved bearing upon the question whether the alleged order was given, and if you find that the only reasonable inference is that an order that the prisoners be killed was given by the accused at the time and place alleged, and that the prisoners were killed as a result of that order, you may properly find the accused guilty. . . . [I]t is not necessary for you to be convinced that a particular or formal order was given but you must be satisfied before you convict, that some words were uttered or some clear indication was given by the accused that prisoners were to be put to death. . . .

Much of the evidence has been given to enable the Court to appreciate the background, the state of the battle at the times material to the several charges and the circumstances under which the alleged offences were committed. As experienced soldiers you will appreciate these factors, some of which are particularly relevant to the question of guilt and others to questions of mitigation of punishment should you find any of the offences proved. . . .

This statement with regard to the duty of commanders is in accord with what came to be accepted as the proper assessment of such responsibility and is in line with the *Yamashita* decision, although it may be considered that the Canadian Judge Advocate required a closer link with the actual crime than did the American court. It is now provided by Article 87 of Protocol I of 1977 that military commanders must prevent, suppress, and report breaches of the Geneva Conventions and the Protocol to the competent authorities. Commanders are also obliged to ensure that those under their command are made aware of their obligations under those documents. Further, reflecting perhaps the experience of the My Lai tragedy, commanders are obliged, if they are aware that subordinates are going to commit or have committed breaches of the Conventions and Protocol, to initiate preventive steps or disciplinary or penal action against the violators. This leaves unaltered the issue of the personal liability of the commander, who is responsible for having ordered, or failed to control his troops so as to prevent, the commission of war crimes. It merely requires a commander to take steps to prevent or punish crimes by his subordinates. Any failure on his part in this connection would be a breach of the Protocol and might not even amount to a crime. His personal criminal liability will still depend on the principles underlying the *Meyer* and *Yamashita* cases.[46a]

Once the International Committee of the Red Cross indicated its intention of seeking to develop the humanitarian law of armed conflict as embodied in the 1949 Geneva Conventions, Canada devoted itself to seeking as wide an application of those humanitarian principles as possible. To this end, Canada's experts sought, insofar as concerned international conflicts, which were the subject of Protocol I, to limit the impact upon the civilian population of the effects of legitimate means and methods of warfare. They

[46a]On command responsibility generally, see ch. X above.

sought, for example, to outlaw area and terror bombing and the use of starvation as a weapon. It is perhaps not surprising that their efforts were only partially successful. Insofar as the former is concerned, the Protocol does make it completely illegal to launch direct attacks against civilians or civilian objects,[47] or to attack civilians with the sole view of terrorizing them,[48] while imposing limitations upon attacks, to some extent by the indirect method of defining military objectives[49] and defining and forbidding indiscriminate attacks[50] and demanding the cancellation or suspension of attacks "which may be expected to cause incidental loss of civilian life, injury to civilians, damage to civilian objects, or a combination thereof, which would be excessive in relation to the concrete and direct military advantage anticipated."[51] As regards starvation, the starvation of civilians as a method of warfare is absolutely forbidden,[52] and it is prohibited to attack, destroy, or remove objects that are indispensable to the sustenance of the civilian population for the specific purpose of denying them for their sustenance value, whether it be in order to starve out civilians, or cause them to move away, or for whatever other motive.[53]

During the Diplomatic Conference held for the drafting of the Protocol, Canada tried to extend the protection of the humanitarian provisions further than the majority of those attending were prepared to concede. Thus, during the discussion on perfidy, when analysing the proposal to forbid the feigning of a protected sign in order to mislead the enemy,[54] Canada proposed that the definition should be wide enough to ensure that when an unrecognized emblem was habitually used to secure protection and was known to be so used, if it were used in an improper fashion so as to mislead the enemy, it, too, should be regarded as perfidy. This proposal, however, even though it would lead to the punishment of those wrongfully displaying it, was opposed by the Arab states on the ground that it would serve as an indirect way of securing recognition of the Red Shield of David which, though used by Israel instead of the Red Cross, and which enjoys *de facto* recognition, is not recognized as a protected emblem in the Geneva Conventions. An equal fate befell a proposal by Canada intended to extend the protection of cultural objects under Article 53. It was suggested that it should be open to the parties to a conflict to inform each other of those cultural monuments which they would be prepared to recognize as protected and so immune from attack. Again, the Arab states contended that this would indirectly involve recognition of Israel. On yet another occasion, in connection with the definition of grave breaches, Canada sought to secure a more specific definition of what is meant by *apartheid*[55] than appears in the Protocol. It was made very clear by the Third World states that what they had in mind was the United Nations concept of this offence, which meant discrimination by white southern Africa against the black populations, and not, for example, Burundi or Idi Amin's genocidal attacks upon the Asian population of Uganda.

During the Committee stages of the Conference, Canada was able to secure acceptance of articles relating to the defence of superior orders and command responsibility. As to the former, the aim was to ensure that the individual soldier would not be able to rely

[47]Art. 51(2).
[48]*Ibid.*
[49]Art. 52(2).
[50]Art. 51(4), (5).
[51]Art. 51(5) (b).
[52]Art. 54(1).
[53]Art. 54(2).
[54]Art. 37(1)(d).
[55]Art. 85(4)(c).

on this defence when the act ordered would have involved commission of an act which the most common of soldiers would have recognized as criminal. The command responsibility proposal reflected the summing up in the *Meyer* case, as modified by the *Yamashita* principle. Both these proposals were lost in Plenary. A more successful result attended the Canadian formulation of a United Nations proposal concerning the protection of journalists engaged in dangerous missions, which, instead of requiring a complete convention, was dealt with in a single article—Article 79.

It was in connection with Protocol II, extending some measure of international legal control to non-international conflicts, that Canada played a more vital and innovative role. It is in the sphere of internecine struggle that, historically, the most extreme atrocities are committed and, until the Diplomatic Conference produced Protocol II, while there was the hope that even in non-international conflicts basic human rights would still be recognized,[56] there was no treaty law other than Article 3, which is common to all the Geneva Conventions. This seeks to ensure that, even in such a conflict, there should still continue to be recognition and application of the minimum requirements of the rule of law. One of the difficulties has always been to determine the threshold of violence and conflict which should warrant departure from the traditional rule of non-interference in domestic affairs, while another has been to impose upon states the need to accept that even rebellious citizens remain entitled to the protective umbrella of humanitarian law.

From the beginning, aware of the essential differences between those who would participate in a non-international, as distinct from an international, conflict, Canada emphasized the importance of keeping the written law relative to the two types of conflict apart, and of the need to keep that relating to non-international conflicts as simple as circumstances would permit. There was little to be gained, and perhaps much to be lost, if the document prescribing the law for such conflicts merely mirrored that for international conflicts, with only verbal changes having been made. Moreover, Canada was conscious of the fact that the traditional view was that international law would only become interested in a non-international conflict when the conflict had reached the level of something like the Spanish Civil War, with both sides being recognized as belligerents, and equally conscious that most of the incidents which had occurred since 1949 in Asia, Latin America, and Africa had not reached this threshold.

The first Canadian draft of a Protocol relative to conflicts of a non-international character[57] was presented to the Conference of Government Experts that met in Geneva in mid-1971. The underlying assumptions of Canada in this field are easily seen by reference to the first paragraph of Article 1 which provides:

> The present provisions, which reaffirm and supplement Article 3 of the Geneva Conventions of . . . 1949 . . . apply to all cases of armed conflict occurring in the territory of one of the High Contracting Parties, involving government forces on one side and armed forces whether regular or irregular on the other side, and to which common Article 2 of the Conventions [defining the nature of an international conflict] is not applicable.

Such a definition would not have included sporadic outbursts of terrorism, riots, and civil disturbances, nor even the sort of incident that occurred at Kent State University. It would, however, have meant some measure of humanitarian control of every internal conflict when the government, being confronted with organized armed forces, albeit

[56]See e.g., "Human Rights and the Law of Armed Conflict," ch. V above.
[57]See 1 *Canadian Defence Quarterly*, 64-67 (No. 2, 1971).

irregular, as distinct from a simple military mutiny, found itself compelled to make use of its own forces to suppress those opposing it. Such a definition would almost certainly have embraced every struggle of an anti-colonial character, and would probably have included within its ambit the situation created by the Irish Republican Army in Northern Ireland.

This proposal was clearly based on the desire to humanize every conflict in which armed forces were involved, whether the struggle had reached the level of an insurgency, belligerency, or civil war. It was, however, far too extensive to secure acceptance, and what was ultimately accepted as constituting the material field of application of Protocol II was little different from a traditional civil war. By Article 1, the Protocol will only apply to a conflict taking place "in the territory of a High Contracting Party between its armed forces and dissident armed forces or other organized armed groups which, under responsible command, exercise such control over a part of its territory as to enable them to carry out sustained and concerted military operations and to implement this Protocol." A definition of this severity makes it difficult to determine how a non-international conflict differs from one waged by a national liberation movement seeking its self-determination which, in accordance with Article 1 of Protocol I, ranks as an international armed conflict, subject to all the rules and principles relative to such a conflict.

Reflecting its concern to cover the majority of incidents and in as simple a fashion as possible, the Canadian draft contained a mere twenty-four articles, whereas Protocol I, as ultimately adopted, runs to 102 articles, plus annexes, and at times during the Conference, it almost appeared as if this was going to be the fate of Protocol II. So great was there a danger of this that, at the end of the Second Session in April 1975, Canada put forward a revised Protocol II,[58] accepting the restrictive field of application just referred to and comprising twenty-nine articles. The covering letter to which this draft was appended repeated this Canadian view:

> It is necessary to warn against any automatic repetition in Protocol II of the more comprehensive provisions, such as those on civil defence, found in Protocol I and applicable in that Protocol to international conflicts. To do so would risk altering the "Material Field of Application" of Protocol I to such an extent that States, with a view to the internal application of the Protocol, would either fail to ratify it or tend to argue for its non-application in situations objectively falling within the scope of the Protocol, thereby leaving, in fact, the victims of these contemporary conflicts without adequate protection.

Canada's view as to the importance of an international legal document concerned with non-international conflicts was expounded as follows:

> (1) The provisions of Protocol II must, individually and overall, be agreeable to all parties to the conflict, whether governmental or non-governmental. There should, therefore, be an obvious, practical benefit to be derived by each party in the observance of these provisions.
> (2) These provisions must be well within the perceived capacity of each party to apply them. They should, therefore, be kept as precise and simple as possible so as to be readily understood and honoured by even a relatively rudimentary organized group under responsible command, etc.
> (3) The Protocol should not be invoked as affecting the sovereignty of any State Party or the responsibility of its government to maintain law or order and to defend

[58]Diplomatic Conference on the Reaffirmation and Development of International Humanitarian Law Applicable in Armed Conflicts, Doc. CDDH/212, 8 Apr. 1975, IV *Official Records* 191.

national unity and territorial integrity by legitimate means; nor should it be invoked to justify any outside intervention.

(4) Nothing in the Protocol should suggest that dissidents must be treated legally other than as rebels. To move in the direction of recognizing the military activities of the rebels as having some degree of legitimacy, is to invite the expectation or even demand for Prisoner-of-War status on capture.

Despite the abbreviated form of Canada's proposals, it appeared, until very late in the Conference, that all these efforts on behalf of those involved in non-international armed conflicts would be lost, and that there would, in fact, be no Protocol II. Ultimately, owing to the efforts of the head of the Pakistan Delegation, a revised draft, largely based on Canada's proposals, was accepted as a compromise and by consensus. Of the final articles, those relating to the personal field of application granting protection of the fundamental guarantees of humanitarian treatment after the end of hostilities and until the persons involved had regained their liberty, those adapting the minimum requirement of humane treatment and the rule of law, those advocating an amnesty at the end of hostilities, and some of those relating to the protection of civilians found their way into the final Protocol. However, many suggestions that would have ensured further modification of the horrors inherent in this type of conflict were lost—the attempt to preserve a visiting and supervisory role for such organizations as the International Committee of the Red Cross; a ban on the carrying out of death sentences until after the termination of hostilities for offences connected with those hostilities, in the hope that by the time peace was restored, national hatreds would have sufficiently abated to permit of mercy; an attempt to control the means and methods of combat so as to forbid unnecessary injury and to safeguard persons *hors de combat*; and proposals for the dissemination and teaching of the provisions of the Protocol so that the civil population as well as the armed forces might be aware of their rights in the event of a conflict, as well as a further effort to secure some measure of international control and supervision so as to achieve limited internationalization of the observance of the Protocol in a non-international conflict.

It is clear from this survey that Canada, has, in fact, played a significant role in the development of the law of armed conflict. It has done this by active measures in the field of the law of prize, by consistently applying the generally recognized law of war and so providing further evidentiary proof of what this comprises, by awakening the conscience of the world to the need to introduce humanitarian measures even in internal conflicts, and by the role played by its own delegations at international conferences in modifying, liberalizing, expanding, and formulating the proposals put forward by others. It is, in fact, a record of achievement that is perhaps not sufficiently known.

INDEX

In view of the constant reference to the various Geneva and Hague Conventions, together with the 1977 Protocols, as well as the Hague Regulations, it has been decided not to refer to specific articles of these in the Index. Equally, reference is made to these documents only when the discussion is of a general character. For the main part, these documents are dealt with by inclusion under specific rubrics.

X, 32, 56, 111-113
XIII, 193
Hague Law, 4, 77, 84, 88, 135, 215, 253
Hague Regulations, 6, 12, 17, 29, 37, 84, 89, 110, 135, 136, 137, 160, 165-166, 215, 225, 235, 243, 247, 263, 267
Hague Rules of Air Warfare (1923), 14, 32, 91, 137, 140, 167
Halsbury, Lord, 46-47
Hare, J.I.C., 48, 53
Harrington, J., 3
Henri Dunant Institut, 39, 41
Henry V, 35, 85, 241
Himmler, H., 225-226
hors de combat, persons, 14, 83, 84, 89, 93, 100, 127, 137-139, 143, 146, 215, 242, 275
hospitals, 85, 86-87, 104-105, 106-107, 109, 113, 120, 143, 147
hospital ships, 30-31, 55-56, 107-109, 112, 113-115, 116-118, 120, 129, 169, 245, 254
hostages, 95
human rights, 83-102, 144, 156, 173, 242
humanitarian law, 3-4, 12, 15, 23, 32, 38, 39, 41, 42, 43, 71, 76, 81, 83-102, 103-134, 140, 144, 145, 159, 167, 171, 200, 210, 216, 245, 255, 261, 271, 273-275, *see also* Geneva Law
humanity, crimes against, 30, 54, 92, 93, 99, 120, 133, 222, 247
Hurtval, Dr. A., 122
Hyde, C.C., 79

identity cards, 37-38
ignorantia juris non excusat, xxi, 19, 27-42, 75, 79, 216, 217, 245, 262, *see also* superior orders
incendiaries, 156, 167, 170, 172-173
Indian National Army, 49, 106
indiscriminate attack, 18, 98, 143, 147, 148, 169, 172, 272
individual responsibility, 90, 95
Institut Henri Dunant, 39, 41
International Committee of the Red Cross, 3-4, 16, 21, 32-33, 36, 39, 41, 81, 89, 96, 98, 100, 106, 109, 114, 127, 130, 147, 172, 251, 271, 275
international common law, 61
international criminal law, 41, 207, 239-252, *see also* mercenaries; war crimes
International Fact-Finding Commission, 21-22, 100, 251
International Institute of Humanitarian Law, 39, 81
Israel incursion into Lebanon, 229-230

journalists, 17, 37, 273
judge advocate, 76-77, 80-81, *see also* legal advisers
jus ad bellum, xix
jus in bello, xix, xx, 88, 135, 154

Kahan Commission Report, 229-237, 251

Keitel, General, 78
Kellogg-Briand Pact (1928), xix, 92
Korean war, 67-69, 119, 249
Kozhevnikov, F.I., 245

Laconia incident (1942), 121, 141
Lafayette Squadron, 185
Lauterpacht, Sir Hersch, 57-58, 59, 171, 243, 244
Lebanon, Israel incursion, 229-230
legal advisers, xxi, 19-20, 28, 38-39, 73-82, 217, 250, 270
Legnanon, G. da, 241
Leipzig trials (1921/3), 30, 55, 170, 244, 245
Lieber Code, 31, 87-88, 104, 156, 166, 242, 263
Loganadan, Lt. Col., 106
London (Nuremberg) Charter (1945), 92-93, 225, 240, 246, 247, 248, 250, 255
London, Treaty of (1930), 90, 169
looting, xxi, 85, 157, 163, 165, 179, 241
Lorimer, J., 183
manuals of military law, xxi, 31-32, 57, 58, 62, 63, 75-76, 83, 85, 160, 166-167, 172, 228
Martens clause, 84, 124, 166, 216, 229
McNair, Lord, 2, 57
medical aircraft, 119, 128, 132, 139, 141-142, 145-146
medical care, 16, 23, 93-94, 99-100, 103-134
medical experimentation, 16, 94, 95, 99, 120, 122-126, 129, 131
medical personnel, 16, 23-24, 86, 94-95, 103-134, 139, 146
mercenaries, 9-11, 15, 175-213, 216, *see also* Angola
  Organization of African Unity, 195-196, 199-200
  Protocol I, 208-211
  Switzerland, 180-181
  United Kingdom, 181-182, 202-205
  United Nations, 193-200, 211-212
mercenarism, 10, 195, 197, 198, 199, 200-202, 205, 206-208, 209, 210, 211-212
military knowledge, 270, 271, *see also ignorantia juris non excusat*
military necessity, 20, 77, 87, 91, 101, 112, 113, 129, 143, 144, 164, 166
military objective, 17-18, 19, 91, 98, 128, 132, 143, 144, 146, 147, 148, 149, 173, 272
missing, 16-17
Mistrali-Guidotti, Dr. L., 103, 107, 127, 133
Mobutu, President, 22
Montesquieu, 3
Moscow Declaration (1943), 246
My Lai, 67, 71, 252, 271

national liberation, 3, 4-9, 11, 24-25, 78, 92, 98, 130, 159, 185, 189-190, 193-200, 207, 208, 211, 213, 215, 228
naval bombardment, 90, 136
neutrals, 21, 145, 147, 157, 183, 192-193, 253, 265
Newman, Cardinal, xxii